California Vieja

The publisher gratefully acknowledges the generous contribution to this book provided by Lisa See and Richard Kendall as members of the Literati Circle of the University of California Press Foundation.

California Vieja

Culture and Memory in a Modern American Place

Phoebe S. Kropp

UNIVERSITY OF CALIFORNIA PRESS
Berkeley · Los Angeles · London

University of California Press, one of the most distinguished university presses in the United States, enriches
lives around the world by advancing scholarship in the
humanities, social sciences, and natural sciences. Its
activities are supported by the UC Press Foundation
and by philanthropic contributions from individuals
and institutions. For more information,
visit www.ucpress.edu.

University of California Press
Berkeley and Los Angeles, California

University of California Press, Ltd.
London, England

Library of Congress Cataloging-in-Publication Data

Kropp, Phoebe S. (Phoebe Schroeder), 1970-.
  California vieja : culture and memory in a modern
American place / Phoebe S. Kropp.
       p.   cm.
  Includes bibliographical references and index.
  ISBN 978-0-520-25804-4 (pbk. : alk. paper)
    1. Architecture, Domestic—California, Southern.
2. Architecture, Spanish colonial—California, Southern.
3. Architecture—California, Southern—20th century.
4. Landscape—California, Southern.   5. Mexican
Americans—California—Social conditions.
6. Memory—Social aspects—California.   7. El Camino
Real (Calif.).   I. Title.
F862.K76 2006
978'.02—dc22   2005028156

Manufactured in the United States of America

17 16 15 14 13 12 11 10
11 10 9 8 7 6 5 4 3 2

This book is printed on Natures Book, which contains
50% postconsumer waste and meets the minimum
requirements of ANSI/ASTM Z39.48-1992 (R 1997)
(*Permanence of Paper*). ∞

For Will,
and for our sons,
Marlin and Darby

Contents

Illustrations

MAPS

Tables

Preface

This book began in La Jolla, California, where nearly all gas stations have red-tile roofs. As a graduate student in the 1990s, I began the research that would yield this book, exploring Californians' fanciful cultural memory of the Spanish past and its ramifications for Mexican-Anglo relations. When I ventured outside the library during those days, I saw a disjuncture between praise for Spanish style and fear of Mexican immigrants in the Southern California landscape. I didn't set out to solve the puzzle of present-day California in my work, but wherever I turned, this mixture of desire and disdain marked the cultural, political, and "built" environment. Though I completed my project from a considerable distance, the Southern California landscape continued to offer me food for thought during my analysis of its memory and continues to do so today.

During my time in Southern California, I noted that most new subdivisions sported names such as Mariposa Ranch and Arroyo Blanco, though many of them mangled the Spanish syntax to achieve English linguistic effects. Stucco and tile were the preferred building materials in housing developments, though the Mesa Apartments where I lived showed no visual allegiance to their Spanish name. The tourist-oriented historic reconstruction of Old Town attempted to create an ongoing Mexican fiesta, with its attached shopping mall, the Bazaar del Mundo, and half-watermelon–size margaritas at the Casa de Bandini restaurant. Small green mission bells peppered the coastal highways heading north out of town, reminding travelers that these thoroughfares were once dusty Spanish roads, frequented by sandal-clad friars and silver-spurred rancheros. Yet in one stretch of Interstate 5, the bells shared the roadside with "Caution" signs depicting a family dashing across the 65-mile-an-hour freeway with a little girl in pigtails in tow. This shorthand reference to the desperate travels of undocumented Mexican immigrants needed no explanatory text for locals, though it sometimes perplexed the uninitiated. When Operation Gatekeeper tightened the border, immigrants shied away from busy roads and attempted perilous high-desert crossings in eastern San Diego County. Local news nightly reported the discovery of bodies throughout midsummer and winter. Public commentators seemed to think the region was on the cusp of an invasion, whether from Mexican immigrants or Africanized killer bees. Meanwhile, Southern California lawns sprouted political signs supporting a series of statewide ballot propositions seeking to deny public services to illegal immigrants, dismantle affirmative action, and discourage the teaching of Spanish in the schools.

This landscape confounded logic. On the one hand, the melodically named streets with red-tile–roofed houses looked back on a romantic Spanish past and highlighted the region's colorful local heritage. On the other, public discourse suggested a disruptive present in which the Mexican immigrants mowing the lawns on these streets seemed to threaten the region. How could these seemingly opposed visions both typify Southern California? Why did people's fanciful memory have such an important impact on the region? The book that follows cannot account for all the idiosyncrasies of Southern California's culture. But, one fact that remains inescapable, in the text and on the landscape, is the powerful influence and lasting effects of memory on place.

Acknowledgments

Besides racking up miles on Southern California freeways, I accumulated a number of personal debts in the years I took to complete this book. I take great pleasure in repaying them now, if only with words. Several institutions generously allowed me both financial support and valuable time. Early on, the Kenneth and Dorothy Hill Fellowship at the Mandeville Special Collections Library at the University of California, San Diego (UCSD), gave me the opportunity to conduct exploratory research; dissertation fellowships from the Department of History at UCSD assisted me at crucial moments. Two grants from the Henry E. Huntington Library—the Chandis Securities Fellowship and the John Randolph Haynes and Dora Haynes Fellowship—supported a substantial portion of my dissertation research, opening the gates to the library's wealth of archival material as well as the beauty of its grounds. A Smithsonian Institution Pre-doctoral Fellowship at the National Museum of American History enabled extended use of several Washington, D.C., archives. A Kevin Starr Postdoctoral Fellowship in California Studies at the University of California Humanities Research Institute supported initial revisions of the dissertation, and a semester of pretenure leave granted by the School of Arts and Sciences at the University of Pennsylvania gave me the time to complete the final editing and preparation of the manuscript.

Archivists and librarians at these and other institutions were invaluable, helping me find not only what I was looking for but also information

I didn't know to ask for. I would like to thank the staff at the following libraries for their willing assistance: Henry E. Huntington Library; Mandeville Special Collections Library, University of California, San Diego; Regional History Center, University of Southern California; Seaver Center for Western History Research, Los Angeles County Museum of Natural History; City Archives, City of Los Angeles; El Pueblo State Historic Park; San Diego Historical Society; Braun Research Library, Southwest Museum; Archives Center, National Museum of American History; National Anthropological Archives, National Museum of Natural History; Smithsonian Institution Archives; Division of Archives and Drawings, Avery Library of Art and Architecture, Columbia University; California State Library; Special Collections, University Research Library, University of California, Los Angeles; National Archives and Records Administration, Pacific Region, Laguna Niguel Office; Fray Angélico Chávez History Library; New Mexico State Archives; and the Laboratory of Anthropology, Museum of New Mexico. Peter Blodgett, Alan Jutzi, and Jennifer Watts at the Huntington; Dace Taube at the University of Southern California; Tom Sitton at the Seaver Center; and Steve Coy at UCSD all lent me their learned perspectives on Southern California as well as their expert archival knowledge. For assistance with images, I want also to thank Jean-Robert Durbin at the Huntington; Morgan Yates at the Automobile Club of Southern California; Jeffrey Rankin at the University of California, Los Angeles, Special Collections; John Cahoon at the Seaver Center; John Blazejewski at the Marquand Library of Art and Archaeology, Princeton University; and Dace Taube at the Regional History Center.

I have had the opportunity to present portions of this work in various forums, and the final product has benefited immeasurably from the thoughtful comments of participants. I am particularly grateful to Lisbeth Haas for her insightful comments on two conference papers, Mike Engh of the Los Angeles History Group for inviting me to present a dissertation chapter, Ian Christopher Fletcher at Georgia State University for encouraging me to rework a talk I gave there for submission to the *Radical History Review,* and Hal Rothman and David Weber for the opportunity to join a Clements Center symposium on cultural tourism in the Southwest. I am also thankful for a weekend of inspiring scholarly discussion and camaraderie at a Miami University of Ohio symposium on Public Culture in March 2004; the joint meditation on issues of space, memory, diversity, and identity came at an opportune moment in my manuscript revisions. I thank all the participants, but especially John Bodnar, Catherine Gudis, Edward Linenthal, Hal Rothman, Mary Ryan, and organizer Marguerite Shaffer.

Earlier renditions of several chapters have appeared in previous publications, and I appreciate permission to republish the revised editions. A version of chapter 2, entitled "In Search of History and Romance on El Camino Real," appears in *The Culture of Tourism, The Tourism of Culture: Selling the Past to the Present in the American Southwest*, edited by Hal Rothman (Albuquerque: University of New Mexico Press, 2003), 38–65; a version of chapter 3, entitled "'There is a Little Sermon in That': Constructing the Native Southwest at the San Diego Panama-California Exposition of 1915," appears in *The Great Southwest of the Fred Harvey Company and the Santa Fe Railway*, edited by Barbara A. Babcock and Marta Weigle (Phoenix: The Heard Museum with the University of Arizona Press, 1996), 36–46; and a version of chapter 5, entitled "Citizens of the Past?: Olvera Street and the Construction of Race and Memory in 1930s Los Angeles," was published in *Radical History Review* 81 (Fall 2001): 35–60.

I was fortunate in graduate school to find a remarkable group of friends, colleagues, and mentors. The cohort of hopeful California historians who collected during my time there offered lively community, swapped archival tips, and contributed significantly to the early stages of this book. My thanks go to Eric Boime, Greg Rodriguez, Sarah Schrank, Rachel Shaw, Abraham Shragge, and Mark Wild. Whether by lending supportive ears or sharing the softball season, Krista Camenzind, Barnet Hartston, John Lee, and Enrique Sanabria helped make UCSD home. The history department faculty and the members of my dissertation committee helped me through the many hoops, intellectual and bureaucratic, that pave the way to a Ph.D. Rachel Klein, Stephanie McCurry, Ross Frank, and Susan Davis together expanded my mind and my bibliography; some of the big questions they posed have yet to relinquish their hold on me. I count myself extremely lucky to have had not one but two superb advisors, David Gutíerrez and William Deverell, whose guidance has been of enormous benefit to me. David's tutelage in the politics of history and Bill's gentle encouragement to tell my own story shaped my thoughts in fundamental ways. They have continued to shepherd my progress far beyond the requirements of the office and have become two of my most valued friends.

Collecting friends and colleagues all over the map is a common academic habit, and I am no exception. Over the years, Douglas Flamming,

Greg Hise, Charles McGovern, Char Miller, Natalia Molina, Becky Nicolaides, Virginia Scharff, Bryant Simon, and Denise Spooner have shared with me their considerable stores of wisdom and kindness. Matt Bokovoy has shared research of mutual interest with the most generous of spirits. At the Humanities Research Institute, my fellow Starr Fellows—Jared Orsi, Glen Gendzel, and Mary Coomes—provided a friendly forum for discussing work in progress and professional issues. For making my various archival stints true fellowships, I thank Angie Blake, Elspeth Brown, Stephanie Cassidy, Pete Daniel, Carolyn Kastner, Regina Koffman, Cheryl Koos, Tehya Kopp, and Josh Piker. Several key individuals have sustained my work in ways that are difficult to measure. Lynda Claassen, at the Mandeville Special Collections Library, offered me a semipermanent home base and always kept a project waiting in the wings for me when I needed gainful employment. Fraser Cocks, at the Dimensions of Culture Program at UCSD, gave me an office, a job, and a friend at a most critical moment. Michael Dear, Rayna Green, and Hal Rothman have each been key advocates and sounding boards. From walks in the Huntington's gardens to research forays into the wilderness, Peggy Shaffer has been a trusted ally, insightful reader, and enduring friend.

I have great sadness that one of my outstanding debts has to be paid posthumously. Though his life ended way too soon and all too suddenly, Clark Davis was one of the most genuinely caring, earnest, and joyful people I have known. I deeply value his support of my work, as well as his perceptive scholarship and wealth of knowledge about Los Angeles, both of which he shared freely. He was a one-man welcoming committee at the Huntington Library, and from my first visit, made me feel part of the in crowd. Lunching there will not be the same without Clark. I hope his star sightings are frequent now and that he knows how much I appreciated his friendship.

The University of Pennsylvania has offered a stimulating atmosphere in which to complete this book. Students in my history and memory seminars have brought fresh perspectives to the table and kept alive my interest in the field. Not only have my colleagues presented a wealth of historical perspectives, but many also found the time to read and comment upon my work. For their interest and shrewd advice, I thank Ann Farnsworth-Alvear, Steven Hahn, Bruce Kuklick, Ben Nathans, Barbara Savage, Tom Sugrue, Margo Todd, and Beth Wenger. I have especially appreciated my conversations with Stephanie McCurry, Kathy Brown, and Kathy Peiss. They improved this book in different but important ways.

Sarah Igo graciously read numerous drafts of the book, expertly edited the writing in key places, and happily shared the travails of revising.

Readers for the University of California Press gave key assessments of the work at various stages. David Johnson and Abby Van Slyke offered helpful blueprints for initial revisions. Greg Hise read both the dissertation and a revised draft, granting me unique feedback that proved helpful well into the third version. Editorial committee reader Vicki Ruiz suggested some beneficial changes and additions and saved me from several crucial errors. Monica McCormick took on this project in its most fledgling form. Her editorial expertise and good cheer saw it through most of the developmental stages, though she moved on before I could bring it home. Niels Hooper willingly stepped in and offered a fresh perspective to guide the final process of editing. I appreciate the efforts of Suzanne Knott, who oversaw production, and Adrienne Harris, who did a superb job of copyediting. Outside the press, two individuals made key contributions to the final work. James Munson, a cartographer at California State University, East Bay, turned my vague directions into excellent maps. Peter Agree at the University of Pennsylvania Press deserves many thanks for crafting the title.

Two remarkable women made substantial investments of their time in this project and have become invaluable companions over the past decade. Erika Bsumek shared her research on the Southwest as we worked our ways through dissertation research and beyond. Her comments on a number of chapters have been extremely helpful, and her ideas about ethnicity, consumption, and culture gave me new ways to think about my topic. Other than my husband, perhaps no one has sweated the details of this book with me more than Theresa Smith. She has read countless drafts, corrected thousands of comma splices, and endured long debates about word choice. Her talents for concise writing and clear argumentation have vastly improved the text. Since our days a desk apart, Theresa has been my toughest critic, given the best pep talks, and shared the longest laughs. The book simply would not be finished without her loyal friendship.

My family has followed my adventures in and out of academia, and for their support I want to thank my stepfather, Al; my father, Li; my in-laws, Myron and Anita; and my late grandmother, Eleanore—the personification of history in our clan. My sister, Chloe, probably can't remember when I was not working on this book, and her entrance into college served as a reminder that it was time to wrap it up. She, however, always reminded me that there was more to life than school. I must be a most fortunate daughter to have a friend, a colleague, and a mom all in one. My mother, Gale, wears all those hats and more, and for her encouragement, strength, and generosity, I am truly grateful.

Most of all, I thank my husband, Will, who embraced my goals as his own and never failed to remind me that we were in this together. His perspectives on Southern California offered plenty of dinnertime debates, and his willingness to keep talking about its Spanish past (and to keep cooking dinner) for so many years has helped me see this book through to its end. Even more, his confidence in me, his laugh, and his daring spirit have lent me the energy to keep working and the reason to quit at the end of each day. To him and to our sons, Marlin and Darby, this book is joyfully dedicated.

Introduction

Can we read the history of a place in its buildings? The skyscrapers of Manhattan; the wooden, wide-porched farmhouses of Iowa; the broad streets of Chicago; the narrow-streeted neighborhoods of Boston; the brick colonials of Philadelphia; the white-columned manors of Georgia; the pastel art deco buildings of Miami all stand witness to the past, conveying the personality and ethos of a place. Even in these days of cookie-cutter suburbs and cloned malls across America, each city and region retains its own look. Yet a city's buildings display more than local character and house more than the history that passes through them. The forces that create, preserve, popularize, refurbish, and market a place's emblematic architecture grow out of local debates about usable pasts and alternate futures. From afar, the red-tile roofs of Southern California appear to reflect a regional affinity for Spanish style and heritage. So plentiful are these stucco-and–terra-cotta structures that they "give back the sunshine stained pink," as architect Frank Lloyd Wright once remarked.[1] On the ground, however, they reflect decades of cultural work. Anglo boosters of Southern California in the early twentieth century worked hard to promote a romantic version of the state's Spanish past in the region. They invested in this cultural memory by fashioning a "built environment"— buildings and other structures of human design that mark the physical landscape—that echoed Spanish forms. This impulse arose both from their desire to honor local history and from their ambition to develop Southern California into a premier American place to live, work, and play.[2]

In Southern California, as elsewhere, memory is like mortar, cementing in people's sense of place. Whether a region's past exists as lived experience or marketed slogan, it stamps a place with a unique character. Even in the forward-looking United States, memories are everywhere in public culture. Often these recollections are in situ, seated in place.[3] Whether born of nostalgia for the well-ordered New England town, the romantic plantation South, or the dusty frontier West, narratives of regional pasts have thrived in the United States in the past two centuries. The turn of the twentieth century, in particular, witnessed a boom in nostalgia, with Americans clamoring for the past in many forms. As Michael Kammen, encyclopedian of American memory practices, has suggested, "Anyone who probes historical sources for this period will be figuratively assaulted by the nation's arsenal of memory devices and by the astonishing diversity of its stockpile."[4] Between the end of the Civil War and the Progressive Era, the hunger for tradition grew in cities and towns across the country. Anglos in Southern California entered the memory business as well, inscribing several regional histories on the landscape. For some, California history had its genesis in Anglo-Americans' arrival on the scene, which was an open invitation for pioneer stories. Gold rush stories were the most popular of these origin myths, although these stories centered primarily on Northern California.[5]

Others knew that California was not, as some pioneers believed, an empty land before their appearance, and those who yearned for a more colorful and venerable story of place turned to a different regional past. Anglos, especially Southern Californians, recast the eras of Spanish mission colonies and Mexican rancho settlements as an idyllic golden age, depicting a picturesque land of pious padres and placid Indians, of dashing caballeros and sultry señoritas—their very own myth of moonlight and mantillas. These dreamy pasts that Anglo-Californians recalled were not their own. Local residents with longer tenures—Indians and Mexicans—played starring roles in the historical set pieces that Anglos assembled for their regional stage. The region's diverse, intriguing, and sometimes brutal history, wrested from the hands of earlier inhabitants, became the raw material from which Anglo-Californians fashioned new memories. The focus on romantic ambiance became both a figurative preamble to Anglo development and a material product of it. First floated to tourists before the turn of the twentieth century, these memories by the 1930s formed a dominant mode in which locals and newcomers imagined the region.

In 1933 Los Angeles promoter of the Spanish past Christine Sterling wrote that "life in Los Angeles before the Americans came was almost an ideal existence," where the men "rode magnificent horses," the women wore "silk and laces," and there were "picnics into the hills, dancing at night, moonlight serenades, romance, and real happiness." Her Spanish reverie was more than nostalgia; it was a telling expression of the California good life to which Anglos aspired, moonlit patios and all. Sterling invoked a by-then well-honed regional image that served boosters' development designs by associating Southern California with a salable historical personality and an enticing lifestyle all its own.[6] Yet this image went beyond the typical booster come-on. The romantic regional memories shaped the cultural landscape, from built environment to social relations. Why did Anglos work so vigorously to stamp the past on their future? Why did they mourn the passing of an idyllic world whose demise they actually hastened by settling there?

Perhaps the answer lies in this feeling of loss. Anglo-Americans who came to the region in the late nineteenth and early twentieth centuries worked feverishly to make their cities the utmost in modern living, and they boasted broadly of their accomplishments. The booster ethos that dominated Southern California's business community, government, and press a century ago was obsessively future directed. Yet, underneath the bravado, Southern Californians were anxious about the relentless pace of progress. They were suspicious of the changes that modernity brought to their lives. They worried that they might repeat the tragedies of eastern industrial cities, with their unruly workers and soot-filled slums. To regain a sense of control over their cultural environment, Anglos retreated into a comforting past. They embraced the Spanish era's apparent romantic chivalry, preindustrial innocence, and harmonious hierarchy as a respite from the ugliness of modern times.

One can certainly make a case that anxiety provokes nostalgia and that uncertainty drives a search for the comfort of a certain past. This theory has provided some key analytical muscle for interpreting the meaning of public memories.[7] Explanations for the early twentieth-century national fascination with the Old South, for example, often follow such a trajectory; white Americans saw their newly industrial society fraying at the seams amid labor unrest, race riots, and teeming immigrants, and they found great psychic relief in a vision of gracious hegemony. As sectional tensions waned, myths of southern racial harmony, plantation elegance, and genteel sociability became more palatable to northerners. From Uncle Remus to Scarlett O'Hara, the Old South came to evoke for many white Americans a happier time and a less hurried pace of life that seemed everywhere in retreat after 1900.[8] In some ways, this relation of present anxiety to past comfort is evident in Southern California. Many people did speak of their dissatisfaction with the effects of progress on their cities and fellow citizens. They wanted Southern California to be modern, but not in the style of New York or Chicago. New residents also said they felt out of place and ill at ease in this landscape that seemed to have no recognizably American past. As this logic would predict, with the pace of change being both too fast and not fast enough, anxiety brewed and nostalgia blossomed.

Blaming modern angst is an attractive option, but to suggest that worry about the present leads directly to the pursuit of relief in the past makes memory merely an instinctive, almost reflexive reaction to change, requiring little thought or action. Romantic visions of Southern California's Spanish past reflected a range of Anglo responses to modernity, from utter dismay to enthusiastic validation. Many boosters envisioned Spanish themes as investments in the future, not withdrawal from it.[9] Anglos advertised regional history to serve their ambitious development plans—using it as a tourist draw and a theme for suburban styles and civic enhancement. The prevailing scholarly premise that such cultural memories emerge from feelings of insecurity about the present does not explain the booster mind-set in Southern California, in which various pasts represented potential catalysts for future regional success. Moreover, the anxiety model posits cultural memory as primarily defensive psychological compensation for groups that feel their fragility. Yet, in the archival record, Southern California Anglos appear to be more frequently confident than nervous. Eager to stay on the leading edge of urban progress, they revealed more than anxiety in their Spanish fantasies. In short, the Spanish past spelled growth, not retreat.

Past and progress may seem to work in opposition, but as this case suggests, they can operate in concert. If Southern California Anglos advanced a regional past in hopes of greasing the skids of progress, then longing for authentic, simple, picturesque pasts could not have been simply wistful pining or therapeutic escapism. Nostalgia participates in modern commodity culture even as it seems to resist it. Like the plantation myth in the South and the colonial revival in the East, in Southern California, Spanish genres were aesthetic styles Anglos might consume as much as products of antimodern longings.[10] Anglos built Spanish-colonial homes by the thousands, not only because they wanted tangible artifacts of the past but also because red-tile roofs showcased a popular style. The

Spanish past offered a good investment of financial and cultural capital in the regional future. Early speculation in the region has largely paid off, as Spanish homes on the Southern California real-estate market today have greater value than their ranch-style counterparts.[11]

Southern California's Spanish golden age offered a comforting past for Anglos, but Anglos did not inherit this past; they produced it. Regional history contained no inherently tranquil memory.[12] The romantic version of history may not have been completely fabricated, but it still required interpretive work that smoothed out conquest, genocide, and war as well as race, class, and religious conflict. Indeed, many Anglos did not initially see the possibility of a Spanish idyll. They judged the pre-Anglo region to be a poor and dusty backwater with little charm. Furthermore, a variety of readings of the past survived in turn-of-the-century Southern California. Some Yankee transplants tapped into a Spanish legacy, while others labeled it worthless. Mexican rancheros and Californios, as California-born Spanish speakers were known in the nineteenth century, burnished their own nostalgia in response to experiences of dispossession following the Mexican-American War; meanwhile, California Indians reconfigured their tribal histories and tradition to survive in the changing ethnic and national context. Anglo entrepreneurs carefully culled choice elements from these versions, silenced others, and rearranged these pieces into compelling regional narratives that spoke to their hopes for the future.

However delightful Anglo depictions of Spanish days came to seem, they did not typically signal a willingness to embrace Mexican or Indian Californians as fellow citizens in the present. Anglo memories drew the region's temporal boundaries to place Anglos at the center of Southern California's future while exiling all others to its past. As the promoters of Spanish style and memory at a Los Angeles marketplace characterized the relationship, Mexicans strolled the streets of yesterday, while Anglos inhabited a city of today.[13] These categories of time—past and present—came to define regional citizenship. Mexican and Indian people clearly could not live bodily in the past. Yet in myriad representations, the past became their natural abode, and they survived into the Anglo-American present only as artifacts, colorful but awkward remnants of another time. While all three groups (and considerably more) continued to coexist within the same regional space, the partition of time sanctioned the social and economic division of the region along racial lines. It generated a racialized understanding of regional identity and belonging, as well as a divided sense of place, that has persisted.

Southern California Anglos did not hatch romantic stories of the Spanish past as a conspiracy to divest Indians and Mexicans of public standing by pretending to celebrate their heritage. They did not have to do so. The nostalgia that took hold at the turn of the twentieth century was unnecessary to the project of acquiring power within the state. More mundane developments in the realms of real estate, law, the economy, demographics, and politics had already put power in Anglo hands by the time the romance got going.[14] Memories of the powerful can help consolidate and protect that power—indeed this reality is an inescapable theme of this book—but both the causes and the effects of their memories suggest more than a calculated manipulation or a devious ruse. The Spanish past figured variously into Anglo city-building projects, desires for a sense of local memory, and a search for a distinctive architecture. Moreover, many Anglos vouched genuine love for and appreciation of Indian and Mexican people and imagined a happy harmony between them and "Americans." Still, ethnic division was central to these visions of the past, giving the neat cleavage of yesterday and today its appeal as well as its consequence.

California Vieja explores the dynamics of memory, looking at how romantic versions of Southern California's Spanish past came to carry cultural weight in the region. The book focuses on the interaction between Anglo memory promoters and Mexican and Indian people during the construction of four venues that gave form and meaning to Southern California's regional memory: a mission highway, a world's fair, a suburban community, and an urban marketplace. Together, these places demonstrate how a set of cultural memories came to dominate discourse about the region as place, shaping both visions of the past and debates about public space and culture. This nostalgic style helped drive Southern California's fantastic growth in the early twentieth century. Anglos built their regional future literally by building the Spanish past into the urban and cultural landscapes. These representations and their vested racial terms thereby acquired a lasting material presence beyond the moment of expression and beyond Mexican-Anglo relations. These cultural memories played significant roles in twentieth-century California, both in the state's changing racial climate and its rise to national prominence.

This Southern California style of cultural remembering and its racial ironies have not escaped the notice of scholars and observers over the years. Farsighted critic Carey McWilliams christened it the "Spanish fantasy heritage" in 1946, deeming it a manifestation of Southern

California's "schizophrenic" mentality. Many observers continue to wonder how Anglos could simultaneously celebrate the Spanish past and denigrate the Mexican present without collapsing under the weight of their own contradictions. Was this fantasy past, as McWilliams intimated, largely a promotional tool that few realtors and boosters sincerely believed, or were Anglos willing dupes of a false version of history? Either way, the disparity between the romantic view of regional history and social life on the ground in Southern California has been the source of much academic incredulity.[15] More astonishing perhaps, as several writers have shown, have been the real-life effects of the regional investment in such fantasies. In the words of one scholar who picked up McWilliams's trail, the construction of the city of the future required a coat of historical whitewash, an institutionalized forgetting of Los Angeles's cultural and economic dependence on Mexican residents in both past and present. Anglos' popular vision of the California past might dissipate modern fears of the Mexicans in their midst by forming a "cultural salve of equal parts dissonance and romance."[16] The romantic past enabled Anglos somehow to comfortably maintain a stance that now appears to be a serious ideological fallacy.

Yet this focus on the past as paradox has made the region's popular history into just one more of the state's many oddities in many people's minds, part of what distinguishes wacky California from the rest of the nation. Ersatz, counterfeit, misrepresentative, ironic, unique: Anglo perceptions of the Spanish past may have been all of these things, but to see them as logical impossibilities, albeit remarkable ones, is to miss a key point. This cultural memory is not simply a West Coast curiosity; it is an example of a central method Americans have used to express race and nation. From blackface minstrelsy to a passion for Navajo blankets, white Americans' ability to disdain and yet desire, to reject and yet possess, was a familiar and consistent strategy for dealing with nonwhite people and cultures in the nineteenth and twentieth centuries.[17] Patterns of cultural appropriation are not so much bizarre as ominously rational (and national). Racial discourses were fundamental to the ways that Southern California Anglos, and increasingly Americans in general, defined local identity, made national claims, boosted economic progress, expressed community, built houses, understood places, and interpreted history. How an apparently whimsical cultural memory accomplished such a task—fusing race and division with regional and national identity and building this amalgam into the landscape—is the story of this book.

How did Southern California become characteristically Spanish but undeniably American? With the region's seemingly opposite definitions of place, Anglos worked to build an image of their adopted region that would complement their national loyalties. Southern California Anglos wanted to contribute to patriotic narratives, but hailing Plymouth Rock, Bunker Hill, or even the Alamo did the region little good. Adapting local memories to national metaphors offered a more workable strategy of place, one that had worked for many hallowed American sites. Thus Anglos sought to assert a Spanish legacy less to counter national stories than to join them. Popular memories put local progress on a higher national plane, celebrating how colonial Spain gave way to American empire and hailing Southern California as the vanguard of American progress and civilization. This movement toward empire, anchored in Spain, created an obliging local context in which nationalism could gain expression.[18]

How regions or localities related to the American nation was changing in the late nineteenth century, which was a time both of healing sectional divides and of defining regional differences. Expansion of the nation's territorial arc strengthened Americans' sense of nationalism but also prompted them to think of themselves as parts of regions in new ways. Regions increasingly came to be defined less by their particular ways of life—as the wheels of industrial capitalism and consumer culture began to roll across the continent—than by their distinctive looks, or personalities.[19] Thus regional definition dovetailed with, rather than diverged from, the post–Civil War rebuilding of national identity. Historical memories became critical to these negotiations. Commemorations of the Civil War, which occupied much public attention in the era, are a good example of this type of self-definition. Commemorations both encouraged national reunion and marked the South with an aestheticized regional past. For many white southerners, national reconciliation came via their perceptions of restored regional pride. Not only did soldiers become loyal bands of brothers in one national family, but praise for Confederate heroism also featured the valiant defense of regional identity. As northern fascination with the romantic myth of the South increased, as tottering old veterans shook hands over the wall at Gettysburg, the national myth did not so much trump regional identity as institutionalize it.[20] At the same time, a mythic version of the West was defining national identity in a different fashion. Buffalo Bill Cody's Wild West shows, historian Frederick Jackson Turner's frontier thesis, Theodore Roosevelt's strenuous life, and the eager eastern audiences they held in thrall all agreed that western experiences produced an ideal American character. This West solidified white Americans' memories of the nation's pioneer heritage, its past triumph over wilderness, and its unlimited promise.[21]

In making these local-national connections, such narratives on the surface appeared to leave out some key actors. The dominant interpretations of post–Civil War sectional reunion failed to recall African-American participation and federal emancipationist aims. The immensely popular mythic West relied upon notions of vanishing natives and empty land. Yet the plantation myth did not render African-Americans invisible, nor were Plains Indian peoples absent from the frontier stage. On the contrary, these groups were necessary components of the myths. How could they be both visible and vanishing? In essence, they became the foils in stories of regional pride and national unity, largely playing the role of permanent outsiders. Nowhere was this process more evident than in Southern California, where Indian and Mexican residents became marginal citizens despite their central roles in Anglos' imagined regional past. Visibility, in this case, did not imply recognition or acceptance but rather the conspicuousness of a stranger.[22]

Southern California's racial terminology complemented a national tendency to distance whites from nonwhites, though it often diverged from other regional patterns. According to the leading local press in the early twentieth century, two groups almost solely peopled the region: Anglos and Mexicans. These labels concealed the great diversity within and between these groups. White Americans, however, learned to use the moniker *Anglo,* for which *American* seemed to be a close synonym, to differentiate themselves from *Mexican,* conflating racial and national identity on both sides. Clearly, not all white Southern Californians were of English origin, and many whites fit awkwardly in this ethnic designation. But in Los Angeles, Russian Jews and Irish Catholics were nominally Anglos (although Chinese were not), at least in comparison to Mexicans. While this division seemed to parallel the career of European immigrants and the consolidation of white racial identity vis-à-vis African-Americans in the East, Southern Californians remained attached to the term *Anglo* as a salient social identification. The term neither referenced individual ethnicity nor implied the lack of one; it simply signaled *not Mexican.*

For Anglos, *Mexican* usually indicated not a romantic regional past but the immigrant present. By the end of the nineteenth century, *Mexican* had become a derogatory term in the popular press and even in the halls of government, and the word masked significant and sizable differences among ethnic Mexican groups. Mexican people, American citizens and otherwise, described themselves in various ways—including *Californios, mexicanos,* and terms tracing their allegiance to points of origin in Mexico—reflecting their attachment to places in the border region or to cultural and generational ties, all of which evolved over time. The category that became *Spanish* referred less to a people than to an era, and the term *Spanish-American,* which could reference Spanish speakers in New Mexico or the Southwest, never found wide use in California. Anglos marshaled *Spanish* at times to establish Europeanness and used the term most significantly to distinguish something, again, from things Mexican. The term *Indians,* too, for Anglos, referenced a regional past more than a group of residents, although Southern California contained a significant, and after 1900, growing population of native peoples who usually referenced themselves by tribal affiliation.[23] This complicated net of racial labeling was in certain ways peculiar to the region, and its reductionist effects played a vital role in producing narratives of regional identity and diversity.

Race became a key method of determining regional and national belonging, in and beyond California. Atlantic City's experience offers a telling example of how racial discourses became embedded in people's sense of place. As urban historian Bryant Simon has shown, many Americans came to the New Jersey resort town to promenade on the boardwalk and announce their arrival as members of the middle class. Yet one of the key ways they did so was by paying African-Americans to push them up and down the boardwalk in wicker chairs. While the drama of social mobility made Atlantic City tick, landing atop a racial ladder was the principal marker of having achieved the American dream.[24] Southern California's Spanish memories offered similarly exclusive fantasies, symbolizing elite aspirations to regional status. Mexicans and Indians were more than servants in Anglo memories. The romantic visions of the Spanish past celebrated them as conduits of the region's unique heritage. This celebration, however, depended upon their explicit differentiation from Anglos. This "festive deployment of race and ethnicity," as one scholar has described the phenomenon, celebrated cultural differences, but largely as commodities available for Anglo possession.[25] The Anglo traffic in Spanish pasts offers an opportunity to examine the centrality of exclusion in many people's sense of place, past, and public culture and to explore how racial difference can become integral to national identity.

Women's role in building Anglo Southern California's Spanish memories highlighted this split in regional personality. Across the United States, women took on public roles in memory production: preserving historic structures, artifacts, and sentiments became a proper avocation for active society women of the late nineteenth century and Progressive Era, and these activities helped create favorable constituencies for suffrage. When few opportunities existed for women to contribute to academic historical dialogue, budding female public historians appeared in leadership positions in cities throughout the nation.[26] This activity was not, however, a tide that lifted all women regardless of race or class. In Southern California, as elsewhere, largely elite Anglo women were able to take advantage of the region's Spanish past as a method of increasing their stature. Indeed, Anglo women were largely at the helm of the venues described in this study. Their stewardship, however, did not lead to a particularly feminist or democratic version of history. For example, many people's fascination with the Spanish era focused on the highly eroticized figure of the sultry señorita. For Mexican women, this role allowed some opportunities for performance work. But it could also confine them, hindering rather than facilitating any desires to participate in Anglo-dominated politics and public culture. Yet when Anglo women donned the señorita's costume for an evening, they gained both celebratory license and credit for preservation. In short, Anglo women profited from the Spanish past while Mexican women appeared to live within it. The dissimilar fortunes of Anglo matrons and Mexican señoritas embodied the racial divergence at the heart of Southern California's Spanish romance.

No one has seen this contradiction more clearly than have the putative objects of Anglo longings: California Indians and ethnic Mexicans themselves. These groups keenly understood the combined effects of Anglos' relegating their culture to a quaint past and segregating them through labor, residence, and language. Anglo nostalgia for a Spanish golden age marked Mexicans and Indians alike as outsiders, if often visible ones, in their own land.[27] Yet, despite the authority of Anglos' romantic memories, the dominant fantasy muted rather than silenced unorthodox versions of the past. As scores of scholars have demonstrated, Mexican and Indian people established lives independent of Anglo typecasting, beyond boosters' narrow renditions of their history, culture, and identities. They remained active, if not formally recognized, parties in the imagining of their public personae. Moreover, Anglo memories forced them to formulate new tactics to contest both the material conquest of California and the rhetorical capture of its past. Scholars' debate over the meanings of the Spanish past for Anglos, as well as the focus on the invented nature of the romantic version, often figures Mexicans and Indians as passive victims. Yet this view cannot account for the fact that the increasing prominence of Southern California's Spanish era in the modern Anglo landscape met with strong Mexican and Indian response. Though dissenting Mexican and Indian voices found little purchase in public culture during the period of Anglo dominance, they outlasted this era and gained ground in later decades.[28]

Such alternative memories are typically assumed to represent the voice of the oppressed, to be genuinely liberating and to offer a truer sense of history than elite versions do.[29] Yet the great variation of such countermemories shows that none had special access to truth or authenticity. For example, Mexican-American theater reputedly preserved a pure tradition of critique, even when it could not air in the Anglo public. Not all ethnic Mexicans adopted this stance, however. For example, Southern California's Padua Hills theater offered Spanish-language plays for an Anglo audience that incorporated romantic myths popular at the time with the tacit goal of improving ethnic relations. Though Anglo run, these productions did give Mexican performers an expanded space for self-representation. As Matt Garcia writes, the meaning of Padua Hills plays is difficult to decipher. The plays seem on the one hand to contribute to Anglo mythologies and on the other to work against them. That these performances resulted from a desire to overturn negative stereotypes and to portray Mexican people in a positive light does not negate the fact that the resulting images constrained Mexicans in other ways.[30] Should we call this kind of theater a form of resistance or cooptation?

How also should we view the elder Mexican-Californian residents in the late nineteenth century, the Californios who reminisced about the days before the Yankees came? They simultaneously waxed nostalgic about the same elements of rancho culture that Anglos later found appealing, bemoaned the loss of their position at the top of a racially stratified labor system, and protested their discrimination at the hands of their American successors. Besides providing some of the raw materials for Anglo romance, as chapter 1 discusses, they hoped to hedge against actively negative views of Mexican-Californians in the mainstream press and the threat of becoming irrelevant to the Anglo historical record.[31] Whether on the stage or with the pen, or simply among their own communities, Mexicans and Indians preserved their memories, if not always in lockstep or in simplistically conceived modes of resistance.

Examining the survival of marginal memories despite great duress is important, but so is the larger context in which preservers of these memories had to maneuver. Ethnic Mexicans and California Indians may have chipped away at the Anglo consensus, but they did not make serious, immediate inroads into the dominant public culture. Anglos designated their visions of the Spanish past as official, and their prevailing regional history held sway over Southern California's cultural landscape for decades. Challengers to this legacy did not start from a clean slate but had to counter what became accepted wisdom.[32] The Anglo appropriation of California's Indian, Spanish, and Mexican past was so forceful that to disentangle romance and history, one would have to unravel race and the nation itself. This task would also require the symbolic dismantling of a built environment that continually reinforces visual connections between Southern California and a romantic sense of Spanishness.

California Vieja examines this enduring landscape in four representative places that I call venues: El Camino Real, the Panama-California Exposition, Rancho Santa Fe, and Olvera Street. Venues are, on one level, physical spaces and buildings that, if not permanent, persist even while accommodating change, often beyond personal memory. Highways, exposition buildings, homes, and marketplaces were ways in which Anglos marked out places on the landscape. That the sites I discuss here still exist testifies to the enduring resonance of the romantic Spanish past. Sociologist Maurice Halbwachs, often seen as the progenitor of modern memory studies, suggests that memory lives and works through social groups. Yet, to last, it must also survive in material things and representations. If memory were simply an abstraction, a mental note, it could neither be shared beyond a personal frame of reference nor become part of public culture.[33] Memory promoters seek to materialize their versions of the past in some fashion, through texts, media, artifacts, and places. The built environment offers particularly lasting material for transmitting memories to posterity and thus for studying their effects.

These venues, however, are more than physical places. They are also arenas for events. Not only do buildings permit reinterpretations as new generations inhabit them, but they provide only an abbreviated form of the memories they embody.[34] People do not passively inherit memory, whether from a person or a building; they actively produce it. If memory is something one has to perform, do, and practice, then historic built environments are most notable when they become stages for dramatizing the meanings of the past in the present.[35] A road, a fair, a suburb, and a street are the outcomes of discussions of how best to build living monuments of memory. These places, their continued popularity as sites both for leisure and for contestation, demonstrate how certain memories retain cultural currency even while under debate. Through this ability to persist and adapt, as much as through its material presence, memory leaves a footprint on the landscape that one can remove only with much effort.

Between 1900 and 1940 Anglos gradually stamped their versions of the Spanish past onto the local landscape. As chapters 2 and 3 detail, wildly popular Spanish memories began as tentative and locally suspect slogans to entice tourists and potential emigrants to Southern California. Anglo promoters had to convince their fellow residents of the utility of the Spanish past in selling the region. Over the first two decades of the century, the argument began to work. As more newcomers arrived, they came with expectations of finding Spanish romance and the good life in Southern California. Where they could not see this vision, they set about building it with ever-greater faith in its regional suitability. Imagining themselves to be latter-day conquistadors, Anglos captured the region's history and territory. Metaphors of conquest from the Spanish past became synonymous with growth and were shorthand for belief in racial and national succession in the region. Between 1920 and 1940 the Spanish past began to surface in the everyday living apparatus in Southern Californian homes and cities. Chapters 4 and 5 illustrate how the Spanish mode gradually came to dominate the landscape as the quintessential built expression of Southern California. The coined architectural idiom of Spanish colonial connoted exclusivity, high property values, and the suburban good life. Leisure experiences keyed to Spanish themes proliferated, often requiring the labor of Mexican people to produce physically and to authenticate the illusions, though their participation unintentionally invited more public debates about the past in the years to come.

To read the history of a place through its buildings requires more than tracing the skyline; one must read broadly into the stories and people behind the buildings. In Southern California, much of this history resides in the ephemeral material of culture: the commercial print and visual media that best capture the expressive nature of these memories. That a narrative developed on stray tourist brochures, the backs of postcards, and magazine advertisements could become a lasting material presence is perhaps surprising. For indeed, the origins of these landmark structures lay not in official records but in yesterday's junk mail. True, these sources are "compromised" in that they are mediated and promotional. Southern California Anglos' "real" feelings, as might be divulged in confessional manuscripts, remain an elusive if highly questionable quarry. Rather, guidebooks, promotional articles, and the like were the ways in which most Anglos accessed the shifting forms of the Spanish past. Anglos' memories developed as they encountered places already defined for them in printed image and text. That individuals could form their own interpretations is of course possible, but the standard views that appear in private representations show that remarkably few views of the past fell outside the romantic range. Such narratives of the past, whether personal or produced, offer sources for accessing the experience of place and the practice of memory.[36] As authors of promotional tracts, boosters of venues, and consumers of memory, Anglos together produced broadly popular views of Southern California's Spanish past and American future. Old California, California *vieja,* was a modern place indeed.

Popular history is often conceived as a sequence of important places. To travel from Independence Hall to the Vietnam Veterans Memorial, from Gettysburg to Ground Zero, or perhaps from Colonial Williamsburg to Disneyland is to relive the story of the United States. The promise of experiencing time in space, which is at the heart of historical theme parks, sends many people to visit places of the past. These places' physical, virtual, or architectural reenactments are not just about personifying a past. They seek to make memories and places meaningful in the present.[37] In Southern California, historical space included old missions and new architecture, fanciful fairs and quaint markets. In public culture, it also came to embody racial divisions and to provide places in which Anglos celebrated their versions of other peoples' pasts. The region may be unique in this regard, but its cultural memories of the Spanish past illuminate the essential, but complicated, relationship between memory and place. Memory places are sites of cultural production and venues for struggles over public space, racial politics, and citizenship in America.

PART ONE

Locating the Past

CHAPTER I

Los Días Pasados

Tales from Nineteenth-Century California

The genesis of Anglo fascination with the Spanish pasts of Southern California arguably was the publication of *Ramona* in 1884. Helen Hunt Jackson's melodramatic romance about an Indian Cinderella painted the region's past as a sublime' historical narrative—tragic, breathtaking, luxurious, and intimate. Readers were enthralled. *Ramona* became the most famous fiction work about Southern California and a national bestseller, inspiring countless fans to visit the book's picturesque setting. In the 1880s and 1890s California tourists carried their copies of *Ramona* along with their travel guides. With the New Englander Jackson as a guide, wealthy easterners spent many a winter tramping up and down the landscape looking for the sites and characters of the story.[1] With the onslaught of these *Ramona* seekers, the transformation of Southern California's memory began. The romance-starved Americans from the East set about resurrecting the forgotten past and refashioning Southern California's history and landscape. Or so goes the conventional wisdom.[2]

However potent, *Ramona* was neither the first attempt to romanticize Southern California nor the last word on the region. Anglos did not have the first claim on an idyllic vision of the Spanish past, nor was this past an abandoned idea they suddenly rediscovered. In fact, Jackson herself relied upon earlier retellings by Californios, whose own idealized construction of *los días pasados,* bygone days, was an altered interpretation of the past.[3] These Spanish speakers' nostalgia for pregringo

times was itself a response to witnessing their own decline and dispossession since the loss of the Mexican-American War, with Anglos treat-
ing their presence and past on the land largely as obstacles to onrushing
progress. In a swirl of alternative stories that sought to define the nineteenth century, Anglo desire for a Spanish idyll arose late and did so
only as Californios' ability to represent such a society began to fade in
the face of American migration and the rising market economy. At this
time, the purposes to which Anglos and Californios put their memories
could not have been more different. *Ramona* represented a bold first
strike for Anglo mining of these memories, but for reasons I discuss
later, the book was at best an awkward vehicle that could not alone
have spawned the transformation of Southern California's built environment. Nevertheless, understanding where *Ramona* came from and
what captivated its early readers can help us understand how Spanish
fantasies emerged and why they had a strong impact on regional culture
and politics for decades to come.

"A PICTURESQUE LIFE"

Ramona opens with a lush description of a Spanish rancho and its matriarch, Señora Moreno, set in the recent past. Moreno is struggling to keep
her family's estate afloat in a new world of American rule. Both author
and subject reminisce about the old days, before the gringos came. "It
was a picturesque life, with more of sentiment and gayety in it, more
also that was truly dramatic, more romance, than will ever be seen again
on those shores. The aroma of it all lingers there still; industries and
inventions have not yet slain it; it will last out its century—in fact, it can
never be quite lost, so long as there is standing one such house as the
Señora Moreno's."[4] Enter the heroine, Ramona, an orphan born to a
Scotsman and a California Indian woman. She comes to live on the
Moreno ranch through the Señora's sister, who had once been the Scotsman's fiancée, and thus is unaware of her ignoble birth. Like Cinderella,
Ramona finds maltreatment at the hands of her adoptive stepmother
despite gathering the adoration of all the other characters. She is
supremely beautiful, innately good, and generous to a fault. To Señora
Moreno's dismay, her only son, Felipe, heir to the rancho and the personification of American stereotypes of indolent Spaniards, worships
Ramona from afar. Both the story and Jackson's rich description of the
setting drew in her nineteenth-century readers. The opening chapters
chronicle daily life: the colors of the sunset, the goings-on of the

servants, the mysterious Catholic devotions, and preparation for the annual sheep shearing. Among the loyal Indian band of shepherds that arrive to perform this work is Alessandro, the young, handsome leader. Alessandro earns nothing but praise from the author and from his fellow characters for his deference and work ethic, yet the relations between the various groups on the rancho—the Spanish Morenos, the mestizo servants, and the Indian shearers—betray a complicated ethnic milieu.

To many people in the nineteenth century, a claim of Spanish heritage spoke to European roots and pure blood, whereas Mexican heritage connoted mixed-race ancestry. Few Californios could prove that their families contained purely Spanish bloodlines, though the term carried that connotation at the time. In this sense, an assertion of Spanish heritage staked claim to class as much as race, aiming to recall noble birth and elite station. The Morenos who owned the ranch were Spanish; their servants were Mexican. *Ramona*'s readers came to see this ethnic divide as a class distinction, having encountered in Texas and other parts of the Southwest a view of Mexicans as dirty and degraded.[5] For Southern California Anglos, the Mexican label also marked a person as an immigrant, no matter his or her nativity. If Mexicans were marked as outsiders, Spanish Californios appeared to have some claim on the region's history; and indeed they often invoked their past in their late nineteenth-century struggle for inclusion in white California society.

The racial factor that purportedly differentiated those who called themselves Spanish from Mexicans was Indian blood. Señora Moreno, though she employed Indians on her ranch, judged them to be an inferior race: "Of what is it that these noble lords of villages are so proud? their ancestors—naked savages less than one hundred years ago? Naked savages they themselves too, today, if we had not come here to teach and civilize them. The race was never meant for anything but servants." Southern California Anglos largely shared this view that the region's Indians were among the least civilized people of the world and had been only partially redeemed by Spanish missionaries. Readers of sentimental fiction may have joined the chorus, but following Jackson's portrait of Moreno as meanly prejudiced, they could also have read Alessandro as a "noble" if "naked" savage.[6]

The racial dynamics in the book make for much of its drama, as Ramona falls head over heels for Alessandro. The possibility of romance between the lowly Indian laborer and the apparently high-born Spanish maiden titillated readers, though such cross-race love was not an uncommon device among Jackson's counterparts in the dime-novel industry.

The señora tries to dissuade Ramona from marrying Alessandro, first by stressing the nobility of her Spanish name and then by shaming her with her Indian parentage. Moreno eventually forbids the marriage and locks Ramona in her room. Ramona makes a daring escape, and she and Alessandro elope. Shorn of her elite comforts, Ramona at first enjoys the Indian outdoor life, as Jackson takes the lovers on a spectacular journey through a lush and beauteous countryside that, for all of California's charms, has no earthly location. Yet the pair's life at a series of Indian villages holds few pleasures and little time for love. The couple is desperately poor, and every effort Alessandro makes to become a good farmer fails. American squatters menace Ramona's and Alessandro's tenuous land claims, and the couple's first child dies due to the negligence of an Anglo doctor. Ramona somehow retains a sunny outlook, but Alessandro becomes distraught and begins to lose his mind. During one of his delusions, he accidentally rides home on the wrong horse. The only true villain in the book, a drunk American cowboy, accuses him of being a horse thief and shoots him dead. Ramona collapses and lies for weeks perilously close to death, and readers prepare themselves for a maudlin Victorian deathbed scene. At the last moment, however, Moreno's son, Felipe, arrives to rescue Ramona from an anonymous death and brings her back to health and to the Moreno ranch, where the señora has conveniently passed away herself. Felipe marries Ramona and restores her honor, yet the two are unable to keep the family's ranch in the face of a determined American onslaught. Seeing no place for Ramona and Felipe in Southern California, Jackson sends them off to Mexico, where Ramona becomes the belle of the city despite a broken heart.

This romantic drama drew heavily on the historical tensions of nineteenth-century California and nearly a century of colonial settlement. Whether this history was familiar or foreign to American readers, Jackson used the successive conquests of California as the background for many of the characters' motivations: Señora Moreno's resentment of the Americans, Ramona's mixed parentage, Alessandro's despair. The author projected her view of Indians' and Californios' feelings about Anglo-Americans' arrival and subsequent power grab. Novelist Albion Tourgée spent much of his career criticizing Southern romantic mythmaking for blurring the emancipationist goals of the Civil War, yet in an 1886 review, he applauded Jackson for putting romance to good use: "The story is laid in California, but it is not altogether our California. . . . Hitherto, fiction has treated California only as the seat of a new civilization . . . gold diggers paradise, adventurers' Eden, speculators'

El Dorado. *Ramona* pictures it as the Indian's lost inheritance and the Spaniard's desolated home."[7] Indeed it was.

"WHAT MISERY!"

The Indian population of Southern California was numerous and diverse before the Spanish arrived to attempt permanent settlements in the eighteenth century. Though the coastal plains and valleys were not as thickly settled as the northern section was, Kumeyaay, Ipai/Tipai, Cahuilla, Acjachemem, Tongva, and Chumash tribal groups (often known later as Diegueño, Cupeño, Luiseño, Juaneño, Gabrielino, Fernandeño, and Barbareño, according to their association with certain Spanish missions) could be found living there in small seasonal villages. Farther inland, Coahilla, Mohave, and other bands peopled the mountains and deserts, if a bit more sparsely. Language, social relations, and political organization separated these groups culturally despite their geographical proximity. Estimates put the total number of Indian residents in the southern region prior to European colonization at thirty-five thousand to forty thousand.[8] These numbers began to decline when European explorers arrived and brought disease with them: European contact had come as early as the mid-sixteenth century, when a few early explorers happened upon San Diego Bay and traded with local inhabitants. The Spanish did not arrive in force, however, until 1769, nearly 250 years after their conquest of Mexico. Southern California represented the far northern frontier of colonial New Spain, and unlike wealthy Mexico, it was poor and inaccessible. When rivals such as Russia and England began to investigate the neglected colony, Spain decided to establish its claim on Alta California more securely. Missionaries and soldiers were dispatched from Baja California to convert native populations and establish governance in the region. San Diego became the site of the first mission and presidio (garrison), and more outposts quickly followed.[9]

Missionaries were a key part of Spanish colonization strategy, because they attempted to gain Indian loyalty through religious conversion rather than brute force, lessening the need for a major military presence. In California, this job fell to the Franciscan order and its local leader, Junípero Serra. The missionaries' aim was to transform Indians into Christian worshippers and skilled laborers for the colony. The padres established mission communities wherever they encountered abundant Indian settlements. By 1792 they had founded six missions in the southern portion of Alta California: from south to north, they were

San Diego, San Luis Rey, San Juan Capistrano, San Gabriel, San Fernando, and San Buenaventura. Attracting Indians with food and European goods, missionaries housed anywhere from hundreds to thousands of "neophytes," as they called their followers. These converted Indians lived in sex-segregated, dormitory housing and performed mandatory labor; once they came to live at the mission, their lives were under strict surveillance by the missionaries; escape was punishable, and discipline, in keeping with early modern standards, was often severe. Because of, or perhaps despite, the harsh regime, mission Indians became the primary productive force for the Spanish colony, as they tilled fields, herded cattle, made olive oil and wine, constructed buildings, designed furniture, produced leather, cooked meals, forged iron, sewed clothing, and accomplished all manner of work on these extensive plantations. Southern California missions produced greater wealth than those in the central or northern portions of the chain, which eventually numbered twenty-one and ended in Sonoma, just north of San Francisco.[10]

Unfortunately, as fast as the Franciscans could recruit Indians, disease decimated their communities, both inside and outside of the missions. In the seventy-five years following Spanish settlement, California Indian populations dropped to one-third of their precontact numbers. The crowded nature of mission life, which brought together several thousands of people used to living in groups of several dozen, accelerated the effects that plagued native populations throughout the New World. European-borne diseases devastated political structures, family networks, village life, and religious traditions. In weathering this onslaught, California Indians alternately adapted to Spanish culture and resisted it. They continued to serve as an indispensable labor force for the colony and found ways to express themselves in European forms of artwork and music. But neophytes periodically fomented rebellion, sometimes killing priests and burning buildings. Others returned to home villages and launched raids on mission establishments, absconding with livestock and produce. Consistent Indian resistance and inconsistent state support hampered Spain's efforts to gain complete control over the native populations of California.[11] A dearth of colonists from Spain and Mexico made matters worse. Few people were willing to live in the rude and remote northern outposts, despite enticements of land, money, and tax exemptions. Spanish population, capital, and trade grew slowly.

When Mexico won its independence in 1821, it stepped up economic development in its province of Alta California with a more liberal distribution of land grants. While colonists took the offers, the enormous size of these ranchos and their mammoth cattle herds increased production more than population. More land became available in the 1830s, as Mexico embarked on a plan to "secularize" the missions, essentially putting them out of business. The Franciscans' agricultural enterprises reverted to the government, which sold off the lands and stock for profit, reducing missions to parish churches. Secularization freed Indians from forced labor but nothing more. Some tried to return to their villages, while others now hired out their labor on the ranchos, often with conditions no better than those at the mission.[12]

Indian labor helped produce a class of Californio rancheros who commanded vast cattle empires and became a closely intermarried oligarchy that had far more power in the region than any arm of the Mexican government. This local sway caused constant tension between the California landed classes and the governors imposed on the area by Mexico City. Californios' wealth depended entirely on the hide and tallow trade, with some sheep raising, grape growing, and grain production for local consumption. While this limited focus left Californios vulnerable when the California economy diversified in later decades, the social organization of this economy, with the Indian peon as the primary laborer, allowed the *patrón* to live in relative luxury. Rancheros did not live as leisured a lifestyle as one might assume, however; Californianas, especially, worked hard to keep the large rancho households running. Still, the social expectations included frequent festivities for marriages, saints' days, rodeos, and other sporting contests. The fiestas and *bailes* that became so popular in cultural memories were gay occasions to be sure, yet they required labor by both Californios and Indians. These social events revolved around the extended family, the essential unit of ranchero life.[13]

Almost as soon as Mexican rancho society set down roots, Anglo-Americans began to arrive and insinuate themselves into the Californio elite. Ambitious young men from Massachusetts and elsewhere married into Californio families by converting to Catholicism and becoming Mexican citizens, as Mexican law required. They adapted to local customs and often Hispanicized their first names, as Liverpool-born John Forster did when he assumed the moniker of Don Juan Forster upon his 1837 marriage to Doña Ysidora Pico, sister of the governor. Typically, however, these American "dons" grafted such acculturation onto American-style economic practices. Anglo-Californio family alliances were thus also economic partnerships, widening trade with the United States. For example, when Bostonian Alfred Robinson arrived in the

1830s as a junior agent for the powerful Bryant, Sturgis and Company, he asked for the hand of thirteen-year-old Doña Anita de la Guerra, daughter of one of the most powerful ranchero families. When the two married, Robinson joined the California gentry while the De la Guerras netted an inside track for the trade of their hides and tallow. While such unions were not the automatic tickets to economic success and membership in the social gentry that they seemed, the image of a beautiful Californiana happily marrying an ambitious American endured among Anglos as an evocative metaphor for the natural cession of land and power. The view of California as a "child bride" appeared to confirm the rightful custody of an American protector.[14]

Other visitors found in Southern California a national opportunity more than a personal one. Falling back on stereotypes of lazy Mexicans, many people believed that Mexico had failed to develop California to its fullest potential. When American travelers saw adobe buildings where they thought wood houses and brick banks should be, they judged California towns to be utterly backward. Richard Henry Dana visited in this era and loved the landscape but not the people; his famous lament in 1843 reflected many Anglo-Americans' sentiment: "In the hands of an enterprising people, what a country this might be!"[15] Such beliefs spurred incipient faith in America's Manifest Destiny to span the continent. The Mexican-American War, begun in Texas, quickly focused on California, which Americans saw as a possible trophy. Few in number and mixed in political leanings, Southern California rancheros mounted only scattered resistance and one pitched battle against the invaders. The Treaty of Guadalupe Hidalgo ceded California along with the area that would become the Southwest to the United States in February 1848 and incorporated promises to honor the rights of former Mexican citizens.

However, these promises fell by the wayside, and the discovery of gold the following month in the Sierra Nevada foothills of California altered the state's social geography nearly overnight. Ethnic tensions between Anglos, Mexicans, and Chinese flowed out of the mines and throughout the state. The hunt for the legendary bandit Joaquín Murieta virtually gave license to assault Spanish speakers, whether they were citizens or not. In the north, Anglo-Americans overwhelmed the existing population; most of the one hundred thousand to two hundred thousand new people who arrived in California by 1852 landed in San Francisco. Californios quickly found themselves to be a small minority in the state that had recently been theirs, but in Southern California the process of attrition was more gradual.[16] Anglos steadily trickled into the region and looked hungrily at the large lands owned by Californios. Squatters first became a nuisance and then a major threat to rancheros, who were forced to defend their ownership to the U.S. government with little documentation that the courts would respect. The high costs of the litigation and significant tax burden compelled landowners to sell off much of their ranches piece by piece. For example, Mariano G. Vallejo, one of the most prominent Californios both before and after the war, saw his Northern California holdings gradually shrink from 175,000 acres to the grounds of his heavily mortgaged Sonoma home by 1874. Overproduction of beef for gold miners in the 1850s magnified financial difficulties, and an extended drought in the 1860s pushed many rancheros to the brink of financial ruin. The rancho economy disintegrated, Anglo entrepreneurs converted small pieces of the giant cattle ranches to agricultural uses, and merchants, bankers, and a small number of manufacturers moved in to service these ventures.[17] When the Southern Pacific Railroad arrived in Los Angeles from the north in 1876, Anglo urban and economic fortunes seemed to be on the rise.

For Californios, however, these events created tough times. The ranchero families that had weathered the early years of American rule became increasingly outnumbered and surrounded in Southern California. As early as the 1870s, they held a mere fraction of the political sway and economic clout that they had had only a decade before. Elite Californios in particular experienced the defeat largely in terms of this dispossession. Where before they had been at the pinnacle of California society as members of landed classes, they now saw their land eroded and their culture engulfed by the Anglo-Americans they had once welcomed. Not surprisingly, many Californios felt this disjunction personally, as the war ruptured the continuity of their life expectations. As Mariano Vallejo wrote to his wife in 1877, "What a difference between the present time and those that preceded the usurpation by the Americans. If the Californios could all gather together to breathe a lament, it would reach Heaven as a moving sigh which would cause fear and consternation in the universe. What misery!" Californios were resentful and disillusioned, painfully aware of their status as social exiles, and constantly reminded of their linguistic, ethnic, and political displacement.[18]

Contributing to the melancholy was a communal fear of eradication, if not from California itself, from the pages of its past. Not only were Californios losing out by measure of population, but they also found themselves at the short end of the historical record as Anglos began to write them out of significance. Exhortations appeared in the Spanish-language press in the 1870s prodding Californios to defend themselves from erasure.[19] Stronger than their frustration with Anglo attempts to silence them, however, was their anger at the increasing misrepresentation of their social history. The 1860s and 1870s witnessed a hardening of anti-Mexican views and group stereotypes, and Californios often had a difficult time extricating themselves from Anglos' blanket indictments. Late nineteenth-century popular culture also contained portrayals of Californios as "lazy, cowardly, and incompetent."[20]

With a common desire to counter such mean Anglo depictions and to keep their own stories alive, Californios developed a strategy that scholar Genaro Padilla has called an "autobiographical impulse." Yet they had few mainstream media outlets in which to air their refutations. The likeliest way for Californio expressions to reach the Anglo majority in the 1870s was through a project of the prolific compiler of state history Hubert Howe Bancroft. In commissioning research for his volumes on Spanish and Mexican California, Bancroft sent emissaries to interview as many Californios as they could locate and persuade to talk. While some remained suspicious of this project, others, like some Vallejo, became convinced that it offered a strategic opportunity to inject Californios into public history. He and other Californios hoped to maneuver their contributions in a way that countered the dominant discourse and hedged against oblivion. Their narratives, Padilla suggests, were "no less than warfare waged within the text of California history. . . . The Californios, who had lost the war and with it their lands and social position, must not lose their papers or their memories of a way of life increasingly maligned by others." So, one by one, they either composed their memoirs or consented to be interviewed by Bancroft's agents.[21]

Intriguingly, however, Californios' testimonials betray little anger on the surface. Their social critique is embedded within otherwise largely nostalgic texts that are reminiscent of Jackson's dreamy portrait. Many, if not all, Californios romanticized the rancho society they had lost. They imagined prewar California as an idyllic, harmonious world, and their descriptions reached longingly back to it. However exaggerated these memories might have been, they offered a clear rebuke to Anglos' malicious characterizations—unlike Jackson's view of the past, which in some ways relied upon the stereotypes. Californios' nostalgia became a mode through which to respond to and oppose their displacement. Their past may have been an invented one, perhaps created out of defeat, but it was also a strategic one. Their romantic remembrance offered a method of dealing with the miserable present. Their past was oppositional as

well as nostalgic: it countered prevailing Anglo theory and contemporary California experiences.[22]

While Californio reminiscences ranged from discussions of important
political events to descriptions of popular dances, three key recurring
topics—class, gender, and Indians—gave their memories an oppositional
impulse. To take the first issue, much nostalgia centered around a desire
to reclaim class position. Rancheros' narratives often excluded California
residents who were not land grantees, except to fondly recall the control
rancho owners wielded over their large labor forces and extended families. Rancheros' lament was for the loss of the property relations in which
they had held sway. This take on the past was not undifferentiated nostalgia for the old days but a very specific one. As scholar Rosaura
Sánchez writes, "The world of Alta California was not an idyllic 'pastoral' society; on the contrary, it was a cattle-raising, labor-intensive,
tallow-and-hide producing economy with a largely 'unfree' labor force
made up of Indian men and women."[23] Indians or mestizos who never
had land to begin with found themselves in even more difficult straits
than did Californios. Few areas of American towns welcomed them as
neighbors, so segregated barrios began to arise in Los Angeles, Santa
Barbara, Ventura, and San Diego. Non-Anglos confronted a dual wage
system, earning less than their Anglo counterparts for the same labor.[24]
In a sense, Californios protested their reduction in circumstances by
pointing to their former high position as landed patriarchs.

Gender, too, offered a clear barometer of the fall from grace in many
male Californio memories. Women's behavior—from "cheerfully
ensconced in the home" to loosening their morals at the dance hall—
seemed good evidence with which to condemn Anglos' low character
and its corruption of their culture. Women's testimonials, though fewer
in number than men's, recall instead their own efforts to subvert patriarchal control well before the American takeover and openly declare
their disappointment with men's inability to defend against it. This
view, however, gained little credit in male memories, either in Anglo or
Californio narratives, which were more alike on this topic than one
might assume. As Antonia Castañeda suggests, Anglo writers like Dana
set up the same dichotomy between good and bad Californianas that
Californio men suggested. In this view, elite women managed to be
paragons of virtue and social butterflies, but without proper control,
they would fall victim to their natural sexuality and promiscuity.[25]

Nor did Californios' portrayal of Indian people differ much from
Anglo views. Indian people often figure into Californio nostalgia as

markers of ethnic difference, at times serving as villains in stories of raids on ranchos and at times appearing as children in need of guidance from superiors. Here was a way to claim a margin of ethnic superiority that Anglos were attempting to monopolize. Californios could not be Anglo, but by separating themselves from Indian blood, they might share European ancestry. Former rancheros expressed pride in their ability to control vast numbers of Indian workers through "natural" dominance. Moreover, they characterized the Indians under their charge much as Anglos did, remembering them as "indolent, ignorant, and reluctant to work." According to Sánchez, such representations were perhaps "doubly ironic, not only because the Indians had carried out all the work, . . . but also because in 1875 the criticism of indolence and derogatory portrayals were being proffered against" Californios themselves.[26]

Perhaps these interpretations appear to be malicious, suggesting that Californios were somehow complicit in the Anglo pursuit of racial hierarchy. However, their options were severely restricted; their decision to claim a genteel Spanish heritage was logical in the face of daunting cultural change. Moreover, their stance was not simply a way to pick on the lower class, women, and Indians; by responding specifically to conditions in the postwar present, it called attention to the oppositional character of Californios' nostalgia and the origin of that nostalgia in the trauma of displacement. Anglos' rendering of this nostalgia echoed some Californio portrayals of the past. The emphasis on gentility, even aristocratic privilege; the split view of women as honorably pure or dangerously sensual; and the denigration of Indian people all carried over into the *Ramona*-inspired picture of the region's past. But, in the new version, these narratives were shorn of their implied social critique. Importantly, Anglos envisioned few of the present-day applications of these memories that were Californios' reason for telling them. While Jackson gained fame for employing Californio informants, Anglos' use of Californios' material told a different story altogether.

"TO MOVE PEOPLE'S HEARTS"

If Anglos read *Ramona* primarily for its intoxicating descriptions of the past, Jackson meant for her novel to serve a pressing public cause, although not that of the Californios. She hoped to expose both Anglo and Californio residents for their maltreatment of mission Indians. For California Indians, the late nineteenth century marked a nadir in population. American laws suggested a loose-constructionist approach to identifying "hostile" Indians and exterminating them; Indians who appeared to be mere vagrants faced sentences of forced labor. Meanwhile, the federal government alternately negotiated and reneged on a series of treaties that squeezed tribes into constricted reservations and frequently evicted them not only from ancestral lands but even from reservations that had been established only a few years before. Furthermore, the lands that the Mexican government granted to Indians in the secularization era, small and tenuous already, were as susceptible to American squatters as the ranchos were. While many Indian communities persisted at the missions, such as at San Juan Capistrano, they did so largely as Spanish-speaking groups that were rarely recognized for their native ancestry.[27]

Woven in with Jackson's tale of romance was reproach for Californians' behavior and attitudes toward Indian people. Jackson, heretofore a writer of sentimental prose and poetry, had become a patron of Indian causes in 1881 while writing *A Century of Dishonor*, a nonfictional account of the abysmal record of the United States' relations with American Indians past and present.[28] When sales were slow, she sent a copy to every member of Congress at personal expense. While the volume caused nary a ripple in the Capitol, she accepted a government offer to prepare a report on the condition of the California mission Indians. Traveling around Southern California with fellow appointee and Los Angeles real-estate promoter Abbot Kinney, she visited Indian villages and crumbling missions as well as a few of the still-working ranchos. At the old Californio homesteads, she found material she would later exploit for the romantic backdrop and charming characters she needed to tempt readers into her remonstration. After filing her official report, Jackson decided to present her protests directly to the public in novel form. In a tale more personal than *Century of Dishonor*, she hoped to "set forth some Indian experiences in a way to move people's hearts." As she remarked a number of times, she hoped that *Ramona* would become the *Uncle Tom's Cabin* of Indian reform.[29]

Yet despite such intentions, the novel did not turn out to be the lightning rod that Harriet Beecher Stowe's work had been for an earlier generation—at least not for its intended purpose. Her audience was primed to respond to the romantic angle more than the social critique. Jackson's style placed *Ramona* less in the company of a protest novel like Stowe's than in the genre of "regional fiction," a popular literary trend in the latter half of the nineteenth century most famously practiced by Mark Twain. Regional novels incorporated, as *Ramona* scholar Dydia DeLyser suggests, "colorful characters speaking in dialects, lavish and loving place descriptions and nostalgic depictions of picturesque folkways" presumed to be fast disappearing.[30] Although Anglo readers might have sympathized with Ramona's and Alessandro's difficulties and cursed their American tormenters, the book's major appeal lay in Jackson's sun-kissed landscape and the quixotic figures that inhabited it. Her portrayal of the Spanish era in California as a happy, leisured existence instead of a lazy, backward past was new and intriguing. Nineteenth-century readers' expectations of and emphasis on these features seemed to distract them from Jackson's message; so did her inexplicably happy ending, in which Ramona and Felipe reconstitute the rancho family, and the tragedy of Alessandro's death is all but forgotten. The couple's retreat to Mexico can be read as a final defeat, but it signals the loss of the Californio culture rather than the grievances of mission Indians.[31] Unfortunately for the author, who died ten months after the novel's release, her romantic regional fiction trumped her social protest.

By choosing to drench her novel in nostalgia, Jackson not only smothered her own critique but also led the effort to package Californios' memories for Anglo consumption. In addition to visiting Indian *rancherías,* Jackson visited several prominent Californio ranchos and families, starting with the home of Antonio Coronel. In Coronel's adobe house in Los Angeles, the author listened with rapt attention to Coronel's wistful remembrances of the old days as well as his theories about the deterioration of treatment of mission Indians. He blamed Americans for the Indians' fate, a perspective that *Ramona* echoed. Yet Coronel interspersed such diatribes with guitar serenades, dance demonstrations with his wife, Mariana, and anecdotes about colorful characters from an earlier age. Coronel had long been a champion of Californio traditions and sought to preserve their prominence in public life well into the American period. He joined the Historical Society of Southern California in its first year (1883) as one of the few non-Anglo members, hoping to perpetuate this Hispanic influence.[32] Apparently, Jackson was so taken with Coronel and his home that she proposed centering her novel around his household, but he suggested she visit some of the more traditional, rural ranchos. He sent Jackson to Rancho Camulos in Ventura County in January 1882, where, he reportedly said, "the original life of a California hacendado could still be studied in all its poetry and importance."[33] Jackson followed half of Coronel's advice, preferring poetry over politics.

Jackson's visit to Camulos comprised only one morning, in which, as she wrote to her partner, Abbot Kinney, the matriarch "Mrs. Del Valle was away from home, unluckily . . . ; but it was a most interesting place, and the daughters, cousins, sons and daughters all as Mexican and un-American as heart could wish." The Del Valle family established Camulos in 1839, through a Mexican land grant of forty-eight thousand acres. Camulos contained grazing lands for cattle and sheep and hills full of citrus groves and vineyards, as well as a settlement of close to two hundred family members and workers, of both Mexican and Indian descent. Despite a decline to fewer than two thousand acres in the later part of the century, the Del Valles managed to maintain their rancho more or less intact, an unusual fact that drew Jackson there.[34] In search of more such exotic atmosphere, however, Jackson again consulted Coronel, who suggested she try Rancho Guajome in northern San Diego County. Whether Jackson actually visited Guajome remains in some dispute, but the legend grew that instead of taking a brief tour, the author overstayed her welcome, taking advantage of the Bandini-Couts family's hospitality, interfering with ranch business, and reportedly trying to set the Indian workers against their Californio employers.[35] Guajome also originated from a postsecularization Mexican land grant, deeded in 1845 to Abel Stearns, an American migrant who had married into the prominent Bandini family of Los Angeles and become a successful merchant and rancher in his own right. Six years later Stearns gave the 2,200-acre tract to his sister-in-law Ysidora Bandini and her Tennessee-born beau, Cave Couts, as a wedding present. Couts steered Guajome through the postwar financial dangers by diversifying along the lines of Camulos. Sheep, wine, and citrus kept the ranch afloat.[36] Jackson took notes, inquired about colorful incidents, and sketched personalities. These visits probably led her to depict Californios' resentment at loss of their homeland to Anglo control in her novel, but she used the visits more to gather evidence for descriptions of the ranchos' faded romantic atmosphere (see figure 1).

With Coronel as her guide, Jackson viewed Camulos and Guajome as representations of a colorful past that persisted only in small pockets of Southern California. In fictionalizing these people and places, she put the emphasis on past rather than persistence. While Coronel and other Californios often used nostalgia to claim a voice in the present, Jackson saw little future for the Californios; packing Ramona and Felipe off to Mexico confirmed the point. She emphasized how out of place and out of time the Morenos were, even as she seemed to regret their ill fortune. Moreover, Jackson anticipated how Anglos would choose to remember Californios when she made the Morenos the prototypical Californios, though the stories she drew upon were in fact often atypical. The Del Valle and Couts

Figure 1. "On the Veranda. Camulos Ranch, Ramona Scenes," ca. 1900. In this unusual image, members of the Del Valle family (Josefa del Valle Forster, James del Valle, Nina del Valle Cram, and Alexander Harmer, an Anglo artist who was related by marriage) pose as characters from *Ramona*. They are staging a scene from the novel on the famed south veranda of their Rancho Camulos home, which tourists soon insisted on seeing as the home of Ramona. Though the purpose of the tableau is unknown, it evokes the Del Valles' ambivalence about being so closely linked to *Ramona*. Family members found tourists inconvenient and often rude, yet they astutely realized that the novel's popularity offered an opportunity for profit. The photograph captures the tension that many Californios felt: Would they capitalize on *Ramona* mania, or would they share the heroine's fate and be forced to leave California to the Anglos? Courtesy Seaver Center for Western History Research, Los Angeles County Museum of Natural History.

families, not to mention Antonio Coronel, were unusual in their ability to maintain their fabled picture of wealth and opulence and a modicum of political influence. As Leonard Pitt writes, the Del Valles "exuded a deceptive air of well-being in the 1880's, considering its [Rancho Camulos's] financial condition" and continued to host elaborate fiestas into the new century. They did so by adapting to new conditions and diversifying the ranch's holdings. Two of the younger Del Valle sons got out of the flagging cattle- and sheep-grazing business, which *Ramona* highlighted, and turned to cultivating citrus and grapes, part of the California agricultural vanguard in the 1880s and 1890s. Couts, a Californio by marriage, actually added to his land holdings in the postwar years, expanding Guajome nearly tenfold and controlling over twenty thousand acres at the time of his death in 1874. Neither was Coronel native to California; he arrived from Mexico at the age of seventeen in 1834 and after the American conquest, assertively joined the new cultural and economic context. He shrewdly manipulated his finances and real estate, invested in urban enterprises, and became a railroad and civic booster like many Anglos in Los Angeles.[37] All three families had significant but uncommon postwar biographies among Californios, for whom loss of wealth and stature was the more common experience.

Atypicality was a hallmark of Anglo memories. Among the Californios to whom Anglos most liked to pay tribute were Arcadia Bandini Stearns and her husband, Abel, who were as atypical as they were legendary in Los Angeles. As a city dweller who was unable to bear children, Arcadia did not share with many of her fellow Californianas the duties of mothering and managing a rancho household. Her life, instead, "literally revolved around entertaining and socializing amongst the new Los Angeles elite" and thus gave credence to the view of Californio culture as a continual round of fiestas. Anglos viewed her life as a kind of "idealized existence" that stood in for the whole of Californio history.[38] Jackson took such surface appearances for the substance of Californio life. Anecdotes, gossip, recollections of weeklong fiestas, beautiful dresses, and romances, became the center of Anglos' fascination with Californio lifestyle. Even if Jackson allowed Señora Moreno some indignation at the American takeover, many of her readers glossed over that aspect of the señora's life to revel in the seeming exoticisms of daily life on the rancho. Anglos missed Californios' original object in recalling these activities: to promote their own history as a lever for future advancement. For all "their old-fashioned fiestas at Camulos," for example, the Del Valles "aspired toward and in most respects attained the status of the new 'better classes.'" In a sense, their "traditional" events, such as the annual Fourth of July fiesta, whose attendees were predominantly Anglo, served as an entrée into Anglo public respectability.[39] But in the end, Anglos focused on the fiestas, the dazzling social life, and the opulence in Californio society, not on Californios' struggles against financial ruin, cultural oblivion, and ethnocentrism in the late nineteenth century.

"QUAFF YE THE WATERS OF RAMONA'S WELL"

Helen Hunt Jackson's novel neither wholly invented nor clearly stole Californio nostalgia. For her, Californio life was scenery, and her story was not about Californios' real lives or troubles but about Indian pathos. Readers followed her lead, coming to California in droves in search of the romantic setting she so breathtakingly advertised. This stampede of *Ramona* fans was possible only because Southern California had begun over the previous decade to make itself more amenable and enticing to tourists. A new set of Anglo-Americans began to discover Southern California, not as a place for business and labor but, as one 1876 book stated, for "Health, Pleasure, and Residence." Consumptives came to recuperate in the region's mild climate, which some ambitious boosters gave the scientific-sounding label of "subtropical." Lavish hotels cropped up to cater to the vanguard of rail tourists. An elite set of white Americans began to "winter" in Southern California. When, in 1887, the Santa Fe Railway broke the Southern Pacific Railroad's California monopoly and established a direct link between Los Angeles and the eastern United States, these tourists multiplied and became thousands of potential residents. A rate war between the two railroads dropped the price of a one-way ticket from Kansas City to the West from $125 to $1. Wild speculation in real estate led to a boom in prices, as hundreds of new towns were platted and sold. The boom collapsed nearly as quickly as it had begun, but in its wake was new incentive to promote the region to tourists.

Southern California Anglos quickly learned to capitalize on *Ramona*'s runaway popularity. Some clever entrepreneurs built the Hotel Ramona in 1890 in San Luis Obispo. Though the hotel looked nothing like the Spanish architecture described in great detail in the book, the owners advertised it in Jacksonian terms: "How pleasantly mellifluous is the name, Hotel Ramona; how suggestive of the dolce far niente of the venerable old San Luis Obispo." Yet readers demanded more than vague references. They wanted to see the actual places and people from the book. A pilgrimage circuit grew up around shrines that consisted of Ramona's "real home," Ramona's Marriage Place, and the "real" Ramona herself, though no one could conclusively pinpoint the identity or location of these destinations. The Santa Fe and Southern Pacific promoted different locations for the Moreno ranch, according to which one lay closer to its own line.[40]

Where Ramona got married was hotly debated, but when Thomas P. Getz opened Ramona's Marriage Place at the newly restored Estudillo house in Old Town, San Diego, in 1910, other contenders were forgotten. Getz's establishment included a souvenir shop, an extensive array of postcard views, its own post office with custom cancellation, lantern-slide lectures on the history of the missions, and rooms decorated in

Figure 2. "The Court, Ramona's Marriage Place, San Diego, California," ca. 1915. Postcard from author's collection.

period style. Visitors could lounge in the picturesque interior patio and drink a cup from the wishing well (see figure 2). How could they not linger? The sign's invitation was irresistible:

> Quaff ye the waters of Ramona's Well,
> Good luck they bring and secrets tell,
> Blest were they by the sandaled friar,
> So drink and wish for thy desire.[41]

Getz promised that visitors would leave "the romantic old adobe with a sense of peace and harmony" and a remembrance of "long warm moon-light nights when filmy mantillas dropped coyly over velvet eyes and gallant caballeros played serenades outside grilled windows; days when everything was Mañana, when love and beauty, toil and bitter struggles, mixed in a kaleidoscope of real and unreal."[42] *Ramona* tourists willingly mixed fact and fantasy in their pursuit of such a feeling. Proliferating souvenir bric-a-brac offered a chance to take a piece of that atmosphere home. Ramona baskets and pincushions were popular, but only the rare visitor went home without, as historian Carey McWilliams noted, a little replica of the bells that rang to celebrate Ramona's wedding. Many people even chose to hold their own weddings at Ramona's Marriage Place, transforming a space that recalled a purely fictional occasion into a site of significant social activity and personal meaning.[43]

Figure 3. "The Real Ramona," ca. 1900. Though the postcard fails to note this woman's identity, she is Ramona Lubo, a Cahuilla whose husband, like Alessandro, was shot for accidentally taking a white man's horse. This coincidence later earned her minor fame and extra income. Postcard from author's collection.

An increasing number of guidebooks and feature articles catered to *Ramona* tourists and heightened tourist expectations of romance. At the same time, they reinforced the assumption that the book was factual. One chronicler insisted that, "Every incident in the story has fact for its foundation, even down to the minutest detail."[44] A glimpse of the "real" Ramona was frequently offered as proof of the novel's veracity (see figure 3). Some promoters cloaked these Indian visits in romantic prose, suggesting where tourists might go to "look upon the dreamy and lazy life of the Indians." Yet most travel guides warned visitors that actual Indians would fall short of Jackson's picture of their beauty and goodness and indeed prompt contempt. One travel writer, claiming that he had located the legendary Ramona, lamented in 1900 that "she is now like all the other Indian women become as they grow older, *greasy* and *slovenly*, . . . She is just as haggard looking and lazy as the other squaws." McWilliams brought this inconsistency between the "real" and imagined Ramona into sharp focus: "The region accepted the charming Ramona, as a folk figure, but completely rejected the Indians still living in the area."[45] Once again, *Ramona* proved to be an ineffective vehicle for prompting recognition of the injustice Indian people had suffered. Far more Anglo tourists visited "Spanish" Ramona sites than Indian ones; many were more interested in experiencing the romantic past than in pursuing redress in the present.[46]

Many of the hosts of *Ramona* sites were initially less than pleased. The Del Valles and the Couts were among the people most perturbed at the hordes of tourists that descended upon their homes demanding to see "Ramony." Rancho Camulos became known as Ramona's home less than two years after the novel appeared in print, when a *San Francisco Chronicle* article identified it as such. When this piece was reprinted as an appendix in new editions of the book, readers found encouragement not only to regard the story as true but to tour its real-life sites.[47] Reginaldo del Valle found that these uninvited guests increased the financial burden on his ranch, which was still under pressure from taxes and squatters. He wrote to his sister in 1888 that, despite the family's tradition of hospitality, "the expenses are tremendous and if we continue in the same manner we will go bankrupt. . . . The strangers that come to see Ramona out of curiosity will have to be advised that we do not have a hotel here and that we cannot provide [for] them." Visitors continued to overrun the estate; a newspaper reported one occasion in 1896 when "a mob of 300 of both sexes took advantage of the opportunity to raid the orchards . . . steal[ing] as many oranges as the time would permit, even invading the private grounds and apartments of the house." Such actions caused the Del Valles to close Camulos to all unknown visitors.[48]

At Guajome, fans encountered the following sign near the entrance: "Notice. Ladies and gentlemen calling here, in my absence, will kindly refrain from assuming liberties in and about these premises that would be objectionable to you if exercised by strangers in your homes. This is private property and must be respected. Sightseers are only tolerated NEVER WANTED!!" Whether the tourist onslaught or Jackson's characterization of Señora Moreno got to her more, Ysidora Bandini Couts was incensed enough to file a defamation suit against the author in Los Angeles County. The case was dismissed when Jackson died, but the resentment lingered. So too did Antonio Coronel's regret; despite his enthusiastic cooperation with Jackson, he found himself deeply remorseful for having unwittingly allowed Anglos to lay siege to Camulos and Guajome.[49]

Neither did all Southern California Anglos jump on the *Ramona* bandwagon immediately. In the late nineteenth century, while many Southern Californians did want sightseers, they agreed with the Couts and Del Valles that *Ramona* had brought a flood of tourists ready to impose their ill-founded preconceptions on the region. *Ramona* dismayed many Anglos and Californios for its wild romantic embellishments and its critiques, which they thought were unfounded. A review in the California literary journal *Overland Monthly* denounced Jackson's depiction, claiming that "somehow, by some impalpable quality put in it or left out . . . [it] misses being *our* California. The truth is that it is probably no one's California; that while every description is true to nature, the story is really laid out in the poet's land, which can never be exactly the same as any region of the realistic earth." Southern Californians felt the sting of Jackson's reproach for their treatment of Indian people and worked to change this impression by disproving her romantic portrayals of native tribes. A San Diego–area newspaper article entitled "Real Ramona and Ramona of Romance" argued that "There is nothing about the squalid adobe of the original character of Ramona connecting her with the lovely creation of Helen Hunt Jackson." Other local commentators decried the "hucksters" that sold the novel's fantasy as fact. Charles Fletcher Lummis, who often promoted Southern California's Spanish motifs, stated that " 'Ramona' is pure fiction. Not one of its characters lived. Among all the falsehoods told to tourists perhaps none are more petty than those of people who 'knew Ramona,' who 'knew Alessandro,' and so forth."[50]

In the 1880s and 1890s many Southern California tourist promoters and boosters were eager to prove that the region contained modern amenities and civilized society. And to many, this task meant separating the place as much as possible from its Mexican past. According to this strand of public opinion, the region was hampered by its association with Mexican people, adobe buildings, and social organization and thus was on a slower path to civilization than the Anglo-dominated northern region.[51] *Ramona* did not help rid potential visitors of the belief that Southern California remained in a rude frontier stage of life. Locally produced guides often included less *Ramona* material than those authored by eastern tour companies. A Boston-based tour company's booklet in 1900 advertised a guided tour of California and guaranteed that customers would see real *Ramona* sights: "On the way we pass Camulos, the home of Ramona, whose stormy love story, in its frame work of mountain and range, spring and desert is so vividly painted by Helen Hunt Jackson. The house in which Ramona lived is pointed out to the traveler, and an ancient and wrinkled Indian woman, living in the vicinity, is said to be the romancist's original." In comparison, an 1894 hotel directory for the Los Angeles area contains no mention of the popular novel, choosing instead to inform its readers that "To-day Southern California has all the material signs of a high civilization. Her population is not rich, hence it is progressive and hopes to become rich, living in the meantime as they could not do in a less favored country."[52] Before Jackson's work, markers of East Coast–style civilization, like hotels, railroads, and city blocks or natural features like the climate, the Sierras, and redwood trees contained the most appeal. Southern California Anglos emphasized these features at least as much as they tapped into the new passion for Spanish romance.

"A STRANGE MIXTURE OF FACT AND FANCY"

In the late nineteenth century, many Anglo-Californians remembered the region's recent past differently than *Ramona* rendered it. Their view of mission and rancho California supposed a dirty and primitive place populated by lazy people that emerged from this backward state only with the arrival of Anglo-Americans. Many people believed, as did one of California's earliest American historians, John S. Hittell, that California was born in the gold rush, rising "as if at one bound from the stagnation of semi-barbarous pastoral life to the . . . restless activity of a refined civilization."[53] We must remember too that the 1880s and 1890s were productive decades for western history and for the mythmaking business in general, as Buffalo Bill, Theodore Roosevelt, and Frederick Jackson Turner each hawked their own versions of the American frontier enterprise. Together these men provided an inescapable context for Anglo-American accounts of California history during this era.

Here we return to Hubert Howe Bancroft, who had collected in the 1870s those significant Californio memoirs that captured the nascent nostalgia of the time. Bancroft's volume on the Mexican era, *California Pastoral,* finally appeared in 1888 and included the Californio narratives merely as props for his argument about the inevitable and proper ascent of Anglo-Americans to dominance in the state. From the thousands of pages of testimonials in his library, Bancroft culled elements of romantic detail but virtually repeated Dana's portrayal of Californios from four decades before. Mexicans, as he unfailingly called California's Spanish speakers, were a people of "inherent indolence," with no patience for farming. Instead, they enjoyed the easier life of ranching, with its attendant dominion over animals and "Indian serfs." Bancroft praised Mexicans for their "chivalrous courtesy" and acknowledged that they wanted for little, but he still accused them of damnable laziness: "Lazy some of them might be, and were, day after day, at morning and at night, lazily they told their rosary, lazily attended mass, and lazily ate and slept." That their memories, nostalgic and idealized though they might be, could fuel such an indictment of their society, appalled Californios who read Bancroft's version. In one case, the author called Mariano Vallejo's recollection of a key event a "strange mixture of fact and fancy" and thus cast doubt on Californios' entire cultural memory. As scholar Genaro Padilla has remarked, at that moment, Vallejo and his compatriots realized that their attempt to broadcast their message through Bancroft's histories "was another Californio mistake, since the Anglo-American historian proved to be as imperialistic as the land grabbers. . . . The Historian had spoken. Vallejo must have stared at the pages before him, stunned and humiliated."[54]

Anglos, with little access to Californio-authored nostalgia except that filtered through Helen Hunt Jackson, presumably read Bancroft's argument differently. In a telling statement that seemed to pervert the old Yankee proverb "Never put off to tomorrow what you can do today," Bancroft claimed that the Californio motto was "Divertirse hoy que ya mañana es otro dia" ("Enjoy yourself today because tomorrow is just another day.") This version both contained *Ramona* fans' picture of a leisured good life and blamed Californio indolence for the American conquest of California. As Bancroft records the successions, Californios "were not a strong community in any sense, either morally, physically, or politically; hence it was that as the savages faded before the superior Mexicans, so faded the Mexicans before the superior Americans."[55] Southern California Anglos would come to romanticize this idleness in much the same way that *Ramona* fans did, but in so doing, they did not reject Bancroft's belief that Anglo-Americans were the rightful possessors of California. *Ramona* did not so much counter this logic as put a softer face on it. Jackson's tale saw much to regret in the American takeover, not least the plight of California Indians. Yet she, like Bancroft, painted the conquest as inevitable and depicted rancho society as flawed in all the same ways: authoritarian, lazy, backward, and prejudiced.

A few local Anglo depictions of Southern California began to appear in print in the 1880s, and they too did not stray far from Bancroft's formula, despite often exhibiting greater generosity toward their predecessors. Horace Bell's 1881 memoir, *Reminiscences of a Ranger; or, Early Times in Southern California,* describes a good deal of amicability

between Anglos and Californios in the rough frontier society he
recalled. The Los Angeles Rangers to which Bell refers were an organized vigilante squad that pursued ruffians and criminals in the 1850s
and wore uniforms that resembled the garb of California caballeros
(cowboys). Bell admitted that he had always been "an ardent and enthusiastic student of Spanish history, and was a great admirer of the
chivalry of the race" and was dismayed that the "California Spaniard"
lost his land and inheritance. But he insisted that the fault lay not at the
feet of the government or enterprising Americans; Californios had only
themselves to blame. "There is not a squatter in all California that ever
got one acre of an honest Mexican grant, unless he purchased and paid
for it; while the truth is that squatters, or more properly speaking,
American settlers on the public domain, were defrauded, by millions of
acres" because of spurious Mexican land claims. Moreover, he explicitly rejected the political objects of Californio nostalgia in offering "a
parting word to the young men of Spanish blood: Pine not over
grandeur gone, of misfortunes past" but instead join Anglos and successful Californios "on a new race of progress" and take a "stand in the
ranks of American progression resolved to carve their way onward and
upward. . . . [M]uchachos, emulate their virtues, their determined
efforts, their industry, and let your own brave hearts be your future fortune." While less dismissive of the Spanish-Mexican presence in the
region, Bell's story remains, as Kevin Starr has suggested, one "of conquest: of how order was brought to the frontier. . . . [T]he movement is
from anarchy to civilization, and the end result is the founding of Southern California."[56] Californios might become members of this new
civilization, but only if they were to shed their past and become like
Americans.

Ironically, however, Anglos were the ones who imagined Californios
as representative only of the past. Californios' nostalgia spoke to their
present condition; Anglo versions, whether romantic or reproachful,
consigned them entirely to a bygone era. These perspectives presented
two different motives and forms for nostalgia. Where Californios
asserted narratives of decline in the desire to assert their continuing
presence, Anglos conceived of the Californio lifestyle as a brief but colorful chapter in a larger story of progress. Anglos did not experience the
Californio trauma of displacement that gave the original nostalgia its
purpose. Their wistful reminiscence had more to do with marking a
poignant comparison of "relics of another age" and "spared pillars of
the past" with their "enterprising Yankee nation," as Richard Henry Dana

said upon his return to California in the postwar years. Converted to the romantic view, Dana composed a eulogy for the Californio past: "How softening is the effect of time. I almost feel as if I were lamenting the passing away of something loving and dear."[57]

For Southern California Anglos at the turn of the twentieth century, *los días pasados* had come to suggest two key images, besides the possibility for tourist profit: a colorful past and the good life. Despite the exaggerations in the *Ramona*-style portrayal of California's rancho society, Californios themselves seemed to be bona fide remnants of a departed time. To quaff the waters of Ramona's well was to drink of the past itself. Some Californios learned to capitalize upon this value-added quality. A later generation of Del Valles affixed a Home of Ramona label to their orchard products, and Cave Couts, Jr., set about remodeling Guajome to fit tourist expectations. Styling himself as "the last of the dons," Couts clearly understood that a good deal of Anglos' fascination lay with Californios' supposed disappearing act. Nothing could have been farther from the Californio agenda in the 1870s than disappearing yet the less headway that Californios made in Anglo society, the more they appeared in Anglo nostalgia.[58]

Ramona's version of the past also seemed to harmonize nicely with the possibility of a graciously civilized and definitively Anglo future in Southern California. Boosters like Charles Nordhoff, Benjamin Cummings Truman, and Charles Dudley Warner offered the region's bounteous climate and landscape as a domestic Mediterranean. More than drawing health seekers, however, Southern California as "Our Italy" suggested a fulfillment of Americans' dreams of a genteel Arcadian society. In this other Southern California self-image, the possibility that a new center of civilization might germinate in the friendly sunshine held great appeal for Anglo residents. As Warner wrote in 1891,

> The picture in my mind for the future of the Land of the Sun, of the mountains, of the sea—which is only an enlargement of the picture of the present—is one of great beauty. The picture I see is of a land of small farms and gardens, highly cultivated, in all the valleys and on the foothills; a land, therefore, of luxuriance and great productiveness and agreeable homes. I see everywhere the gardens, the vineyards, the orchards, with the various greens of the olive, the fig, and the orange. . . . It is the fairest field for the experiment of a contented community, without any poverty and without excessive wealth.[59]

This image of the Southern California good life was not so far from *Ramona*'s halcyon days. Though fusion of the Spanish metaphor with

Anglo lifestyles would wait for another day, Jackson's renderings vibrantly evoked the bucolic and genteel landscapes that local Anglo promoters foresaw. Eventually, even many Anglo skeptics caught on to the possibilities of envisioning and promoting the region in these Jacksonian terms.

CONCLUSION

The parallel development of California's image of the good life in past and present, along with the steady proliferation of *Ramona* guides and venues, have led many historians to see *Ramona* as a watershed in the region's "self-consciousness" and obsession with its Spanish past. *Ramona* appears in many accounts to have single-handedly overturned earlier versions of local history and inaugurated the romantic turn that continued unabated.[60] Indeed, the Anglo turn to Spanish romance is difficult to imagine without Helen Hunt Jackson's assistance. Yet *Ramona* has received too much credit. First, the book's nostalgic mood and style were not original. Jackson and her readers subsumed the Californio version under an Anglo imprimatur, but the Del Valles and Coronels and their compatriots were both her ghostwriters and pro- tagonists. As Rosaura Sánchez remarked evocatively, "In a war of position . . . one does not turn over one's weapons to the enemy for safekeeping, unless, perhaps, it is the only way of ensuring their storage and survival." Faced with the danger of erasure, Californios chose to tell their stories, even if they could not control the way Anglos would read their stories. They did not "disappear, ignored of the world," as Mariano Vallejo had feared, but rather their legacy began to appear across the Southern California landscape. And, however difficult to access, their narratives remain in play, as scholars like Sánchez and others have brought to light.[61]

Loaning one's history, however, can be a perilous gamble. Mistrans- lation can have lasting effects, as Santa Barbara matron Doña Maria de las Angustias de la Guerra was horrified to learn. Genaro Padilla revealed that English translations, down to recent decades, have consis- tently mutilated a key statement she made to Bancroft's interviewer. Her argument that "The taking of the country did not please the Californios at all, and least of all the women" became "the conquest of California did not bother the Californians, least of all the women." The erroneous translation provided fodder for generations of Anglos, who believed that Californios were receptive to conquest and lackadaisical in their resistance.[62] This unfortunate example offers a revealing metaphor for the way Anglos used Californio memories. Southern California Anglos continued to rely upon Spanish speakers as authenticators, but mostly for the surface details of an idealized lifestyle rather than the substance of their lives.

For example, Antonio Coronel's words appeared in print in local English publications for decades after his death. The Los Angeles Chamber of Commerce's promotional magazine *Land of Sunshine* published interviews with him in 1895 to validate the locations of both Ramona's home and the Camino Real, and a number of *Ramona* tourist guides quoted him as a reference for Jackson's assiduous on-the-ground research. As late as 1929, a portion of his Bancroft interview was translated for *Touring Topics*, the auto-club monthly. Titled "Things Past: Remembrances of sports, dances, diversions and other domestic and social customs of old California," the excerpt was entirely descriptive and betrayed little of his perspective on either Mexican or American times.[63] Anglo versions like *Ramona* were often light diversions that presented life in isolation, apart from Californio experiences as a whole.

But there are other reasons that *Ramona* could not have been the lone muse for Southern California Anglos' fascination with the Spanish past. As an eastern transplant and tourist rendering, the *Ramona* myth did not wipe away competing local memories, Californio or Anglo. Nor could it independently consolidate the romance into the inescapable marker of regional identity that its version of the past would later become for Anglo residents. No doubt, it was an important catalyst. The book and tourist pilgrimage provided a springboard for newfound nostalgia. More important, perhaps, it gave the Spanish past an Anglo author. Like Bancroft, Jackson transcribed and translated *los días pasados* for Anglo audiences. Just as she made Indian people both central to and invisible in the process, she allowed romantic details to smooth over political agendas. Yet had *Ramona* remained the sole expression of this nostalgia, no matter how popular, Anglo cultural memories of the Spanish past would not have achieved the regional magnitude that they did. Only by assembling homegrown fantasies— divested of Jackson's strident, if ignored, social critique—and installing them in the built environment did Southern California Anglos integrate the Spanish past into their regional memory and sense of place. *Ramona* represented the Anglo deed to the Spanish past. The next question is how Anglos built upon this acquired landscape.

CHAPTER 2

The Road

El Camino Real and Mission Nostalgia

In 1870 Father Osuna, a wandering Mexican friar, drifted up from Baja California and found himself in San Diego, a town undergoing a transformation thanks to an influx of ambitious Anglo city boosters. As one historian of nineteenth-century California repeated the tale, "His sandals and robe so startled San Diego that the marshal jailed him on a charge of lunacy and had him extradited—a perfect example of the Yankees' total lack of understanding of or empathy for the era of the missions."[1] Though perhaps apocryphal, this story suggests Anglo-Americans' attitudes toward the Spanish mission priests who had colonized California earlier in the century. Even after the furor over *Ramona*, neither tourists nor locals were likely to visit the old Spanish missions that dotted the coast between San Diego and Sonoma. Guidebooks did not recommend including a mission on a sightseeing tour. No visitor facilities existed at the abandoned missions, and the ones still in use functioned primarily as Catholic parish churches, not as places where the upstanding Protestant Yankees who constituted the bulk of the California tourist market were liable to venture. Even souvenirs of missions warned visitors away. For example, one stereograph card presented stark images of San Francisco's Mission Dolores on one side and on the other gave tourists the local outlook: "This Mission Church is an adobe building erected by the Spanish Catholics when San Francisco was not. It is still regularly used and the interior is just as dirty and tawdry as any other church of the kind in any of the smaller towns of the coast. The graveyard contains the remains of

Governors and Soldiers whose names are associated with the early history of California but would hardly interest you."[2] Why tourists might want to purchase a view of a building of such apparently scarce appeal is unclear; if they defied caution and went inside, they must have done so only out of a sense of morbid curiosity.

Yet in increasing numbers, by the 1890s and 1900s, both tourists and residents in Southern California began to find these old structures and the past they conjured endearing as well as bizarre. Locals began to see new promotional possibilities and potential tourist markets in the sites. Few people would have predicted, however, that by 1931, Father Junípero Serra, founder of the Alta California missions, would be one of the state's two marble representatives in the U.S. Capitol statuary hall. The Franciscan stood next to statues of George Washington, Ethan Allen, Samuel Adams, and other more famous eighteenth-century patriots. More than hailing the Spanish missionaries as the first Europeans to settle in California, this formal recognition of Father Serra prefigured American California in the founding of Spanish California. A generation before, only a handful of Anglo-Americans in California would have recognized Junípero Serra's name, much less anointed him a national hero. The dramatic rise in the status of missions from hardly interesting oddities to essential state emblems was remarkable but not inevitable. What accounts for this near-complete reversal of Anglo-Californian sentiments about the missions?

At the turn of the twentieth century, the meanings of missions remained up for grabs, and Southern California Anglos were at best ambivalent about them. The Anglo struggle to build a mission road, a latter-day El Camino Real, began a long regional investment in cultural memories of the Spanish past. There was much work to do, because the raw material for this transformation was an unlikely set of decaying buildings strewn in inaccessible portions of the state; yet for this reason, the missions were perfect candidates for repurposing as remnants of a romantic past. Local Anglo citizens' efforts to rehabilitate them physically and symbolically required a significant collective reinterpretation of the missions' place in modern California. Both for the Anglo promoters who imagined the mission road and the tourists who narrated their travels upon it, these efforts represented a good deal more than *Ramona* reveries. Whereas nineteenth-century Anglos viewed missions (and mendicant friars) as incongruous parts of the landscape, after 1900 Southern Californians began to work out a historical narrative that made missions perfect embodiments of their vision for the region—ones they hoped tourists wanted to see. They fit their newfound nostalgia for the passing romantic era into a timeline that culminated in their own presence on California's shores. El Camino Real encouraged Southern Californians to put themselves in the padres' sandals and imagine a direct lineage from the European colonizers to themselves. Unlikely though the missions were, they offered Southern California national landmarks of the highest appeal.

"LET US HAVE OUR SPANISH AFTERNOON"

For most commentators before the turn of the twentieth century, the missions seemed incompatible with a modern American state. With scant local and tourist interest, many of the stone and adobe buildings languished in disrepair and relative obscurity. With a few exceptions, the missions had been sold to private parties, abandoned, and left to molder since the 1840s.[3] Information about missions was available in the tomes of historians such as Hubert Howe Bancroft, and images of them appeared in the photographs of then-unknown Carleton Watkins, who began to document their decay, but few tourists found much to interest them. Founded between 1769 and 1823, the missions made only token appearances in guidebooks and souvenirs before the 1884 appearance of *Ramona*. Guides to California preferred to showcase examples of East Coast–style civilization—hotels, resorts, city blocks— or features of landscape and nature. Tourists' memory books and photograph albums emphasized places such as the Del Monte Hotel in Monterey, San Francisco mansions, Chinatown, and the Big Trees grove of redwoods—not Franciscan missions. The growth of the Southern California tourist market in the 1870s, 1880s, and 1890s paralleled railroad development in the region. Railroads aimed to keep passengers close to their lines and thus concentrated visits in a few cities and destination resorts, many of which hosted tourists for several months at a time. If asked, most tourists would have said they had come to Southern California for the climate rather than the history—to see exotic plants, not people.[4]

Even when tourists started to seek out the missions on their *Ramona* tours, the buildings remained mere side trips on the typical California itinerary. Part of the problem was accessibility. Outside the orbits of passenger trains and resort hotels, mission sites offered meager lodging and accommodations. The Southern Pacific advertised a limited tour of the missions in 1898 that evidenced these difficulties. It promised visits to San Gabriel, Santa Barbara, Monterey, and San Francisco but bypassed three significant missions south of San Gabriel completely and offered stagecoach excursions to others.[5] While the remoteness of many missions discouraged special trips, few tourists clamored for more chances to visit the out-of-the-way places. Even among *Ramona*-mad tourists, missions were often the least interesting sites in their pilgrimages, certainly far less inspiring than Ramona's Marriage Place or her "real homes" at Camulos and Guajome. Guidebooks, souvenirs, and albums of the 1890s tended to replicate tours of the previous decade, adding a few missions or *Ramona* sites as afterthoughts.[6] Where missions were adjacent to resort hotels in Santa Barbara or San Diego, tourists took note but did not find them especially alluring. One 1887 article about Santa Barbara in the New York travel magazine *Outing* largely described the area's landscape, climate, and leisurely atmosphere. It recalled the mission era as a delightful time but saw little evidence of such delight in the town's buildings.[7] Slowly, tourists began to include missions in their usual rounds, but excitement about the romantic possibilities of a mission tour remained absent.

Tourists steered clear of the missions not just because the sites were out of the way but also because their guidebooks hinted that missions would be out of place in a typical tour. Authors had difficulty reconciling the crumbling missions with their pictures of modern California. Charles Franklin Carter was just one writer who found them out of place: "To see Capistrano, or San Luis Rey, or Santa Ines, is almost like visiting a foreign land, and why should it not seem so? California was, less than 75 years ago, a foreign land to us, just as Mexico is to-day." Some tourists, incidentally, remained unsure of the United States' hold on the territory, inquiring of a Los Angeles paper in 1896 whether an American needed a passport to travel there or would need an interpreter. The missions, thus were just one representation of the questionable Americanness of the region. As Carter said, they represented a past "totally unlike what one is accustomed to in other parts of our land, . . . oriental in character."[8] Such exoticism offered an exciting prospect for some visitors, perhaps, but marked the missions as outside the nation's normal bounds. Similarly, prolific guidebook author James Steele confessed to some discomfort with the disjunctive images the missions conjured. He meditated publicly on the problem in an 1892 commentary:

> The crumbling towers of these ancient temples keep one all the time wondering if this be any lawful portion of the great American inheritance and perhaps one sometimes wishes them entirely out of the way.

Daily the incongruity between the then and the now becomes more striking and daily the crumbling walls remind more strongly of a modern
usurpation of what was meant for other uses. So long as they shall stand
there is a feeling that this is not entirely a Saxon country. Flowers and
eternal summer are not the natural surroundings of the race.[9]

The missions made sense to Steele and other Anglo observers at the turn
of the twentieth century only insofar as the buildings recalled an era and
a people that had no logical place in their conceptions of American
California. Steele was ambivalent; he offered both an opening for past
beauty and a rationale for razing the structures. For the incongruous
missions to become tourist attractions and regional emblems, they
would require a historical framework that located Anglo-, or Saxon-,
Americans in a landscape of flowers and mission ruins.

Whether Anglo-Americans could prosper in sunny Southern California
was a question of some anxiety for contemporaries. Charles Dudley
Warner, a prolific essay writer and one-time editor of *Harper's Magazine,* retired to Southern California and became one of its strongest
early boosters, popularizing the idea that the region was "Our Italy," as
he called it in one of his pamphlets. But even Warner was unsettled by
the seeming disjunction between race and place. He wrote in a local
periodical about the prevailing belief that much of Anglo-Saxon
progress and civilization was due to the struggle with harsh climate in
northern Europe, whereas tropical climes produced the backward and
lazy cultures that Anglos stereotypically associated with black and Mexican people. Warner stated unequivocally, "The black races have thriven
physically but have never produced anything worthwhile in civilization
in a tropical climate." He spoke to his readers' worry when he pondered
if Southern California's "flowers and eternal summer" would serve as a
similar drag on "Anglo-Saxon energy and thrift." Would their "intellectual faculties [become] atrophied"? This question was, he suggested,
a matter of "great interest and of practical importance . . . in regard to
the experiment in Southern California. Will the settlers hold their northern vigor and enterprise, or will they follow the example of the former
occupiers, the Spanish Americans?"[10] The question was, for many, a
vexing one.

Southern California appeared to observers like Warner to be an
"experiment," a trial Anglo civilization whose success was not guaranteed. "We have here a substantially Anglo-Saxon race, a settlement
largely recruited from climatic conditions much more severe and
extreme than Southern California has, and thrown into a climatic region

that produced the sort of happy-go-lucky, *mañana* condition in which the country was under Mexican rule and influence." Here Warner reprised the standard nineteenth-century indictment of Californios for their indolence, equivocating about whether the malady was racial or environmental. Warner himself believed that Anglos would take a best-of-both-worlds approach and build a modern paradise, combining their efficiency and ambition with a greater "grace of life, ease of living, . . . and enjoyment of existence" than might be found on eastern shores.[11] Insofar as Anglos thought about associating their region with a distinctive mode or style, they decidedly imagined Southern California in these terms of the good life. This landscape of leisure was largely the environment that tourists sought there: a place with pretty views, a healthful climate, and gracious architecture. Anglo locals were sometimes skeptical about whether a society, much less an economy, could thrive on this formula. Some elite refugees from the East, particularly in retreats like Pasadena and the Arroyo, modeled this nascent California lifestyle, but most Anglos had ambitions to implant East Coast–style civilization in a dusty outpost at the southwestern edge of the nation.

At the turn of the century, then, champions of the missions were few. Two Los Angeles librarians formed the Society for the Preservation of the Missions in 1892 and embarked on lecture tours to publicize the missions' plight and to solicit donations. In three years, they raised only ninety dollars and accomplished no substantial work. In 1895 they turned over their entire treasury and membership rolls to Charles Fletcher Lummis upon his founding of the Landmarks Club in 1895.[12] This decision was rather prescient because Lummis became one of Southern California's most tireless boosters of the region's Spanish legacies as well as one of its most eccentric public figures. By 1895 Lummis was already well on his way to fashioning himself as the premier authority on the Spanish and Indian past of the Southwest; in that same year he took over a small chamber of commerce magazine, the *Land of Sunshine,* and turned it into a powerful promotional machine, advertising the region, its romantic charisma, and his own personality, not necessarily in that order.[13]

Lummis used the Landmarks Club and the *Land of Sunshine* as his personal bullhorns and implored other organizations and media outlets to promote the significance, even the indispensability, of the missions to Southern California Anglos. The case he and other authors initially made in the pages of local magazines centered on the missions' anomaly and obscurity, not their regional appropriateness. That few people shared these activists' fondness for the queer old places is evident in their own pleas for support. Anna Picher, one of the society's founders, lamented in 1895 that the name *El Camino Real* is "not often uttered," and is "unknown to Americans." Five years later the complaint was the same: "Are there not enough people, enough Californians, who have the means to raise the paltry sum required with which the walls [of Mission San Antonio di Padua] could be restored and the roof replaced? Or is the reproach going to be made to the people of California in the years to come that they were so careless, so commercial . . . that they would not make the effort to save the historic landmarks on their soil?"[14] Even this dedicated band doubted they could save the missions from destruction.

The anti-Spanish fervor of 1898 presented another obstacle to gaining mission devotees. Nervous business backers of Los Angeles' fledgling spring festival, *La Fiesta,* chose to cancel the celebration in 1898 because of worries about how to cast their Spanish-themed events as patriotic observances. But anti-Spanish sentiments did not spring solely from the war. In 1897 in the Northern California literary journal *Overland Monthly,* John E. Bennett presented a diatribe about the missions that resonated with the coming wartime invective throughout the state. He accused the Franciscan missionaries of corruption, hoarding wealth only to "squander [it] on ecclesiastical pomp" and personal luxuries. Why preserve them, he asked, when "they were citadels of tyranny?" Even among those skeptical about the missions' place in California, Bennett's critique was unusually vitriolic, and he was largely alone in his call to let the adobe crumble. His linkage of Spanish colonization and slavery, however, was far from unique in the discourse about Cuba. His judgment of the missions pointed a symbolic finger at Spain, past and present: "[T]he mission was a plantation; the friar was a task master"; though "the mission fathers had it in their power to make citizens of the Indian, they chose to make them their slaves. . . ."[15] Such an interpretation lent little romance to the mission era.

More surprising was the ability of some of Bennett's contemporaries to denounce Spain for colonial cruelty in Cuba and beyond while finding worth in the remnants of Spanish California. If Indians were slaves, an 1899 observer wrote, they were "happy for the most part in their slavery." F. A. Ober wrote for a Los Angeles newspaper the same year with admiration for these missions and their "architectural attractions and interesting associations" and commendation for the Spanish in locating the "choicest continents and islands" for colonization. He coupled this approval with a chastisement that reflected Spanish-American

War rhetoric: "there was nothing providential for the Indians, however, for wherever the Spaniard landed there he immediately exercised despotic sovereignty." The author found the missions out of place, seeming "rather to pertain to Spain or Mexico than to the United States" and considered them a problem yet to be resolved: "the question has often been asked: what good purpose can these old missions serve today?"[16] The article concludes, as did many at the turn of the century, that the missions offered only quandaries.

Despite these early setbacks, mission preservationists began to gain some followers. After 1900 mission advocates began to stop lamenting the poor state of mission buildings and to embrace a nostalgic, sentimental mood. The end of the Spanish-American War factored significantly in this shift, though it seemed to have little direct impact on mission memories. Not only did the war remind Americans of the long history of Spanish colonization in western lands, but its conclusion also enabled Anglo-Californians to put Spain, now a defeated nation shorn of its empire, into a definite past. A visitor to Santa Barbara mission reported that "From the moment of crossing the threshold, the spirit and charm of the yester-years seemed to wrap us about, and to breathe from every object of its primitive furnishing. . . . It was all so like a bit from out the bygone centuries that had the good Fra Junípero Serra himself appeared . . . who has long since moldered to dust beside the mission walls, or, indeed, some haughty grandee booted and spurred and fresh from the court of Ferdinand and Isabella, had passed in procession before us, I think we could scarcely have felt a thrill of surprise."[17] As remnants of this distant past, the missions began to win converts, both among travelers and locals. By 1902 the Landmarks Club managed to raise funds to repair roof tiles at San Juan Capistrano and to shore up walls at San Fernando. The club also recruited a number of energetic mission defenders, several of whom later took the lead in the Camino Real campaign. The most vocal of these recruits was a newcomer from Boston. Harrie Forbes arrived in Los Angeles with her husband in 1895 and quickly became an enthusiastic member of the Landmarks Club. A honeymoon tour of California a decade earlier had already piqued her interest in the missions. Forbes was so taken with them that she made papier-mâché models of mission bells upon her return home. Though her fascination might have been greater than most, more and more people seemed to share her sentiments.[18]

Forbes was among the first people, however, to declare that this brand of romantic history was more than odd residue of the past and to recognize that it could become a particularly appropriate regional emblem. She explained in 1904 to the *Los Angeles Examiner* that "we do not need to go back in California to Colonial teas. Let us have our Spanish afternoon and our Indian dances."[19] Perhaps a newcomer's perspective was necessary to give Anglos a way out of the mission predicament. Forbes described the Spanish past not as anomalous but as analogous to a more familiar national past. Southern California boosters had been trying to prove themselves equal to the East in modern terms, but Forbes declared that in the realm of history at least, they ought not mimic other regions. In the attempt to link the region to the nation, to make Southern California definitively American, this strategy offered confidence in local distinctiveness and relied upon non-Anglo ethnicity to provide it. Yet one had to stretch to see Forbes's elevation of Spanish and Indian themes as inclusive. Forbes's leadership emphasized how fitting the missions were as symbols of "our" history—that is, the history of Anglo-American Southern Californians, even those as recently arrived as she. Using possessive terms for the Spanish era in a novel way, Forbes filed a new claim upon the mission past.

"THE NEW HAS COME TO THE RESCUE OF THE OLD"

As the desire for Spanish afternoons grew, a group of Southern California Anglos hit upon an idea for showcasing the missions' romantic possibilities. These local boosters imagined a single road linking the twenty-one missions, where travelers might undertake a complete mission tour. If tourists had yet to show their enthusiasm for such a circuit, the institution of a permanent road on the landscape would invite them to drive it. Promoters decided to call the road El Camino Real, a name whose historical origin was ambiguous but that held some local currency and a good amount of flair. Though their preferred translations, "the royal road" or "the king's highway," added an appealing note of European glamour, the more colloquial meaning of "the state highway" applied as well, since a state highway was exactly the type of road this group wanted to build. To persuade the state of California to build this road, however, lobbyists had to prove that a mission route could offer more than nostalgia; they had to demonstrate its economic potential. Here the mission enthusiasts reversed their earlier position. Instead of pleading for donations, they asserted that proper promotion of the Spanish past could pay dividends in tourist dollars. The coalition of business backers and romance seekers that gathered to push the Camino Real

cause came up with a winning formula that swayed the state at large
and opened the missions to a wealth of new meanings.

Formal work on the road began in 1902, as the scattered supporters
of the missions gathered to form a statewide association and to turn the
obscure route into a unified state highway, paved for efficiency and pub-
licized for recreation. Plans for El Camino Real were the subject of hear-
ings at the statewide meetings of the Federation of Women's Clubs and
the Native Daughters of the Golden West.[20] These efforts netted a
number of allies, but the larger organizations hesitated to pursue the
plan. Harrie Forbes, frustrated by the lack of initiative in her own California Federation of Women's Clubs, put her considerable energy and
resources to work and quickly widened support for El Camino Real.[21]
Appealing to booster interests on a number of levels, she organized a
powerful, if not always unified, coalition. Forbes recruited likely associates in local preservation organizations, historical societies, and
women's clubs, but she also won the allegiance of the good-roads
movement and automobile advocates. Members of the state's Anglo
elite jostled for influence in this group, yet debates among Camino Real
supporters reveal conflict between individuals who in other ways were
remarkably similar: they were Anglo, elite, Protestant, self-ascribed
Progressive, and relatively new to California. In this homogeneous context, these conversations highlight the differing beliefs about the purposes of the past within the region.

Women's clubs were key to the coalition. Though some of the clubs'
leadership had been reluctant to take on El Camino Real alone in the
past, many of the club members readily joined Forbes's effort. Forbes
had used women's clubs as an avenue to local prominence, joining several groups within the first year of her residence in Los Angeles. For a
woman who could not join the Native Daughters of the Golden West,
admission to the Friday Morning Club or the Ebell Club, or leadership
in the Federated Women's Clubs, symbolized elite status, both in affluence and reputation. Once welcomed, Forbes drew on this network of
prominent clubwomen to mount her campaign, and in turn, El Camino
Real lent her a viable civic platform. Leading clubwoman Clara Burdette
seconded her efforts and suggested that history projects offered women's
clubs good opportunities for public visibility: "most of the towns of California have a thread of romance woven into the fabric of their history.
And the individual club would confer a bonus . . . by editing a booklet-
history of its town."[22] California's Progressive Era women identified the
Spanish past as an issue on which they might gain a public voice.

In this effort, California clubwomen were ahead of the national curve; not until a decade later did the General Federation of Women's Clubs declare that historic conservation would be a central goal. That women should stand as the preservers of "all that is good in the civilization of the past" was an argument meant to enhance their role as champions of the civic good in modern times.[23] Targeting the past served women well in the long fight for suffrage. In California, after the crushing defeat of a suffrage measure in 1896, white women began to reorganize under the banner of civic altruism. This strategy, they hoped, would help build the case for women's civic participation gradually but deliberately, enhancing the belief that women are civic persons, boosters even.[24] Much like the "municipal housekeepers" who espoused improvements in children's welfare, public health, immigrant Americanization, and urban parks, these historical housekeepers were able to increase their authority in civic matters by positioning themselves as virtuous guardians of a family of citizens. Promoting the past was a safe, seemingly nonpolitical cause for women to join, yet this focus helped expand their opportunities for work, expression, and influence in the public arena. By 1911 this strategy bore fruit in the successful achievement of suffrage in California, nearly a decade ahead of the nation at large.

If the role of historical housekeeper was paying off for many women at the turn of the century, it was not without its own exclusions. Many of Southern California's elite women's clubs included prominent Californio women. For example, members of the Sepulveda and Del Valle families belonged to white women's clubs. They lent the clubs a touch of aristocracy, and the clubs in turn confirmed their acceptance in Anglo society. Nevertheless, a brouhaha over remarks by Caroline Severance in 1902 threatened this tenuous exchange. Severance was a pioneering clubwoman and former abolitionist who had retired to Los Angeles. She made an awkward defense of the Friday Morning Club's whites-only policy by expressing her amazement at the illogic of barring "our own southern blacks, while receiving socially representatives of other dark races, Spanish, Italian, East Indian, etc." Californianas protested their relegation to the "dark races," and in the debate that ensued, as historian Gayle Gullett found, both Severance's supporters and detractors placed the Californio elite in an "intermediate racial position. They were not white, as were Anglo-Saxons, but neither were they dark in the same sense as working-class Mexicans, Indians, or African Americans. . . . They were Spanish American ladies, not Mexican women."[25] The acceptance of a few elite Californios called attention to their exceptional status, reinforcing both the general racial rules (against Mexicans, presumably) and the assumption that clubwomen were, by and large, Anglos. Interestingly, the impressive clubhouses these Anglo women erected at the turn of the century were often built in Spanish style. In the ethnic context, however, this architecture suggested not the clubs' diverse membership but their use of the Spanish past to enhance their public standing. This stance had consequences for people beyond the Anglo women who invested in local history to support their desires to become civic activists.[26] Though Forbes herself appeared to be a single-minded promoter of El Camino Real, the project clearly served as a vehicle for Progressive women's larger causes, and these women understood it as necessarily an Anglo enterprise. The desire to win fans to the idea of women as public actors, defenders of history, and promoters of the civic good gave the Spanish past a boosterish cast, a patriotic purpose, and a definitively Anglo set of guardians.

Advocates for roads and automobiles saw a means to their ends in the historic highway, although the two groups surprisingly did not act in concert. Camino Real leaders readily made common cause with the good-roads movement. These Progressive road boosters promoted state responsibility for improved transportation as a means of rationalizing national infrastructure. In this sense, they endorsed the growing belief that each state had a duty to fund the construction of a comprehensive highway system. The state highways, according to one California commentator, presented a "problem calling for the highest engineering science, the greatest financial skill, and the best legislative sagacity of an intelligent people." One state official described the roads as a California disgrace and called the seasonal mud that mucked up dirt roads one of the "relics of barbarism." Better highways, these advocates argued, made for both a better economy and a better civilization.[27] In such a formula, good roads were an objective that no legislator could sensibly oppose. Still, joining forces with these sympathetic preservationists could only assist their argument that road building improved the state on many levels.

The choice to make common cause with automobile and good-roads advocates rather than railroad companies was a bold move. Railroads remained the dominant mode of tourist travel, even though Southern California was an early leader in car culture. Though by 1902 the good-roads plank had gained wide acceptance, in theory if not in practice, the early automobilists who hoped to drive on these new highways remained controversial. Few people saw the expensive, unreliable horseless carriage as anything but idle amusement for the wealthy; most preferred reliable roads for the familiar mode of horse-drawn transportation. Forbes was ecumenical and solicited automobilists' support, to the chagrin of other Camino Real boosters who thought the noisy contraptions would ruin the atmosphere of a romantic past. Specifically, she persuaded the Automobile Club of Southern California (ACSC) to embrace her plan. Founded in 1900 as one of the earliest organizations for automobile enthusiasts, the ACSC campaigned for public acceptance of the motorcar and supported the growing ranks of drivers.[28] Its influence in Southern California, where automobiles proliferated faster than in other regions, made the ACSC a power broker for any road agenda. Auto-club leaders saw in the Camino Real campaign the potential to increase statewide acceptance of their machines. In turn, the growing clout of cars and their drivers encouraged many tourist-oriented businesses and city boosters to back El Camino Real, banking on the potential of increased traffic.

At the 1904 statewide convention to organize the El Camino Real Association, automobile activists took the greatest share of podium time. Still, clubwomen and good roadsters—as well as chamber of commerce presidents, local elected officials, and business owners—had a chance to contribute their ideas. Little consensus emerged from the meeting. All the attendees wanted to have a mission road, but they could forge no initial agreement on its fundamental purpose or route. Clearly, however, Southern Californians would be the ones to do the squabbling. Twenty-six California cities sent representatives, but attendees from cities in the southern part of the state and Los Angeles residents in particular dominated the discussion. In fact, over 60 percent of the delegates hailed from Santa Barbara and points south. Neither section included any attendees with Spanish surnames or Californio connections.[29] This commonality did not override the acrid debates that developed about leadership and emphasis among these otherwise likeminded civic boosters.

While Harrie Forbes and other female club members played significant roles in the early publicity for and organization of El Camino Real, women accounted for barely one-quarter of the attendees at the first convention. Most of these female representatives were clubwomen, largely from the Native Daughters and the Federated Clubs.[30] Perhaps this low representation reflected the fact that many of the official delegates were city and county officials. Evidence of brewing dissatisfaction with the female leadership among a few male boosters, however, suggests something else at work. Charles Lummis indicated as much in a 1904 column in *Out West* (successor to *Land of Sunshine*). He praised women's energy, their constant "Pulling on the Bit" and "Communal Desire to Go," but he judged this enthusiasm undirected, wasted in "talk . . . fiddle . . . and dreams." To accomplish "something Real," Lummis suggested, these women required a man's leadership. He applied this principle to El Camino Real in a backhanded compliment to women's initiative: "it is only fair to remark, in passing, that while it is now high time for men to take hold who know what's what, eighty per cent of this whole Camino Real momentum is due to women."[31] Privately, Lummis and fellow Camino Real supporters grumbled about these public women. Lummis's letters spread rumor and doubt about Forbes's and other women's abilities and interests, accusing them of "serving nothing but . . . personal ambitions" and suggesting that they were "not the class of people who should run such an enterprise." Lummis did not want upstart women like Harrie Forbes cutting into the great personal influence he believed he had in matters of Spanish-Californian history. He assessed Forbes's character in letters to various Camino Real advocates: "she is very nervous, and excitable, and uninstructed, and ignorant of things she deals in. On the other hand, she is very energetic and apparently a hard worker. If we can break this kind of a bronco to some harness it will be a good thing all round."[32] With this startling image, Lummis explained that Forbes should not lead but could help pull the Camino Real bandwagon, with himself presumably at the whip.

Such anxiety testifies not only to Lummis's personal eccentricities but also to the level of women's involvement in the cause. If anything, Lummis understated the case; women were the primary force behind the preservation and booster organizations that bolstered El Camino Real, precisely because these groups provided growing spheres for women's public leadership. Harrie Forbes captured the public eye, garnering a full-page article on her life in the *Los Angeles Examiner* in 1904. The spread included a favorable review of the guidebook she had authored the year before. *California Missions and Landmarks and How to Get There* went through eight editions and lent her local authority on mission issues, which Lummis regarded as his sole province. Given the resentment that he and others harbored against Forbes's fame, women's public role carried certain risks. When supporters officially founded the El Camino Real Association in 1906, Forbes chose not to bid for the presidency, serving instead as secretary of the Los Angeles branch, and later as vice president while her husband, Armitage Forbes, held the top post.[33] Behind these male executives, she was able to maintain her stance of civic altruism as well as her vocal leadership. Many club-women recognized the advantage of involving men in their public causes, not for need of direction but for want of funds. As Camino Real supporter Eliza Keith put it, "No organization composed entirely of women has the same opportunity of raising funds as have those whose membership embraces independent businessmen and capitalists and state legislators."[34] Though Keith and others understood that women's ability to influence public opinion would rise in proportion to their coffers, and thus to their cooperation with men, they also knew this cooperation entailed some cession of their leadership roles. Forbes tenaciously clung to her de facto control of the organization, but the latent gender tension remained.

Women and men in the Camino Real organization fell on both sides of a major debate about the appropriate emphasis for the road itself. The *Los Angeles Times* named these opposing camps "sentimentalists" and "automobile scorchers."[35] The former group stressed the need to adhere to strict construction of historical authenticity, while the latter argued that the road would be worthless unless made practical for commerce and transportation as well. Harrie Forbes was one of the few who initially believed that the road could accomplish both goals, combining her nostalgic desires and business acumen into one vision for the road. For the others, however, intense disagreement about which master the road would serve—past or present—threatened to break apart the Camino Real coalition. But before a final rupture could occur, boosters discovered that their quarrel suggested a highly salable contrast, a compelling juxtaposition of modernity and nostalgia that would govern Camino Real rhetoric in the future.

Automobilists maintained that a road that wandered among the hills, bypassed the heart of cities like Los Angeles, and strayed far from travelers' amenities would be a failure. Not only would few follow it, but no one would want to build such an impractical road. Sentimentalists feared that if they pursued a more efficient approach, severing their links to the mission past and its historical romance, their project would lose its unique appeal. Their fledgling El Camino Real Association might "become an adjunct to the National Good Roads Association, thereby losing the distinctive character implied by the adoption of the Camino Real idea." Lummis, the sentimentalists' self-appointed spokesperson, warned more pointedly that the goal of automobile enthusiasts was "the shortest road from the south to the north. . . . In other words, a thousand-mile speedway for red-devils."[36] Planning the route became a protracted battle between the two sides. When sentimentalists insisted that any deviation from the true trail of the padres would be sacrilege, compromise appeared improbable.

On a practical level, however, the hedge against historical heresy—an "authentic" padres' route—proved difficult to maintain in the face of daunting geography and competition among local boosters to get their town on the road. The research alone proved to be far from simple. The Los Angeles branch of the El Camino Real Association, under Forbes's guidance, began to peruse old church and rancho documents, interview old-timers, and survey the region. Popular travel writer and colorful booster George Wharton James decided in the meantime to try to locate the original route on horseback. James, a locally known authority on diverse topics, including the Spanish era, penned dozens of books on the subject, most of which outsold Lummis's efforts. Accompanied by a *Los Angeles Examiner* reporter, he attempted to trace the southernmost section between San Luis Rey and San Diego. The object of the journey was to determine the "feasibility" and "practicability" of the El Camino Real Association's goal of reestablishing the old route. Five days of orienteering led them to the disappointing conclusion that only five miles of the "true historic route" remained in use. Large sections of the road ran under private fences and were alternately built upon and overgrown. This experience led James to regard as folly the project of determining the authentic route, let alone rebuilding it. "To those who contend that the real and only Camino Real can be located and followed I have nothing more to say than that 'though I had the gift of knowledge and tongues and prophecy and spoke with the tongues of men and of angels,' my ability were nil compared with that of the locator of the old Camino Real."[37] James's claim was worrisome. The history was not just sitting out there waiting to be discovered; it had to be reconstructed, even created.

The apparent impossibility of achieving authenticity caused trouble for the association. It led some Northern Californians to besmirch the very idea of remembering the road. In the summer of 1904 a *San Francisco Chronicle* editorial alleged that a continually traveled, definitively named road called El Camino Real was "a myth—probably always was." Echoing the automobilists, the author endorsed the road project for practical reasons but remarked that "nobody would care a fig if they choose to call it El Camino Real, although it would show more horse sense if they called it a name that would advertise themselves rather than after some legendary king who built an imaginary road."[38] James Miller Guinn, local historian and prominent member of the Historical Society of Southern California, also found specious the proposition that El Camino Real was the only important highway of Spanish California. His own surveys showed "fifty or one hundred old caminos reales that anciently existed in California." Guinn asked, "Which one of these shall [they] designate as the *real* one?"[39] Such skepticism not only undermined the sentimentalists' case but threatened to stall the association's momentum with their claims that El Camino Real did not exist.

This issue of authenticity left the El Camino Real Association in a bit of a fix. Though association members were increasingly under pressure to make the road practicable, they could hardly abandon their totem of authenticity, lest the whole enterprise be declared a fake. Guinn had intimated as much, suggesting that the so-called Royal Road was "a new discovery made by recent arrivals." The association dredged up old interviews with Californios to testify to the mere existence of the road. Leaders pointed to Anna Picher's interview with Don Antonio Coronel, published in 1895 in the *Land of Sunshine,* in which the elderly Californian supposedly verified the route, name, and romance of the old road. Coronel himself was no longer around to assist with the map, and few boosters consulted Californio descendants as anything other than symbols of authenticity. The process, and the dilemma, remained in Anglo hands. Ventura County Camino Real activist Mrs. M. E. Dudley warned her colleagues that the route might "deviate a few rods" from the original path, but "to go into wild and unauthenticated trails would bring ridicule." Extensive research (or the appearance of it) might shield the association from such a fate. Her own progress report detailing the meticulous research in 1907 set out to establish "the facts of history." But her description of the committee's goal of identifying "the main traveled road" in the Spanish era allowed greater freedom to identify a practical route.[40] James, who had exposed this problem first, suggested an even better rhetorical solution. Meeting modern needs like gradual grades for automobiles and links between important towns, he argued, paralleled the padres' own alterations; they had changed the route due to seasonal constraints or newly discovered shortcuts. The route therefore, could be approximated "near enough for all sentimental and practical purposes."[41] Modern surveyors could plan the route in the spirit of the padres if not in their actual sandal tracks.

Camino Real advocates jumped on James's compromise as a way to escape the critiques of Guinn and others. Their internal disagreements

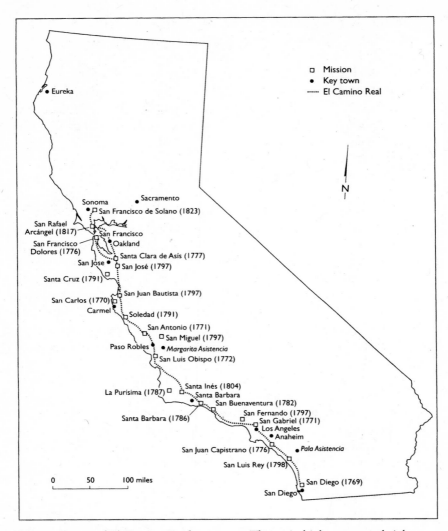

Map 1. Route of El Camino Real, ca. 1910. The main highway passed right by some missions, while other missions were on branch roads. Adapted from a James Munson map.

had put the project in jeopardy, and sentimentalists and automobilists closed ranks to choose a route and preserve their road. The years of research allowed them to make a good show of historical authenticity, but the agreed-upon course did not validate a singular path (see map 1). It excluded certain remote outposts on the central coast but incorporated some subsidiary sites that gave the road a reason to run through significant modern cities. The Plaza Church in downtown Los Angeles, which was not a mission but a regular pueblo church for the villagers, found itself on the main road, while important missions such as San Fernando and Carmel were shunted off to branches of the road.[42] If this compromise resembled a defeat for the sentimentalists, they didn't bill it that way. Even Lummis was convinced, writing in *Out West* that "those who care for the lessons of history and those who are simply seeking a good road" could share El Camino Real; the association, he said, "found that these two interests are twins."[43] In fact, the agreement about the route allowed greater accommodation between sentimentalists and automobilists.

Once resolved, the dispute netted these advocates a valuable rhetorical device. The resident Camino Real booster at the *San Francisco Examiner* charted the path to James's compromise and pointed to its symbolic mileage. That "these men with choo choo cars" were largely underwriting the organization's budget led her to conclude that "the automobile is a good friend to El Camino Real. The New has come to the rescue of the Old. The auto men have contributed coin that the King's Highway may be once more the chain that links the venerable mission of the padres and the California people."[44] This solution was a popular Progressive turn: using new scientific tools to reestablish familiar order. Moreover, it enabled celebration of American progress in a way that chastising Californians for neglecting the missions could not. It allowed Southern California Anglos to pursue simultaneously the seemingly divergent paths to the missions' past and modernity. Connecting the padres and the people would be the automobile, a symbol of the modern era. By placing this triumphalist spin on a vexing practical dilemma, the association helped claim the Spanish past for California's new Anglo inhabitants.

"MONUMENTS IN CONCRETE"

The rhetorical strategy that highlighted the contrast between modernity and antiquity proved to be the association's most secure accomplishment. When mission enthusiasts set out to build El Camino Real, they had not yet worked out this interpretation; rather, it grew out of the discussion they had to have about how to sell the Spanish past. Camino Real supporters had to sell their interpretation first not to tourists but to the state of California: Why should the state build the road at all? In the resulting lobby-and-leaflet campaign, linking nostalgia and progress was indispensable. Appealing to Progressive-minded politicians meant using the language of good roads and invoking trust in engineers to design and build such roads. Good roads offered Progressives a seemingly attainable, noncontroversial goal that could demonstrate the judicious use of modern science for social betterment and in this case, for historical preservation. Accordingly, Harrie Forbes chided Californians, "we of modern time and methods," for abiding conditions the padres themselves would have abhorred. "Is it then not time," she asked, "that we urge and thoroughly support the project for the betterment of our roads when by so doing we reap the benefit and sustain the supremacy of progress?" The title of her article in *The Grizzly Bear,* the organ of the Native Sons and Daughters of the Golden West, stated the relationship succinctly: "Good Roads Means Restoration of El Camino Real."[45] Modern technology could be not only a social savior but also a historical one.

Several years of petitioning by Camino Real and other good-roads activists resulted in the State Highway Commission, whose charge was to survey routes for a potential state-highway system. Governor James N. Gillett, though a machine Democrat who often opposed Progressive measures, proposed a bill in the waning days of his term to fund a state-highway system. With this development in the spring of 1909, Harrie Forbes believed the construction of El Camino Real was at hand: "through the Governor's Good Road Bill I see El Camino Real looming up in the near distance." She claimed to "have the ear of the Engineering Department that will handle the $18,000,000 bonds for the State Highways."[46] Forbes hoped to influence the choices ahead, pushing state engineers toward the association's preferred Camino Real route. Her hunch proved correct; surveyors for the planned coastal route did recommend a similar path. One report mentioned El Camino Real by name, recalling the "[r]omance . . . built into the roads . . . laid out by the padres when California was Spain."[47] In November 1910 the state-highway bond passed a statewide vote by a narrow margin. Survey work was still under way when the highway commission realized that the initial sum would not be nearly enough to complete the system. Voters approved two more state-bond issues during the decade to finish the highways, sixteen million dollars more in 1916 and an additional forty million dollars in 1919. Engineers spent the money as quickly as they could, improving existing roads and grading new ones, building bridges, and cutting passes. Nonetheless, they could not keep up with the growing traffic of automobilists in the 1910s and 1920s who clamored to drive El Camino Real and other routes before the roads had been paved.[48]

Throughout this process, Forbes was determined to keep El Camino Real at the top of the state's road agenda. Helping her make the case were the mission bells that had begun to sprout up alongside the association's route. These bells arrived on the road as a result of a 1906 plan of the association's Los Angeles section to mark El Camino Real with road signs. After forging agreement on the route in 1904, Camino Real boosters tossed about for the next task that could generate publicity, attract donations, and further actual work on the road. The association's assets were much too meager to fund private paving; the more ambitious the plan had become, the more people realized that state funds and labor would have to build the road itself. The El Camino Real Association needed to find an activity that would not only give the road more name recognition but also increase public pressure to build state highways in general. Los Angeles leaders came to see that road signs could accomplish this task when they witnessed the success of the ACSC's program to mark Southern California roads with directional signs. These projects had lent the auto club much of its early authority; and its visible signs endowed it with the aura of an official agency long before the state took over the responsibility of marking roads. Camino Real prospects might similarly brighten if the association were to mark the length of the route with signs designating "The King's Highway."

The Los Angeles section of the association expanded on the ACSC's approach and decided to mark the road not just with a sign but an "emblematic and appropriate guide post" that would amplify the romantic ambiance that members associated with El Camino Real. None other than Harrie Forbes suggested the idea of a "mission-bell guidepost." She submitted a design for a replica mission bell hung from a tall standard that curved at the top like a shepherd's staff. Each pole held a "guideboard" listing directions and distances to the nearest missions, north and south. The El Camino Real Association heartily approved both the idea and the design, adopting the mission-bell guidepost as the "official road marker" for the whole highway. Forbes secured a copyright and design patent to make this design exclusive to El Camino Real. The Los Angeles section then led the way in marketing these road markers, erecting the first mission-bell guidepost in August 1906 at the Plaza Church with a festive ceremony (see figure 4).[49]

The bell program netted a wide set of supporters and drew more attention to the El Camino Real Association. Forbes's goal was to install

Figure 4. Mission-bell guidepost, Plaza Church, Los
Angeles, ca. 1906. Photograph by C. C. Pierce. This item
is reproduced by permission of The Huntington Library,
San Marino, California.

a mission-bell guidepost for each mile of the six-hundred-mile length of
the road. She solicited funds from a wide variety of groups and individuals to carry out the project. In the *Grizzly Bear,* she appealed to "any
person or any society that may be interested in the project of marking
the highway" to write her for information about the price, installation
process, and locations that needed markers along El Camino Real. She
reeled in town-boosting branches of the Native Sons and Daughters,
women's clubs, and local governments with the bait of a "brass memorial tablet" affixed to the guideposts naming the donor.[50] The orders
began to pile in on Forbes. During the first three years of the project, she
sold 57 bells, each of which cost twenty-five dollars plus the cost of
shipping and assembly. By 1910 90 bells hung by the highway, and two

years later, the count was up to 120. In 1915 Harrie Forbes boasted that 400 guideposts now marked El Camino Real, with a bell a mile between San Diego and Ventura. The eventual total for the project was 459, slightly short of the goal for the six-hundred-mile highway, but still a frequent sight along it.[51]

The bells began to have a cultural impact early in their life span. Travelers followed them even when only a small number were in place. Especially before the road became a unified highway, guidebooks often gave directions by them. In 1911, when there were still fewer than one hundred bells along the entire route, *Thorpe's* automobile guidebook instructed drivers between Santa Ana and San Juan Capistrano to make a turn at a particular mission-bell guidepost. In 1912 one tourist recalled her experience navigating by the bells. "From the very first we came to depend upon these beautiful signposts and if we were ever uncertain about our route, our doubts were instantly downed when someone raised the welcome cry, 'There's a bell!'"[52] This level of recognition could only benefit the association's advertisement plans. In fact, the bell guideposts netted Camino Real advocates more advantage in influencing the route than they had anticipated. Because the association reserved sole power in the placement of guideposts, it could mark its favored route without interference. Once placed, these signs lent a quality of permanence and unity, indeed a physical existence, to a route that had yet to become anything more than a path outlined in promotional pamphlets. Despite all the early wrangling, the association created the expectation of a road without paying for the actual construction.

While the growing renown of the bells must have pleased their purchasers, the business the bells generated satisfied their producers even more. Harrie Forbes, the author of the design, owned the factory turning out the mission-bell guideposts. Bell making apparently began as a hobby for Forbes, who had a foundry built at one of her residences on 31st Street in Los Angeles. She assured the purchasers that the bells were a nonprofit operation, with the twenty-five-dollar purchase price defraying the cost of materials and labor only. Nevertheless, by 1914 the Forbeses decided that they could make a business out of the enterprise. Harrie and her husband founded the California Bell and Novelty Company to manufacture replica bells and other souvenir items for Camino Real tourists. Far greater profit lay in this expanding tourist market than in production of the guideposts, of which there would be a limited number. Mission souvenirs, including bells small and large, proved to be a profitable product for the Forbeses, who at the time operated the only bell foundry west of the Mississippi.[53] The Forbeses also profited from another Camino Real connection, though this time they were dependent upon the success of El Camino Real as a state highway. They owned one of the largest gypsum mines in California, gypsum being a key ingredient in cement. Their mine had supplied much of the gypsum in the cement for the Owens River Aqueduct and, later, for much of the state highway.[54] The Forbeses' interest in the romantic El Camino Real could not be divorced from their stake in the commercial one.

Yet Harrie Forbes's interest in El Camino Real was not mercenary. From all appearances, her devotion to the project was genuine, sparked not by a profit-making scheme but by an insatiable desire to re-create the romantic mission experience she had first glimpsed. Nevertheless, her commercial interest was part and parcel of her sentimentalism, though in public life she had to emphasize the latter. As she confessed in 1904, "if I went into such work for profit I would have no disciples and my work would avail nothing. I love the romance of California and I work for its interest alone."[55] Forbes was indeed aware of the stigma that profit attached to her causes and to women's causes in general. Charles Lummis's attack on her as a "promoter" carried subtexts about gender, judging keen commercial ambitions to be unseemly for women. She thus positioned herself as a sentimental volunteer, not a resourceful entrepreneur. The mission-bell guideposts were a quintessential example of Forbes's delicate public balance. They symbolized a romantic past, but at the same time they improved tourist access and created a market for related products. In fact, Forbes had to demonstrate the economic potential of the missions. Southern California boosters had been loath to promote the missions until El Camino Real proved a good bet. The popularity of the Spanish past depended upon its profitability, almost as much as Forbes's own credibility depended upon her maintenance of a public identity that befit a female volunteer unconcerned with profit.

Even as she invoked the role of the historical housekeeper, Forbes launched projects that furthered the common commercial interest that many Southern Californians had in the success of El Camino Real. For all their propitious connections, the Forbeses were not unique. Boosterism fueled California businesses, as public and private interests converged in local promotion. The association with El Camino Real offered a new outlet for this public/private partnership, enabling local promoters to develop a link with the romantic past and thus tap into new markets and audiences. One by one, coastal cities and towns began to recognize the unrealized value of their historic associations. They began to heed the words of people like John S. Mitchell, president of the Los Angeles Chamber of Commerce, when he spoke to a group gathered to commemorate the Landmarks Club's restoration of the roof of the San Fernando Mission in 1910: "It took us a great while to realize that the Missions had anything but a sentimental interest. But if we were slow to learn, we have learnt our lesson at last. We realize today that the Missions have not only a commercial value but the greatest! We realize today that the Old Missions are worth more than money, are a greater asset to southern California than our oil, our oranges, even our climate!"[56]

Once in process, El Camino Real attracted the attention of a number of astute investors. While established real-estate developers, architects, restauranteurs, and hoteliers joined the El Camino Real Association, others of them ventured into new commercial interests on the road itself.[57] During the 1910s the growing number of California auto tourists began to note the increase of hotels and service stations that made their trips more comfortable. Travel writer A. L. Westgard told his readers in 1912 that the "route offers a good hotel at the end of each reasonable day's riding distance, thus insuring the tourist comfort for himself and all needed attention for his motor." The Los Angeles Chamber of Commerce detailed in 1916 thirteen Camino Real hotels where travelers might lunch or stay the night. One tourist described her lodging in San Juan Capistrano, Las Rosas Inn, as "a pleasant country home turned by some enterprising woman into an inn."[58] The efforts of the enterprising innkeeper were undoubtedly copied up and down the highway, as new businesses began to compete for the vacation dollars of Camino Real tourists.

The town of Paso Robles, in southern San Luis Obispo County, provides a good example of the road's potential benefits for local businesses. The hot springs there had led to the creation of several spa hotels, but the isolated location kept Paso Robles from becoming a major destination. Once El Camino Real ran through town, however, automobile tourists began to regard Paso Robles as an obligatory stop along the drive. *Thorpe's* guide in 1912 mentioned the town and its fine hotels as a must-see. "Here we spend the night and take a medicinal bath, whether we need it or not." El Camino Real was, for Paso Robles, a tourist pipeline. The Paso Robles Hot Springs Hotel opened about 1920, inviting affluent guests to enjoy an immaculate Victorian-style hotel and modern spa facilities amid a Spanish atmosphere. Its brochure made explicit connections to El Camino Real, calling nearby Mission San Miguel the "Paso Robles Mission." The front cover pictured a brown-robed padre drinking water from a rocky spring, with the white wooden hotel in the background. The brochure used the El Camino Real Association's rhetoric, highlighting the hotel's modern "comfort and luxury in striking contrast with the dusty trail of the Padres, who, walking El Camino Real from Mission to Mission, refreshed themselves with the waters of these wondrous Springs."[59] Paso Robles took the idea that the new saved the old and made it a tourist amenity that town boosters could sell and that people wanted to buy.

The most famous hotel for seekers of Spanish romance was Frank Miller's Mission Inn in Riverside. Midwestern and Protestant by birth, Miller became one of Southern California's foremost boosters of the Spanish past. Though neither a mission nor El Camino Real could be found nearby, he took a small tumbledown inn in the 1890s and over the next three decades, transformed it into a veritable "Spanish Revival Oz" and a lucrative business. Riverside became a focal point of mission tourism as a result. The Mission Inn's architectural whimsy, rich decoration, and maze of patios, courts, and domes made it a one-of-a-kind place where tourists might indulge visions of mission luxury. Miller also conceived of the idea for a mission play, based upon Oberammergau's Passion play, and recruited John S. McGroarty to write it. McGroarty was a Pennsylvania-born journalist and sentimental poet turned *Los Angeles Times* columnist and local booster. The spectacle he dreamed up—which combined music, melodrama, dance, and pageantry—opened in 1912 and played to packed houses in a mission-style theater in San Gabriel for nearly two decades. By 1929, some two and a half million tourists, locals, and schoolchildren had seen his version of California history, which celebrated the padres, lamented their demise, and suggested that Anglo-Americans could redeem the present by remembering the past. The Mission Playhouse included a miniature El Camino Real, complete with diminutive mission models, that patrons could walk through on their way into the show; on the way out, some were surely inspired to take the full tour.[60] The road and its related booster business promoted each other as people invested in productions of the Spanish past for an increasingly eager market.

The success of El Camino Real suggested that there was gold to be mined in the mission past. Images of this history had, after all, prompted the construction of the first state-highway system in California, a major Progressive goal. As the ACSC said in retrospect in 1915, El Camino Real was "seized on as a great State highway . . . with the promise of paved boulevards to come. These monuments in concrete to the achievements of California's first civil engineers [the padres] are no less real gifts to the world than were the missions themselves."[61] This rhetorical combination of progress and nostalgia made disbelief in a romantic version of the Spanish past nearly slanderous. Residents, travelers, and tourists on El Camino Real began to reference the missions more and more in identifying the hallmarks of the region's landscape. Why Southern Californians believed the Spanish past could accomplish such good work for regional identity and memory had everything to do with its apparent good work for the regional economy and infrastructure. That the road had been built with state investment and commercial interest meant that it was likely to remain. Yet how it came to represent something more than a tourist slogan or a lobbyist tool is a story that is less about the road than its riders.

"THE ROMANCE WHICH LINGERS IN BROKEN ARCHES"

Automobile tourists began to drive El Camino Real even before the road had received the attention of engineers. In their newfangled contraptions, they traveled the new highway with great zest and wrote copiously about their trips. Narratives of El Camino Real during the first quarter of the twentieth century had many authors, though these writers were overwhelmingly white and hailed from the middle to upper classes. Some were promoters of the campaign, whose journeys served to advertise their efforts. Others came from the tourist industry, producing guidebooks and postcards for sale or penning articles for travel magazines. Still others were local historians, writing descriptive pamphlets about portions of the road or individual missions. But many were simply tourists, from near and far, who wrote formal diaries of their trips, perhaps for publication, or assembled albums of photographed memories. Nearly all the writers participated in tourism in some way, taking the mission road with an eye to the new sensibilities of the tourist experience.[62] Despite the fact that Camino Real tourists generally traveled on their own (not on guided tours), their accounts echoed each other, repeating key themes, interpretations, images, and prose. If tourists and writers could conceivably depart from this consensus, few did.[63] The concurrence of tourist accounts is all the more remarkable in light of the absence of the now-familiar museum-style displays or descriptive signs at the missions themselves. Tourists either wandered the mission grounds alone, guidebook in hand, or paid a resident caretaker or priest to show them around. No standard tour presented itself to visitors.

By 1915 a common feature of the mission tour was the automobile. Over the course of the Camino Real campaign, California became a mecca for automobile tourists, a "motorist's paradise," according to one travel writer. The state led the nation in cars per capita, and the number swelled with the ranks of wealthy wintertime tourists who brought their autos with them. Camino Real boosters not immodestly proffered their creation as the best in tourist experience: the "autoist's royal road," one author called it, while another predicted that El Camino Real was "destined to become the most popular automobile tour on this whole continent."[64] Thus by the 1910s tourists commented on the multitude of cars on El Camino Real. A 1915 guidebook mentioned that "a constantly increasing stream of motorists flows by the rude portals of these California Cathedrals." Typical was the note on the back of a Santa Barbara–mission postcard: "We have lizzied California so much."[65] Promoters geared the mission road to the automobile, and tourists responded, making the Camino Real tour definitively a motorized experience.

For all the concrete poured on the road, promoters still had to address two key areas of discomfort about the missions: the recentness of the structures' demise and their apparent incongruity in modern California. Promoters could sell this road, but would tourists buy it? The new promotional logic, on the one hand, distanced the mission past from modern life by associating it with bygone romance and glorifying the ruins. On the other, by eulogizing the Indians as a vanishing race and lionizing the padres as California pioneers, Camino Real narratives reassembled the region's apparently disjunctive history into a logical progression, indeed a racial succession. If the missions had earlier been too close and confusing for comfort, in Camino Real rhetoric they became both distant and coherent. Pushing the mission era further back in time, and further from Anglos, allowed history to unfold in a predictable, almost leisurely sequence from primitive to colonial to modern eras. Camino Real promoters thus offered travelers places in the mission landscape and roles in its timeline. Tourists, clearly defined as part of this modern stage of civilization, could be part of the rediscovery and restoration of the missions, again being part of the new that would save the old. Driving modern automobiles to visit ghostly ruins, Camino Real tourists enjoyed the repeated passage over the threshold from present to past and back again. El Camino Real, with its vicarious time travel, was an early twentieth-century thrill ride.

To build this time machine, narrators of El Camino Real had to push the missions into the past. The further the missions receded into

memory, the more they came to represent a lost romantic life. Mission
days appeared in promoters' tales as brave ones, full of religious devotion and courage, quaint customs and picturesque landscapes. For one
guidebook, just the name *El Camino Real* "summons visions of a vanished age, an idyllic epoch, a time of Missions, and siestas and lan-
guorous existence in a land of golden plenty."[66] For all the florid
language and hyperbole of these accounts, the repetition of such sentiments established El Camino Real as a conduit to romantic experience.
Many tourists explained their motives for taking a Camino Real tour in
exactly these terms. One travel diarist began his memoir by recalling his
initial anticipation: "we feel that we shall find in the crumbling, vine-
covered ruins a glamour of romance and an historic significance that
would make our journey worth while even if it did not take us through
some of the loveliest and most impressive scenery in the world."
Another hoped that on his journey from mission to mission, he might
"slowly, leisurely, becom[e] acquainted with the beautiful legends and
history connected therewith . . . for in their history lay the charm and
romance which appeals to one so."[67] At first glance, this purple prose
might appear to be liberal embroidering by tourist promoters on the
make. A few Camino Real tourists did find some fault with their guidebooks' promises when views and visits fell short of the astoundingly
picturesque.[68] But however disappointed some visitors may have been
in their encounters with mission romance, their sincere expectations
suggest how readily they adopted the tone of romanticism.

The Southwest was becoming a popular outlet for fast-growing interest in exoticism and romance. At the turn of the century, white tourists,
archaeologists, and developers discovered the lands of the American
Southwest, viewing them alternately as an American Orient, the real
Indian country or "our Italy." Altogether foreign to the climate, landscape, and demographics of the eastern or midwestern United States,
the Southwest remained a mysterious place for many Anglo-Americans.
When the railroad began to make the region more accessible, curiosity
about its exoticism replaced apprehension.[69] In California, the Mediterranean metaphor was particularly appealing. On the East Coast,
Mediterreaneanism was the offshoot of a more widespread cultural
affinity for romanticism in the era. From the newfound popularity of
figures like Joan of Arc and various architectural revivals, a fascination
with "romantic historicism" took hold of elite communities in the late
nineteenth and early twentieth centuries. For many people, romance
depended on historic associations; the modern era appeared to have few

opportunities for the romantic brand of heroism or drama of yore.[70] Tourism, as a modern industry, gave travelers a secure way to view exotic peoples and landscapes supposedly trapped in the past without losing their moorings in the present.

When Camino Real writers invested the missions with the romance they found wanting in their own time, they began to distance themselves from the Spanish past. The power of recalling the past lies in its determined vagueness, its invocation of a time both distant and indistinct, and its fundamental irretrievability. One Camino Real tourist summed up this relationship in 1912: "the old Mission buildings with their quaint architecture speak very tenderly of the past, the broken past which will never be revived."[71] If romantic life resided only in the past, then labeling the missions romantic placed them too in a bygone age. Camino Real writers cleaved California history into two distinct periods: the romantic mission era and the modern world. Under the influence of romanticism, travelers on El Camino Real severed connections with the past even as they coveted it.

What did people seek in their journeys to the past? Their quarry was not likely to be the profit and distinction that local boosters sought. Perhaps advertisements such as the following rare one for a Southern Pacific rail tour of El Camino Real enticed them: along the trip, tourists could happily lose themselves in "an aroma of romance and an atmosphere of historic association that blends and envelops like a fine ether the materialistic sense of modern life." Such invitations promised escape, a temporary hiatus from the pressures of twentieth-century living. Alternatively, writer Ruth Kedzie Wood fashioned her auto trip to Santa Barbara as a promenade, an imaginary visit to "Sevilla's Avenue of Delight." Momentarily succumbing to the illusion, she asked, "who that has a touch of the Spaniard in him (and her) but loves to ride out in a carriage?"[72] Her escape was not just to the past but to a foreign land, a virtual visit to the Spain of literary imagination. That the presence of the Santa Barbara mission could transform her motorcar into a Spanish carriage spoke to the desire Camino Real tourists had for the idea of escape. In this formula, the more anachronistic the missions appeared, the more precious was their romance, and thus the more popular they became. This kind of tourism exoticized the past by casting missions as products of a distant age and a foreign people. Ironically, this perspective also made the mission past a consumable product of the modern market that tourists claimed they were trying to escape. Indeed, the missions receded into a hazy, bygone era in direct correlation to

Figure 5. "Ruined Arches at San Juan Capistrano Mission, Cal.," ca. 1910. Images of Capistrano often placed its broken arcade in the extreme foreground, strengthening the allusion to classical ruins. Postcard from author's collection.

their increasingly frequent appearance in the present as tourist attractions and California landmarks.

For mission tourists and writers, proof that the missions belonged to the "broken past" was the fact that many of the structures were literally broken, in ruins (see figure 5). The discourse on ruins in promotional articles, guidebooks, and tourist diaries both added to missions' romantic allure and pushed them further back in time. El Camino Real renewed tourists' interest in sublime and picturesque landscapes, a desire that harkened back to mid-nineteenth-century romantic aesthetics. In this pursuit, tourists betrayed nostalgia for an earlier form of tourism that offered seemingly less standardized, less industrialized contemplative tours than twentieth-century promoters hawked.

Rhetorical meditations on mission ruins called forth writers' most sentimental impulses. The author of a 1914 guide prepared her readers for a visit to Mission San Antonio de Padua, a structure in nearly complete ruin. Instead of bemoaning its appearance, she remarked, "its very ruins are piles which speak of mystic beauty." Guidebook and feature writers suggested that visitors could have the most profound mission experiences at those in ruins. "Pathetic though lovely," missions evoked the "sad sublimities of departed glories" and possessed "all the melancholy beauty of moss-grown decay."[73] A verse in *Overland Monthly* offered poetic homage:

> "[M]y heart broods over the missions
> And leans to the crumbling stone.
> They are touched with supremest pathos;
> They feel they are old and gray
> In your absence, O holy padres,
> In the sunlight of today."[74]

One author beseeched his readers, "I beg of you to visit this ancient ruin, as you will be repaid by an impressive view, particularly on a moonlight night, when the imagination clothes the ruined Mission with all the beauty and magnificence of its former days."[75] Ruins presented opportunities for transcendent experiences that took tourists beyond standardized vistas and run-of-the-mill romance.

For novelist Eleanor Gates, missions perhaps even harbored ghostly echoes. The Minnesota-born Los Angeles resident summed up her sunset visit to ruined Mission San Antonio by pondering, "If the ghosts of good men ever walk at San Antonio, they walk at that twilight hour." She was not alone in this conclusion. As late as 1934 a travel diarist recalled that a twilight mission visit made him believe "he hear[d] the chants of the padres, the pad of bare feet of the long line of neophytes filing in to vespers." At these times, he imagined, "the ghosts linger."[76] Keen observer Charles Francis Saunders, a frequent contributor to various California publications, tried in 1915 to identify the quality that so intrigued people about the ruins: "one hardly expects to meet ghosts in California. We are too new, and also, I think, there is too much sun. But if ghosts there be in this hustling century and this most modern of States, then certainly the Missions are the places where one might expect to see . . . them." For early twentieth-century residents of Southern California, the missions appeared to be the most remote representation of the region's past. The fact of ruins provided critical evidence for the necessary distance or, as one scholar has said, a "dramatic discontinuity" between the missions' romantic origins and modern life. Missions had a "touch of human antiquity" that the newborn towns and cities of California lacked.[77] Missions were the most tangible remnants of this history that tourists could visit.

So popular did the mission ruins become that many tourists looked skeptically at locals' attempts to restore them. Whereas early mission enthusiasts had begged for restoration funds, Camino Real tourists often lamented their predecessors' earnest efforts. At San Luis Obispo in particular, where shingles replaced the tile roof and white clapboards covered the adobe walls, tourists found the rebuilding distasteful. Traveler and trailer-camping pioneer Hi Sibley remarked that "there is something incongruous about curtains in the windows . . . wicker chairs and chaise-lounges in the patio." The restoration, not the mission, now seemed regionally inappropriate, turning the building into an "ugly New England meeting house," as one guidebook claimed.[78] Camino Real writers wrestled with the problem of restoration itself. British globe-trotter and travel writer Thomas Murphy spent three summers motoring through California and came to the conclusion that "while it is desirable that any mission be restored rather than fall into complete ruin, it certainly is to be regretted when the work is done so injudiciously as at San Luis Obispo." Restoration entailed loss of the ruin. San Luis Obispo disappointed because its crumbling walls had been "sheathed in boards."[79] With modern accouterments and sturdy walls, the missions seemed not like missions at all. Not only had travelers come to expect the ruins, they had come to see the missions' natural state as one of ruin.

Camino Real writers established the credentials of their mission ruins by likening them to European cathedrals and medieval ruins, comparing them favorably to England's abbeys and Romanesque basilicas. One travel writer found that "the legacy of romance which lingers in broken arches, piles of adobes, and quaint Spanish names, . . . goes a long way to supply the deficiency of our country in that element which makes European travel so interesting." Diarist David Steele observed in 1917 that missions were "among the few monuments of a country that has nothing very old." During World War I, when travel to Europe was impossible, this allusion to European-style sites was particularly relevant.[80] The European pedigree of the Spanish missions and their ruined state allowed promoters to hint at a grander regional past than the East Coast and its "ugly New England meetinghouses" could muster. Travel writer A. L. Westgard submitted that the missions' "deplorable state of disrepair . . . emphasizes the old age of the wonderful structures and lends an added charm to their inspection." While the buildings themselves, built largely at the turn of the nineteenth century, were often less than one hundred years old at the time these tourists visited them, visitors often described them in terms of antiquity. Murphy called them a "bit of old world medievalism," and another traveler suggested that "in the eerie moonlight these have the appearance of an ancient Grecian pile." One writer reached back even further: "Though it [California] is the youngest part of the youngest among the great nations, its monuments and relics reach back beyond man's vision into the prehistoric past."[81] As writers pushed missions back into a hazy prehistoric past, the further away from modern California their heyday seemed.

The ACSC placed the romantic reading of mission ruins into a logical narrative trajectory of California history in 1915:

> More splendid in their melting glory than the Cathedrals of the Old
> World, California's dust-brown missions call the motorist to the trails of
> yesterday over the highways of today. Wearily waiting for the inevitable
> end, when their tired walls have at last melted to the dust from which
> they sprang, when rain and wind have called earth's own back again,
> these ruins sleep majestically on the rounded breasts of their native hills.[82]

More than anything, the ruins naturalized the end of the Spanish era in California, providing an organic explanation for the region's chronology. One travel diarist intoned, "La Purisima's work is done. Earth to earth, ashes to ashes, dust to dust!"[83] In such interpretations, the demise of the missions was inevitable—the result of a natural rather than a historical process of change that had vaulted Anglos to regional dominance. Emphasis on the structures' ruined state reminded people that the missions' days were over and that their only occupants were ghosts— perhaps many more than their visitors might have supposed.

"IN THE FOOTSTEPS OF THE PADRES"

Camino Real writers linked the ruined missions to those who had once peopled them: the ghosts of a small band of heroic missionaries and a supposedly vanished race of California Indians. Both padres and Indian people fit into assigned places in the new regional and national history, representing the primitive and colonial stages of the state, as distinct from modern tourists. These historical narratives began to reconnect these ancient, exotic, and romantic ruins to a recognizable American story. California had participated in the ascension and expansion of the United States. Native people and Spanish padres were crucial to this past but remained ghostly and quizzical figures in the present. When tourists visited California missions, they rarely saw Indians, even when native people stood right in front of them. They viewed either empty, roofless structures overgrown with grass, or operating churches that catered largely to Spanish speakers. Though many visitors saw these parishioners as "wretched Mexican families . . . the poorest of the poor," more than a few were in fact Indian people. Yet, as one guidebook writer informed his readers, "not a vestige of an Indian remains." Either way, Indians were not present in the way that tourists might have expected to see them, perhaps with blankets or feathers.[84] Their absence prompted the oft-repeated assumption that their people had largely vanished from the earth; any living Indians appeared as mere remnants of a dying culture. One guidebook made this relationship clear: "Where oxcarts creaked, where padres walked, twentieth century fliers are hurtling, still the dust is the same, the walls are there, and still, under the shadow of the self-same cross, the children of the missions, the Indians, are waiting for the end."[85] Just as mission visitors assumed that the adobe missions would soon crumble back into the earth, propelled by inescapable forces of nature, they believed that erosion and disappearance were the fates of the missions' Indian dwellers.

Population numbers of the time seemed to confirm the Anglo presumption of inevitable native extinction. The Indian population in California was at its nadir in 1900, at around 15,000, a precipitous decline from some 150,000 in 1845.[86] Visual evidence corroborated the assumption. The most popular tourist images of Indians showed the oldest-looking people available. Photographs displaying elderly native people, often identified as mission Indians, proffered improbable ages, from over 100 to ridiculous estimates as high as 180 years. A *Land of Sunshine* report, "The Oldest Californian," imagined one Tulare man as a potential object for restoration. "Old Gabriel, chief of a now extinct tribe of Tulare Indians died six years ago . . . at the reputed age of 151 years. . . . It was a matter of pride with us, nearly all Californians born and bred, to point to our old Indian, the oldest man in the world; and to know that our kindly clime had nourished one who lived to a century and a half. Would that a benevolent Landmarks Club could have preserved him to us!"[87] The Landmarks Club did, in fact, focus more on helping buildings than on helping people, contributing to the resiliency of the one at the expense of the other. Postcard and photograph captions frequently related native people to the crumbling adobe settings that surrounded them. In one image, "Ancient Belles of San Luis Rey," three aged women sit on the grass in front of a ruined colonnade (see figure 6). The text on the reverse suggests that these women "helped build the mission" ninety-five years before.[88] If the missions were eroding away to nothingness, would not these women soon disappear as well? With Indians represented only by the oldest people one might

Figure 6. "Ancient Belles of San Luis Rey," 1893. These women, Luiseño Indians in all probability, are not identified by name. Photograph by C.C. Pierce. This item is reproduced by permission of The Huntington Library, San Marino, California.

imagine, viewers logically assumed that as a group, native people would soon die out—and die of natural causes—in line with their prescribed fate in the ascendance of civilization.

The concept of the vanishing race buttressed the assumption that the missions' demise was a natural event; it both reflected a social Darwinist logic and validated national and racial succession in California. Though the trope of the vanishing race was neither new nor unique to California, Camino Real tourist narratives adopted it in assembling the state's time-line and relating it to a larger national story of continental conquest. As an *Overland Monthly* writer decreed in 1901, California Indians were "rapidly passing away under the march of civilization, and will in the near future be so totally obliterated and lost as to be but a memory of the past."[89] The march of civilization appeared to be unstoppable, a force of progress that gradually emptied the landscape of its native inhabitants and logically led Anglo-Americans to possess the land.

Even among tourists who voiced regret about the disappearance and hinted that Anglo-Americans shared the blame, the verdict remained the same: the vanishing was inevitable. As Thomas Murphy reckoned the situation, because of "the American conquest . . . the once happy and industrious natives were driven back to the hills and their final extinction seems to be at hand." Despite some regret, most writers absolved the United States from any responsibility. One writer reasoned, as did many, that the California Indians, whom he termed "a race without laws or rules, following the common animal habits of savage life," were becoming extinct because of those inherent faults, in this "decadent condition perhaps for centuries." They were, he said, "already a dying race."[90] This writer laid the responsibility for extinction at the feet of the Indian people themselves.

Anglo-Californians' remembrances of native people, however full of nostalgia, rarely failed to characterize them as degraded. If Indians were picturesque within the historical confines of the mission system, in these narratives, they appeared as an inferior race, perhaps the lowest race in a North American hierarchy. One author of several MacMillan guidebooks, Trowbridge Hall, deemed them "altogether . . . a lazy, filthy people, 'more beastly than the beasts.'" Another writer, Nolan Davis, agreed: "It has to be accepted as incontrovertible fact that these Indians were the most stupid, brutish, filthy, lazy and improvident of the aborigines of America." This habitual portrayal of California Indians as the lowest of the low rationalized their extinction, which seemed assured by the turn of the twentieth century. This view depicted an inferior race giving way to one more evolved, even as it elevated the role of the mission in the civilizing drama of colonial endeavors, be they American or Spanish.[91] Mission nostalgia softened the blow by making the disappearance picturesque but only reinforced the assumption that extinction was a fait accompli.

Though Spaniards' arrival in California hastened the decline of the native population, Camino Real narratives celebrated Franciscans not for their grisly effects but for their goals of converting and civilizing the indigenous people. The lower was writers' estimation of Indian people, the loftier was their praise for the padres and their difficult tasks. One early writer judged the Franciscans' efforts Herculean, given the "intellectual and moral caliber of the natives—lazy, dull, cowardly, covetous, and weak of will." In these writings, native people were in great need of these missionary enterprises. Like many of her fellow tourists, New Yorker Mary Crehore Bedell applauded the padres for ministering to the California Indians: "it was very impressive to me to see the enormous amount of good work the early Mission Fathers did in this wild country, which was in quite a state of savagery when they built these Missions."

When she looked at a mission, she thought of the "high-minded attempt of some great men to raise the Indian out of his ignorance and superstition." Even Nolan Davis, on the same page that he labeled California Indians the "most stupid" of all American natives, complimented the Franciscans for trying to "turn them into self-respecting, moral, law-abiding citizens." The padres became the heroes of El Camino Real, for having taken the lowly "Digger" Indian "and out of him made a tiller of the soil, an artisan, a producer."[92] The padres and their "good works" marked essential chapters in Camino Real writers' stories of California's progress. Though Indians and Spaniards made the missions together, Anglos saw themselves as inheritors of a glorious European, and Christian, past, not a native one.[93] Not only did tourists split their representation of the past along racial lines, between heroic padres and savage Indians, but they admired the dominion of one over the other.

While Camino Real tourists applauded the padres for their civilizing efforts and appreciated what they saw as a successful conquest, several crucial omissions made their happy memory possible. The devastating effects of disease on native people, intensified by gathering them in crowded mission communities, scarcely found mention in tourist texts. While references to Indian extinction in the present day abounded, few writers noted the high rates of death at the missions themselves. This death rate was readily observable in mission records, though not in grave-yards, as the missions' gated *campos santos* were filled with the individual, engraved headstones of Franciscans but few separate graves and little mention of the thousands of Indians buried elsewhere on the grounds. The other typical mission experience that was excised from Camino Real writings was discipline. Though the padres reportedly performed no forced conversions, once an Indian entered the mission for residence, he or she could not voluntarily leave. Those who departed were often treated as runaways and, if caught, punished severely. Labor was also compulsory, and shirking one's duty in the fields or kitchens could sentence an Indian worker to a number of lashes. Unsurprisingly, perhaps, guide-books never noted the locations of the old whipping posts.[94] If these forms of discipline did not depart significantly from eighteenth-century custom elsewhere, to imagine the kindly, heroic, pious padres as the arbiters of corporeal punishment would have been unthinkable for romance-seeking tourists on the modern El Camino Real.

Tourists preferred to envision the padres as traveling companions and often wrote of their desire to see their tours through the padres' eyes. Eleanor Gates sub-titled her serial travel diary in *Sunset Magazine*

"A Gasoline Pilgrimage in the Footsteps of the Padres." With a classic preamble, Thomas Murphy also invoked the metaphor of pilgrimage: "like many a pious pilgrim of old, we set out on the King's Highway. . . . We shall follow in the footsteps of the brown-robed brothers of St. Francis." Junípero Serra, first leader of the California missionaries, was tourists' companion of choice. Baltimore schoolteacher and travel diarist Letitia Stockett confessed that over the course of her tour, Serra had "become a real and living person, traveling down El Camino Real beside us."[95] Whereas a mission tour turned Indian people into ghosts, it brought Father Serra back to life.

Mission-bell guideposts helped keep the padres alive as tourists spun along the road. The four hundred iron bells provided more than signage; they came to represent "testimonials," even "witnesses," to the padres' "achievements, . . . heroism, . . . and sacrifices [in] plant[ing] the Christian religion and the best traditions of Spain among the savages." They called to mind, for poet and publisher Alice Harriman, religious markers of antiquity: "its [the road's] commemorative bells, placed at timely intervals along this Padres' Path are an everlasting testimony, . . . as distinctly attractive as the shrines once dotted along Rome's great artery, the Appian Way."[96] As shrines, the guideposts lent the Camino Real tour a purpose, making the missions more than items on the must-see list; it was a personal pilgrimage to discover the origins of American civilization in its far southwestern outpost.

The concept of religious pilgrimage, however, posed a dilemma. Though the missions appeared in Camino Real writings as landmarks of civilization and romanticism, they also commemorated a Catholic project. Given the resulting religious implications, the degree to which tourists and Southern Californians disregarded conflict with Catholicism is surprising, especially when one considers that, with a few notable exceptions, patrons of El Camino Real were overwhelmingly Protestant. Historian Carey McWilliams noted this odd fact as well: "Not one of the numerous pope-baiting fundamentalist pastors of Southern California has ever objected to this community-wide adoration of the missions."[97] When Lee McConville wrote about El Camino Real in a 1910 diocese newsletter that "it has ever been a manifestation of man's profoundest religious faith to undertake pilgrimages," he referred to the Catholic tradition of visiting the relics and tombs of saints.[98] Why did Protestants go on pilgrimages?

How Southern Californians, largely Protestants themselves, negotiated this idiosyncrasy speaks to the meaning of the missions' religious metaphor for them. The religious project of the padres did carry significance, earning high marks for the missionaries not only for their secular good works but also for their effort to bring Christianity to the wilderness of California. Along with lavishing praise on the padres for being the first "pathfinders, horticulturalists, vineyardists, and irrigationists of California," Episcopalian Eliza Keith and other Camino Real writers credited the Franciscans with creating "Christian communities in the midst of heathendom."[99] Yet praise for the religious purposes of the missions typically focused on the role of the padres themselves, not on the particularities of Catholic faith or colonization. The relationship between Indian neophyte and Franciscan priest received special attention in tourist writings. Narrators assumed that the missionized Indians had elevated the padres to the same level of heroism that they did. As Maria Antonía Field explained in one of the rare Californio-authored guides, "Indians clung to the Fathers like little children to their parents, and from the vices of paganism, under a healthy and kind rule drawn for them by the wise Father, Christian virtues took a deep root in at least a great many of these poor 'children of the soil.'" Anglos' even greater focus on the padres' good works in tutoring needy Indians suggests, as did historian Kevin Starr, that "for all its luxuriant images, the mission myth fundamentally celebrated the Protestant virtues of order, acquisition, and the work ethic." This myth pictured "Spanish California as a busy utopia, without labor troubles and with Father Junípero Serra as the original booster."[100]

Nevertheless, commentary on the denominational awkwardness of mission remembrances appeared often enough to indicate that the issue had yet to be resolved. James Steele, even as he attempted to dismiss the discomfort, suggested that questions remained. "It would not only be no impropriety, but would be a fitting and proper thing if his [Serra's] statue should be set by Protestant hands in every Californian town and his heroic story told in every public school." While claiming a pandenominational significance for Serra, Steele still felt the need to declare the fitness of Protestants' celebration of a Catholic hero. Others occasionally reported their encounters with proselytizing priests or visitors at the missions. Charles Francis Saunders recalled debating with a Catholic tourist at Mission San Jose, "when I expressed my pleasure as a Protestant in seeing such historic buildings preserved, she acquiesced, adding with a gentle loyalty to her own creed that I liked, 'Yet not as dead monuments, but as living instruments for the extension of the Faith.'"[101] Saunders's meeting suggests tension between Catholic and

Protestant views even within common admiration. Protestants like Saunders used the missions for historic purposes, representing them as part of the past; his Catholic friend viewed them as institutions of continuing salience. Her suspicion that the Protestant preservation impulse assumed the missions to be "dead monuments" was justified, as the fawning praise for ruins attested.

In explaining the loss of the golden age, Camino Real writers saved their special wrath for Mexico and its policy of secularization. Part of a postindependence plan to divest the church of its wide temporal and political power, this policy aimed to downgrade the California missions into simple parishes. Effected in the 1830s, the policy turned over the church's valuable lands to private enterprises, granted small parcels to native people (many of which were subsequently lost), and released the land from mission control. To Camino Real writers, this policy was calumny. They called it "the dread order of secularization," "a disastrous scheme," a "Bunda of secularization and pillage," and a "polite term for political robbery." They blamed the removal of Franciscan power for the natives' subsequent decline. The end of forced labor and conversion did not mean freedom for Indian people in this rendering; it spelled vagrancy, neglect, starvation, and death. Many writers attributed the secularization plan to base Mexican moneygrubbing, a "desire to pay her [Mexico's] debts with other people's property." This explicit act of greed "sounded the death knell to this dream of patriarchal government."[102] Unwilling to find fault with the padres' efforts, writers made secularization and the Mexicans the scapegoats for both the apparent Indian extinction and the assumed poor development of California on the eve of American annexation. Just as Reconstruction was demonized by both northern and southern whites in the late nineteenth century, secularization served purposes of unification.[103]

The common denunciation of secularization left room for resolution of Protestant-Catholic tension. Dating the golden age to the zenith of Franciscan power, Camino Real writers portrayed the missions as places of pilgrimage at which all Christians could honor the padres. As one poet characterized the legacy of the padres, "The past and the present are one,/ And one is the war that we wage,/ And one is the Lord over all,/ Unchanging from age unto age."[104] Such verses appealed to the unity of Christians; made into symbols of antiquity, the missions suggested a pre-Reformation unity of faith as well. A unique poem by Camino Real promoter Mrs. M. E. Dudley in the farcical dialect of a midwestern migrant echoes this accord.

> I wonder what the Padres think who first this road surveyed,
> To see the pesky Protestants a takin' of their grade.
> I've always been a hearin' since I was 'bout knee-high,
> that Catholics and Protestants don't mingle in the sky,
> But times out here are changin' and thoughts and roads grow broad,
> Because the folks that's livin' now all worship the same God.[105]

While describing the disturbing sight of Protestants on El Camino Real, the poem suggests a growing ecumenicalism. Yet Southern California, and Los Angeles in particular, was well-known at the time for being solidly Protestant (at least among Anglos). As scholarship has shown, turn-of-the-century civic politics and social institutions remained firmly in Protestant hands, in numbers that would grow increasingly disproportionate to the number of Protestants in the population. The Los Angeles Chamber of Commerce, among other booster organizations, promoted policies and encouraged migration aligned with the Anglo-Protestant community it represented. In the first two decades of the century, national Protestant organizations cited Los Angeles as an "Ideal Protestant City" and a "Model Christian Community." Although Protestant control declined in the 1920s and 1930s, it had established a regional agenda that waned more slowly. As the region grew more heterogeneous, both ethnically and denominationally, as long as Catholics "did not challenge the power base of civic culture, or threaten community consensus, Protestants took little notice."[106] Anglo-Protestant Southern Californians had few qualms about celebrating the Spanish-Catholic mission past because Anglo-Protestant Southern Californians directed the celebration.

The presentation of regional history in Camino Real narratives began to assemble a linear progression of Indian, padre, and American. Though Mexican secularization did not advance progress, it provided the necessary interval of ruination and a catalyst for a triumphant American ascension. The religious element seemed to add further proof. By showing the Catholic missionaries inevitably giving way to the Protestant pioneers, Camino Real history not only explained the dominance of Anglo-American Protestants in Spanish California but legitimized it as the end result of a long march toward civilization. The mission era became a romantic interlude in a longer ladder of progress, with adobe ruins, a vanishing race, and old-world religion making room for Anglo-American modernity. The story of American triumph over primitives and Europeans, which made the Southern California story one of racial succession, thus linked regional history with national history.

"TO COMPLETE THE AMERICAN CONQUEST"

Camino Real advocates, tourists, and writers made the missions seem a safe distance away from their modern world and yet happily compatible with it. They found that their reverence for the missions could serve a purpose in the present, acting as a standard-bearer for the Anglo-American image of regional character. While tourists and boosters sometimes took different meanings from El Camino Real, they joined in their affirmation of the road's American identity. By continually asserting their own presence in the historical narrative, Southern California Anglos implicated the missions in America's national destiny. Camino Real writers imagined the missions as an endorsement of American conquest, linking California past and present to the nation through a common celebration of progress. They imagined the padres not just as heroes but as patriots. Missions and bells were not simply reminders of a romantic past but physical markers of American conquest. A tour on El Camino Real became a metaphorical reconquest of California.

As strange as this view might seem today, Camino Real writers believed that the Spanish colonizers deliberately planted a harvest for Americans to reap and that the missionaries anticipated their own demise at the hands of a worthier force. For many Anglos, missions had been "outposts of *our* first civilization" and "the earliest relics of the beginning of civilization on *our* great Pacific Coast." One Camino Real booster proclaimed that the "glorious achievements" of the "good friars, who planted the Christian religion and best traditions of Spain among the savages," formed the "foundation for *our* present Western civilization." Californians began to honor Junípero Serra as "*our* first citizen" and his colleagues as the state's founding fathers. A monument in Riverside depicted "the beginning of Civilization in California" as Serra ministering to the Indians; the plaque specifically honored him as "Apostle, Legislator, Builder" of that civilization. In 1913 state leaders declared November 24th as Serra Day, a state holiday.[107] As one local interpreted the history these memorials commemorated, "the padres fulfilled a broader mission than that which they sought to accomplish in their religious zeal. They brought the seeds of civilization to our fair shore, and sowed them with care. Behold today the result—a higher, happier, loftier civilization than ours the sun has never shone upon." The belief that the Franciscans, typically reliable monarchists, were friends of a fledgling United States, or even supporters of the American Revolution, became as common as it was surprising. Whether by negligence or predestination, the padres' deferral to Americans was an inevitability in these accounts. One Camino Real supporter intriguingly noted in private that the United States was "following Spain around both oceans, gradually picking up the pieces of the old Spanish Empire."[108] Though missions had begun as colonial outposts of Spain, for tourists, their ruins became a confirmation of American conquest.

Acceptance of American empire and conquest, in California and across the nation, was a contested process during turn-of-the-century decades. The debates over the appropriateness of a republican empire and the so-called white man's burden affected the development of a Camino Real myth.[109] Camino Real boosters' admiration for conquest grew in the decades following the Spanish-American War, which on a national level, both prompted public questioning of conquest in Spanish terms and marked the opening for American empire. The seeming romance and harmony of the Spanish past in Southern California became evidence for the propriety of American empire. By 1916 George Wharton James was giving the Spanish conquest effusive praise. "What a wonderful movement was that wave of religious zeal, of proselytizing fervor, that accompanied the great colonizing efforts of Spain . . . Conquistadors and friars—. . . both were full of indomitable energy and unquenchable zeal, and few epochs in history stand out more wonderfully than this for their great achievements in their respective domains."[110] Conquest was good for the soul and for the nation.

El Camino Real incorporated numerous reminders of American conquest and progress in California. From the American flags that waved in front of many missions to the postcards that pointed out the key events that took place at the missions during the Mexican-American War, missions became not simply reminders of California's romantic past but sites that commemorated its conquest. As the caption of one such postcard informed tourists, John C. Frémont had quartered his soldiers at Mission San Fernando "on their way to Los Angeles to fight the Californians . . . to complete the American conquest."[111] But the most common physical markers of modern America along El Camino Real were the automobiles that conveyed tourists from mission to mission. Southern California Anglos came to see the missions as part of American history as they wrote, or drove, themselves into the story. With constant reference to their own novel automobile journeys, tourists themselves became the link between the mission past and modern America. As Eleanor Gates recalled, "as we spun along, I could not help but think how the brave old padres had to plod over this same way. . . . They would have marveled at us!"[112]

Figure 7. "Mission San Fernando, California," ca. 1910. Postcard from author's collection.

Automobiles provided a ready example of the superiority of modern life because drivers generally believed that their vehicles represented the pinnacle of progress. Automobilists on El Camino Real admired their own machines, the "marvelous speed of our new powers," the "power and swiftness . . . [of] the blast of our motor engines." By the 1920s writers even began to cloak the automobile in the romantic language typically reserved for the missions themselves: "The satiny highway gleams under the light from auto-lamps where the modern pilgrim speeds, even at night, over the historic day-path of the Padres."[113] Coupled with nostalgia for the past and glory in conquest, the praise for motor-driven progress cemented the celebration of the missions in a consistently hierarchical view of history that put tourists at the wheel.

One of tourists' favorite Camino Real activities was, predictably, taking photographs. The image they enjoyed posing for most, however, is less predictable: In photo after photo, the consistent subject is tourists' cars. Tourists sought to document the presence of their automobiles at the missions, whether or not they themselves appeared in the car or in the photograph at all. Such car-focused images appeared in guidebooks, magazines, albums, and travel diaries. As figure 7 demonstrates, tourists could even buy postcards that replicated the experience for them, offering views of anonymous automobiles in front of various missions. Twice in the 1920s mission-car scenes graced the cover of *Touring Topics,* a Southern California travel magazine published by the ACSC; the August 1925

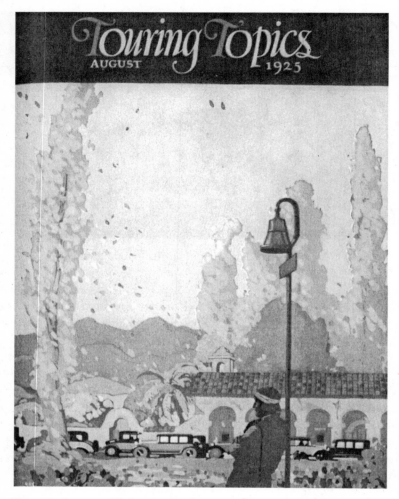

Figure 8. Autos on El Camino Real, cover of *Touring Topics*, August 1925. With an Indian leaning against the mission-bell guidepost, gazing out over a full parking lot in front of the mission, this magazine cover captures tourist desires both for modern experiences and past relics. Artwork by Raymond Winters. Courtesy of Automobile Club of Southern California Archives.

cover appears in figure 8.[114] Often, images that literally cut and pasted a car under a ruined mission arch recalled the incongruity between the missions and modern life. And yet the experience of building and touring El Camino Real allowed Southern Californians to see this juxtaposition as perfectly natural.

El Camino Real demonstrated people's attraction to two seemingly opposed perspectives. On the one hand, it made hay out of the gap between the modern and the primitive. Travelers were drawn to the novelty of parking their fresh-off-the-assembly-line vehicles in front of the missions, which had quickly become known as the best ruins America had to offer. By visiting, they appeared to be the new that might save the old from its final demise. The contrast in the image was compelling: the future and the past locked fleetingly in the same frame. On the other hand, Camino Real history stressed the logic and harmony of linking past and present in a natural progression. This myth was exhilarating to people not so much because it located the missions in an appropriate place in the past but because it personalized this past. It allowed Anglo-Americans—tourists and Southern Californians alike—to locate themselves in the mission landscape. Photographing their automobiles in front of ruined missions, tourists might visualize their place in the timeline—that is, at its pinnacle. Even while making missions definitively of the past, these activities did not put them in the past. Visits and photographs anchored the missions firmly in modern times as foci for the expanding tourist market. Designating the missions part of the exotic past ensured their persistence in the future, both as physical sites and as inspiration for new nostalgic styles.

Camino Real tourists expressed desires not only to picture but to experience this conquest for themselves. One way they did so was by triumphing over the road itself. However much drivers admired the modernity of their vehicles, early automobiling was anything but luxurious. Motorists gave up many modern comforts. Touring on winding dirt roads, open to the sun and dust, "with meager springs and little padding, . . . was an arduous, bumpy, drafty ordeal," historian Warren Belasco reported.[115] El Camino Real was little help. Despite some work by the state, even into the 1920s the road remained incomplete. Many sections still had inadequate bridges, pavement, or maintenance, and El Camino Real continued to be a largely imaginary road marked only by mission-bell guideposts. Drivers had to work hard to keep their cars on the road. Not only did they have to deal with mechanical breakdowns and up to 30 percent grades, but they often had to ford streams, dislodge tree stumps, and have horse teams tow their vehicles out of the mud. Compared to the relative luxury of a Pullman coach, these conditions were rustic.

Automobile tourists converted these drawbacks into a rationale for their journey. They would conquer these barbaric roads and emerge victorious, much like the Spanish padres had before them. Drivers welcomed the skill and ingenuity the roads demanded and recorded their difficulties in great detail. Diaries included extensive commentary and photographs of machines proceeding along muddy roads, hanging up on large boulders, or negotiating hairpin curves. Conquering these wretched roads was an achievement that drivers, and even their petrified passengers, recalled with satisfaction. In the struggle to navigate less-tamed territory, the automobile appeared to offer a more intimate and individual touring experience than was possible by train. Automobile and tourist promoters certainly billed the often-exasperating experience that way. *Sunset Magazine* recommended a western automobile vacation for the man "who thrills in an elemental contact with the reality of nature."[116] Here was a chance to wrestle with a version of the hardships the padres had faced: to confront and tame savage nature.

"IT IS NOT OURS"

While conquering the roads proved to be an exhilarating adventure for the thousands of drivers who packed their bags and toured El Camino Real, this adventure paled in comparison with the prospect of symbolic conquest of the Indian people themselves. Empty missions did not offer Anglos much opportunity for contact with the supposedly savage people the Spanish had tried to civilize. In one rare instance, Anglos decided to repopulate a mission and to try to finish the civilizing project the Spanish missionaries had begun more than a century before. Their chance came in 1902. The site they chose was Pala Asistencia, an outpost of Mission San Luis Rey in northern San Diego County that the Franciscans had established in 1816 to reach Luiseño Indians living in outlying regions. After secularization and American annexation, the land passed into private Anglo hands, and the residents scattered. Government records show that sixty-six Luiseño Indians still lived there in 1890, a small group compared to populations in villages nearby.[117] When Anglos heard that Indians were still living at a mission site, they were surprised but largely assumed that the group was a remnant population that would soon die out. An 1899 poem about Pala by Charles Keeler evokes this belief, mentioning the Luiseños' continued existence and their death in the same stanza: "Still come, when the bells in the tower call,/ The Indian folk from afar,/ But the presence of death steals over all/ In the shadow of Palomar."[118] Here was a semifunctioning mission, with Indians still on-site. At no other station on El Camino Real could tourists view an approximation of the mission era. While Pala's remote mountainous location made it an improbable tourist destination, Keeler's romantic prose pointed to future discovery by Anglo tourists.

Meanwhile, thirty miles to the southeast, the ancestral villages of a number of bands of Cupeño or Ipai people were sitting on Warner's Ranch, land claimed by American settlers who intended to develop the area's natural hot springs into a tourist resort. Unable to purchase their original lands from the American ranchers, the Cupeños were forced by the federal government to cede their homes to the American claimants. The local Indian agency asked Charles Lummis to head a committee of Southern Californians to locate new lands for the three hundred people about to be uprooted. Two tribal delegates, Salvador Nolasquez and Ambrosio Ortega, surveyed various properties along with the three-member Anglo committee. After the committee's first meeting, Lummis suggested for the second time that the government purchase Warner's land and allow the Indian people to remain. Being rebuffed, the committee then evaluated various locations for their suitability for agriculture, social life, and support for native activities, like basketry. The area around Pala scored well on these criteria, being a fertile valley with streams and fields. The government accepted Lummis's recommendation to purchase nearly 3,500 acres in the Pala valley, expanding the small Luiseño reservation already there, and to move the Warner's Indians, as Anglos called them.[119] With the exception of George Wharton James, few people noted the irony of the situation, for Pala had been Indian land once before. Americans were moving an evicted people to a place from which they had evidently uprooted a different group of native people a generation before. James asked, "Whence had these and their descendants gone? How had they been deprived of their land? . . . Now it had to be bought back again."[120]

Ignoring the historical irony, Lummis argued that the best reason to favor the Pala purchase was that "this valley has been the home of Indians from time immemorial . . . , selected three-quarters of a century ago by the Franciscan missionaries as the site for a Mission." This reasoning, rather than James's doubts, struck a chord among Southern California Anglos. Lummis's own Landmarks Club undertook minor renovations at the Pala chapel between 1901 and 1903, in preparation for welcoming new parishioners. Harrie Forbes found "romantic possibilities" in the thought that Pala could be "repeopled with the remnant of a dying race." She hoped that this project would be an example that could be replicated up and down El Camino Real, where "the mission

Indians could, as of old, sell their wares and dwell according to the customs of their ancestors." Though mission life clearly was not part of
Indians' ancestral tradition, for Anglo enthusiasts of El Camino Real,
bringing Indians back to the missions, where they believed natives were
once content and controlled, made perfect sense. As one observer later
said, "the coming of this sizable congregation of those whom the Franciscans first and lastingly connected seemed to indicate a certain historic
fitness."[121] Southern California Anglos saw the eviction of the Warner's
Indians as a return, the homecoming of a strayed people to the mother
mission. The chance to remissionize the Indians was an exciting one for
Anglos, entitling them to some of the credit given the padres.[122] Here
was an American conquest worthy of the heroic days of old.

Southern California Anglos congratulated themselves on the high
quality of the land they had purchased as well as the historical harmony
it presented. Not only did they assume that the arrangement would
please the Warner's Indians, but they decided to move other bands slated
for eviction to Pala as well.[123] Anglo commentators who observed the
distressing process of eviction incorporated it into the Camino Real
rubric of romance and progress. Ruth Kedzie Wood called the May
1903 procession, led by the U.S. Army, a "picturesque hegira"; another
Camino Real narrative transformed it into "a small counterpart of the
incident that gave rise to the sad idyll of Evangeline."[124] Moreover,
soon after the Indians' arrival, a group of Southern California Anglos
proudly announced that they had secured the transfer of the deed to the
mission church back to the Catholic Church "in trust for the Indians."
So committed were these mission enthusiasts to re-creating an imagined
past that they made no attempt to establish a Protestant presence at
Pala, instead encouraging the Indians' Catholic worship.[125] For Anglos,
the mission picture was now complete.

For the Cupeño people, the experience was anything but picturesque.
Evidence shows the Cupeños' opinions to be clear on this point: most
did not want to go to Pala and once there, did not find it the promised
mission paradise. Though Nolasquez and Ortega, the Cupeño representatives on Lummis's committee, had cooperated in trying to secure the
best land on which to relocate, they did not represent all tribal members' opinions. Cecilio Blacktooth, captain of the Warner's Ranch Indians, registered opposition to relocation to the committee in 1902. He
tried patiently to explain that which "place we like next best to this
place where we always live" did not matter. "You see that graveyard
over there? Here are our fathers and grandfathers. . . . We have always

been here. We do not care for any other place. It may be good but it is not ours. We have always lived here." When the agent again asked what place would they like next best, Blacktooth asserted that "if we cannot live here, . . . we will go into the mountains like quail and die there, the old people and the women and the children." Indeed, a few elderly people did hide in the hills while the army brought most of Blacktooth's people to Pala with whatever possessions they could carry on their backs.[126]

When the Cupeños arrived at Pala, conditions did not live up to their rosy billing. Moreover, the commingling that Anglos saw as a reunion of tribes at the mission instead caused difficulties. The various villages of Cupeños found themselves thrown in with traditional enemies, particularly those of San Felipe and Agua Caliente. Never happy at Pala, significant numbers of them fled back to relatives at other reservations. The securing of the Pala church also failed to have the hoped-for effect, as the first priest assigned to the parish put a fresh coat of whitewash over native decorations, causing great "irritation and bitterness" among the now-outnumbered Luiseños at the reservation. Worse were the uninsulated temporary houses that the government provided. Drawn from dispersed rural settlements, the compact village setting and lack of proper sanitation facilities resulted in a crowded situation that increased the occurrence of illness and death, particularly among children and elders—ironically, re-creating mission conditions more closely than the committee had anticipated.[127] Over the next ten years, however, under the watchful eyes of government Indian agencies, both Cupeño and Luiseño groups tried to build homes, farms, and communities.

With new publicity about the relocation episode at Pala, Southern California Anglos slowly began to make the difficult trek to see the place for themselves. Pala was not on the main Camino Real route, and the road to it was extremely rough, discouraging the more casual mission tourists. But consistently larger numbers made their way out to see Pala's annual festival of San Luis at the end of August in the decade after the relocation. One of these was Eleanor Gates, who had written a three-part travelogue for *Sunset* about her Camino Real tour in 1912. She reported on her visit to Pala in a follow-up piece in 1913. Gates was initially perplexed by the scene she encountered. "These were not the *kind* of Indians we had expected to see. And where were the time-honored, semi-savage customs we had promised ourselves?" The festival seemed to her an entirely "familiar Fourth-of-July" affair with tug-o-war, baseball, and prizes for husbandry. But when night gave over to traditional dances and games, she was pleased to see "the years rolled back, sweeping us with them. . . . This was early California! Here were Palatingwas [sic] and their friends, celebrating—with tribal dances, and old songs, and enthralling gambling games." She enjoyed the "unrestrained" celebration but noted that the Indian policeman provided "the Link—between Past and Present; between Washington-on-the-Delaware and the Pala Reservation."[128] What was going on at Pala? The new mission villagers were not behaving as many had expected them to, but neither were tourists entirely displaced. What had happened to the remissionizing project?

Pala did not fulfill Lummis's vision for it because the people most interested in seeing the mission, Camino Real enthusiasts, were not the only ones influencing the new settlement. The boosters had considerably less sway over events at Pala than did the federal government or the native people themselves. For example, while tourists hoped to see a semblance of traditional or mission Indian life, the U.S. Bureau of Indian Affairs (BIA) waged an extended campaign to discourage the Cupeños from performing old dances, games, rituals, or social practices. The bureau feared that traditions would slow Indians' assimilation into white society and thus directed its local superintendents to monitor these activities. By the early 1910s, the Pala agent reported to his superiors that the Indians there performed dances only "for the purpose of attracting the attendance of white visitors," and those who did so were quite elderly, by and large. By 1918 the agent "freely predicted that upon the death of these few Indians, whose life-expectancy is quite short, the dances will disappear, and no one will be left who can conduct them." Evidently, the agents had some trouble enforcing these rules. In their annual reports, discussion of the dances and songs always appeared under the Law and Order heading; outside of these reports, local agents corresponded about how best to punish those who performed anything that the agents considered "obscene."[129]

A second attempt by BIA agents to transform Cupeño culture (and that of other Southern California Indians) was to replace the Indians' annual fiesta with an "agricultural fair." Fearing that the fiestas provided an outlet for traditional activities, especially gambling, they worked to redefine the event. By the early 1910s agents believed that Indian people were eager to take part in the fairs, putting up their produce for contests. With the apparent increasing interest in agriculture, the government saw fit to install an irrigation system at Pala, the lack of which had handicapped the profitability of Indian farming operations. Most Indians, however, could find little employment on the reservation, so men worked for Anglo ranchers and younger women became domestics. A few women wove baskets to sell; this industry netted them one thousand dollars in 1915, most of which came from sales to visiting tourists. Residents at Pala were more successful at selling these baskets and selling them on-site than were Indians at other reservations in the area, which could boast no mission as an additional attraction for tourists.[130]

Though tourists and government officials were at odds over the image of Indian people they wanted to see, Cupeños clearly could adopt a range of representations depending upon the situation. The Indians confronted two differing images among Anglos—as representations of a vanishing primitive past or as pupils taking a course in civilization—and negotiated their way between them. Tourists were sometimes useful: they bought baskets and likely brought money to the reservation in other ways. They also provided a handy excuse to perform traditional dances despite specific prohibition by BIA agents. Yet, perhaps to gain assistance with their farming operations, the Indians often participated in government-sponsored agricultural fairs, to tourists' disappointment, even as they continued traditional fiesta activities in a new context. What the Cupeños thought of tourist expectations and government dicta is difficult to assess, but they likely could find reasons to conform to or confound them at different times.

A few locals and tourists suggested that Cupeño lives extended beyond their mission performances to include the present day. Unlike many fellow Anglo visitors, Thomas Murphy recognized that the current Pala residents were not the original inhabitants. He told the story of double eviction and expressed his hope that "tardy justice will make some amends for all that the red men about Pala have suffered at the hands of their white brothers." James praised the bucolic landscape and tidy cottages that native people had produced at Pala. He gave the native people credit for making the best of a bad deal and for transforming themselves from a "crushed, disheartened, half-starved, and almost dependent people . . . into an industrious, energetic, independent, self-supporting, and self-respecting tribe."[131] Despite the paternalism and preference for assimilation that these comments reveal, Pala offered Anglo visitors like Murphy an opening to envision Indian people as other than remnants of a romantic band of mission neophytes.

The story at Pala was ambiguous. It was not exactly the scenario that Anglos had envisioned when they embarked on the remissionizing project. Indian people did not prove to be as easily tractable as the mission buildings were, a limit that Anglo romantics would confront again. The absence of native people, identified as such, at other missions enabled Anglos to imagine a direct connection between themselves and the padres. The living Indian presence at Pala forced Anglos to subtly alter the meaning they assigned to the mission. Perhaps some Anglo visitors envisioned an alternative to Indians' inevitable disappearance or contemplated the possibility that Indians might have a different mission memory from that of Anglos, one that presumably included stories of disease and disfranchisement. Native people at times found that increasing Anglo interest in the missions generated revisions in and a resurgence of their own interpretations of the past. Yet however Anglos reconceived their relationships to the Spanish past after a visit to Pala, they did not typically abandon the rubric of conquest. As "thrifty ranchers," as one observer called the Pala residents, Indian people seemed to prove American conquest as securely as the vision of harmonious mission communities testified to Spanish dominion.[132] That the government could "civilize" these native people appeared to be as important an accomplishment, albeit a paradoxical one, as returning them to a picturesque state. Not only could Americans retrace the padres' path, but they could surpass the Spanish missionaries who had come to civilize the Indians two centuries before but left the task incomplete.

This shift from Spanish to American dominion became clear at the celebration of the one hundredth anniversary of the Pala mission in 1917, when a *Los Angeles Tribune* reporter observed that "a large American flag was run up over the mission by the oldest Indian on the reservation, Chaves Cliperosa, who claims to be 113 years old and says he helped build the mission. . . . All the Indians removed their hats and pledged allegiance to the flag."[133] Instead of sitting beside crumbling adobe, this elderly Pala man raised the American flag. Anglo-Americans could see themselves reflected in the scene, just as they could imagine themselves retracing the padres' steps in their swift automobiles. For Southern California Anglos, the imaginative and physical conquest that had created this "real Indian village" by force linked their picturesque version of regional history to a decidedly national story.

CONCLUSION

Probably the most tantalizing aspect of El Camino Real for those who sought it out was its tender of a vicarious experience of conquest. As Anglo tourists drove the mission road, they did more than gaze wistfully at the missions: they saw themselves on a romantic adventure of their own. Many early automobilists adopted a patriotic stance, describing their trips as a means of reclaiming their own land and rediscovering their own history. An early automobile advocate specifically promoted "the rediscovery of America by the automobile." Imagine, he asked, "how much more thoroughly Columbus could have discovered America had the good Queen been able to pawn an extra jewel to place an automobile . . . at his command!" In their automobiles, Americans thus might lay claim to their own country by playing Columbus, or Serra, and discovering it "as they never have discovered . . . [it] before."[134] On El Camino Real, one might encounter a romantic regional past and a sense of national identity. The mission tour allowed Southern California Anglos to link the two.

An Automobile Club of Southern California guidebook claimed the missions for the nation in 1915. "Now, these missions are not the relic of any creed. They are the property of the people of the United States in a finer sense than that given by deed or title. Like the battlefield of Gettysburg, like Plymouth Rock, Bunker Hill and the Liberty Bell, they belong to the soil of the Nation—they are the nation's wards."[135] In that group of national landmarks, the Spanish missions appear to be the likeliest candidates for a game of "which one of these things doesn't belong." In the interpretations that Camino Real writers worked out, the missions could spark just as telling a remembrance of national achievements as the other, more familiar monuments of patriotism. So regionally ingrained had this connection become that in the following decade, Southern Californians pushed through statewide acceptance of the enshrinement of Junípero Serra in Statuary Hall at the U.S. Capitol. Over the objections of some northerners, who chose New England–born minister Thomas Starr King as the other state figure, Southern Californians argued successfully that Serra was a fitting symbol for California. This vote marked Serra's ultimate transformation into an American patriot.[136] With a cross in one hand and a miniature San Carlos Borromeo mission in the other, Serra stood as a model citizen, commemorating California for the nation.

El Camino Real changed the way that Southern California Anglos viewed the mission past. In less than two decades, Anglo tourists and boosters converted people's considerable uneasiness about the missions' foreignness into local pride for unique landmarks and then into a national symbol of the state itself. Charles Lummis declared success in 1916: "Our long and lonesome and tiresome campaign of education has borne fruit. The good roads and the automobiles have helped us very greatly. A generation ago only a few people cared anything about the Missions. Now everybody cares about them."[137] El Camino Real brought many Anglos into agreement about the Spanish past, even if they cared about it in different ways. Tourists sought a journey to a romantic past that affirmed their modernity. Locals hoped that, as regional emblems, the missions would help them find a place in the nation and its history. Linking Southern California's Indian story to the national trajectory—a vanishing race, a closing frontier—gave El Camino Real broad appeal among Anglo-Americans, Southern California residents and visitors alike. Indian people found useful positions in complying with or contesting the romance, but new Anglo memories made their disappearance as a people and a culture central to the public narrative, decisively shaping the regional context in which they operated. Despite Lummis's declaration, not everyone became a romance-starved Camino Real tourist; isolated skeptics of the abounding sentiment for the Spanish past still harrumphed at the fantasy. Nevertheless, so many people incorporated the romantic versions of the road's history as an origin myth for the region that critics would forever be unable to extricate the missions from the cultural and physical landscape. El Camino Real made the crumbling adobe of the Spanish past a permanent fixture in Southern California.

CHAPTER 3

The Fair

*Panama-California Exposition
and Regional Ambitions*

In 1915 a Camino Real tourist would have found the mission road anchored at each end by an exposition. The year was notable for the opening of the Panama Canal, and California played host to two expositions to celebrate the event. At one end of the state, San Francisco put on an expansive world's fair, the Panama-Pacific International Exposition, where visitors could see an array of foreign and domestic exhibits amid towering Beaux-Arts and neoclassical buildings. At the other, San Diego hosted the Panama-California Exposition, which was dedicated to an explicitly regional display and showcased Southern California in a fanciful Spanish shell. With ornate architecture, costumed guards, strolling guitarists, and speeches honoring the conquistadors, San Diego's exposition elaborated on the regional theme of Spanish romance at a new and monumental level. It inspired widespread admiration, with visitors lavishing praise on its flowers, buildings, and atmosphere. Beyond the usual didactic displays of products and machinery and the motley conglomeration of concessionaires, the feature that enchanted visitors most was the thoroughly Spanish setting.

San Diego's Spanish style resulted from a deal struck between the two exposition cities. San Francisco hosted the official world's fair, while San Diego put on a regional show.[1] Despite, or perhaps because of, the diminished sphere of the Panama-California Exposition, it became a significant venue for furthering the Anglo-dominated discussion about Southern California as place and about the role of the Spanish past within the region. The debates between and among Anglo city boosters, fair designers, and spectators drew on the Camino Real experience but did not replicate its approach or appeals. A number of San Diego Anglos active in promoting the road became exposition planners, and while El Camino Real had paid local dividends, the fair promised advertisement on a much broader, national scale. Whereas Anglo fascination with the missions continued to cultivate a wistful nostalgia and a compelling mix of romanticism and modernity, the exposition fully invested in the future, anticipating Southern California's vital position in a mighty American empire. Spanish style became key to this expression, as fair boosters transformed a romantic vision of the region's still-unsettled identity into a confident metropolitan spectacle that thoroughly hitched the Spanish mode to regional ambitions. Anglo boosters of San Diego in a sense liberated themselves from El Camino Real's decaying historic structures and the lockstep of mission history. Seeking less a conquest of the past than one of the future, they assembled a Spanish legacy befitting their bold plans and limited only by their imaginations and their budget.

Local desires for growth and the imminent opening of the Panama Canal both influenced this new incarnation of the Spanish past. The canal would connect the West to the nation in new ways, and San Diego boosters badly wanted to show that their city was poised to lead this new era. Spanish-Californian history, as a reminder of a global colonial project, became an emblematic idiom in which to imagine an American imperial future. Homages to Spanish adventurers and monarchs were everywhere at the exposition, often overshadowing reverence for the humble padres. The regional chronology that Camino Real writers worked out, the Indian-Spanish-Anglo succession in America, went on display, linking Southern California definitively to a larger story of national progress and even human evolution. Native people of the Southwest were thus visible and key elements of the exposition's overall message. As supposed subjects of domestic dominion over primitives, Indian participants at the fair extended the colonial theme. Native people found ways to operate within this structure, negotiating their relationship with exposition officials, evading visitors' expectations, and using the fair for their own purposes. Nevertheless, Indian people, along with the kaleidoscope of displays and exhibits, found themselves overwhelmed by a promotional barrage that stitched Southern California, the Spanish past, the Panama Canal, and Anglo-American imperial destiny together in a comprehensive thematic net. How this logic took shape in the civic landscape and influenced regional uses of Spanish style resulted from the process of planning the fair's built environment, the designs of its social architects, and the experiences of participants and spectators, from Southern California and elsewhere in the nation.

"THIS IS NOT A ONE-HORSE TOWN"

In 1900 San Diego was a small city with big ambitions. Many of its seventeen thousand residents, themselves recently arrived, believed theirs would be the premier California port city and believed themselves "the fortunate children of an opulent land."[2] Such grandiose urban dreams must have seemed laughable to their counterparts in Los Angeles and San Francisco. San Diego's population had declined since the real-estate boom of the 1880s. Without a direct rail line, the city had stagnated while Los Angeles grew rapidly. At the turn of the century, it remained barely one-tenth the size of Los Angeles. Thus the small cadre of Anglo city boosters in San Diego harbored a bit of an inferiority complex as they pursued urban growth and kept expectations high. As Los Angeles and San Francisco settled uncomfortably into the shared title of principal California metropolis, San Diego scrambled to catch up. The city's dimming prospects led San Diego boosters to the idea of staging a world's fair to advertise their city to the nation and to outpace rivals. From the initial proposal for the event, ambitions for growth held sway and influenced the final product. Yet selecting regional slogans, historical genres, and didactic emphases that would encourage growth proved to be a more complicated affair than first appeared.

For all the grand rhetoric, Anglo leaders in San Diego puzzled about how to pursue growth. They wanted a city with more clout, to be sure, but other than pursuing a bigger body count, they were unsure what path of urban development to adopt. They admired Los Angeles' might but were wary of following its example—offering material incentives to industry to locate there—and they expressed unease at the masses of workers and the clouds of smoke that they assumed came with crowded cities and factories. Their ambivalence about the side effects of the industrial cure prompted San Diego boosters to test the efficacy of building an economy around suburban living, genteel consumption, and the outdoors—in short, the nascent California good life. Accordingly, they encouraged the migration of consumers to fuel the city's mercantile economy, home seekers to invest in its abundant real estate, and the health minded to enjoy its vaunted climate and outdoor recreations.

Except for a long-time desire to make the city an important navy base, which many San Diegans naively believed meant investment without smokestacks, members of the San Diego Chamber of Commerce rarely discussed attracting new industry as one of their goals. Nor did the body spend much time worrying about a labor force, preferring to attract home seekers with money to spend rather than workers willing to earn. The chamber's target audience for new migration was thus implicitly Anglos, not Mexicans. Though by 1900 Anglos already outnumbered ethnic Mexican residents and controlled the city's economic and political institutions, the proximity of the border and the recentness of the demographic change made Anglo boosters keen to distance San Diego from Mexico as much as possible.[3] Just as early commentators expressed ambivalence about the missions and were eager to make California fully Anglo-Saxon, so did San Diego leaders wish to transform their border town into a model Anglo-American city, if one without a significant laboring class. Could a place have both regional economic prowess and a livable, leisure-oriented city? The optimists in the city clearly believed these two goals were compatible.

From their positions in the chamber of commerce, these boosters largely dictated the city's politics during this period. In San Diego, an Anglo, conservative, and male mercantile elite charted urban and business objectives.[4] In this way, the chamber, and the exposition boosters that sprang from it, differed somewhat from the Camino Real leadership, which had greater female participation and a vaguely Progressive bent. When these San Diego leaders anointed the growth imperative as the sole custodian of the local economy, they shaped urban culture and politics in distinctive ways. The growth philosophy, despite the vagueness of the method, organized the expression of urban goals and problems around the city's ability to appear enticing. Though a beautified past became an important element of the booster appeal, the growth-at-all-costs mind-set squelched debate about civic purposes in several ways. San Diego's leaders wielded growth with all the subtlety of a billy club, repeating the need to grow whenever civic dissent threatened to upend the booster agenda.

One prominent local booster exemplified this leadership and its approach. John D. Spreckels, capitalist and scion of a family with a $25 million sugar fortune, invested heavily in the San Diego economy and became a major financial backer of the exposition. In 1910 approximately one of every fifteen city residents worked for a Spreckels-owned company. John Spreckels's businesses, among others, assumed continual growth and typified the San Diego economy; among his interests were a commercial importing company, three major street-railway systems, a ferry franchise, the city's main water utility, the already-famous Hotel del Coronado, theaters and public amusements, and two of the three daily newspapers, the *Union* and the *Tribune*. Though residents sometimes grumbled about Spreckels's power, they could not ignore his capital and commitment to the city's development.[5] Spreckels used his near monopoly on publishing to keep the city behind him. Through his main newspaper, the *San Diego Union,* he constantly reminded his readers of the growth imperative. During the first two decades of the twentieth century, atop the masthead of every morning's *Union* appeared current population figures and cumulative annual amounts of building permits under the heading "Watch San Diego Grow." Whether one read the figures as hopeful or troubling, Spreckels's message could not be clearer. Despite a steady population increase, San Diego continued to lose ground to Los Angeles. Underlying the encouraging progress reports was a frantic desire to keep pace.[6] The subtext of "Watch San Diego Grow" was grow or die.

In this atmosphere in 1909 local banker Gilbert Aubrey Davidson, then president of the chamber of commerce, proposed that San Diego host a world's exposition. Given that San Diego was a small city, Davidson admitted, "we cannot hope to have a second Chicago fair [like the World's Columbian Exposition in 1893] but we certainly will be able to make lots of noise with an exposition that will bring many thousands of people here." *Union* predictions that the exposition would triple the population easily won over local boosters and the chamber. A large group of them immediately filed articles of incorporation for the Panama-California Exposition Company (PCEC).[7] The officers of the PCEC, including first vice president John Spreckels, were prosperous businessmen—all men—mostly bankers and real-estate developers, whose success was predicated on growth.[8] Under their leadership, the PCEC appealed to like-minded San Diegans to purchase stock in the company and to vote for a million-dollar municipal bond to help pay for the exposition. Despite this involvement of public funding, the exposition was largely a product of private entrepreneurial efforts, and the local leadership of the fair reflected this emphasis. An almost exclusively male commercial elite ran the enterprise from beginning to end.

Anglo women's absence from this group of exposition planners, in comparison to the central roles they played in the Camino Real project, is as striking as it is puzzling. Perhaps women did not participate at significant levels because of the exposition's obsessive focus on business and growth. Though these themes were clearly important to El Camino Real proponents as well, at the fair they nearly overshadowed the rhetoric of public history. Moreover, if leadership drew primarily on business executives, then few women fit the profile necessary to ascend to higher levels of the fair organization. Alternatively, maybe many of the women who were likely to find the exposition a useful public platform were in 1909 and 1910 otherwise occupied, as the battle for suffrage in California heated up. The temporary nature of the fair may have made the project appear to be a less useful outlet for women's energies. The PCEC did engage a women's auxiliary committee, which included a long roster of members, but this group apparently did not seek a broader role in either the design of the fair or the civic goals it implied. The auxiliary's major work was to set up rest areas for female exposition visitors. Whether Anglo women found fewer opportunities for or saw fewer rewards in participation in a San Diego fair, their absence was unusual. Nevertheless, many were apt to count themselves part of the broader growth consensus that in San Diego came to stand for the public good.

The exposition's growth formula appeared to offer the simple solution San Diego leaders wanted, bringing visitors, money, and fame without the hassle of industry. Leaders promoted the fair to the populace on this basis. A stock advertisement in the newspaper claimed that the exposition "ought to double your business, Mr. Business-Man." On a wider scale, the PCEC advertising campaign hinted that a world's fair would link the far southwestern city with the nation at large. One PCEC director believed that the exposition was the ideal vehicle to "let the people of the country know that this is not a one-horse town." Another director declared in the *Union* that San Diegans would reject this national advertisement and growth catalyst at their peril: "Now is the time for San Diego to be a city or lay down and be out of the running for good and all." With the twin enticements of growth and fame, stock in the exposition sold quickly, and a bond issue passed by a wide margin in the fall of 1910. The *Union*'s editors could hardly contain their excitement. An exultant editorial congratulated the voters for choosing the exposition and all its attendant civic promises: "San Diego the Unconquerable, the Irresistible, and the Incomparable!"[9]

Consensus was less clear, however, when the PCEC began to sketch out initial plans for the exposition. What kind of growth the fair would prompt and who would cash in on it became vexing questions. Growth and the middle-class good life did not always go together, nor did they automatically benefit all citizens. This disconnect was laid bare in a major early struggle over where to locate the fairgrounds. The city's 1400-acre City Park just northeast of downtown, appeared to be a sensible choice. The Olmsted Brothers, a nationally famous landscape architecture firm and the PCEC's choice for designing the grounds, proposed situating the exposition in the southwest corner of the park on about 100 acres. The firm believed that preserving the naturalistic character of the rest of the area was important so that city residents could use it during and after the fair. Though the sons of Frederick Law Olmsted were accomplished fair designers, they had inherited loyalty to the "greensward" park plan from their father, the architect of New York's Central Park.[10] But the PCEC's newly appointed director-general of the fair, D. C. Collier, claimed to need more space, hoping to attract as many exhibitors as possible and arguing that a bigger exposition meant greater returns in growth. The southwestern site was hemmed in topographically and had little room to expand. Therefore, the PCEC preferred a site in the very middle of the park that would accommodate its plan of 350 acres and would allow for almost unlimited expansion.[11] With the support of a number of elite San Diegans, the Olmsteds objected vehemently via telegram, claiming that the city would violate its duty to its citizens "to ruin park by putting exposition in middle of it." The San Diego Hotel and Roominghouse Keepers Association complained as well, arguing that the new site was too far away from the city's lodging facilities. Other residents suggested that this move went too far for growth, damaging the character of the city itself; a few accused PCEC board members of promoting the exposition only to aid their own enterprises, not to benefit the city as a whole.[12]

The grumblings about uneven growth dividends cast suspicion on boosters' motives, but the partnership of urban development and private enterprise was not a new one. The central site would more easily facilitate the building of a new streetcar line from downtown through the park and on to new suburbs on the other side. Collier owned many of those new subdivisions, and Spreckels's commuter-railway franchise was almost certain to win the contract for the new line. Though the city had so far prohibited tracks across the park, it would have to transport visitors to the park from downtown hotels during the fair and would likely grant a complete right-of-way afterward. Moreover, Spreckels had threatened to withhold his pledged stock payment of two hundred thousand dollars until the central site was assured. The PCEC had run up early debts in anticipation of the bond issue and stock pledges and needed Spreckels to deliver his promised contribution to remain solvent. Spreckels and Collier asserted that their interest was not selfish, as they believed the whole city stood to gain from their developments.[13] The PCEC was inclined to agree and chose the central site, though in doing so they forfeited the services of the Olmsted Brothers, who resigned in protest. The Olmsteds would have been displeased anyway. As map 2 shows, the fair eventually grew to occupy more than six hundred acres, nearly half the park, and Spreckels's Electric Railway Company did win the right to build a line through the park.[14] Two visions of the city clashed over this seemingly simple decision of location. Should urban development favor current or future residents?

Exposition boosters abhorred such internal squabbling. They carefully managed San Diego's image so the city might appear to be of one voice on the fair, discouraging argument on any point, however small. Despite solid support for the exposition, sponsors tried to project a unity that simply did not exist. The *Union,* for example, used the fact that the twenty-member Pressmen's Union purchased ten shares of PCEC stock as proof that the exposition had the backing of all organized labor in the city, a statement open to considerable debate. Moreover, fair boosters kept up a deliberate campaign to squash dissent, painting any objections to the PCEC as disloyal to the city. As Spreckels employee and PCEC-board member William Clayton stated, "there is no room for a minority opinion . . . There are some people who are not in harmony with the Panama-California Exposition. . . . They must be convinced to change their minds." In growth-obsessed San Diego, it would have been risky to take the stance that the PCEC's plans, much less the fair itself, was counter to civic interests. The *Union* pitched in to keep the grumbling to a minimum, issuing continuous articles backing the exposition. One piece, "Boosters, Knockers and the Cities They Build," portrayed the opposition as "not city builders." Instead, it called them "parasites on the enterprise of other men, barnacles on the keel of the ship of progress." Chamber of commerce boosters went so far as to ask the *Union* to close its columns to any opinions disparaging the fair. The editors eagerly complied with the request for censorship, snickering that malcontents had "the inalienable right to hire a hall."[15] Exposition boosters and the PCEC presented a unified San Diego, but their defensive claims bespoke some nervousness about losing control of the city.

San Diego was not a quiescent city on the eve of the exposition. First, the 1910 census results had been disappointing. Boosters had hoped

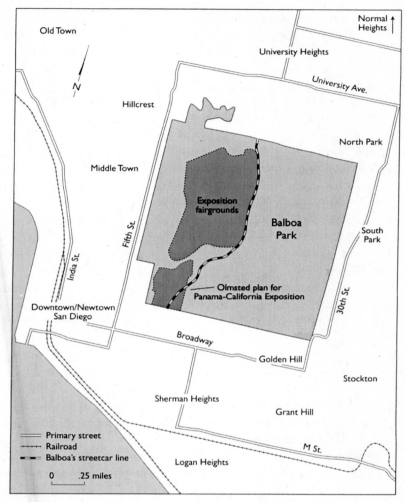

Map 2. San Diego and Balboa Park, ca. 1910. This map shows the two proposed locations for the fairgrounds as well as surrounding suburbs and Spreckels's streetcar line. Adapted from a James Munson map.

that the city population would reach sixty or seventy thousand, but the total came to less than forty thousand, still just a little over 10 percent of Los Angeles' population. Furthermore, vigorous local socialist organizing belied the appearance of social harmony. Despite the fact that San Diego was firmly in the control of the Republican Party, Socialist candidates frequently appeared on local ballots, and in 1904 the Socialist Party presidential candidate, Eugene Debs, came in second behind

Theodore Roosevelt, outpacing the losing Democrat, Alton Parker.[16] To add to the radical undercurrent, in 1912 the Industrial Workers of the World (IWW) launched a free-speech movement in the city. San Diego leaders moved quickly to repress the agitators. Several exposition directors, along with other leading citizens, took part in vigilante actions, beating, intimidating, and literally tarring and feathering IWW members. Socialist and feminist activist Emma Goldman required a police escort to leave the city safely, and as she did, many Anglos cheered their victory.[17] Nevertheless, both the uprising and its repression heightened urban tension and indicated considerably less accord than boosters presumed.

For Anglo boosters, the onset of the Mexican Revolution during the planning years complicated efforts to manage the city's image. The predicted fallout—immigration, radicalism, anarchism, and confiscation—heightened many Anglo-Americans' fears of their neighbors just to the south. The revolution forced locals to take notice of transnational radicalism, including the presence of exiled Mexican agitators in the Southwest. Particularly incendiary were rumors of the Plan de San Diego, which proposed reclaiming lands lost in the Mexican-American War by killing all Anglo men in Texas over the age of sixteen. Many Americans anticipated U.S. intervention, even the annexation of Mexico, to quell the disturbance and the perceived threat to American security. Local boosters worried that rumors of war with Mexico would place the Panama-California Exposition in jeopardy.[18] How could the fair entice tourists to a danger zone? How could boosters advertise the region if it appeared full of strife rather than promise?

Urban and international turmoil at this public moment placed San Diego's harmonious image and potential for growth at risk. The success of the exposition became even more crucial to local boosters. In the years before the opening of the gates, exposition backers maneuvered the design and promotion of the fair in response to the evolving regional context. The exposition had to counter the radicalism emerging on San Diego's streets and Mexico's border and present instead an image of the city at its most perfect and a region at its most productive. For all the marketing to newcomers, exposition planning also contained a message for San Diegans and Southern Californians, Anglo and otherwise. Just as fair and growth boosters engineered the newspaper for national consumption rather than local debate, they wanted locals to see their region through the eyes of tourists. To do so, they needed to present it as a place to see as much as to live in, a place with a distinctive look and character rather than a conglomerate of competing interests.[19] This rhetoric encouraged residents to behave in essence as tour guides, projecting loyalty to the city as a whole and enjoying the pleasures of its ample good life.

"A NEW EL DORADO"

Against the volatile background in San Diego, the medium for exposition boosters' message was crucial. What look would the fair give the region? How would this miniature city model the larger whole that surrounded it? Because San Diego had lost the official world's-fair designation to San Francisco, it had to relinquish any claim to federal support or recognition and could not invite international exhibits. These terms might have discouraged other cities, but San Diego boosters saw the restrictions as a new opportunity. Here was a chance to be more than an attractive host city or a mere stage for the art and culture of the world: The region itself would be both the site and the object of display. Though earlier fairs, notably the White City of Chicago's 1893 World's Columbian Exposition, had clearly offered themselves as ideal urban paradigms, the local focus allowed San Diego's exposition boosters to create the fair as a microcosm of their vision of civic belonging, regional identity, and future development. Boosters planned the exposition as a glimpse of "the golden-lined future promise of the Southwest."[20] If this approach could not claim San Diego as the preeminent port of entry on the Pacific Coast, it proved to be an effective alternative strategy for increasing the city's renown. What boosters did not anticipate, however, was that this conception gave the exposition an influential role in articulating the regional identity of Southern California and the greater Southwest, on both a national and a local stage. As Collier boldly predicted, "Those who have dreamed of California, of the California that is pictured in all our literature and told about in song and in story, will find the land of their dreams in San Diego in 1915."[21] The standard the PCEC set for itself was high. The group wanted a theme that would get both visitors and residents to imagine an ideal California.

Equating the region with Spanish romance, an approach that was already attracting visitors to El Camino Real, offered a promising choice. In the first public statement of plans for the fair, the PCEC's 1910 *Fore-Glance* tested the possibility. "Spanish Pageantry to live again. . . . The so-called mission style of architecture will pay tribute to the memory of the venturesome seventeenth-century [sic] Spanish padres who first anchored in San Diego bay and there laid California's cornerstone. . . . The history of California's earliest civilization will be impressed on the entire Exposition."[22] This early focus drew upon the interest in missions and California's own history but seemed unsure of its footing. A "so-called" legacy was a thin one upon which to build. However evocative missions had come to be, could they symbolize future growth as boosters wanted them to? Fair backers searched for a way to broaden the Spanish theme.

The Park Commission decided in 1910 to rename City Park in honor of the fair. Residents came up with a number of possibilities, again suggesting divergent local viewpoints: Pacific, Horton (after Alonzo Horton, an Anglo city founder), Silvergate (an invented city nickname), and Balboa (the sixteenth-century Spanish explorer), though, surprisingly, no Serra. The board, composed entirely of PCEC directors, unanimously chose to commemorate Vasquez Nuñez Balboa, famous in part for being the first European to sight the Pacific Ocean from the Americas (though not San Diego). According to the *Union*, the board chose the "hardy Spaniard," for whom they thought the Pacific Ocean ought to have been named, partially as "tardy compensation" for this four-hundred-year slight. The *Union* believed the choice particularly appropriate because associating the park with a dashing conquistador would complement the PCEC's aims to showcase Southern California as a grand and glorious place.[23] Balboa Park foreshadowed the merger of nostalgic sentiment for the region's Spanish-colonial past with the imperial civic ambitions that animated exposition boosters.

A more extensive trial run of the Spanish theme—which melded mission references with conquistadors, carnivals, and *Ramona*—took place at a four-day festival to break ground for construction of the exposition in 1911. Along with presenting speeches and ceremonial shovels, the PCEC put on costume balls, athletic contests, concerts, fireworks, and historical pageants. The opening-night spectacle included a reenactment of Cabrillo sailing into San Diego Bay. The explorer stand-in was hailed as a king and borne to city hall on a sedan chair carried by a group of ten leading citizens costumed as Indians, although their outfits resembled those of Plains Indians more than anything Californian or Southwestern. In a contrived scene of welcomed conquest, a greeting party met Cabrillo, including one Queen Ramona who presented him with the key to the city. PCEC publicist Winfield Hogaboom described the scene in this way: "That night old Juan Rodriguez Cabrillo, brave old mariner of the romance days, reincarnated, came again to San Diego in his caravel of old."[24] Historical pageants in the following days set the stage for the fair's narrative of regional progress. The first performance gave an overview of California history, beginning with the mission era and concluding, as the official program said, with "the first permanent development of San Diego . . . and the awakening of imperial enterprise throughout the Southwest."[25] The next day's parade included depictions of conquistadors defeating Aztec armies, Balboa claiming possession of the Pacific Ocean, Franciscans baptizing Indians, Americans taking down the Mexican flag, and Neptune joining the oceans at the Panama Canal.

The third day's pageant concentrated on the missions. It presented twenty-one floats, each featuring a miniature mission building and historical characters. For example, the first one, of San Diego itself, included Don Gaspar de Portolá trailed by twenty of his soldiers and forty Indians leading horses. The description of the La Purísima Concepción float tallied several "groups of Indians bearing wheat, oats, barley, and driving cattle and sheep gaily decorated, marshaled by monks." Floats near the end displayed the Anglo-American era, parading John Frémont and his soldiers, American and Mexican flags, fur trappers, and forty-niners. Though no floats represented the coming of bankers, farmers, or railroad magnates, the tableau clearly culminated in a triumphant American destiny. According to *Mission Play* author John S. McGroarty, the purpose of this sequence was to "impress upon people the march of time in the magnificent Southwest, the land of sunshine, and of wastes redeemed."[26] Together, the parades and historicized ceremonies suggested powerful symbols on which the fair might draw, including Spanish colonization, Indian deference, racial succession, and American conquest.

In addition to demonstrating the didactic potential of this historical theme, the celebration's pastiche of historical and romantic allusions produced a carnival spirit. Invitations to the ground breaking had imagined it in precisely those terms. A Santa Fe Railway pamphlet advertised the event as a holiday where "once more across the stage will march padres and peons, señoritas and cavaliers and all the sunny life of centuries ago." The cover of the PCEC's program included colorful clowns and Renaissance revelers with the caption "4 Days of Pageantry and Carnival." Indeed, the PCEC opened one city block for dancing at Queen Ramona's Masque Ball.[27] This and other balls offered attendees an occasion to indulge in the fantasy that had proved so alluring to Camino Real tourists and to experience a bit of the Spanish past for themselves. Yet the fair celebrations went one step further by offering

Spanish-themed entertainment that invited Anglos' direct participation. This approach was quite popular, and its success prompted the PCEC to move away from a strictly mission-oriented theme.

Fostering a sense of disorder amid the presentations of historical order might appear to be a contradictory action, yet the combination worked to local boosters' advantage. The carnival temporarily turned society upside down, not so much along class lines as along lines of race and time. The *Union* reported the transformation of the local ambiance as a "newly created fairyland, . . . an excess of animal spirits" and a "desire for harmless mischief." It suggested that the "colors of the old Spanish-Californian days, red and yellow, got into the blood."[28] Projecting themselves backward into a premodern Spanish past, Anglo revelers demonstrated the appeal of a participatory romance. Yet the deliberate costuming of the city and its residents highlighted the fact that the historical inversion was an exception to the normal, American order of things. Moreover, this joint civic celebration encouraged civic unity beyond any level that a didactic parade could impose. As historian David Glassberg has noted, such events "addressed urban resident and tourist alike as members of fun-loving crowds," not as citizens with competing political agendas.[29] Even in its planning stages, the fair began to promote loyalty to city and region by generating shared styles of popular culture, the most important of which was a fanciful and entertaining memory of Spanish California. Though the spectacle as a whole might not have reflected citizens' views of the city or understanding of history, Spanish themes became common cultural currency in the region and began to preclude other ways of imagining place, past, or perhaps even politics.

The architecture of the fair was thus crucial. It would carry the weight of booster visions for the city and determine how residents and tourists saw it—in a romantic Spanish light rather than in political terms. The PCEC hoped to find an ideal candidate for chief architect—a nationally famous designer who could produce a style evocative of this fanciful past. John Galen Howard of Berkeley expressed interest but was quickly turned down because his Beaux-Arts style had few specific regional references. The PCEC initially stated a preference for Irving Gill, a San Diegan who had trained under the Chicago modernist Louis Sullivan. Gill's style was a modern version of the mission-revival style that had flourished briefly in California in the previous decade. His buildings were distinctive for their complete lack of ornament and their commitment to geometric form. Gill presented the PCEC with an opportunity to make the exposition design a memorable architectural statement of modernism.[30] But selecting Gill would be a risky decision. Gill's unrelenting modern treatments eschewed the showy decoration and monumental scale expected of expositions and did not readily lend themselves to the romantic fantasies that PCEC planners were coming to see as fundamental to the exposition's program. Collier suggested that the board's vision of Spanish style should include both "simplicity *and* . . . richness of ornamentation." Prominent California architect Elmer Grey believed that historical association required some ornament: "were the great cathedrals of Europe, the manor houses of England, or the chateaux of France possessed only of such qualities as his [Gill's] work possesses they would be poor work indeed."[31] Gill's work reminded the PCEC too little of the Spanish past and too much of the disquieting modern city.

Before the Olmsted Brothers had quit, they had suggested an eastern architect, Bertram Grosvenor Goodhue, who had expertise in a variety of Spanish styles, from colonial and baroque to the florid churrigueresque. Having traveled extensively in both Spain and Mexico, Goodhue considered himself an authority on these styles, publishing numerous architectural books on the subject.[32] The PCEC saw immediately that Goodhue brought qualities that Gill could not: a national reputation and a romantic treatment of Spanish style. Goodhue wanted the job, believing it offered a "chance for fame," and he lobbied heavily for it. He encouraged the PCEC's doubts about Gill and pressed several well-known California colleagues to write to the PCEC on his behalf. John Olmsted reported to Goodhue that he had "argued your reputation good for publicity."[33] This possibility was too tempting for the PCEC to reject. At the end of January 1911, the group offered Goodhue the job, and he enthusiastically accepted. In a letter to his brother, Goodhue exclaimed that San Diego was a place where he "went, saw and conquered without much, if any difficulty. The thing is not a tremendously big affair, and doesn't pretend to rival San Francisco, but . . . there is a chance to make a charming group." The *Union* anticipated that he would make the city an architectural landmark. For a fee of twelve thousand dollars, his two-year contract called for him to select the architectural theme of the exposition, design the permanent buildings, and supervise the overall planning and design. Goodhue and the PCEC found a mutual "chance for fame" in the Spanish regional theme.[34] Goodhue's romantic baroque style promised to deliver not only the fanciful mood the PCEC wanted but a model that San Diego could emulate.

As exposition planners converged on the choice of a whimsical Spanish theme, they tested its applicability to booster ambitions for growth and progress. The *Fore-Glance* suggested the PCEC's desire both to preserve "the romance of long gone days" and to hasten "more wonderful progress for the future throughout this great American Southwest." How could these two objectives be successfully integrated? The combination would be important if fair planners were to persuade new migrants, investors, and locals to buy into the booster vision of the region's future. The fair's chief publicist suggested this logic: The Panama-California Exposition would "condense into striking, dramatic scenes the picturesque history, political and economic, and the wonderful resources, developed and undeveloped, of the territory."[35] Telescoping the region's past, present, and future into a singular linear narrative gave the Spanish theme greater import, providing a meaningful as well as decorative idiom. In proposing to use the past to predict the future, the PCEC put a traditional world's-fair strategy to a decidedly regional purpose. The fair could offer a glorious version of the Spanish past of Southern California as a harbinger for coming American success. This past was a far cry from the romantic pathos of mission ruins or the pious sandal-clad padres; it called to mind silver spurs and cities of gold.

The Panama Canal itself, the pretext for the exposition, provided an outlet for boosters' most imperial ambitions. The canal solidified the region's link to the rest of the nation, and not only in terms of transportation and commerce. San Diego Anglos fused their regional boosterism with the canal's nationalist implications. A *Union* article explaining the reasons for holding the exposition called the canal a "big American ditch" that would discourage "any nation who may want to pick a quarrel with Uncle Sam." Given that San Diego sat on the nation's extreme southwestern corner, city boosters were eager to assert their national allegiance. Fair publicity touted the appropriateness of San Diego's hosting a celebration for this national, indeed international, event. "It is fitting that San Diego should make the occasion [the fair] fully worthy of the event [the Canal opening], not only because that event is to be the beginning of a new and glorious history, but because San Diego herself is destined to play a great part in this splendid history."[36] The canal symbolized the region's future. Yet the seeds of Southern California's destiny also supposedly existed in its Spanish past, its once and future position as a hopeful outpost of a most powerful empire. Though Alta California never brought Spain the wealth or power that the Latin American colonies did, Anglo boosters of Southern

California often ignored that disparity and imagined the region as awash in New World riches. Bertram Goodhue saw an integral connection between the canal and the region's Spanish-colonial past: The canal represented the "triumphant realization . . . [and] the culmination of the Spaniards' search for a Western route."[37] As had Camino Real advocates, exposition boosters suggested that Anglo-Americans were "picking up the pieces of the Old Spanish empire," inheriting the conquistadors' mantle and continuing their conquest.

Thus the exposition related the history of California as one of national succession. Indeed, it cloaked the American future with the metaphorical grandeur of the Spanish past, envisioning the Anglo development of Southern California in the coming century as a conquest just as glorious as the exploits of the conquistadors and missionaries. "This great empire, in 1915, looming largest on the horizon," the *Fore-Glance* suggested, beckoned as "the new land of opportunity next to be conquered by peaceful settlement." An image of the region as empire and a model of growth by conquest governed exposition messages from then on. In his opening-night address at the exposition, PCEC president G. Aubrey Davidson put an end to the five tumultuous years of debate and threw open the gates with these words: "Here is pictured this happy combination of splendid temples, the story of the friars, the thrilling tale of the pioneers, the orderly conquest of commerce, coupled with the hopes of a new El Dorado where life can expand in this fragrant land of opportunity."[38] In proclaiming the coming of "a new El Dorado" in the Southwest, Davidson tried to link past and present, growth and conquest, and tourist and resident in a vision of the region as a rightfully won, historically appropriate American paradise. This booster vision dominated the physical and rhetorical impression of the exposition grounds, a place that Anglo leaders could control more easily than the city itself.

"MAGIC CITY ON THE MESA"

The Panama-California Exposition ushered in 1915 with a spectacular midnight celebration on New Year's Eve. Fireworks and electric lights brightened the darkness, and San Diego became the host of a two-year party. Initial reviews were overwhelmingly positive. From the perspective of tourists, midwestern newspapers, architectural critics, and Southern Californians alike, the little fair that could was a brilliant success. As Emily Post summed up her visit, "The San Diego Exposition was a pure delight." With special rates for rail travel and the concurrent

draw of San Francisco's Panama-Pacific International Exposition, which
would open in March, the fair's attendance and popularity soared.[39]
The regional vision that visitors encountered was a study in contrasts.
Boosters' dual intentions to display the region's romantic history while
encouraging future development led to designs that juxtaposed regional
antiques with cutting-edge technology, a Spanish past with Anglo
progress, and a European legacy with Indian people. Visitors reported
their experiences in these dual terms, at once appreciating the fanciful
Spanish style and applauding modern methods.

The image that first greeted visitors was the architecture and
ambiance of Spanish romance. Publicity beckoned visitors to "this
magic city on the mesa, . . . dreamed of by Cabrillo four centuries ago
and by the succession of conquistadores and padres who followed."
The entrance to the fair was striking; crossing the high-span Puente de
Cabrillo, visitors saw the tiled dome and campanile of the California
Building and walked through a wide gateway that afforded a glimpse of
a broad avenue lined with trees and tile roofs. As one visitor recalled his
approach, "From the moment that you cross the Puento [sic] to the
Exposition, you see only beauty." Descriptions and guides complimented the Spanish-colonial buildings and their designer, Bertram
Goodhue. One fair visitor even wrote the architect personally to express
her "great pleasure in the beauty of this San Diego Exposition. . . . [T]he
whole has given me one of the keenest artistic delights I have ever experienced." Many comments confirm that Goodhue successfully created
the impression he wanted; his plans called for "a city in miniature,
meant to recall to mind the glamour and mystery and poetry of the old
Spanish days." The words of the reviewers repeated this mood. One
author found herself in a dreamland, a "fairy Spanish city, . . . a sweet
and restful land where 'castles in Spain' seem realities; a land in which
you loaf and invite your soul."[40] Goodhue's buildings struck the tone
the PCEC wanted, transporting visitors to a Spanish dream city.

Architectural critics believed that this effect was possible because of
the designer's extensive use of ornament. Local designers applauded the
move from the more austere style of the California missions to the flam-
boyant stage of Spanish-colonial style, which they claimed could be a
"style as complex and rich as the Baroque of Europe." One writer called
the combination of Spanish baroque, colonial, and Moorish styles a
"wonderfully effective, boastfully rich style of architecture." Despite
some critiques of the fair's architecture as "the spirit of the Renaissance
gone mad" or an "architectural crazy quilt," most area designers judged

Goodhue's Spanish-colonial style "historically and logically appropriate," and they clamored to replicate it in their own commissions. Goodhue's fearless blending of "broken pediments, curves, twists, flutes, [and] scallops" produced, according to one architect, "theoretically a sort of architectural buffoonery, yet actually a style of strange and peculiar delight." Goodhue's approach at the Panama-California Exposition would touch off a Spanish-colonial building spree in the later 1910s and 1920s. But observant commentators could already guess at its impact. Frank Miller, proprietor of the Mission Inn in Riverside, predicted that "Goodhue's work at San Diego will be felt for generations to come in every town and village of California."[41] It still is.

That the style bore little resemblance to the missions or any other structures the Spanish built in California mattered little. The bygone era of castles and conquistadors to which many people referred had no precedent in California's days as a remote and relatively poor Spanish colony. For direct reference, commentators had to reach further back and farther away. A Santa Fe Railway guide, for example, described the exposition as a "a walled city of the fifteenth century, its architecture reminding one of the Alhambra, the old Mexican cathedrals and the still older edifices of the Moors." Several writers thought the architecture outdid that of Spain itself. Architect William Templeton Johnson said of the California Building, "There is no finer façade in Spain and the tower holds its own with the gorgeous towers of Cordova and Seville." Another visitor remarked simply, "So Spanish in feeling—yet so rarely equaled in Spain." PCEC boosters rectified the geographical disjunction by imagining that the Spanish would have built more extravagantly in California if they had had the means. The exposition was thus "a city such as Cabrillo and his men must have dreamed of as they stood, perhaps, on that same lofty mesa, and looked down to the sea."[42] Boosters took Camino Real advocates' solution—building in the spirit of the padres rather than replicating their efforts—one step further. They created a time and a place that never existed. Freed from mission adobe and California history, the designers of the Panama-California Exposition created a wholly new invocation of the region's past, mixing historical metaphors with the same aplomb that they mixed building styles.

The spatial plan and sculptural program of the fair continued the medley by frequently referencing famous people from the Spanish past. Navigating the fairgrounds required knowledge of a who's who of Spanish explorers. As map 3 shows, not only were there the Cabrillo Bridge and the Plaza de Balboa, but Calle Cristóbal and Calle Colón took visitors

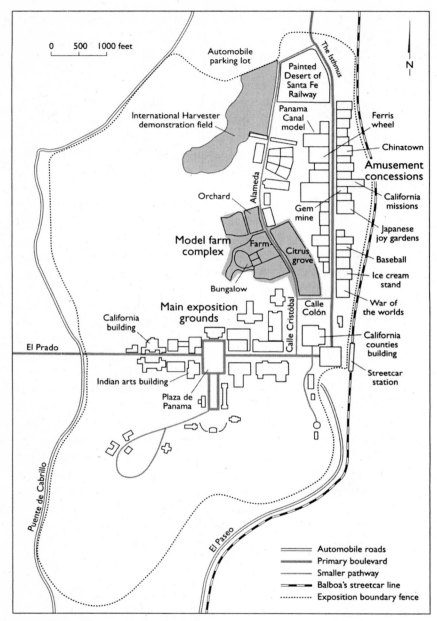

Map 3. Panama-California Exposition grounds, 1915. Adapted from a James Munson map.

Labels within map:

0 500 1000 feet

Automobile parking lot

Painted Desert of Santa Fe Railway

The Isthmus

N

Panama Canal model

Ferris wheel

International Harvester demonstration field

Chinatown

Amusement concessions

Alameda

California missions

Orchard

Gem mine

Japanese joy gardens

Model farm complex

Farm

Citrus grove

Baseball

Bungalow

Ice cream stand

Main exposition grounds

Calle Colón

War of the worlds

California building

Calle Cristóbal

California counties building

El Prado

Streetcar station

Indian arts building

Plaza de Panama

Puente de Cabrillo

El Paseo

Automobile roads
Primary boulevard
Smaller pathway
Balboa's streetcar line
Exposition boundary fence

from the main boulevard, the Prado, to the amusement midway, the Isthmus. Visitors thus trailed Columbus again from the Old World to the New. Numerous statues anchored points on the map. The group that stood above the entrance to the main exposition building, the Casa del Prado, embodied California as a classical goddess, showing her shepherding two boys, one Spanish and one Indian. In adjoining niches sat Columbia and Queen Isabella, the latter of whom appeared to have bequeathed her mantle as California's protector to the Anglo-American women with whom she shared the ledge. A Santa Fe Railway guide noted the inescapability of such references: "Reminders such as this of the Spanish explorers and conquistadores are everywhere."[43]

The richly ornamented entrance to Goodhue's California Building received much comment. A youthful Padre Junípero Serra stood at the top of the doorway with the shield of the United States above his head; around the door clockwise were Charles III of Spain; Juan Rodríguez Cabrillo, the first Spanish explorer to sight San Diego harbor; Gaspar de Portolá, the first Spanish governor of California; Sebastian Vizcaíno, who gave San Diego its name in 1602; Father Antonio de la Ascencion, a Carmelite historian who accompanied Vizcaíno; Father Luis Jayme, a Franciscan missionary killed by Indians in 1774; George Vancouver, the first English navigator to visit San Diego; and Phillip III of Spain.[44] The array of monarchs, sailors, and missionaries reflected the way in which fair designers used regional history as a grab bag of references, with little attempt to impose consistency. As one publicity piece described the doorway, "It is a roster of kings and priests, navigators and historians, heroes and martyrs." Local booster and leading city retailer George White Marston saw this willy-nilly gaggle of "saints and heroes" as a perfectly appropriate group. In dedicating the California Building on opening night, he asked, "Do they not set forth the past and present of California's life? Are they not true symbols of her glowing history and her wonderful to-day?"[45] While George Vancouver, the lone English explorer in the group, might seem out of place, his presence testified to the Anglo claim on California. Having Serra nearly carry the U.S. shield reinforced the point that the Spanish conquest of California had been an obliging precursor to the Anglo-American one.

There was more to the magic Spanish city than its buildings, however. The PCEC, remembering the success of the atmosphere at the ground breaking, made these statues come alive as costumed employees. Together, buildings and actors formed parts of the overall illusion: "The Spanish city is one of . . . tiled domes and fantastic towers, archways

Figure 9. "In a Tropical Garden," Panama-California
Exposition, 1915. The building behind these Spanish-
costumed performers is the Indian Arts Building. Postcard
from author's collection.

from which hang old mission bells, . . . a cool patio . . . , a fountain
plashing, a caballero leaning lazily against the wall . . . , or the troupe of
Spanish dancing girls whose bright colored skirts are awhirl to the hum
of guitar and the click of the castanet."[46] Dressed as various Spanish
types, employees animated the architecture and put visitors in the mood
for Spanish romance (see figure 9). Guidebook vendors wore riveted

pants, pointy sombreros, and ranchero-style jackets. Garden attendants donned plain work clothes but tied colorful sashes around their waists. Female workers, often selling mementos and refreshments, had varied costumes, but photographs typically find them in tiered, lace-fringed midcalf-length skirts, scarves of contrasting colors around their waists, simple white blouses, and lacy vests or tasseled jackets.[47]

The PCEC hired for the duration of the fair a group of "Spanish" singers, actors, and dancers to perform "whenever they could please or interest the visitors." Whether the members of this troupe were Hispanic in ways other than their costumes is unclear, but they played a prominent role in creating the "lazy spirit of romance and a recollection of Spanish tradition" that permeated the exposition. Visitors frequently asked them to perform the following scene, which became a frequent sight along the Prado: "Seated in a balcony . . . , the visitor may glimpse a daughter of Old Seville, and beneath the balcony her Spanish lover, strumming his guitar. The visitor is in the Old World now; in old Spain, perhaps, or the capital of some republic to the South of us." Caballero and señorita were Spanish romance personified. An advance report enticed visitors with details; this company would also include "dancing girls . . . , thirty of them . . . imported bodily, castanets and all, from Barcelona, Seville, and old Monterey, thirty sloe-eyed, nimble-footed señoritas who will, without fee or price, gyrate to the rhythmic swing of Spanish melodies."[48] The curve and sway of the dancers would carry the baroque architectural flourishes out into the streets.

The sultry, dark-eyed señorita was a key figure in the imagined moment that fair designers sought to evoke; indeed, she appeared in Southern California Anglos' Spanish fantasies too many times to count. On postcards and in publications, film, and popular songs, the señorita evoked an eroticized variation of the ethnic theme. While the señorita gyrated openly on the main boulevards of the exposition, a dime show on the Isthmus, the Sultan's Harem, was closed down for the indecency of its female dancers.[49] Protected by the fair's immersion in the Spanish past (and a little more clothing), the Spanish dancers escaped such charges. The figure of the dancing señorita symbolized the romance and pleasure that many Anglos sought in their reenactments of the Spanish past. She epitomized the Anglo version of rancho (as opposed to mission) days in California, suggesting one continuous fiesta during which revelers could give themselves over to dancing and laughter. Yet by and large, fair visitors did not join in the dancing, preferring to watch the dancers enact this fantasy for them. The señorita embodied for them the

Figure 10. Balboa guards (Pinkerton detectives), 1915. Lined up on the Prado, these guards resemble a marching band more than a police force. Courtesy Seaver Center for Western History Research, Los Angeles County Museum of Natural History.

spirit of revelry and the "animal spirits" and "desire for harmless mischief" that attendees at the ground breaking had so enjoyed. These desires came to reside in the body of the "Spanish" woman herself, marking the difference between old Spanish days and modern Anglo life in Southern California.

Figures of order as well as revelry received fanciful costumes. The exposition police squad became the "Balboa guards" and wore pale-blue military-style uniforms, decorated with bars and epaulettes, and white and gold plumed hats. Guidebooks praised their costumes along with their policing performance. "The Guards, in their bright, light-colored blue Spanish uniforms, with yellow and black bars, form an exceedingly ornamental as well as useful branch of the Exposition efficiency organization." As widely advertised as the resplendent outfit was the professionalism of the police force—Pinkerton detectives, no less. Two rows of guards formed the subject for the postcard (see figure 10), which bore a complimentary caption: "so smoothly did the opening celebration come off that they did not have to make one arrest despite record-breaking crowds." A reporter from the *Denver Post* lauded this success, even linking the costumes to the maintenance of order: "everything is under the strict supervision of the Pinkerton police force, whose brilliant blue uniforms, slashed with gold braid, make their presence conspicuous."[50] This link between uniform and function was a potent combination. Far from diminishing the Pinkertons' reputation, Spanish romance offered a beguiling language in which to express underlying images of order.

The Pinkertons' Spanish makeover paralleled the metamorphosis of Spanish explorers into American patriots. Much as Columbus became a "Yankee hero" at the 1893 World's Columbian Exposition in Chicago, here Balboa, Cabrillo, and Serra helped legitimize a new version of empire, from the real Isthmus of Panama to the cities of Southern California. A plaque in the fair's California Quadrangle honoring Serra exemplified this sentiment: "To the memory of Fray Junípero Serra and to his fellow pioneers whose saintly devotion and dauntless courage established Christianity and civilization in Alta California, 1769–1915."[51] By extending the date from 1769 to 1915, the present time, PCEC leaders stretched out the project of conquest. Not only did these boosters include themselves as partners in Serra's project, but they also called for new pioneers to take up a different kind of struggle for regional dominion.

"CARVING A GREEN EMPIRE OUT OF THE GRAY DESERT"

Inside its beautiful buildings, the exposition presented visitors with a dazzling array of the products of progress. Showing manufacturing processes, scientific discoveries, transportation methods, tools, and goods, the exposition offered a detailed plan for developing the region and making it the exemplar of the nation. The *San Diego Union*'s review of the exposition's first year stated that in essence it was a "concentration in a small space of the whole life of the new West."[52] The Panama-California Exposition promoted a wide range of development possibilities, from naval industries and gem mining to mercantile displays and aeronautics. The most-emphasized regional opportunity, however, was agriculture. In exhibit halls, surrounding gardens, and demonstration fields, visitors learned of the vast potential of Southern California cultivation. The fair presented the region as a cornucopia in waiting.

Many of the fair's displays were predictable, including, Emily Post sighed, the typical "bottles of fruit in alcohol, sheaves of grain, arches of oranges." The sculptural displays of citrus fruit were monumental but by then routine, as California had been sending towers of oranges to every exposition since the Chicago one. Nevertheless, the sheer volume of agricultural products could not have failed to impress other visitors. But if the exposition was to grab their attention, a publicist suggested, it would have "to show the actual scenes of carving a green

empire out of the gray desert, to visualize the carving process by transforming, before the visitors' eyes, a plot of primeval sagebrush into a
highly productive farm by means of a model, complete irrigation
system." The boosters believed that only a lavish display of fruit and
flowers growing on-site would convince the metaphorical "Illinois
tourist" who arrived believing that the Southwest was "a kind of
national sandpile especially designed for invalids, pueblo Indians, cow-
punchers and prospectors, a parched waste aggravated by copper
smelters."[53] The PCEC wanted to correct this misconception with elaborate proof of the region's natural fecundity.

The first plan was to cover the entire exposition grounds with lush
greenery. Unlike other fairs, which had "cramped quarters . . . , heat and
dust and turmoil," the San Diego exposition would showcase a city of
"space and verdure and a joy of Nature, . . . the wondrous growth of
tree and vine and flower which spreads its lavish beauty over all." Compared to gardening efforts at previous expositions, which the PCEC publicist described as "monotonous clumps of puny bushes," the San Diego
fair was "one vast botanical garden, [with] the finest, rarest specimens of
plant life growing and thriving in the open air." Publicity called visitors
to "the land of the orange and the olive; the land of flowers and sunshine
and joyous perpetual springtime. The land of delight." The orange and
the olive were products of Spain and the Mediterranean world, and the
profusion of plants on the fairgrounds added to the appearance of a
romantic paradise. To drive the point home, the PCEC arranged to have
young women hand out small bouquets to visitors on the Prado, a particularly effective technique in January and February.[54] If late nineteenth-
century observers believed Anglo-Americans should be wary of living in
a decadent land of "flowers and eternal summer," PCEC gardeners presented the region's floral bounty as theirs for the asking.

The planting was the most impressive aspect of the fair for many visitors. Those who found the architecture and themes less appealing than
advertised could not help marveling at the gardens. One correspondent
who scribbled her disappointment with the fair in general on the back of
a postcard conceded that "the grounds are beautiful." College president
M. Carey Thomas judged the "Spanish Renaissance *over* emphasized"
but believed "the planting . . . most lovely." Emily Post, whose overall
impression of the exposition was positive, reserved special adulation for
the greenery: "And how things did grow! Some of the buildings were
already covered to their roofs with vines, and benches shaded by shrubs
that we treasure at home in little pots!" Bertram Goodhue was one of the

few people who thought that the foliage was out of control. He complained about how thickly it covered his buildings: "[they] have hung tropical verdure over everything in a way I have never seen in Mexico or Spain."[55] Even Goodhue's grumbling testified to how successfully the fair presented Southern California as a land gifted by nature.

The lush garden owed less to the spontaneous gifts of nature than to a specific PCEC plan. Given that San Diego's annual rainfall measured less than ten inches, plants required intentional design and abundant watering to overgrow the exposition in the year or so of preparation. In the local trade journal *The Architect and Engineer,* one review admitted to significant intervention in natural processes. "By the liberal use of dynamite, by plowing and harrowing and incessant watering," the dry canyons have been made "to bloom into a succession of great gardens which probably have no peer in the country." Despite the desire to illustrate Southern California's natural fruitfulness, visitor-oriented publications also acknowledged human direction: "The riot of colors, the handiwork of God and man and the implicit confidence with which nature has responded to man's touch combine to make this spot a place of beauty."[56] The ability to make the desert bloom testified to the exposition's theme of human progress as well as its need for natural beauty.

A more direct display of the landscape undergoing transformation was the highly popular Model Farm exhibit. Jointly operated by several exhibitors, the Model Farm demonstrated the apparent affluence and ease of modern Southern California farm life. The seventeen-acre tract contained a fruit-bearing orchard, vegetable-laden garden, and grain-stocked field (see figure 11). While the Southern California Counties Commission sponsored the farm itself, International Harvester supplied the machinery in a display of its newest technology for mechanized farming. Visitors commended the company for not relegating the machines to an exhibit hall but showing them in action. Fair visitors gathered in great numbers to watch electric sheep shearing, compressed-air cow milking, and orchard pesticide spraying. A special theater showed government films on reclamation and agricultural projects, including *Romance of Irrigation.* A stereograph of the Harvester fields claimed that "by this exhibit it is hoped that the visitors will not alone see the lick it's done with but that they will also see an opportunity for themselves in doing the part that remains undone." Visitors were invited to test-drive tractors and try out the other farm equipment for fun. Commentators insisted that these machines and methods produced amazing results. One guidebook claimed that the combination of irrigation and

Figure 11. Citrus orchard, Model Farm, and view of exposition buildings, 1915. The model bungalow appears in the center of the image, while the tall tower and dome in the background on the right mark the California Building. Courtesy San Diego Historical Society.

scientific cultivation would yield a "riotous profusion," producing five times the crop as by "old style methods."[57] Modern methods removed farm drudgery and displayed Southern California rural life as the promised new Arcadia.

Whereas the fields at the Model Farm demonstrated the work of farming, the model ranch house aimed to show a more leisured lifestyle. The house, dubbed by many sources "a typical California bungalow," came furnished, landscaped, and fully equipped with modern appliances, including electric vacuum cleaners. The display became such a favorite that the Counties Commission developed blueprints to sell to visitors. Though, as built, the bungalow cost a startling four thousand dollars, publicity contended that "it isn't the picture farm of a wealthy man who goes to California to retire among formal gardens. It is intended to be a model for the man of moderate means, and it may be copied on a smaller scale by the farmer of less worldly substance." Nevertheless, the costly modern amenities were a significant part of the appeal for both men and women who dreamed of release from the onerous tasks of farm life.[58] The agricultural life that the exposition advertised was that of a contented family farmer, modern and affluent. The display dismissed the negative connotations of farm life—its hard work, isolation, and unpredictable fortunes—as alien to the Southern California landscape.

Mechanized farming, irrigation, and spectacular yields were bona fide aspects of California agriculture, but small family farms were hardly the norm. Instead, corporate agriculture controlled vast tracts of land, which were worked by a permanent, migratory, and largely non-white agricultural labor force. As opposed to the idealized life on the Model Farm, San Diego's real hinterland was the Imperial Valley, a low-lying area of the Colorado Desert. With extensive efforts to draw water from the Colorado River, including one giant mistake that resulted in the Salton Sea, the irrigated valley began to produce tremendous yields per acre and significant wealth for owners. By planting enormous tracts of land, using lots of water, and hiring untold numbers of workers to do the harvesting, growers produced impressive amounts of lettuce, grapefruit, cantaloupe, and cotton. At the time of the exposition, the valley was well on its way to becoming one of the richest and most productive agricultural areas in the United States. That part of the exposition rhetoric held true, but the Imperial Valley did not contain a million model farms. Rather, it typified a California system that people would later call industrial agriculture or "factories in the fields." Its laborers were a succession of American Indians and Japanese, Hindu, Filipino, and Chinese people and, by the 1920s, mostly Mexican immigrants, who often worked in excess of ten hours a day in temperatures that routinely exceeded one hundred degrees in the summer. Hired as seasonal workers at low wages, these men and women took the drudgery out of farming for Anglo growers.[59] The valley's name testified to its approach to farming: imperial.

If the oppressive conditions in Imperial Valley were not yet a fore-gone conclusion in 1915, the fair's advertisement that seven hundred thousand model farms would become reality in the Southwest proved woefully mistaken. Nevertheless, the exposition held out a popular vision. Visitor David Steele took from the Model Farm the impression that to "the man and woman who is [sic] weary of the smoke and grime and nervous tension of the city," the Model Farm "whispers the call of the land, a land of fertility and loveliness, of cheer and productivity." The San Diego Union did more than whisper in an exposition review article entitled "Virgin Soil Calls Willing Toilers Westward." San Diego, it claimed, invited people from played-out midwestern farms and congested cities. "The undeveloped land in San Diego County, many thousand acres, needs these families." Postcards sold at the fair included views not only of the Model Farm but of "San Diego's Back Country: Valleys of Orange, Grape and Olive." President Davidson echoed the call to "all who are tired of the futile grind of city life and who will turn to the West to work out the realization of their hopes and aspirations."[60] This rhetoric painted Southern California cities as exempt from the ills of eastern urbanization and explicitly drew upon established assumptions about the West as a way out, a land of redemption.

If Frederick Jackson Turner closed the frontier at the 1893 World's Columbian Exposition, San Diego threw it open again. But what did the San Diego exposition's focus on nature and agriculture have to do with Spain? On the surface, little connection existed. Few such allusions were made at the agricultural exhibits, in high contrast to the rest of the exposition, which dripped with Spanish romance. The relationship was oblique but evocative. The model farms and lush flower gardens reminded visitors of the legend of California as a new Arcadia. The rural abundance echoed the expansive Spanish idyll; together they beckoned people to the good life and vested the look of Southern California, urban and rural, with Spanish ambiance. Offering the glory of past Spanish conquests did more than provide a conveniently romantic idiom for the fair. Whether the fair's reference was to past explorers or new acres, it called present and future Southern California Anglos to complete an unfinished conquest, furthering growth and development of the region.

"MEMORIALS OF A VANISHED RACE"

In striking juxtaposition to the Model Farm stood the Painted Desert, an extensive display of several hundred living members of southwestern Indian tribes, their dwellings, and crafts. The PCEC drew explicit comparisons between these two exhibits and classed them into two contrasting paradigms: "There are shown the primitive agricultural methods—just over a cedar post stockade from the tract where the methods of the white man are being shown. There is a little sermon in that." If the Model Farm pointed the way toward modern development of the Southwest, then the Painted Desert displayed its antithesis, the squandering of resources and ignoring of opportunities. The exposition arranged a series of such instructional pairings intended to highlight Anglos' regional accomplishments. Commentators and visitors used the presence of Indians on the grounds, whether in flesh or bone, as a clear vantage point from which to measure Anglo progress. Native people thus became a central object of the fair's nostalgic and imperialistic celebrations, the "little sermon" writ large.[61]

Indian displays at American expositions had become something of a tradition after the P. T. Barnum–controlled exhibits in New York's 1853 fair, although they were not so routine as to be any less popular. While early expositions typically presented Indians as dangerous and savage, later fairs like San Diego's tended to show them as docile and colorful. In the forty years that distanced the 1876 Centennial at Philadelphia from the 1915 fairs, the Indians suffered their final military defeats, removal to reservations, intensive scientific study both through anthropological observers and archaeological excavations, and increasing tourist interest.[62] Thus the purpose of display shifted subtly from proving that the Indian threat was swiftly vanishing to showing the pacified Indian as a cultural artifact, not a political force. Rendered nonthreatening, native people appeared in many white American imaginations as ideal primitives.[63] The Panama-California Exposition straddled the ideological divide between the violent, vanishing primitive and the pacified primitive and cleaved its native exhibits along these lines. The Painted Desert, a Santa Fe Railway/Fred Harvey Company exhibit, invoked the emergent tourist view of Indian culture as picturesque, giving visitors the opportunity to watch Indian people in performances and to purchase their crafts. Adopting an alternative approach, the Smithsonian Institution sponsored extensive anthropological and archaeological displays that placed skulls, facial casts, and wax figures in "habitat groups" on view, adding evidence to the belief that Indian people were largely dead and gone. Together, these displays invested the Southwest in a wider cultural narrative of racialized human progress.

The San Diego fair featured the science of anthropology prominently, as if to corroborate the ascendance of human civilization in the Southwest. The PCEC early on announced its intention to make the "science of man" a highlight at the fair, proposing to trace human evolution via archaeology, anthropology, and ethnology. In an early publicity report, Charles Lummis predicted that the exposition would "show the origin and growth of every human industry to date; the growth of Man in the New World from savagery to highest civilization." In this sense, the exposition's presentation of human and racial evolution aligned neatly with its hopes to raise the region to the apex of national progress. Again, the focus on human science was not necessarily unique; most world's fairs, including the 1893 World's Columbian Exposition and San Francisco's concurrent Panama-Pacific Exposition, contained anthropology departments. Yet the PCEC sought to raise the stakes by making its "never-before attempted ethnological and archaeological exhibit" one of the fair's centerpieces. In hiring prominent anthropologist Edgar L. Hewett as director of exhibits for the entire fair, the PCEC signaled its intention to use the scientific display of human progress as one of its governing themes.[64]

The PCEC invited nationally renowned scientists to contribute to this project, particularly the Smithsonian Institution, whose imprimatur would give San Diego definitive scientific authority and an unmistakable link to a national enterprise. Hewett recommended that the PCEC offer a significant role to Aleš Hrdlička, a physical anthropologist at the Smithsonian. Hrdlička convinced his Smithsonian superiors that mounting an exhibit at the Panama-California Exposition would advance and popularize anthropological study. PCEC funding provided an opportunity to add "highly desirable skeletal material from regions and races which are but poorly or not at all represented in our [Smithsonian] collections."[65] Thus the San Diego fair could claim, by contributing directly to national repositories, that it was more than a marginal outpost of the United States. A major focus of Hrdlička's plan was to discover where American Indian peoples had come from and to demonstrate their racial origins; these questions were important subjects in American anthropological research of the day. If he could present physical evidence to solve this evolutionary puzzle, he might make a significant anthropological statement at the fair, and PCEC leaders certainly hoped this vision would materialize. In the years between his 1912 contract and the 1915 opening of the fair, Hrdlička and his associates conducted acquisitive expeditions in Alaska, Siberia, China, Tibet, Peru, eastern Europe, Ukraine, Mongolia, and Africa. They found and exported a large number of skulls (218 from Mongolia alone) and other bones for use in the exhibit. Despite some difficulties in extracting these remains, Hrdlička pronounced to his superiors later in 1912 that he had discovered "conclusive evidence" of the origins of American Indian races in eastern Asia.[66] A decade before the Scopes trial, Hrdlička's exhibits of evolutionary evidence were likely to attract significant scientific and popular attention.

The PCEC gave Hrdlička space to array his proof in the California Building, one of Goodhue's signature buildings at the fair. Director-General D. C. Collier explained in a letter to the Smithsonian that this placement would draw particular attention to Hrdlička's exhibits, which would link American Indians with the display of native peoples around the world. Here Hrdlička was to show "the development of the species from lower animal forms, . . . [and] the great epoch-making steps in human progress." The "exhaustive exhibits of . . . the native race of America" would serve as benchmarks to measure both trends.[67] Perhaps visitors were surprised that the California Building contained no display of California products. Instead, a stereograph caption informed visitors, "It enshrines the memorials of a vanished race. Its architecture is befitting the theme . . . [for] here are seen the most important works of a civilization that rose, came to the zenith of its power, and fell just at the time of the appearance of the old world visitors."[68] The relation of the building and its contents could hardly go unnoticed. The murals under the main dome depicted the European discovery of America and the conquest of the West in glorious terms, while below sat the skeletal remains of the continent's original inhabitants. Under one roof, art and science repeated the same messages of regional history, national advancement, and racial succession.

Hrdlička's exhibits covered five large sequential exhibit rooms, and as visitors proceeded through the rooms, they found "proof" of a natural hierarchy. The first room contained a library of journals and seminal books, portraits of eminent scientists, field equipment, and a laboratory, providing evidence of the authority of science that would legitimize the information to come. The exhibit in room two, *Remains of Ancient Man,* included skeletons of early humans and other primates to demonstrate the theory of evolution and present Hrdlička's evidence for American Indians' origin in Asia. Room three proposed to survey the "life cycle of present man, from ovum to most advanced senility." It did so, however, by comparing a wide variety of people along racial lines, using sculpted plaster busts to represent the physical types of each race at various ages. Hrdlička concentrated here on "the three principal races of this country, namely, the 'thoroughbred' white American,' (at least three generations on each parental side), the Indian, and the full-blood American negro*[sic].*"[69] Culminating in the last two rooms, the exhibit sought to explain the reasons for this racial diversity. Here Hrdlička grouped all humanity again into three main races—white, yellow-brown, and black—each including numerous subgroups. The key feature was a series of skulls representing these subraces. By measuring cranial capacity, an erroneous signifier of intellectual ability that some scientists ascribed to in the nineteenth century, Hrdlička grouped the skulls along an evolutionary racial scale from primitive (black and yellow-brown) to advanced (white). Hrdlička's impressive collection of skulls appeared to reveal a hierarchy of unprecedented detail.

The skulls gained the publicity Hrdlička had hoped for. The *Union* produced a feature on the collection in the spring of 1915, calling it "an exhibit of the most intense human interest." Many of the skulls contained evidence of deliberate cranial surgery, a sight the newspaper called "savage." Commentary on this practice raised old assumptions about Indian violence, bringing to mind the potent cultural image of scalping (with which it had nothing to do) rather than attempts at lifesaving medicine. Visitors' reactions to this exhibit were difficult to gauge, though many people saw it. One guidebook author indicated that perhaps visitors did not know quite what to make of all the skulls when he called it "horrible but interesting."[70] Nonetheless, the repetitive viewing of skulls must have created a consistent impression that Indians were vanished and gone.

If the skulls themselves did not make abundantly clear the implications of this understanding of racial order and evolutionary progress, commentators were ready to explain. A biology professor at San Diego State Normal School wrote an article for the *Union* in hopes of guiding visitors' experience in the anthropology exhibits. He believed that Hrdlička had proved the theory of human evolution and that his readers would agree if they followed the exhibit carefully. The lessons he hoped they would draw, however, were as much social as scientific. If enough people acknowledged the truth of evolution, he argued, "Man will strive more and more to control the forces of nature and make them work for his lasting welfare. There will be an enlightened program favoring courageously the survival of the fittest human beings." Hrdlička would likely have agreed. Interested in eugenics, or as he said, "man's evolution in the future, with its possible regulation or control," Hrdlička structured his exhibits to adhere to such plans. The leap from evolutionary theory to social Darwinism (and even eugenics) was one that expositions of the period encouraged. Studies like Hrdlička's and their popular interpretation placed all other races "hopelessly behind the white man" as crainiometry appeared to offer scientific proof of a natural hierarchy.[71]

The message in San Diego, however, did not so much focus on the spectrum of races as seek to categorize Indian people specifically in a racial system. In discovering Indian origins in Asia, Hrdlička added the other races for comparison and as elaboration on the evolutionary lesson. The interpretation of his results thus placed Indian people on a lower stratum of the evolutionary chart than the later, European arrivals in the New World. Though this interpretation had been largely unquestioned in several centuries of European expansion, translating the religious or cultural understanding of racial separation into the new science of man was significant, even if evolutionary theory remained controversial. The scientific language and the authority of important institutions lent the belief in racial succession a measure of legitimacy beyond that in the narratives that tourists constructed on El Camino Real. If both narratives grew out of intuition more than scientific method, as we define it today, the professional apparatus at the fair, like the model anthropologist's laboratory, endorsed the region's racial chronology. Moreover, while the display of Indian skulls echoed familiar narratives of the vanishing race, the interpretive scaffolding also gave credence to belief in an essential Indian primitivism.

"SO PRIMITIVE . . . YET SO PICTURESQUE"

Though the anthropological work of scientific validation could be found throughout the fairgrounds, the exposition's most popular Indian exhibit sat near its outer reaches. Sponsored, built, and advertised by the Atchison, Topeka and Santa Fe Railway, the ten-acre Painted Desert contained buildings resembling the pueblos at Taos and Zuni along with Navajo hogans, Apache teepees, the Trading Post—where fair visitors could purchase curios and souvenirs—and a resident population of some three hundred southwestern Indian people. Though the Painted Desert display was theoretically an entertainment concession, PCEC designers saw it as an extension of their work elsewhere. Hewett proclaimed that "no one should miss the Painted Desert. . . . Here the Indians are at work at their usual occupations, some making pottery, others designing silverware, and still others weaving baskets." The Painted Desert was the focal point of the fair's Indian display. Its peopled landscape gave life to the skulls and evolutionary charts in other exhibits, demonstrating the evolutionary order in action. According to Hector Alliot, chief curator of Charles Lummis's Southwest Museum in Los Angeles, the living Indians animated the science for the "throngs of visitors, delighted with the inspiring sight of 'live Ethnology.'"[72]

To reach the Painted Desert, visitors had to leave the world of Bertram Goodhue's grand buildings on the Prado and pass through a jumbled amusement midway—the Isthmus.[73] Like all American fairs since the Chicago exposition, the Panama-California divided its grounds between the educational and the entertaining, the beautiful and the bizarre. The Prado was civilized, stately, orderly, and gleaming white;

the Isthmus was a dense jumble of thrills that associated eroticism, drugs, violence, backwardness, motion, noise, and quaintness with non-white people. It was like an ethnic bazaar in which exoticism became a commodity and visitors became strolling shoppers. PCEC planners intended the Isthmus to be "weird, fantastic *and* instructive," and they succeeded.[74] The Isthmus housed several notable ethnic-oriented concessions, including the morally suspect Sultan's Harem. At the Underground World, ten cents allowed visitors passage into a Chinese opium parlor, where they were enticed to "take a slumming trip through the underworld with competent guides, who will explain in detail life of the underworld showing opium and gambling dens in full operation, torture and white slave dens."[75] The most unusual display was the War of the Worlds, a multimedia extravaganza depicting destruction of New York City by an alliance of African and Asian armies in the year 2000. An advertisement billed the cyclorama as "A thrilling thirty-minute performance on the largest stage in all the world. . . . Magnificent Scenic Spectacle is the only one ever constructed depicting air ships and aeroplanes in realistic combat."[76] The Isthmus attractions offered a strange brew of Anglos' ethnic fears and fascinations. Whatever educational value promoters attributed to the Painted Desert, it lay at the northern end of the "hilarious world" of Isthmus entertainments that visitors had to navigate to get there.

The Painted Desert, as a commercial concession, fit in with the ambiance of the Isthmus. The Santa Fe Railway and its promotional partner, the Fred Harvey Company, designed the Painted Desert as a tourist experience, a prequel to a southwestern vacation. This type of exhibit was not new to the Santa Fe, which had participated in world's fairs since 1893, when it launched its plan to increase tourist traffic at destinations along its route. The Harvey Company spearheaded this project and set out to create a southwestern tour that was exciting and safely luxurious, not dissimilar from boosters' plans for Southern California. The Harvey Houses at the Santa Fe's railway stations in the Southwest became oases, offering a predictable American menu served by an impeccably uniformed all-white waitstaff of Harvey Girls. Meanwhile, Harvey's writers, photographers, and traders recast the region's climate and culture—the desert and its Indian inhabitants—as the setting for grand adventure, picturing the region as a land of enchantment where happy artistic natives played at primitive life. Without venturing more than a few steps from the train, a visitor could buy handcrafts from a Harvey Indian employee at the railway's Hopi House and then stay at one of a chain of deluxe hotels styled in a sumptuous conception of Indian rustic. Countless visitors and consumers found their Santa Fe/Harvey-led encounters with the exotic Southwest to be unique, transcendent experiences.[77]

By offering fair visitors this vacation in miniature, the railway hoped that the Painted Desert would entice new fare-paying tourists. The railway instructed its ticket agents to stick to just such a formula: "The most unique scene along the Isthmus is the Painted Desert Exhibit of the Santa Fe. . . . Remember that the Santa Fe itself runs through an enchanted land, with its Grand Canyon, its Pueblo Indians, its Petrified Forest."[78] In an early proposal for the Panama-California Exposition, Harvey designers predicted that Pueblos would be a good draw. "In no other portion of North America are tribes to be found at present so primitive in both life and thought, yet so picturesque." The Harvey Company had done so much work already to publicize Pueblo peoples as picturesque that even for a California-focused fair, these groups seemed to be a more logical choice than mission Indians. The initial schema called for tribes to live in individual villages following the same geography as the rail route, with a miniature railway taking visitors around the grounds. As the budget escalated to several hundred thousand dollars, the Santa Fe scaled back its plans. The designers concentrated instead on trying to make the most authentic, or rather the most primitive, representation possible. "The houses would be furnished as they were in ancient times and the Indians would be in ancient costume. Characteristic native vegetation would be planted about the houses and a true picture of ancient Indian life re-constructed even to the native Indian dogs." Besides providing pets, the railway brought in old fence posts, yucca plants, and chili strings and worked to conceal modern necessities such as electric lights.[79] The Santa Fe wanted to make every detail of the Painted Desert conform to visitors' expectations of "real" Indian life.

Harvey Company designers made their living presenting "authentic" experiences of the Southwest to the touring public. Tourists took trips like those on the Santa Fe Railway in part because of a common desire to encounter places and moments that appeared to transcend the everyday world and transport them into past realms and primitive cultures. As the Santa Fe perceived its customers' desires, authenticity and primitiveness were intimately related; the more primitive was a house, a basket, or a person, the more authentic people presumed it to be. Why white American tourists and consumers craved encounters with primitive authenticity during this era is a question scholars continue to contemplate.[80] Neither the PCEC nor the Harvey Company puzzled much about this question. For the one, providing an authentic experience highlighted the sermon of progress: If Indians were really primitive, then Anglos, in their visible divergence from Indian ways, must be really modern. For the other, it meant preserving a valuable commodity, indeed protecting its near monopoly on primitivist tourism in the Southwest. Harvey went to considerable lengths at its tour stops and at the Painted Desert to uphold its famed reputation for producing authenticity for visitors, offering "real" crafts, "real" buildings," and "real" Indians.

The Harvey proposal for the exposition recommended that Indian people work not just at the fair but on the construction crew; it suggested at least "two dozen Indians, representing the cream of the pueblo region" be sent ahead to build the exhibit. Harvey wanted these crew members not so much for their knowledge as for their authenticating presence: "The advertising plan of having Indians build the pueblo cannot be overestimated." The railway began to collect dividends on this plan even before the fair opened, when the arrival of several Pueblos in San Diego in the summer of 1914 caused a stir. The *Union* gave the Painted Desert free advance publicity when it reported that "San Diego will soon have an Indian band. Chief Florentine Martinez, who is building the Indian village on the exposition grounds for the Santa Fe railroad, received word today that fifteen more redskins from New Mexico will reach here within the next few days." The paper also extended an invitation to the Indians to make a public debut in the Fourth of July parade. The fact that "Indians themselves did the work of building" became a valuable publicity tool, legitimating the exposition's reproductions before they had even been built.[81]

Nevertheless, the railway hired a non-Indian employee, Jesse L. Nusbaum, a colleague of Hewett's at the Museum of New Mexico, to supervise construction.[82] A *Union* feature on the work in progress in August 1914 sketched out a scenario that symbolized public understanding of the relationship between Nusbaum and his Indian workers. The reporter claimed to witness a conversation between Nusbaum and Julian Martinez, member of the San Ildefonso pueblo and husband of a soon-to-be-famous potter. Nusbaum noted that the replica pueblo copied original features, including "doors without nails or hinges, ladders without joints or screws, rough edges, unfinished surfaces, crude lines, everything for outward appearance just as the modern workman would not do it and just as the Indian did." He then asked Martinez, "Am I right,

Julian? Beginning to look like home?" The article reported Martinez's reply this way: "the picturesque Julian, who speaks English to his friends, smiled an eager sensitive smile, and murmured: 'You bet.'" Despite this necessary Indian endorsement, the reporter concluded that "there can be no doubt about its human author, Nusbaum."[83] The image of Nusbaum instructing his Indian pupils in building their own homes resonated throughout the exhibit and out into the fair at large, once again suggesting that the new was saving the old; modern Anglos were preserving Indian culture.

In the eyes of the local press, Nusbaum's scientific credentials gave him access to the Indian mind and the ability to showcase it to the public. The *Union* described Nusbaum as one of "the white men who spend their lives in the Southwest and who know the manners and the very thoughts of the Indians . . . and who alone could direct the labors of their Indian workmen toward the best results." Another publicity article claimed that "it is difficult to tell which are the genuine relics and which are those created by the genius of the white man."[84] Nusbaum was more than willing to accept the accolades for successfully conjuring a sense of authenticity at his reproduction. On the back of a photograph he snapped during construction, which showed Indian laborers building the adobe structures, Nusbaum wrote, "Zuni pueblo for the Painted Desert built by Jesse L. Nusbaum. This is just a small part of the building I have put up so far."[85] Nowhere did he mention the workers in the photograph, who were clearly the ones building the pueblos. Nusbaum, and by extension the Santa Fe Railway, presented Indian people as the product of white expertise, installing himself as the authority on Indian authenticity.

However, Nusbaum could not look authentically Indian. For that contribution, the railway planned to bring in dozens of families and craftspeople to live and work at the Painted Desert throughout the exposition. The proposal stated that only "real Indians" would do. "The villages would be inhabited during the Exposition by small groups of carefully selected Indians, typical and representative, and versed in making articles prized and sought by whites. The sale of such articles would be large and the profit sufficient to defray the expense of bringing the Indians and maintaining them while there." The Santa Fe Railway could carefully select these Indians from its own cadre of employees and craft sellers. Craft sales were important, not only for the Santa Fe's revenue but also as part of the tourist experience. The Harvey Company promoted the consumption of Indian goods, whether handmade baskets

Figure 12. Swarm of tourists at the Painted Desert, 1915. Courtesy Seaver
Center for Western History Research, Los Angeles County Museum of
Natural History.

and blankets or mass-produced postcards and souvenir booklets, as an
integral part of a southwestern vacation. For this reason, the proposal's
suggestion to exhibit Indian people as they were "before coming into
contact with the civilization of the white man" fell by the wayside.
Crafts produced on-site were not to be shown in traditional uses; rather,
Indians "will be seen bringing their wares into the trading post to
exchange them for food and white man's clothing."[86] The Indian
employees who lived at the Painted Desert display thus added to the picture of authenticity that the Santa Fe had created, even if they engaged
in activities that elsewhere might have been judged inauthentic. The
simple fact that an item was "handmade by an American Indian," as
product labels often advertised, obscured the producer's position in a
modern economic nexus.[87]

After paying the twenty-five-cent admission, visitors entered the
Painted Desert, where they encountered a scene of crafts, adobe, and
people (see figure 12). Directly in front of the entrance were twin pueblos, one resembling Zuni and the other, Taos. Across the grounds, visitors
might trip over ladders leading into underground kivas, beehive-shaped
ovens, and broken wooden carts strewn about for artistic effect. To one
side sat several craft areas, hearths for firing pottery, and the Trading
Post. Behind the pueblos were encampments of the "nomadic tribes"
and a plaster model dubbed the Cliff Dwelling. Beside willow-branch
homes and huts, Navajo and Apache artisans worked at looms and
fashioned silver. The scene was, the *Union* proclaimed, "the most
impressive display of Southwestern Indian life" ever produced.[88]

Visitors seemed to agree. Tourist David Steele marveled at how the Painted Desert managed to include "all that was native to the old Southwest, of Indian, Adobe, even Cliff-Dweller, Antiquarian and Prehistoric." Emily Post's visit to the "Indian Village" was one of only two Isthmus attractions she paid to see, the other being the scale model of the Panama Canal. She too found the display quite comprehensive.[89]

Guides told visitors that the scene they were seeing was real. In response to skeptical tourists' questions about why Indian people would agree to take part in such a display, guides responded that the Indians "are not idle and are not in white man's clothes, but are living just as they have lived and their ancestors have lived for centuries." Far from presenting the Painted Desert as a performance, railroad advertisements suggested that the exhibit was "a section of Indian life lifted out of its own environment and set down in modern surroundings. You seem really to be looking at a bit of the Southwest enchanted land, with its high coloring, old houses and strange peoples." The Santa Fe concluded by indulging in a bit of self-congratulation: "The illusion is perfect." So well had the railway achieved its illusion of authenticity, in fact, that most commentaries announced that the Indians believed it too. The PCEC publicity director likened the Painted Desert to an "open reservation," where native people did not produce the illusion but rather lived within it, apparently oblivious to the change of venue. Visitor E. L. Hubbard wrote that the exhibit contained "actual living Indians, as here revealed in houses, homes, gardens, kivas and the manifold duties of these Children of the Desert played out in unconscious manner right before our eyes."[90] While many visitors surely understood that the railway's creation was a temporary display for their benefit, they still recognized it as a chance to peer through a window into real Indian life.

Commentators often observed that the Indians themselves could not alone have built the replica since they could neither recall their own history nor conceive of the passage of time. PCEC publicity writer Mark Watson declared that the railway had to complete extensive scientific research to reproduce the ancient habitats because the Indians themselves had forgotten how. "Perhaps a fair estimate of the difficulties under which the scientists labored can be drawn from the fact that the Indians themselves had not the slightest idea of the time which had elapsed." Nusbaum's goal was to repossess this lost time: "My job had been to seize the relic of time, to transport it, and this I did with their cooperation."[91] Time was a space in which Indian people could exist but not act. They could move within it but not beyond it. For the Anglo builders and visitors, Indians lived in the past as "their ancestors have lived" but were unaware that time had passed them by.

When native people did venture beyond the Painted Desert, fair visitors found their presence more difficult to interpret, though no less fascinating. Were they still primitives if they rode in cars? One of the most popular postcards at the fair was of blanket-shrouded Pueblo women riding in an "Electriquette." These electric wicker carts were available for fair visitors to rent and ride around the exposition grounds and were the only motorized vehicles allowed. Electriquettes were novelties of modern engineering, and for people who bought the postcard, the image of Pueblo Indians riding in them made for an amusing juxtaposition of the modern and the primitive. Such images brought Indians into the present for a brief moment, but only to show how incongruous they appeared in modern settings. The *Union* eagerly reported on the exploits of Painted Desert Indian employees on excursions around the city in similar tones. Describing one such trip in a motorcar, the newspaper related, "Chief Florentine was given his latest heart's desire yesterday afternoon and placed at the wheel of a speedy automobile. . . . The chief was an apt pupil and learned to operate the car without any accidents."[92] Only with uncomfortable laughter could the exposition explain Indians in automobiles.

Despite curiosity about such moments, the Harvey Company hired Indian people not to showcase their modernity but to represent a primitive past and package it for white consumption. Producing artifacts that visitors could easily purchase and display themselves was a key element of the Painted Desert, and indeed of any Santa Fe Indian project. The Santa Fe brought to San Diego skilled and professional craftspeople, including the later-renowned María Martinez, a Tewa potter from San Ildefonso whose use of glazed black ceramics both recovered a dormant traditional method and popularized it for a new audience. Despite Martinez's and other artisans' modern applications and sophisticated assessments of what would sell on the tourist market, the antiquity of these crafts was the major drawing card. The *Union* commented, for example, that "they [the artisans] are weaving rugs and blankets in the same designs that were made a thousand years ago." Visitors attended daily demonstrations of blanket weaving, pottery making, silver working, cloth embroidery, and bread baking. Guidebooks and postcards never failed to mention the craftspeople, to express admiration of their work, or to encourage numerous purchases. In fact, observers could hardly separate the artists from the objects they produced. Watson hinted that "should one care to buy a rug he can see it woven or he can see his pottery made or his bead waistcoat embroidered."[93] Indian artisans often appeared in descriptive texts only in reference to the objects they made. Painted Desert postcards and souvenirs typically pictured the Indians in the act of pounding silver, firing pottery, weaving blankets. The products and the practice of making them by hand verified the authenticity of the makers. The objects thus symbolized Indian culture more than the Indians themselves did, because one could verify the authenticity of the objects, purchase them, and take them home.[94]

Though the Painted Desert based its appeal on primitive authenticity, with Indian craft production as a centerpiece, it also relied on older ideologies, depicting both the crafts and their Indian producers as vanishing entities. To visitor E. L. Hubbard, the Painted Desert embodied "a civilization fast becoming but a memory of things that were." The prospect of extinction made the encounter with living representatives more enticing than it would have been otherwise. Yet while visitors might have believed in the trope of the vanishing race, they still had to confront the fact that Indians still existed. The Painted Desert, like other such representations of Indian people during the era, thus walked a narrow line of interpretation that some commentators have called "salvage ethnography." Though Indian individuals might physically remain, their traditional ways of life were disappearing and thus required preservation. The Painted Desert preserved an image of Indian culture that clung to a primitive past and did not allow for change. As the authors of the Painted Desert proposal counseled, "Now is the last time that such an exhibition of our Indians of the Southwest can ever be arranged. Only the older people remember the old life and ways, and every year priceless information is lost as these aged persons pass away one by one. . . . The rescuing of the customs of these Indians from oblivion will be an asset to the Santa Fe."[95] The Santa Fe positioned itself as the guardian of this vanishing culture; in fact, it was preserving only its own version of authentic Indian life.

The Painted Desert was popular for its living display of real Indian people who moved, danced, and made crafts. Yet it also owed its significance at the exposition to its relationship to the fair's other Indian figures in wax and bone. By presenting Indianness as an identity in decline, the Painted Desert thus harmonized with the scientific displays and the exposition as a whole. By using disappearing Indian culture as proof of progress in this explicitly regional fair, the exhibit also linked Southern California and the Southwest with similar narratives across the nation, where Indians providentially appeared to recede (or to surrender to pacification) before an advancing America. The Santa Fe used this popular myth as a lucrative tourist draw, advertising the exposition as a chance to witness the last gasp of an exotic culture before it vanished forever. Showcasing Pueblo people as ideal primitives may have seemed to slow their disappearance, rehabilitating their culture for white Americans' consumption, but it did so only to position the Indians forever on the threshold between modernity and oblivion. The exposition enabled its visitors to move back and forth through time, viewing Indian people in all stages of their evolution and presenting them as oddities amid modern technology, either living picturesquely on the Painted Desert or existing as preserved skulls in the California Building.

"THE PRETEND PUEBLO"

The two narratives, Indians as vanishing and Indians as primitive, formed a great deal of the fair's promotion of its native displays. Guidebooks, newspaper reports, and postcards minimized a third metaphor that we see in retrospect, that of the Indian as modern. The Pueblos in Electriquettes and Chief Florentine's driving lesson were features of the exposition experience (and its Indian display) as well. The insistence on Indian primitiveness created the white expectation that native people existed in modern time only as anachronisms. Their appearances outside the Painted Desert temporarily ruptured the belief that they did not share the time in which white Americans lived; interpreting those moments as incongruous ones soothed the breach in time. This view could not close the gap completely, however, because Indians' performance as primitives ironically necessitated their visibility in the modern white world. As Philip Deloria has noted, "stories of Indian modernity" trailed many such shows, from Buffalo Bill's Wild West on. "They appeared in images of Indians in the gondolas of Venice or playing Ping-Pong backstage. When Wild West Indians hopped into cars or learned to ride bicycles, the inextricable sameness of the Indian and white worlds reared an unexpected head."[96] Encountering Indian people seemingly offstage opened this third possibility, a conception of Indian-white relationships that looked beyond the rubric of primitivism, though that choice was unusual amid the rhetoric at the fair and in American culture.

But to imagine these narratives as entirely for Anglo purposes would, of course, be misleading. How did the Indian people who worked the Painted Desert describe their experiences in San Diego? If the first two storylines—of vanishing people and primitive people—dominated visitors' consciousness, the third focus on modernity moved to the forefront in Indian perspectives. Indians at the fair were aware of the stage on which they performed, and they communicated this understanding in ways both subtle and dramatic on the Painted Desert and beyond. If native people were not able to alter significantly the exposition's public narrative of regional empire and progress, their presence continually undermined the attempts to relegate Indians wholly and bodily to the past.

While fair planners led visitors to believe that the Painted Desert was a place where Indian people lived exactly as they might have lived in their pueblos and villages, Indians themselves likely experienced it as a place to work. Whatever viewers believed, it was not home. With Indians living apart from families and communities for extended periods (some stayed from the summer of 1914 through the end of the following year), homesickness and dissatisfaction were common, although the Painted Desert occasioned fewer such reports than previous world's fairs had. María Martinez later recalled that "one of the nicest fairs was San Diego" and that the large number of "families from San Ildefonso and the other pueblos" made the experience less isolating than it could have been. Still, the native people came to the exposition as performers and artisans. The Harvey Company endeavored to reproduce village life, with its dances, ceremonies, and crafts, as authentically as possible for visitors. The more the company strove for authenticity, the more it required Indians to perform. When Martinez called the exhibit the "pretend pueblo," she communicated her understanding that these performances did not represent Indian realities.[97]

In relation to Indians' regional population, the number of Indian people joining the Harvey troupe was small, and members of a given pueblo or tribe often divided over whether participation in this white cultural forum would aid or harm their people in the long run. This split was evident among those of San Ildefonso pueblo. Tuyo, a member who did not work at the fair, wrote to Charles Lummis in February 1915 to complain that "the old ladder that was at the Old Estufa in this village was stolen and it is supposed that some white 'rogue' with the help of some *mean* little Indian got away with it. . . . It is supposed it was shipped to some far off point maybe to the Exposition in California." The writer clearly had no sympathy for Harvey's attempt to make a more authentic pueblo by stealing artifacts that belonged to his San Ildefonso home. The exposition for him was a source of frustration.[98]

Nevertheless, as various scholars have shown in studying Indian performance in Wild West shows, some Indians had a number of good reasons to take these acting jobs. Not only did the work afford a rare opportunity to travel and a chance to interact with people outside of their communities, but performance also offered comparatively reasonable pay and an opening to display skills and arts that might communicate a more positive image of Indian cultures. For Indians who worked for the Harvey Company, travel and interaction with tourists might have been relatively common, but the prospect of extended employment in tourist businesses after the fair was another potential benefit. Moreover, enacting a contrived cultural image of themselves for a white audience may have been strange, but it was perhaps no less strange than living amid the shifting cultural contexts at home. For example, trying to explain the decision of Hunkpapa Sioux leader Sitting Bull to participate in Buffalo Bill's Wild West shows, scholars suggest that he obviously would have preferred the traditional hunting life of the Great Plains for which he fought. But when that life became no longer practicable under U.S. Army control, working in the show offered a rational alternative to remaining at Standing Rock reservation amid its hunger, poverty, and grief. While employment at the Painted Desert did not represent for Pueblo people the only option besides confinement by the American military, like the Wild West Show did for Sitting Bull, the rapid incursion of Anglo ranchers, traders, and tourists into Arizona and New Mexico in the early twentieth century had changed the region's political economy and affected Pueblos' life choices.[99] Their reasons for pursuing the show option had everything to do with the modern world.

Painted Desert builders and artisans revealed conflicted feelings about the work, but the economic opportunity the fair represented could not be denied. María Martinez wanted to go home early, as she did not particularly enjoy the work, least of all the daily pottery demonstrations for large crowds of onlookers (see figure 13). Nusbaum persuaded Martinez to stay by promising that the fair would build her fame and create a future market for her art. She decided to "stick it out" so that she could "get better known, . . . like advertising" for the future of her "pottery-making business." She would later recall fairs as not particularly enjoyable work but as good moneymaking opportunities, and she said that she "like[d] the tourists because they buy pottery." Reportedly, not only did she parlay her work at the fair into a sustaining career in clay, but she also used some of her earnings to purchase an automobile

Figure 13. María Martinez making pottery at the Painted Desert, 1915. Martinez is seated in the middle, shaping a pot. Courtesy San Diego Historical Society.

upon returning to New Mexico, a typical choice at the time for many Americans who found themselves with a little extra cash.[100]

For native participants without Martinez's budding renown, the Painted Desert's economic returns were more short-term. Dionicio Sanchez, a San Ildefonso worker who had come to help construct the pueblos, reportedly told the *Union* that he had to return home temporarily to help his father with the harvest and tend to an ill brother. Sanchez understood that his absence imposed difficulties on his family but admitted, "I don't want to go back, and I will come back here as soon as I can. We like it here."[101] Though the article neglected to state why Sanchez preferred staying at the fair and used his statement as evidence of the Painted Desert's authenticity, his desire to remain in San Diego likely spoke to the opportunity it represented. Hired at a meager hourly rate, like those working at Fred Harvey's Indian buildings along the railroad, Indian workers made most of their money from craft sales at the Trading Post. Harvey Company officials believed that such operations "amount[ed] to but a small sum . . . a negligible profit," and noted that admissions and "other concessions . . . will outsell Indians." The company wanted Indian craftspeople to do well at the fair but perhaps not so well as to venture out on their own. Nevertheless, both Nusbaum and exhibit director Hewett offered Painted Desert Indian workers additional exposition employment, as janitors for example, if at a lower rate than that of white employees.[102] As Dionicio Sanchez hinted, the work presented opportunities that were not easily found at home.

While Sanchez and Martinez may have appreciated this chance, Indian workers did not blindly accept the Harvey Company line. They negotiated their positions relative both to their employers and to visitors. While guidebooks insisted that the Indians were never "in white man's clothing," and all officially produced images showed them in traditional dress, hints exist that Harvey had a difficult time retaining control over their costumes. Indians did wear contemporary clothing and use modern amenities on the Painted Desert from time to time. Whether they did so out of protest or merely out of habit, supervisors had to be on the alert to manage the appearance of primitive authenticity. During a previous exhibit, one Harvey supervisor had had to remind his agents that the Hopi performers they hired "should wear their native costumes during the time they are at the exposition . . . [and] should *not* wear suspenders." In initial proposals for the San Diego fair, designers suggested that "Each Indian could be given a bare room to finish in the style most typical of his pueblo, and *with certain restrictions,* proceed with it as he thot [sic] best." The need for restrictions showed when critic Geddes Smith noticed steamer trunks and kitchen clocks inside the Indians' pseudoprimitive homes.[103] Suspenders and clocks posed problems for the impression of authenticity. Certainly these accouterments were not supposed to exist in the highly idealized and tightly controlled Santa Fe/Harvey vision of the native Southwest. Clearly, while hired Indian participants helped produce the image of traditional villages that the tourists came to see, they retained some control over their clothing and living quarters, despite the efforts of the company.

Moreover, Indian participants had their own methods of dealing with tourists. Martinez remembered that she and her fellow workers would listen carefully to the "many rude questions" and "funny things" the tourists would say out loud, assuming Indians did not understand English. Martinez recalled, "Indians pretended they did not understand what was said, and then they had something to laugh about when the white people had gone home and the Indians were alone on the fair grounds." More than laughing to themselves, however, they often played little jokes on the tourists. Martinez's husband, Julian, had fun with fairgoers' assumptions. When San Diego exhibit guides told their charges to speak to Julian because he spoke English, Julian would sometimes joke, "What you want to know, lady? Me heap big chief. Me know everything." In response to visitors' frequent inquiries about his marital status—especially whether both María and her sister Ramoncita were his wives, Julian always had a witty reply. Often he would answer yes; other times he would confuse visitors by saying that one was his wife and the other his grandmother. A few times he shocked his questioner, by replying, "Me no got no wife, lady. Me look for one. You marry with me, huh?" María's biographer claimed that she did not enjoy these encounters, though she clearly shared the joke and understood the aim to tease the "watchers." What she did not like, mostly, was having people watch her hands while she worked at her pottery. The tourist at the Painted Desert was, in the later words of Santa Clara potter and poet Nora Naranjo-Morse, *tse va ho,* "someone not afraid to stare." Visitors might have laughed at Julian, but they generally did not understand that the joke was on them.[104]

Not only did Indian people understand that they were performing, they took on the task of playing themselves. As Deloria has noted, there is a "long tradition of Indians playing Indians, a tradition with a certain bicultural sophistication and an array of meanings clustered around labor, adventure and conviviality." Clearly, Julian Martinez tapped into this tradition when he performed simultaneously for the benefit of a white audience and for the amusement of his Indian compatriots. Fair rhetoric, however, suggested that he and the other Indian workers were not acting but rather reenacting their traditional lives. In fact, whether on the Painted Desert or not, Indians were expected to continually perform their Indianness, to toe the authentic line. While all about them visitors moved and talked, Indian people were to sit and be Indian. This requirement indeed entailed great feats of performance and was perhaps the withering burden that so exasperated Julian's wife, María. Yet we should not assume that Indians were thus trapped by white representations. Deloria is right to warn scholars not "to mistake the rhetoric used in planning white cultural domination for the actual encounter, which proved far more complicated." Despite the constraints of white expectations and primitivist imagery at the Painted Desert, Indians found ways to shift the interpretive ground and even subtly to undermine it. Whether they meant certain actions to be political acts or not, their decisions to ride in Electriquettes, keep clocks in their quarters, or tease tourists implicitly challenged the social and cultural order.[105]

That historians have scant evidence to analyze Indian perspectives in these exchanges between performer and audience and between employee and employer is unsurprising given the situation in which Indian people found themselves. Their double entendres and modern presentations of self could hardly compete with the mass production of primitivist commentary about them. The Santa Fe Railway and the PCEC controlled the interpretation and distribution of Indian and Painted Desert images. In fact, the two bodies wrangled over which one of them would have ultimate jurisdiction. As a condition of participating in the fair, the railway insisted that it retain rights over the distribution of Indian images: "We have the right to sell our own pictures of Indians and scenes along the Santa Fe line and of our own exhibit, buildings, and Indians."[106] In the dispute between the two corporations, the possibility that perhaps native people might hold some ownership over their own images was never raised. In this context, Indian opportunities for self-presentation were limited.

Even visitors at times got a chance to represent Indianness. One summer evening at the fair featured an Indian Costume Carnival during which people in Indian dress were admitted free of charge. As the *Union* reported, "In place of light, airy summer costumes, Indian garb will predominate on the Isthmus tonight for the white people taking part in the Indian costume prize contest." The photographs of "pretty girls" in "Hiawatha costume" showed that a hodgepodge of feathered headdresses, deerskin frocks, and moccasins—vaguely resembling Plains Indian dress—counted as Indian garb in the contest. Fair promoters didn't insist on regional authenticity here and had no costume police—perhaps because Indian people were not allowed to enter the contest.[107] When whites played Indian, the performance was evident and the costume was obvious.

However authentic the Painted Desert appeared, no amount of promotional ink could make it Southern Californian. While the fair intended to display the Southwest at large, the emphasis on Southern California was strong everywhere except for the Indian displays. The slippage was significant. California tribes had representatives among Hrdlička's skulls, but no permanent living display of California Indians could be found on the fairgrounds. The Santa Fe Railway had originally planned to include a few Californians on the Painted Desert, including Mohave and mission Indians, but for unknown reasons, decided against adding what they derisively called "primitive Diegueños, . . . Naked desert Indians, [or], 'mountain rats' of the Mohave."[108] Santa Fe designers' decision to leave California out of their southwestern diorama left the overall impression that native people were already out of the picture in Southern California, part of its past. To see living Indians, one had to take the railway to the more remote climes of Arizona and New Mexico.

The one notable exception to this absence of California references came at the end of August, when the PCEC invited a number of Southern California tribes to hold their annual summer fiestas on the fairgrounds. Reportedly all the tribes in San Diego County agreed to take part, and more than two hundred mission Indians from the La Jolla, Los Conejos, Pauma, Rincon, and Pala reservations lived at the exposition for four days. This event represented a change of venue but continued by other means a traditional function of these fiestas, which was to promote cultural exchange between Indian bands from far away. The PCEC invited plenty of tourists as well, and many came to witness the scene that it advertised: "strange ceremonials, dances, and athletic games peculiar to the Indians." While this fiesta represented an opportunity for California Indians to demonstrate such traditions—such demonstrations were often heavily restricted on reservations—the event was not meant to be a static display of authenticity. The experiences of traveling some distance, learning new dances, and exchanging goods were traditional parts of fiestas. The customary exchange of culture and economic trade at fiestas had survived the onset of Anglo attendance and would likely continue at the fair. Moreover, it gave many native Californians a chance to visit the fairgrounds when they otherwise might not have been able to. During the fiesta, these local Indian people not only performed but also frequented the fair's concessions as visitors.[109]

The press negotiated the simultaneous primitive performance and modern presence of native Californians at the fiesta using a narrative of assimilation. Alongside advertisements of the quaint and exotic customs appeared affirmations of Indian conversions to "civilized ways." One report reversed the typical portrayal of California tribes, emphasizing instead that "the Mission Indians are neither gamblers nor drunkards and their morals are of a high standard." Another *Union* article praised the Pala Indians for "Forsak[ing] Chase for Quiet Farm Life; Kindness Makes Aborigines Thrifty Ranchers." Perhaps to strike a comparison with the display on the Painted Desert, the author asked about these representatives of the prudent Indian farmer: "his colors, his paint, blanket and arrows—where are they? He threw them aside with his bitterness and hatred for the white man." Instead, Indian people capitalized on a government-installed irrigation system and thus "so utilized their advantages that a desert place has been turned into a garden and a half-starved despondent people have been transformed into an industrious, energetic, independent, self-supporting tribe."[110] If Indian people had not disappeared from the California landscape, the reasoning went, then those who remained had ceased to act like Indians, instead joining Anglos in developing the land.

Clearly, the Painted Desert was indeed a pretend pueblo to the Indians who participated in the exposition. For María and Julian Martinez, it was a game of make-believe they played in hopes of increasing the market for their pottery. For Dionicio Sanchez and others, their San Diego sojourn was a hiatus from the pressures at home or a chance to earn money for other purposes. For Palas, the Painted Desert must have been as foreign as everything else at the fair, for pueblos bore no resemblance to their traditional dwellings. The existence of these Indian perspectives did not overturn the dominant Anglo-American understanding of the Indian as authentic, primitive, exotic, colorful, and soon to vanish. The high visibility of Indians at the exposition must have had an impact on visitors. Indians' ubiquitousness at the fairgrounds seemed to contradict the frequent refrain that they would soon perish from the earth. Perhaps the repeated insistence that Indians were vanishing was a response to the visible presence of Indian people. Southern California Anglos had to say that Indians were vanishing because in fact they were not.

CONCLUSION

Indian displays formed a crucial part of the Panama-California Exposition's overall themes of regional advertisement, booster ambitions, and Spanish magic. Like the juxtaposition of the Model Farm with the

Painted Desert, the presence of Indians was supposed to set the emphasis on progress in high relief. The exposition both affirmed Anglos' belief in their own racial success and encouraged them to keep the wheels of progress turning. The closer Indians appeared to get to the vanishing point, the greater seemed the Anglo advance. Indians would not vanish from Southern California or the Southwest; by 1915 their numbers were beginning to rebound, and they never abandoned the field to Anglo narrators of the region. In the imagining of Southern California's past after the exposition, however, they would drown in the adoration of all things Spanish. The Panama-California Exposition was the last venue during the era to feature Indians so prominently in its display of the region's history. Its argument that Indians had passed away into an increasingly distant history must have been persuasive for most Southern California Anglos. The idea that Anglo visitors took away from the fair was not the primacy of Indians in the region's past but the possibilities of using a Spanish idiom to express a regional identity. The clamor for Spanish design that followed the fair demonstrated that Anglos had found something meaningful in the theme. The exposition showed that a fanciful version of the Spanish past could convey sentiment and ambition, nostalgia and progress, region and empire.

Spanish style also seemed equipped to express the urban dreams at the center of exposition boosters' plans. As a catalyst for San Diego's growth, the exposition worked. Over three and one-half million visitors descended upon the city, and one long-time San Diego resident later recalled that the fair "really opened San Diego." By 1920 San Diego's population had risen to almost seventy-five thousand, and though the city still failed to close the gap with Los Angeles, it continued to expand beyond its one-horse-town origins and never lost its keen sense of rivalry.[111] In retrospect, the fair suggested that a "good-life" economy might pan out after all, if on a smaller scale than in Los Angeles. Though San Diego might never be as orderly or as important as boosters wished, its consistent orientation toward visitors continued to guide local politics. For Southern California Anglos, the fact that an artificial Spanish city helped build a real American one was a message they took to heart.

PCEC leaders wanted the exposition to advertise Southern California as a center of civilization, and the grandiose scale and European references of the Spanish past conveyed this theme in dramatic fashion. The Spanish past had come a long way since the pleadings of mission preservationists. Here was the Spanish legacy as imperial spectacle, designed to impress, spur growth and development, and inspire booster dreams.

Moreover, it raised the accompanying ethnic/national narrative to institutional status. As one commentator wrote, the fair dramatized the confrontation of "Latin" and "Saxon" people in which "the weaker was absorbed by the stronger, but with the passing of the weaker they left a legacy of their art and culture which the survivor has gladly possessed to beautify and decorate his own. We have received this tradition gladly; we have made of this romance the background of our own history."[112] The exposition clearly took possession of the region's past, celebrating both the Spanish era and its end. Conquest, even more at the fair than on El Camino Real, became a comfortable metaphor in which Anglos could imagine their role and purpose in the region. By building elaborate Spanish castles in service of American regional empire, the fair represented Anglo-American conquest as a mantle rightfully won and confidently worn.

Perhaps the theme of conquest seems commonplace by 1915 exposition standards, and the addition of a Spanish metaphor may seem unnecessary to making such a claim. Indeed, such invocations of progress and empire typified most world's fairs of the era. Both American and European hosts flaunted their new imperial triumphs and technological accomplishments, linking progress, national pride, and white racial superiority.[113] In fact, the very familiarity of this logic provided Southern California Anglos with an effective bridge to larger national stories; the Spanish metaphor brought the conquest home. The exposition made a new regional empire seem possible—limned in Spanish style and wrought of modern technology, population growth, racial hierarchy, urban harmony, and Anglo-American progress. Like the Pinkerton detectives in powder-blue costumes, the Spanish mode proved to be a malleable language for articulating both order and difference and arbitrating between past and present, primitive and modern, East and West, and Anglos and others. The fair's Spanish style had as much regional impact, architecturally and culturally, in the decades to come as it did upon the exposition grounds.

But for Southern California Anglos to make full use of this promising regional idiom, they had to figure out how to translate the monumental scale of the fair into everyday life. So far, the Spanish past had provided fodder for nostalgic reveries and imperial lessons, largely put on display for visitors. But even for boosters, the region was a place to live as well as an exotic place to visit. How would locals live with a Spanish look? How would Anglos inhabit the role of conqueror at home?

PART TWO

Living with the Past

CHAPTER 4

The Home

Rancho Santa Fe and Suburban Style

In 1924 Ramona and Zorro built a house in Rancho Santa Fe, a stylish planned suburb north of San Diego where Spanish-colonial architecture was the rule in both domestic and public buildings. Mary Pickford, who had performed the first screen version of Helen Hunt Jackson's heroine in D. W. Griffith's production of *Ramona* in 1910, and her famous husband, Douglas Fairbanks, who starred as the title swashbuckling Californio in *The Mark of Zorro* in 1920, made news with every move they made. Thus their announcement that they would set up a retreat called Rancho Zorro at Rancho Santa Fe was a publicity coup for the fledgling community. The arrival of Hollywood royalty at a time when stars' lifestyles were beginning to be noticed, emulated, and marketed lent the place an immediate cachet. Moreover, the stars' endorsement of the Spanish style could not have been more fitting. Where else could Ramona and Zorro live but in a Spanish-Californian mansion? If the 1915 Panama-California Exposition had demonstrated the possibilities and popularity of Spanish-colonial style to Southern Californians, Pickford and Fairbanks brought the style home.

Mary Pickford did more than move into a Spanish-style house. She became an advocate for the adoption of Spanish colonial as Southern California's emblematic architecture. Speaking to the Southern California chapter of the American Institute of Architects in November 1926, she argued that "the Spanish influence in California is one of the greatest charms our state possesses, a precious heritage second only to our

climate, . . . [I]t should be preserved in every way possible." For her
taste, the bricks and columns of eastern colonial forms had no place in
Southern California. Instead, she argued that Spanish architecture was
"ideal for the California home."[1] Pickford here entered into a brewing
architectural debate in 1920s Southern California. Since the 1915 San
Diego fair, architects had become obsessed with pinpointing a characteristic regional architecture. Despite widespread admiration of Bertram
Goodhue's imposing style at the Panama-California Exposition, architects
initially doubted its applicability to the home. In the decade after the
exposition, however, uncertainty about Spanish style disappeared.
Adaptations of Spanish-colonial style dominated the landscape by the
late 1920s, acclaimed as the quintessential built expression of Southern
California. The development of Rancho Santa Fe both grew out of this
pursuit of a logical regional style and became a defining moment in its
articulation. The community was, in Mary Pickford's words, a "show
place" both for the style and the region.

Pickford and Fairbanks could not have chosen a more telling spot to
build their hacienda in 1920s Southern California. The elite subdivision
of Rancho Santa Fe both pioneered and typified many suburban trends
in the era. The community's preplanned amenities, cost minimums, and
restrictions—both architectural and racial—were part of a development
vanguard. The specific dictate for Spanish-style architecture was quite new
and made Rancho Santa Fe distinctive, if not unique. Moreover, the
tract's developers, architects, advertisers, and residents delved into the
function as well as the form of Spanish-colonial style, seeking to transfer the feeling of the fair into everyday life. What meaning could one
draw from owning a piece of this regional myth? How would the Spanish past look as private property? Theirs was a new attempt to perma-
nently fuse the good life and the Spanish mood. Earlier venues had
hinted at such a possibility, but Rancho Santa Fe took the next step and
tried to transform Spanishness into a durable regional commodity.

Anglo residents found in Spanish style something more than an aesthetically pleasing style for a house. The style appeared to grant an
"imagined proprietorship" over the region as a whole, its history and
essence.[2] Southern California real estate traded heavily on the region's
look and ambiance; in seeking Spanish-style homes, many buyers sought
access to the Southern California lifestyle.[3] Spanish-colonial architecture became a superb conduit to that idealized good life. It personalized
the past, allowing Anglo homeowners to live their own Spanish
romances. Rancho Santa Fe's example, pitched to a self-conscious local

elite, including Hollywood stars, suggested that residents reenact the life of the Spanish dons for the modern age. Buyers responded to this opportunity to assume the role of ranchero, a life they envisioned as full of leisure, class privilege, and European flair. This drama of possession entailed refiguring racial rhetoric, particularly in the context of rising Mexican immigration and Mexicans' presence in the labor force. Though the task was not simple, linking Spanish architecture, the suburban good life, and racial hierarchy at Rancho Santa Fe produced a potent combination. Its perceived promise of regional ownership echoed throughout the community of Southern California Anglos.

"THE NEED OF A TRULY SOUTHERN CALIFORNIAN STYLE"

Rancho Santa Fe owed its hallmark suburban style to a corporate blunder. The Santa Fe Railway purchased the nine-thousand-acre tract in 1906 and planted it with a species of eucalyptus trees it believed would make good railroad ties. After cultivating several thousand acres, railway officials discovered that these trees twisted as they grew and produced wood unable to hold a spike. They were now in a quandary as to what to do with this large parcel of land, distant from both San Diego and Los Angeles (see map 4). Before the railway acquired the land, the area was known as Rancho San Dieguito and was used largely for stock ranching, originally by the family of Don Juan María Osuna. As the first alcalde (mayor) of San Diego, Osuna procured the land from the Mexican government in 1836. Unlike many of their neighbors, Osuna's heirs were able to secure title to the grant immediately following the Mexican-American War. But by the 1880s they too lost most of their land to Anglo squatters, debts, taxes, and default on high-interest mortgages. By 1906 family holdings had been reduced to about two hundred acres surrounding the original adobe home. The Santa Fe Railway reassembled the original grant by buying both the Osuna parcel and other San Dieguito lands owned by Anglo ranchers.[4] But stock ranching did not appeal to the railway as a good alternate use, and for a number of years the land sat idle.

In 1916 an ambitious local developer, Ed Fletcher, who had a keen eye for both real estate and water potential, convinced Santa Fe officials that they ought to subdivide the land for residences and intensive agriculture. Fletcher promised that with the development of water resources, this land might produce thousands of pounds per acre of valuable citrus fruit, all to be shipped by the Santa Fe Railway. Moreover, water would

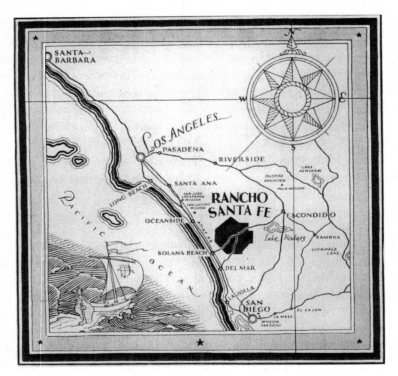

Map 4. Location of Rancho Santa Fe, ca. 1925. This map originally appeared in a promotional brochure, which suggested that the trip to Rancho Santa Fe from Los Angeles was an easy four-hour drive. The size of Rancho Santa Fe is somewhat exaggerated. The inclusion of mission locations and the Spanish galleon off the coastplay up the Spanish theme. Courtesy Burlington Northern Santa Fe Railway and Department of Special Collections, University Research Library, University of California, Los Angeles.

make possible the establishment of several towns along the currently vacant coast, providing a stable base of passengers.[5] The railway hired Fletcher and gave him five years to see if he could make the proposition pay. Fletcher oversaw the construction of a dam and reservoir and organized two irrigation districts. He leased parts of the tract to Chinese and Japanese farmers and directed them to prove the effectiveness of the land for cultivating fruits and vegetables, particularly high-profit items like avocados and oranges. Despite impressive harvests, these farmers' leases expired in early 1923, with renewal made difficult by California's recent Alien Land Laws. Fletcher envisioned the tract's ultimate development differently anyway, more along the lines of the

Panama-California Exposition's presentation of San Diego's backcountry as a landscape both productive and genteel—in Fletcher's words, "a place to live in comfort."[6] Such plans did not include Asian farmers.

As confident as Santa Fe officials and Fletcher were that this plan would pay off, the concept remained an experiment. The developers were following a relatively new path of residential development in the midst of a post–World War I recession that had depressed the building industry. Instead of platting empty lots and letting buyers create their own community ad hoc, developers began to make considerable preparations in landscaping and infrastructure. To better guarantee return on this investment, many developers included deed restrictions that would preserve the planned environment. The Santa Fe Land Improvement Company (SFLIC), which took over management of the tract for the railway from Fletcher, was at the forefront of this trend. Its planners debated not whether to restrict Rancho Santa Fe properties but only what kind and how many restrictions to attach to the deeds.

The SFLIC believed that many aspects of commercial and social life were in need of control. The SFLIC imposed minimum costs for structures and landscaping as well as prohibitions against a wide range of activities, from using service animals, building cemeteries or reform schools, and posting real-estate advertising to failing to pull weeds and allowing property to be "sold, occupied, let or held by any person other than one of the white or Caucasian race."[7] Most of these provisions were standard boilerplate for deed restrictions at the time. The SFLIC's plan differed from others in the extensive architectural control the company intended to hold over buyers. Owners had to submit plans for building their own homes to the Santa Fe Railway for approval. Surprisingly, buyers were eager to accept these abridgments of their property rights. Opened for initial sale in 1922, the Santa Fe development got in on the ground floor of a regionwide jump in residential-housing starts prompted by Southern California's suddenly booming population.[8]

The question that Santa Fe planners confronted, however, was what architectural style they should adopt for their new tract. Should they limit the area's architecture with a general aesthetic standard, or should they designate a mandatory style? The Santa Fe was not alone in pondering these questions. Architects, builders, and buyers in the region were actively considering similar issues. Local trade journals like *The Architect and Engineer* and deluxe monthly magazines like *California Southland* frequently discussed what Southern California's characteristic architectural style should be.[9] At the time that the SFLIC was planning Rancho Santa Fe, area architects would likely have given the company conflicting answers to this question. When architects looked at Southern California's built environment, they saw more stylistic problems than solutions. Many blamed the "shoe-merchants" who branched out into the business of "designer and builder" without professional training. Others found that the import of eastern architects, who were inattentive to local conditions, particularly climate, resulted in styles incongruous for the region. The editors of *California Southland* ridiculed amateurs and newcomers alike as "incompetent imitators" who "sell 'art-chee-tect-chure' by the yard."[10]

Goodhue's success notwithstanding, Spanish style had so far been no hedge against these miscarriages of design. At the turn of the century, enthusiasm had run high for so-called mission style. Spurred by Charles Lummis, among many, architects plumbed the mission era for models, borrowing historical references from local Franciscan buildings for commercial and residential structures.[11] The popularity of the mission style increased along with mission tourism. The style debuted on the national scene at the World's Columbian Exposition in 1893, where Northern California designer Arthur Page Brown collected the architectural flourishes of several missions in one elaborate California Building. But mission style never triumphed.[12] Many Southern California designers found missions to be limiting architectural templates. As Herbert Croly grumbled in 1913, attempts to "adopt the peculiarities of the Mission Style in the design of contemporary American houses have been almost wholly grievous in effect. The missions contained in their architecture much that was rudimentary and awkward and uninformed," though due less to the padres' ignorance than to lack of materials and skilled labor.[13] Moreover, missions' ecclesiastical origins made them difficult to adapt to residences and thus less useful for complex spaces than for spaces to hold large crowds, like railway stations. Though mission-style buildings never disappeared from the region, architects were less enthusiastic about the style on the eve of the San Diego fair than they had been two decades before.

In the meantime, several viable architectural alternatives to the mission style had appeared. The turn-of-the-century arts and crafts movement inspired numerous architects to create the so-called California or craftsman bungalow, done in a more lavish version by the Greene brothers of Pasadena. In the 1910s New England colonials and English cottages sprouted up all over Los Angeles County, making their claims on the region. A San Diego County example of this tradition was the

Stratford Inn at Del Mar, built in 1908 as an "Elizabethan type." A promotional brochure claimed that the inn's style was a good match for the region, "architecturally . . . unsurpassed in its suitability for the location." As late as 1926 at least one architect suggested that a French-country style, with rounded turrets, shake roofs, and shuttered windows could meet "the need of a truly southern California style which will take the traditions of early days, mix them with a due regard for climatic conditions and modern building materials, and make of this conglomerate a creation truly indigenous."[14] With little agreement, a wide variety of regional possibilities flourished. Croly's "The Country House in California" in *The Architectural Record* pictured craftsman bungalows, Greene & Greene houses, Italianate villas, and Greek revivals. *California Homes by California Architects,* published by *California Southland,* featured mission houses as well as gothic, English-country, colonial, and ranch styles. In 1916 leading Los Angeles architect Elmer Grey catalogued successful treatments of Spanish, Italian, French-chateau, Mexican, and Hopi-pueblo models. This observation led him to conclude that the only constant was stylistic fusion: "California seems to welcome to its fold the architectural styles of widely different countries, naturalizing them as her own, and perhaps it will be seen ultimately that her peculiar province is just thus to harmonize the styles of other climes and her own distinctive style to consist of beautifully welded hybrids."[15]

None of these examples or theories, however, matched the enormous regional impact of the Panama-California Exposition. Bertram Goodhue's Spanish-colonial style broadened the mission style and unlocked a global trove of historical references, drawn from Spain and Europe as well as Latin America. Though the fair did not end the debate, it did shift the weight of popular and architectural opinion back to the Spanish side. In 1920 *The Architectural Forum* proclaimed that Goodhue's design was "the greatest single factor influencing the present growth of good Spanish Colonial architecture in California."[16] Grey, already a devotee of the style, had come to the same conclusion a year earlier. In his exploration of the subject in *Architecture,* Grey declared it "Southern California's New Architecture." His remarks about its rising popularity give a sense of the impact of both the fair and the Spanish style.

Any one who should journey to southern California now after not having been there for a few years would . . . be struck with the latest development of style. . . . Especially during the last three or four years, many, if not most, of the important buildings built there have been done in what, for want of a better term, is called "Spanish." A similar tendency was, of course, noticeable prior to that time which had its beginnings in the inspiration of the missions; but it received a fresh, a different, and a much more powerful impetus with the designing of the World's Fair buildings at San Diego in Spanish Colonial.[17]

After the exposition, Grey explained, the "somewhat obscure characteristics" of Spanish architecture became "a definite and popular flame." Many architects agreed with him that the Spanish-colonial style, as Goodhue had demonstrated it, offered a regional architectural resolution.

How to apply Goodhue's stunning new Spanish style to less monumental buildings presented some difficulties. Translating the grandiose public buildings to private, everyday homes would not be a seamless process.[18] A few architectural critics judged the modernization of Spanish-colonial style to be disturbingly incongruous—the awkward designs of amateur builders. One architect called the use of Spanish style for otherwise thoroughly American houses "an architectural anachronism, Nordic invasion of the Mediterranean, Attila again in Rome." In even stronger words, an architect writing for the *Southland* suggested that adapting the Spanish style to diverse California tastes and adorning it with clashing elements like Japanese gardens, formal clipped hedges, and driveways was "Our Architectural Tragedy."[19] Goodhue had had the freedom to create an imaginary Spanish environment and did not have to concern himself with the practical matters that were necessary in living spaces. While designers were eager to follow in his footsteps, the problem of keeping Spanish architecture recognizable while converting it to modern uses was a perplexing one.

Doubters began to find themselves in the minority, as a number of key western architects decided to promote the Spanish style at least in part as a vehicle to raise their professional prestige. In this reasoning, the perceived difficulty of the style helped them make their case to the public about the value of hiring an architect. Spanish colonial was a new, unique, and complicated style. As locally renowned designer Arthur Benton had warned in 1911, "There have been many intelligent attempts to follow the Mission architects, but it is not an easy road for the modern designer. Sixteen-inch walls will not give the effect of six foot ones. Walls pierced by many windows will not have the repose of unbroken masses."[20] Benton himself could ably design in Spanish style, having designed one version of Frank Miller's Mission Inn (1907) in Riverside and later the Mission Playhouse in San Gabriel (1927). Many of his domestic commissions, conversely, resulted in craftsman bungalows. If even an accomplished architect like Benton showed reticence to design Spanish homes, how could the public trust the shoe merchants, contractors, or eastern-minded architects to produce successful examples? Local designers contended that Spanish style required the services of a local architect. By endorsing Spanish style as the quintessential Southern California style, many architects thus hoped to boost their own professional prospects.

With this goal, architects began to itemize the requisite ingredients of true Spanish-colonial style, though great variation existed. The red-tile roof was axiomatic, though it might appear in any color along a spectrum from light pink to burnt clay. Other oft-mentioned features included plain, light-colored walls of plaster, adobe, or stucco. Windows typically sat in deep insets with decorative metal grilles, wooden shutters, or the occasional adornment of narrow balconies. Ornamentation could be rich but usually remained confined to small areas; for example, ceramic-tile borders might set off generous areas of plain wall surface. Plans varied greatly, but a typical addition was a patio, either in the form of a Spanish-style interior courtyard or as an area to the rear or side of the house. Elmer Grey believed that the patio was a crucial element; in a tiled court, he wrote, "California becomes not alone a very beautiful part of our country, but one also redolent of romance, history and tradition." Taken together as the Spanish-colonial style, he claimed, these features were "the fundamental characteristics of the logical architectural style for the Pacific Southwest."[21]

As architects began to articulate their preference for the Spanish-colonial style and as their clients started to demand it, the style was dubbed the most appropriate one for the region. Advocates mustered several reasons to support this claim. The comparison of Southern California's climate with that of southern Spain and the Mediterranean struck a familiar and credible chord with Southern California Anglos. Moreover, this architectural style harmonized with the rising infatuation with the Spanish past, either in the form of mission nostalgia or in the kind of revelry suggested at the exposition. In 1921 *The Architect and Engineer* reported that clients were "enthusiastic . . . to return to the Old Spanish style of building, the pioneer architecture in California." In this view, Southern California Anglos who enjoyed touring El Camino Real would applaud the construction of a Spanish-colonial house on Coronado Island, where Grey believed Junípero Serra's first party had landed. In fact, he insisted, "none could be more fitting."[22] In this way, architects adapted not only the Spanish style but also the rhetoric of the romantic Spanish past to describe their own designs.

Depicting the Spanish style as appropriate for Southern California's climate and history, architects insisted that Anglos in the area had earned the style as a regional birthright. As *California Southland* commentator Mabel Seares explained, "California has a very rich inheritance. Selected by the hard test of a pioneer transcontinental journey, her people are the descendants of a virile race. Swept over by the adventurous and imaginative conquestadores *[sic]* of Spain, the land has traditions of great value which make the building of all Europe our storehouse."[23] Architects forged a new and significant regional link to the European past, not to mention an almost organic connection between the old Spanish land and the American people who now possessed it. If architects could implant Spanish architecture on the landscape, they could underwrite a far-reaching statement of the Spanish past. Beyond building Spanish-colonial houses, they used the rationale of an appropriate legacy and a rightful romance and thus further identified the region as the natural home of Spanish style. This position was a more insistently local claim than most of those made at earlier venues. It boosted Southern California architects and targeted Southern California buyers, promising ownership of Spanish memories on a more immediate and personal level than tourists, even local ones, could achieve on El Camino Real or at the Panama-California Exposition.

"THE SIMPLICITY AND CHARM OF A SPANISH VILLAGE"

Developers planning Rancho Santa Fe undoubtedly listened in on these architectural debates. When in 1921 the SFLIC had to decide which architectural style to mandate at the tract, it cast its lot with the designers favoring the Spanish-colonial style. Yet the planners faced a practical problem: how to translate this rhetoric into a suburban community they could sell. Their goals outstripped those of the architects, as they sought to make the Spanish look more than a style for houses but the theme for a total home environment. The SFLIC chose one of the few local architects who had experience in animating such a theme. Richard S. Requa and his firm, Requa and Jackson, were leading proponents of the Spanish-colonial style in San Diego. Santa Fe planners admired Requa's success in Ojai, a small town in Ventura County. Requa gave Ojai's main business block a Spanish-colonial facelift in 1919 and continued to supervise plans for new building, which had to adhere to form.[24] Here as elsewhere, Requa incorporated European examples in his design and believed that all architects should take extended study trips to Europe. In fact, European travel was one of the key catalysts for the development of the Spanish style in California. World War I hampered the architectural grand tour, but the end of hostilities brought about a renewed round of pilgrimages and publications.[25] Together, Requa's European experience and local corpus made him a leading choice of the SFLIC.

Requa authored two significant records of his architectural travels during the early 1920s: *Architectural Details of Spain and the Mediterranean* in 1926 and *Old World Inspiration for American Architecture* in 1929. The books reproduced hundreds of his photographs from around the Mediterranean—from France and Italy to Algeria, Gibraltar, Morocco, and North Africa, but overwhelmingly from Spain.[26] Though the SFLIC did not have access to Requa's publications at the time, the volumes offer insight into his approach to Spanish style, one that the SFLIC must have liked. Requa used his photographs as evidence for the Spanish colonial's regional appropriateness. In *Architectural Details,* he expressed hope that the images might prove useful "in developing a logical and appropriate style of architecture for California and the Pacific Southwest." In justifying his itinerary and the fact that more than three-quarters of the included plates were from the Iberian peninsula, Requa agued that Spain, more than other Mediterranean countries, held the greatest interest for Californians because "southwestern America was discovered, explored, and settled by adventurers and missionaries from southern Spain."[27] Like so many of his colleagues, Requa relied upon history to explain the style's regional appropriateness.

Perhaps the SFLIC also found his emphasis on the humbler forms of Spanish architecture appealing for home building. Requa explicitly distanced his style from Goodhue's, whose extravagant and monumental designs might have served for an exposition but, as Requa claimed, presented problems for domestic applications. Requa hoped to show that plain villages provided more worthy and useful styles to modify for American domestic uses than did castles and cathedrals "concocted during the florid, decadent period." As plate after plate in his books demonstrated, he preferred "the simple, even primitive structures which best exemplify the character of the people. . . . It is this honest, naive simplicity that gives those interesting old buildings their real charm and merit." Requa did not stand alone in this claim; several European-traveled designers suggested a similar approach. Randolph Sexton, author of a competing architectural guide to Spanish style, argued that "the peasant dwelling or farmhouse of Spain offers perhaps the most for adaptation to American needs. Its chief character lies in a pleasing combination of simplicity and dignity."[28] Requa and his cohort hoped that by mediating between the awkwardness of the missions and the grandiosity of the exposition, these simple house models would be more profitable prototypes.

Yet Requa's resolution imposed its own dilemmas. How does one design homes for wealthy Americans based on peasant models? This question becomes even more pressing when, as Requa suggested, these humble homes become modern, using new materials and sporting the latest appliances. He suggested in *The Architect and Engineer* that "if we of Southern California are to develop a real architectural style, that will be vital and satisfying and live through the coming generations, we . . . should look to the Mediterranean for inspiration, suggestions and ideas, but our buildings should express in their design and treatment the spirit of the Twentieth century." Neither Requa nor others who promoted this amalgamation appeared to notice the irony in this idea. Not only were these peasant houses to serve as models for grand residences at places like Rancho Santa Fe, but they also were the product of the very amateur builders that architects elsewhere scorned for ruining good design. One local architect praised peasant designers for their very lack of training in the pages of the *California Southland,* a principal lobbyist for professional architects. Peasants, this author claimed, "have never tried to solve the complex problems with which we are confronted today and for that matter the utter simplicity of their plans is refreshing. The simplicity of plan, combined with an understanding of the possibilities of a warmer climate, a judicious use of whitewashed walls, tile roofs, and natural planting are perhaps the greatest lessons we can learn from these peasant people of Spain."[29] Despite the rhetorical inconsistencies, Requa remained confident in his ability to marry peasant and professional, primitive and modern, in a happy union of stucco and tile.

In the end, however, Requa did not have to grapple with this self-imposed predicament at Rancho Santa Fe. Though Requa and Jackson accepted the contract the SFLIC tendered in 1922, the commitment of time, with construction stretching out for years, and the distance from the firm's downtown San Diego offices, made the commission difficult to fulfill while maintaining other projects. After sketching initial design concepts, Requa assigned the entire project to a young associate, Lilian Rice.[30] The assignment was a significant opportunity for Rice, whose single-minded devotion to the project and eagerness to establish her reputation made up for any lack of experience. Rice may not have been as well-known as Requa, but she came with some impressive credentials. Native to Southern California, she was among the first and very few women to graduate from the University of California, Berkeley's School of Architecture, earning her degree in 1910. Though for her sex, Rice's accomplishments were exceptional, her stylistic development was typical of the era. Major influences at Berkeley included such well-known figures as university architect John Galen Howard and the Bay Area designer Bernard Maybeck. Upon her return to San Diego, she worked with Hazel Waterman and Irving Gill and studied Goodhue's exposition buildings firsthand.[31] Hired at Requa and Jackson in 1921, she traveled to Spain at the firm's expense in preparation for the Rancho Santa Fe job. Requa gave her the task of studying small-town and village arrangements. She returned with detailed designs for the village center: Spanish buildings with tile roofs, colonnades with deeply shaded walkways, homes close to the street with private patios in the center, and just off the main street, a small inn fronted by a large veranda.[32]

This town center was just the beginning for Rice. During her tenure at Rancho Santa Fe, she designed nearly the entire built environment in the tract. Between 1922 and 1929, she completed eight major public structures, including the commercial block, offices, and the elementary school. Her major business, however, came from home builders (see figure 14). As the SFLIC's resident architect, Rice collected many commissions from home buyers who were impressed with her work on-site and pleased with the convenience of her services as resident architect. She designed fifty-eight single-family houses, two duplexes, and two apartment buildings at Rancho Santa Fe.[33] Spanish style was for her a conduit to professional success. As some Anglo women had found on El Camino Real, promoting the Spanish past could be a route to public acclaim in an otherwise limited field. Female architects in this era, even ones of Rice's talents, found their prospects bleak. Most female graduates of architectural schools, few though they were, had difficulty sustaining steady careers. They encountered obstacles to employment at firms, and they rarely received commissions for major public works or received much work at all beyond residential or landscape design. Many women architects chose to fortify their positions in the latter domains, arguing publicly, as did Rice, that their gender naturally suited them to home design, allowing them to tap into women's natural instincts. In *The Architect and Engineer*, Rice claimed that "the woman who is to

Figure 14. Exterior of a Lilian Rice home, Rancho Santa Fe. Home of C. A.
Shaffer, *Rancho Santa Fe Progress,* July 1927. While the landscaping was
clearly incomplete, this house featured a large patio, shaded arcades, and a
covered balcony on the second story. This item is reproduced by permission of
The Huntington Library, San Marino, California and the Burlington Northern
Santa Fe Railway.

live in a house usually has the most to say about exposures, arrangement of rooms, size of rooms, etc., and I find that being a woman is a
genuine help to me in working out these details."[34] Thus, on the one
hand, Rancho Santa Fe represented a major break for Rice, allowing
her steady work and establishing a career-long reputation. Yet on the
other, her work there limited her scope largely to domestic architecture
and pigeonholed her as a scribe of Spanish style.

How Rice would negotiate the merger of peasant homes with distinctive estates was important to developers. Her buildings would form
the heart of Rancho Santa Fe's Spanish look and appeal. Could she
accommodate modern needs and use contemporary materials while
maintaining the appearance of a humble old Spanish village? She
remained dedicated to Requa's vision of simple peasant architecture,
but she had to develop elaborate methods and ruses to camouflage the

incongruous modern conveniences her wealthy clients were loath to give up. She knew, as another architect noted, "Southern Californians could not live in huts of reed," no matter how picturesque they might be.[35] Rice finessed the problem by simultaneously asserting the authenticity of her designs and using artful illusions. She used various techniques to make new materials look old, drawing on methods developed by colleagues and inventing a few of her own. As architectural journals and advertisements suggested, electric lights could be hidden in hand-wrought iron fixtures, new types of furniture could be made in weathered wood, and heated bathrooms could disguise their elements with decorative hand-painted tile. A former assistant recalled that Rice sometimes aged hand-hewn beams by instructing builders to "build a huge bonfire, big enough for these beams, and burn them and watch them and turn them, keep turning them until they're charred, and then . . . take wire brushes and brush them down. That's the only way we'll get that weathered look like they've been washed around in the sea or just laid out on Palomar Mountain somewhere."[36] That Spanish peasants or early Californians never sought such a deliberately battered look mattered less than the appearance of homes with history literally burnt into them.

Underneath the scorched beams sat some of the most modern equipment of the era. Lilian Rice's kitchens, for example, were fully electric, with dishwashers, incinerators, ventilating fans, extra refrigerators, and floor-to-ceiling automatic lazy susans. Contemporary descriptions highlighted both these conveniences and their disguise. A notation in the *Southwest Builder and Contractor* described a Rice house as a "rancho type residence" with stucco walls, tile roofing, and wrought-iron fixtures on the one hand, and electric heating and refrigeration and a three-car garage on the other. Yet descriptions also emphasized Rice's efforts to mask these modern elements. As figure 15 shows, "Inside, those buildings have every modern American appliance and yet their romantic atmosphere is preserved. . . . The hall lights look like rusted lanterns by castle gates in ancient days, though the light, of course, is electricity."[37] The contrast between the new and the old remained both uncomfortable and compelling. The novelty of an electric light bulb in a rusted iron fixture continued to beg mention despite Rice's valiant attempts to veil the modern technology behind a veneer of age.

Perhaps her aim was not to hide modernity entirely but to keep it hidden in plain view. Electric light is not supposed to emanate from rusty lanterns, so concealing the contemporary nature of the fixtures in

Figure 15. Interior of a Lilian Rice home, Rancho Santa
Fe. Home of Mary B. Allen, *Rancho Santa Fe Progress,*
September, 1927. This Rice design featured a heavy
beamed ceiling and electric-candle wall sconces. This item
is reproduced by permission of The Huntington Library,
San Marino, California, and Burlington Northern Santa
Fe Railway.

a way made them more noticeable. Rice's peasant houses looked
authentic, but she never claimed they were facsimiles. One can imagine
homeowners pointing out to their guests how ingeniously she had
hidden the new light in the old fixture, though in calling attention to the
disguise, they revealed rather than kept the secret. The cleverness of
Rice's claims to authenticity allowed homeowners to traverse the apparently enthralling divide between past and present on a daily basis. This

Figure 16. Gas station with a red-tile roof, Rancho Santa Fe. Designed by
Lilian Rice. Though the filling island stands apart from the service building,
Rice's gas station echoes several key details of The Village Well, particularly
the window grill and the wooden roof supports (see figure 17). This photograph
originally appeared in *The Architect and Engineer*, February 1924. Courtesy
Mandeville Special Collections Library, University of California, San Diego.

tension was evident throughout Rancho Santa Fe. She designed the main
business block to display not bustling commerce but "the simplicity and
charm of a Spanish village." Reviewers, such as *Los Angeles Times*
pundit Lee Shippey, judged her attempt successful: "The shops are so
softened by true Spanish feeling that the commonplace of commercial-
ism is disguised."[38] Garages, shops, offices, and other public buildings
all had their true characters draped by thick stucco walls and wrought-
iron window grilles, though few visitors were likely to miss these buildings' modern functions.

Of all the public buildings Rice designed, perhaps none received more
attention than the gas station (see figure 16). Here she attempted her
most ambitious masquerade, putting a tile roof over the filling island to
make it seem less out of place. In the minds of many visitors to Rancho
Santa Fe, she succeeded. Shippey likened the station to a picturesque
corner of a Spanish town: "[it] looks like a quaint old village well,
around which native flowers grow, and it is probably the only filling station in America that speeding motorists halt their cars merely to look
and admire." Another early description drew the same conclusion.

Figure 17. "A Village Well in Spain," from Richard Requa's
architectural tour. Photograph from his *Old World Inspiration
for American Architecture* (Los Angeles: Monolith Portland
Cement Co., 1929). Courtesy Marquand Library of Art and
Archaeology, Princeton University, and Lehigh Southwest
Cement Company.

"What you might have mistaken for a town well or town pump is a
gasoline filling-station." This "mistake" must have been intentional on
Rice's part. Her design echoed a photograph of a village well that Requa
included in *Old World Inspiration*. As figure 17 shows, it pictured a
similar tile-roof–topped island with women and children gathered
around. Requa's caption reads "these watering places are the scene of
greatest activity in the small communities from early morning until late
at night."[39] In the fast-growing automobile culture of Southern California, the gas station stood in a curious functional analogy with the more

traditional vision of the well. However unmatched a 1920s gas station and a rural village well might be, these commentators understood that the Spanish theme provided stylistic glue between them; it made the primitive modern, the mundane picturesque, and the incongruous appropriate.

The Spanish-colonial style was a product of 1920s Southern California, not a remnant of traditional Spain. Rancho Santa Fe's application of Spanish style to the modern home illustrated how successful and popular this architecture could be as a regional emblem. It helped solidify the architectural consensus that the Spanish colonial was the "logical and appropriate" style for Southern California. Though the transformation was not a seamless one, producing a Spanish-colonial home for Anglos domesticated the regional past. No longer foreign and exotic, the Spanish past became in Anglo imaginations an organic feature of the landscape. Still, the quality that repeatedly drew people in was its novelty and the charm of its seeming incongruity. Like photographs of automobiles in front of missions, the electric light in a rusty lantern and a gas station trimmed in red tile drew attention to themselves, to the artifice of the historic connection. The ability to seem at the same time familiar and unusual lent the Spanish style its particular regional magnetism.

"THE KIND OF NEIGHBORS YOU WILL LIKE"

The look and style of Rancho Santa Fe may have been dictated by the SFLIC's architectural restrictions, but its full splendor emerged only as people bought land and built homes. The development company had to figure out the best way to sell potential buyers on the community and the image it had in mind. The advertising plan that the SFLIC undertook in 1922 promoted the developers' image of the community and its ideal residents. Thus it highlighted the Spanish architecture not for its peasant origins but for its suggestion of affluence. Lilian Rice provided the template, but the evocative advertisements that presented Rancho Santa Fe to Southern California's elite prompted people to hire her. In this region and era marked by high residential mobility and rampant speculation in real estate, Rancho Santa Fe offered itself as a stable retreat. Los Angeles historian Robert Fogelson has said that Anglo-American home seekers in the 1920s wanted their new neighborhoods to be "spacious, affluent, clean, decent, permanent, predictable and homogeneous." When Rancho Santa Fe advertised that it contained

"Fifteen Square Miles of Uniform Beauty," it offered fulfillment of such desires for homogeneity and for a controlled environment.[40] As a whole, the abundant 1920s advertising conjured Rancho Santa Fe as the perfect community, merging a nascent Anglo suburban ideal and elite aspirations with Spanish style.

Marketing Rancho Santa Fe required careful design. Even as the ground breaking began, Ed Fletcher urged the SFLIC to begin planning the promotional campaign. Fletcher first suggested that the company select a more memorable name for the development than the one the SFLIC had been using: San Dieguito. "Mighty few people can pronounce the word San Dieguito," Fletcher warned, "to say nothing of spelling it." Moreover, this name failed to capitalize on the property's association with the Santa Fe Railway, which had already created a formidable brand in the Southwest. Fletcher stated a preference for Santa Fe Park, Ranch, or Rancho as labels more "wholesome," "logical," and "euphonious."[41] Santa Fe connoted enough Spanish flavor through association with the railway but did not tax Anglo tongues. Again, the SFLIC agreed with its chief local consultant and eventually adopted the moniker Rancho Santa Fe.

Developers also wanted advertising efforts to reflect the character of the community they were designing. Many real-estate operations in the 1920s tried to entice customers with free lunches, bus tours, circus tents, entertainment, and the hard sell: "buy now or pay more later."[42] The SFLIC's admen worked to distance their publicity from the taint of these fly-by-night promotions. Theirs would be "an unusual and high class piece of literature," offering neither spectacles nor ultimatums. Early advertisements used a genteel approach. "You are cordially invited to visit the Rancho. . . . If you do not find the location and the development is what you are looking for, you will at least be received with courtesy and you will be under no obligation to purchase." In the real-estate climate of the decade, this approach constituted a significant departure.[43] In addition to instituting its own paid advertising, the SFLIC invited newspaper and magazine reviewers to the tract in hopes of garnering favorable reports. As one adman realized, "A cleverly descriptive article in . . . a magazine would be of greater benefit to us, if followed up by our own letters and literature."[44] While developers began by placing ads in the Sunday real-estate section of the *Los Angeles Times,* upscale Southern California magazines like *California Southland* and *Touring Topics* proved to be the most evocative outlets for the Rancho Santa Fe advertisements. Ads appeared almost monthly in these two publications between 1924 and 1929. The ample illustrative and descriptive material used the color, space, and glossy paper to full advantage. These efforts to set Rancho Santa Fe apart in its advertising style underscored the messages in the ads.

Deed restrictions became a centerpiece of the promotional message. Early, single-column newspaper ads highlighted the benefits of restrictions, which they promised would "Protect Investment, Create Values, and Build a Prosperous Community of Real Southern California Homes with Perfect Harmony of Architecture and Landscaping." Magazine ads continued the refrain: "A scientifically planned, highly restricted community will provide assured income, harmonious environment and growing values"; "[r]igid yet highly desirable restrictions protect your investment here at Rancho Santa Fe"; "[r]igid, yet most sensible building and cultural restrictions assure a permanence of uniform charm and beauty."[45] The repetition of the message indicated that definitively associating Rancho Santa Fe with restrictions was a major goal of advertisers. Newspaperman Lee Shippey lent his pen to the cause in 1923 when he praised the tract as "probably the most highly restricted area of its size of any kind in the world." The developers were so pleased with his review and his favorable nod to restrictions that they reprinted the article as one of their own leaflets.[46]

In addition to showing the positive results of restrictions, advertisements reminded readers of the dangers that unrestricted property posed. According to one 1926 ad, Rancho Santa Fe's restrictions performed "a vitally necessary exclusion of uncongenial neighbors" who might cause others' investments and contentment to suffer. Scare tactics, elsewhere absent from the sales pitch, appeared in the advertisement of restrictions. What use would your investment be, one missive asked, "when unsightly wayside vending and service stations destroyed the beauty of the approach to your home—unrestricted outbuildings marred the landscape—neglected orchards adjoining you menaced the health of your own carefully nurtured plantings?" All that was necessary for this disaster to occur, the ad warned, was "ONE MISTAKE OF YOURS," but at Rancho Santa Fe this situation would never come to pass. A promotional article in *California Southland* contended that its residents "need never fear that a neighbor may build a house that spoils theirs. Architectural harmony must prevail on every hill." Restrictions defended the property against these perceived threats, as these advertisements made clear: "No untoward influence can creep into Rancho Santa Fe to mar beauty."[47]

Neighbors, both desirable and menacing, played key roles in these ads. They were prime indicators of the class of residents the SFLIC sought. One ad that appeared in eight Sunday-morning editions of the *Los Angeles Times* in 1924 offered Rancho Santa Fe as the site for "your California home. Sold only to qualified buyers. The kind of neighbors you will like." Copywriters used many other euphemisms that were similarly imprecise yet conjured a specific profile. The exhortation that "only permanent, beauty-loving residents are wanted" implied that residents were able to finance a particular standard of beauty. An ad praising the 1920s California-bound migration of "successful America" claimed that "everything that people of character and means require for residential surroundings was provided." The passengers in these "Covered Wagons of 1927," according to this ad, were not pioneers on the make but executives at the top of their class.[48]

Later advertisements discarded the euphemisms and began naming names. Applauding owners' prosperity openly, one bulletin boasted that "more than 200 thinking people from all over America who have achieved material success have bought country estates here on which to enjoy the fruits of that success." Other ads listed the occupations of Rancho Santa Fe's residents, the heads of "some of America's foremost families." In semianonymous descriptions of twenty-eight select owners, fourteen are described as capitalists, corporate officials, or bankers, with others in real estate, advertising, or the film industry, including "America's most famous motion picture couple," a barely veiled reference to Douglas Fairbanks and Mary Pickford. A few residents were listed by their social affiliation, including "a scion of one of Boston's oldest families" and "a member of one of Southern California's most prominent families socially." Following the extensive list came the assertion that the list represented a random selection. Not only did the "complete list contain many more families of equal prominence," but the "actual names [would be] gladly given to genuinely interested parties on request."[49] References both vague and specific assured Rancho Santa Fe's potential residents that they would find the right kind of neighbors, people like them.

Rancho Santa Fe advertisements also touted the coarser measure of the pocketbook. Ads hesitated to bill the subdivision as extravagant but rarely failed to include financial as well as social markers. While the ads used language similar to that in other real-estate advertising of the time, assuring readers that terms were fair and land was affordable, the home prices they listed became increasingly prohibitive. The terms of sale required a larger and larger up-front investment as the decade progressed. Costs increased in absolute terms as well; by the end of the 1920s per-acre prices had more than doubled.[50] But more significant than the rising prices and rigorous terms was the fact that Rancho Santa Fe began in 1927 to advertise specific lot prices, amounts sold, and the general prosperity of residents, often under the heading of "Typical Estates Now Available." Instead of vague language encouraging all people to inquire, including "men with but modest incomes," advertisements now listed figures that could only appear exclusionary.[51]

Moreover, the touted minimum construction costs and fast-track building schedules posed an additional class barrier. A commonly advertised requirement was that property owners must, within one year, plant their orchards or build their homes, of a certain minimum price—in some areas, no less than five thousand dollars; in others, fifteen thousand dollars. Even if purchasers might work through the terms and come up with the money for the lot, they immediately had to make a substantial investment in these projects. The SFLIC offered no financing for building or planting; those activities, as the ad stated, were "cash considerations." Advertising these restrictions assured buyers that they were joining a community of people as elite as themselves. "If you can qualify for home ownership here, you have many wonderful and exclusive opportunities. It is the place to make your dreams come true."[52] The ostentatious display of prices and numbers in Rancho Santa Fe's publicity was ironic, because the advertisements' target clientele was clearly those for whom money was no object.

Highlighting recreation was another way that Rancho Santa Fe advertisements sold the community's class character. The availability of a multitude of recreational possibilities was a much more important facet of the publicity appeal than was proximity to jobs. Rancho Santa Fe was fairly remote from any center of nonagricultural work. Some residents might commute to San Diego, about twenty-five miles away, but the suburb catered more to those who might manage their business remotely or for whom Rancho Santa Fe represented a retirement or vacation spot or a secondary home.[53] For this set, the SFLIC offered an abundance of leisure pursuits. A 1927 ad promised that outdoor sports would be available year-round and reported that the accompanying "flair for enjoyment of life" epitomized Rancho Santa Fe. Several ads pictured "the fortunate country gentleman and his family" gardening, horseback riding, boating, and playing tennis. They reported the construction of extensive bridle trails, an outdoor theater, and most prominently in later ads, a golf course. Organized by residents in September 1927, the Rancho Santa Fe Country Club planned a $200,000 golf course, to be designed by the famed golfer Max Behr.[54] Leisure defined the activities of Rancho Santa Fe residents and thus came to define the landscape, class character, and advertising possibilities of the subdivision in significant ways.

Living the good life among congenial neighbors in Rancho Santa Fe conferred membership in an elite class of Southern California Anglos. If the architects used peasant metaphors to describe their designs, the advertisements assured potential buyers that they would find no such plebeian neighbors. Where would the peasants fit in then? One might think the peasant claim could helpfully mask class pretensions, but neither Rancho Santa Fe developers nor residents adopted this ruse. They preferred to imagine their homes as grand estates where peasants had other roles.

"SOMETHING OF THE GRAND MANNER OF THE SPANISH DONS"

That Rancho Santa Fe solidified residents' elite status through a Spanish mode was significant. Architecture was key on more than aesthetic grounds. The Spanish-colonial style and its historic allusions extended the imagined proprietorship to include the region and its past. Advertisements touted the mandatory style for its suggestion of Old World grandeur. One proclaimed that "pure Colonial Spanish architecture in civic center and handsome homes today perpetuates memories of historic past and harmonizes with charming contours." Many ads enticed buyers by saying that a design staff awaited them, ready to share the results of their search of "the Latin countries of the world for charming bits of authentic detail to embellish Rancho Santa Fe homes."[55] Later advertisements reassured buyers that their desires for a Spanish mood could accommodate their modern needs. "Modern homes are being built that architecturally conform to early California—stucco walls and red tile roofs; walled gardens and patios all recall the days of the Dons. . . . A sincere effort is being made to preserve the historical atmosphere and the remains of old Spanish occupation." Whatever the modern amenities, a romantic past was part of the ambiance available with each parcel at Rancho Santa Fe. So sold was Lee Shippey that he mused, "One half expects to see a long-lashed, fan-guarded señorita step out to smile encouragement to a serenader."[56] Spanish style appeared to offer an entrée into the Southern California good life.

The marketing campaign traded heavily on the public's growing fascination with the life and landed estates of the Spanish dons. This focus was a new slant on regional nostalgia. Though an idyllic vision of rancho life had appeared in *Ramona,* the heroism of conquistadors and mission fathers had taken precedence in Southern California Anglos' cultural memory. By the 1920s, however, with leisure time on the rise, the picture of a festive and unhurried lifestyle held renewed appeal, and interest in the Spanish-Mexican ranchos of the mid-nineteenth century came into fashion. A 1929 pamphlet put out by the Title Insurance and Trust Company, the region's leading title agency, typified this newfound attraction to old cattle ranches. This little brochure, *The Romance of the Ranchos,* printed a colorful map of the region circa 1846 that outlined the boundaries of Californios' vast holdings. It invited residents to locate their homes on one of these tracts and to imagine "California cut up into Ranchos like a crazy quilt. . . . Picture a people browned by the sun, happy, prosperous, and carefree. Picture a white-walled hacienda on each of the ranchos, every one open with a never failing hospitality and welcome. That was California when the Americans took it."[57] Once distancing themselves from this legacy, Anglos now came to embrace, even to seize, the romantic vision of Spanish rancho life that Californios themselves had recalled and embellished before the turn of the century. Southern California Anglos' attraction to this heyday of the dons testified to the malleability of the Spanish idiom. Moreover, as Anglos had fashioned other pieces of the region's past to draw cultural lessons and boost development, they now tailored the rancho era to emulate modern lifestyles.

Encompassing the whole of the old Osuna family rancho, Rancho Santa Fe was well positioned to capitalize on this new prestige. The dons cut an appealing aristocratic figure, and few ads failed to mention that the land comprised a grant from the king of Spain to Don Juan Maria Osuna. Publicists chose to ignore the fact that Osuna's grant came instead from the Mexican government, as they were loath to squander the link to royalty. Spanish land grants presumably hosted the romantic rancho life that Southern Californians so coveted, replete with fiestas, fandangos, and flower-bedecked señoritas. During this time of increasing immigration of Mexican laborers, calling this scenario a Mexican life would have raised a number of questions, as well as Anglo eyebrows. The class connotation was crucial to imagining this lifestyle as a leisured good life rather than as unseemly rowdiness. To reckon the dons as the predecessors of an Anglo elite entailed a new configuration that corroborated Mexicans' position as laborers rather than symbolic ancestors. Accordingly, ads described Juan Maria Osuna as a Spanish gentleman and highlighted his achievements as a dashing military officer and the first mayor of San Diego. When Osuna built his family home, an SFLIC notice read, so began the "adventure and romance, the building and planting of Rancho Santa Fe." Southern California Anglos might share this adventure and royal legacy by building their own homes there.[58]

While the advertisements articulated this relationship only in short references, the friendly reviewers whom the SFLIC invited to write about Rancho Santa Fe explored the idea that Anglos of more modern days might partake of past romance in more depth. Of these writers, John McGroarty's 1922 piece most explicitly imagined Rancho Santa Fe as an ideal bridge between past and present. In a familiar ploy, the developers reprinted his article for *The Architect and Engineer* as one of their own brochures, under the new title of *The Endless Miracle of California*. *Mission Play* author McGroarty's endorsement alone constituted superb publicity. Yet his dramatization of the tract's history was the action that helped make Rancho Santa Fe an appropriate stage for this revival of the days of the dons and gave Southern California Anglos the starring roles. McGroarty focused on the Osuna family's lifestyle, describing it as a leisured, genteel existence full of "happiness and contentment, of peace and plenty. . . . It is the same story with the story of so many other of the old Spanish families of California—the first Overlords of the land. Romance has no more golden or glamorous pages."[59] Though not the first expression of this view of Californios, McGroarty's characterization of the dons as "overlords," a veritable aristocracy, had particular resonance at a place like Rancho Santa Fe.

McGroarty continued his review of the rancho's history by telling the sad story of the fall of the Osunas, pointing out that they first lost the war and later their land to the Americans. Despite the woeful tale, which ends with Osuna's son committing suicide, McGroarty hailed the next chapter in the history of the rancho as a triumph. "[T]he world did not end for the San Dieguito when the story of the Osunas ended. Nor did the miracle of California end." Enter the Santa Fe Railway to carry the Osunas' mantle.

> Came then upon a fate-blest day a long time lover of California, W. E. Hodges, Vice-President of the Santa Fe, inspired to weave imperishably into the vast fabric of his beloved railway the romance and the beauty of this historic region. . . . [T]here would rise upon the sunny hills and

winding valleys of the old lordly domain of the Osunas a model community, the like of which perhaps has not yet been seen in all the world.
There was and is a vision of smiling orchards, beautiful homes, luring
roads and forest aisles, of lawns and gardens. A community that shall be
sufficient unto itself, with its own intimate yet ample life. . . . Now we
see history repeating itself on the Rancho Santa Fe.[60]

The "endless miracle," as McGroarty saw it, was the continuation of
this good life in modern days by the land's new possessors. McGroarty
imagined Rancho Santa Fe residents, Osunas all, as inheritors of the
romantic tradition.

The Santa Fe Railway purchased the site of the Osuna home; the
company was the direct agent of the end of the family's possession of
the land. Yet in McGroarty's representation, as in its own publicity, the
railway appeared instead as a valiant defender of historic preservation.
Advertisements told of the extant, almost one-hundred-year-old Osuna
home, which stood on the tract as "a relic of the Dons." A *California
Southland* writer decreed the SFLIC effort to restore the home to its
former glory a "great humanitarian work." Elsewhere, Shippey wrote
of his fear that the rancho would lose its historic atmosphere under the
control of the Santa Fe Railway. Yet in an action that he judged an
amazing feat for a "soulless corporation," the railway had instead
"decided to reserve it for the building of America's most perfectly
planned community and to so restrict it that not only would the old
ranch house and all the other relics of the past be preserved, but the new
buildings erected should also seem a part of the romantic past."[61] Just
as the Santa Fe Railway had positioned itself for the tourist market as
salvage ethnologists of vanishing Indian culture, so it now fashioned a
reputation as champion of a faded Spanish romance. By association, it
suggested that residents, too, performed a public service by perpetuat-
ing Spanish style in their private dwellings.

More than saving Osuna remnants, however, SFLIC developers
hoped to advertise that the lordly life of the dons was still available at
Rancho Santa Fe. Publicity material repeated the refrain month after
month. One pamphlet claimed that buyers would find "an authentic
recreation of the charm and quaintness that characterized this golden
region when vaqueros rode their vast domains. . . . Here on these
orchard estates. . . people are living care-free lives, in something of the
grand manner of the Spanish dons who held this and neighboring lands
originally under grant from the King of Spain." As the king of Spain
seemed to hold considerable influence over real-estate values in 1920s

California, so did the dons appear to offer a beguiling prototype of the ideal suburban lifestyle. A review in *Sunset* claimed that the Dons led a life of leisure and that the "most serious business of Don Juan Osuna and his spirited cronies was to pass the time pleasantly and joyously." The author reported that at Rancho Santa Fe, "men of vision are reviving, on the very spot made romantic by the colorful lives of the Spanish dons, such elements of early California atmosphere as will fit logically into the scheme of modern existence." So appropriate was this bequest that the landscape itself confirmed it: "in fact, the ancient pepper trees planted by Don Juan Osuna's own hands now cast their shadows across the patio of a modern Rancho Santa Fe-an." If Anglos might partake of "the same smiling orchards" and "the same spirit of joyous living," then fulfillment of the promised good life was at hand.[62]

At Rancho Santa Fe, the romantic parallel to the life of the dons went beyond leisure to encompass attitudes toward social order and the production of wealth. Perpetual fan Lee Shippey associated both the dons and Rancho Santa Fe residents with a manorial prerogative. He recalled early California history as "princely days when the old dons lived in California in almost feudal splendor." McGroarty, too, encouraged Southern Californians to aspire to an older style of household management, inviting them "to rear their sunny rooftrees and to fling their glowing orchard slopes where once a Spanish overlord ruled his rude domain in unchallenged mastery." The picture of the dons as feudal lords is debatable but suggested an evocative vision of elite privilege to ambitious residents. The repeated feudal allusions often reflected Old Regime Europe more than frontier California or Mexico, but perhaps this implication was intentional. Rancho Santa Fe thus presented wealthy Southern Californians with a chance to establish their own domains. One ad intoned, "Winding drives. Shady trails. Wooded knolls. Ocean vistas. Beautiful flower gardens. Landscaped walks. Rose-covered pergolas. Perhaps a little private lake. The witchery of friendly old California mountains. An imposing Spanish home crowning a hilltop—are these your dreams?"[63] This 1925 notice advertised not a home but a manor, where one might rediscover feudal splendor and regain an unchallenged mastery.

To enact the vision these advertisements described, buyers needed more than a house; they needed an estate. Developers began to incorporate the idea explicitly, subtitling Rancho Santa Fe in its publicity as "Gentlemen's Estates" or "Country Estates." As one ad said, "Successful Americans from all over the nation are establishing *family estates* on

the broad sunny mesas of an old Spanish grant."[64] The term *estate*
implied the presence of several desirable amenities in the 1920s real-
estate market. First, when pitched against the fear of urban problems,
the idea of a country estate offered a counterpoint of quiet landscape
and a quiescent public community. An advertisement whose heading
read "When Your Spirit Rebels Against Too-much-city" made this contrast clear. "If the strain of your city life is wearing you down . . . If
crowds and traffic jams and relentless noise have frayed your nerves to
the breaking point . . . come down to Rancho Santa Fe. Make your permanent home here in the soothing influence of rural beauty. Escape life's
discordant notes."[65] Estate owners might escape the democratic tumult
of crowds and live as lords of the manor. Second, ownership of an estate
connoted the possession of substantial land. The dons were, after all, a
"landed aristocracy," at least according to Shippey. Rancho Santa Fe
ads highlighted the fact that nearly all the tracts included significant
acreage, and many contained working orchards. That the trees were
not for show and that they produced both fruit and income—in fact
"most gratifying incomes"—added to the appeal. "Far from being merely
a plaything or a lure for idle dollars, Rancho Santa Fe was intended by
its sponsors, and is today, a productive undertaking, creating new
wealth for Southern California in the form of sub-tropical orchard
products."[66] Homeowners might thus be estate owners in more than a
rhetorical sense.

To be lords of the manor, then, Rancho Santa Fe buyers needed peasants to work the land, and their orchards needed tending. Boosters had
portrayed citrus culture as an idealized existence since its inception in
the 1870s. Fruit and wealth seemed to drop from trees with little human
effort required. Despite such rosy portraits, however, citrus production
necessitated specialized knowledge and considerable labor.[67] Lest
potential buyers at Rancho Santa Fe have to plan, manage, and work
these orchards themselves, advertisements assured them that labor was
available to them. The satisfaction of living on a traditional homestead
was available to residents whether they "may dig and cut and trim and
plant, with [their] own hands, or vicariously." The administration of
the tract included an Orchard Maintenance office where a homeowner
could go for horticultural advice and services. A reviewer extolled the
benefits of this assistance. "Think of having the advice of an expert hor-
ticulturist to tell each man what will grow best on each grand slope,
guiding him in his choice of location as to whether he may grow avocados, oranges, lemon, apricots, peaches, pears or olives."[68] Even those

for whom Rancho Santa Fe remained only a seasonal home could have an orchard because they could employ, for extra fees, regular supervision and workers. The plan offered a ready-made estate, where owning an orchard did not necessarily imply that one would work the land oneself. With staff agronomists and dependable irrigation, living at Rancho Santa Fe did not require a return to feudal farming. Much like the Model Farm at the Panama-California Exposition, these homes were thoroughly modern manors. Yet, with their own staff of workers tied to the land through the larger corporate entity, they provided a kind of seignorial privilege. Perhaps the peasant metaphor introduced by local architects fit in best at Rancho Santa Fe in this way—not as a design muse but as a feature of the social landscape.

When Rancho Santa Fe advertisements nourished the desire to live the life of a Spanish don, they proffered a nostalgic notion of class, a world in which money came with land and estates came with workers. Of the many advertising slogans promoting Rancho Santa Fe during its first decade, perhaps the most evocative was the one that dubbed it "A Place for Discriminating People." This full-color, full-page 1926 advertisement (see figure 18) combined the tract's class and historic appeal, depicting a tidy orange orchard, an expansive Spanish-colonial home, and a neatly attired Anglo couple on horseback. It asked readers, "You intend to own a real home someday, in the country with city conveniences; a permanent place with ample room in a select neighborhood, with all-year outdoor living joys, do you not? You are particular about environment and have not found the right district yet?" Rancho Santa Fe, the copy proclaimed, offered the definitive answer to these questions. Amid its Spanish architecture, orchard lots, and prosperous residents, qualified buyers would find a stable, predictable, ordered world; a uniform expectation of beauty; and "a lovely land without a shack, without a jarring note."[69] Rancho Santa Fe had thoroughly fused the notion of the Southern California good life with the Spanish idiom and made both features definitive markers of class. What Rancho Santa Fe proffered most clearly was an imagined proprietorship, a grant from the original overlords, the dons themselves.

"NEVER LET IT BE SPOILED"

Once taking possession of this legacy, Rancho Santa Fe's new residents wanted to protect it in perpetuity. The SFLIC's deed restrictions mandated compliance for only ten years. By late 1927 leaders and residents

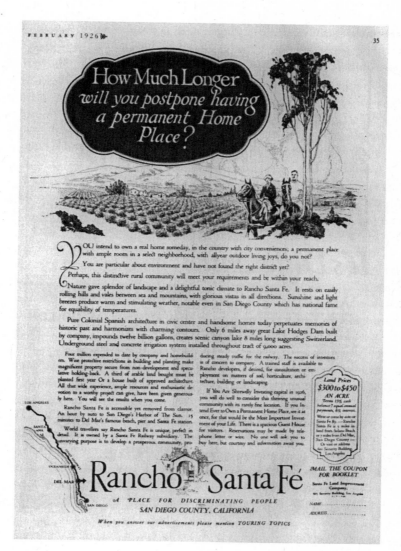

Figure 18. Rancho Santa Fe advertisement, *Touring Topics*, February 1926. This ad dubs the development "A place for discriminating people." Courtesy of Automobile Club of Southern California Archives and Burlington Northern Santa Fe Railway.

of Rancho Santa Fe realized that a decade was too short to ensure the lasting character of their community. They decided to install an even more complex system of restrictions through a permanent homeowners' association. Their effort to draft, publicize, and ratify the resulting *Protective Covenant* offers a revealing gauge of Rancho Santa Fe residents' acceptance of the advertised ideals and the community values they wanted to protect. In some ways, this internal campaign replicated the arguments for the good life that appeared in the public advertising. Yet the covenant went beyond the market message to tie Spanish architecture and real-estate values to a particular racial order. Rancho Santa Fe's ability to maintain and enforce this image suggests that the notion of the good life that the place enacted so alluringly was a restrictive one. In fact, its appeal and preservation depended upon its exclusivity.

As deed restrictions were becoming more common throughout Southern California, so was the movement to make them permanent through homeowners' associations and covenants.[70] Here again, Rancho Santa Fe remained in the regional forefront of community planning when a group of residents decided in 1927, with the first of the deed restrictions due to expire in five years, to form an association. The residents believed that something ought to be done "to make it forever impossible to permit any activity or improvement in the project that might deteriorate values or make any neighborhood less desirable as a place to live." Encouraged by SFLIC officials, this group of homeowners engaged as a consultant Charles H. Cheney, a respected city planner in the region who was well-known for his participation in the design of Palos Verdes, a community as restricted as Rancho Santa Fe. Both locally and nationally, Cheney was a vocal promoter of the type of restrictive covenant that Rancho Santa Fe residents wanted.[71] At his suggestion, a number of residents quickly filed articles of incorporation for the Rancho Santa Fe Association, a homeowners' body that would devise the protective restrictions and later enforce them.[72]

While this stage of planning was accomplished quickly, a considerable task remained to convince the other residents of the value and efficacy of this method of self-government. Having a covenant was a deviation from municipal organization and a significant abrogation of private property rights, which homeowners had to surrender voluntarily. Advocates of the covenant undertook their campaign on a number of individual, private levels; a public record of this negotiation appeared in the pages of the Rancho Santa Fe monthly newsletter, published by the SFLIC. First issued in July 1927 as *Endless Miracle* and later changing

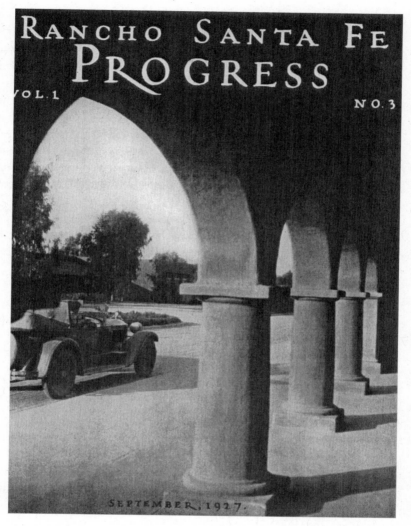

Figure 19. The *Rancho Santa Fe Progress* community newsletter, September 1927. This cover image shows the arcade on the main business block, designed by Lilian Rice. Reproduced by permission of The Huntington Library, San Marino, California and the Burlington Northern Santa Fe Railway.

its name to the *Rancho Santa Fe Progress*, this sixteen-page newsletter had a magazinelike layout but operated as a local forum and discussed new homes under construction, orchard profits, school events, society notes, and organization of the golf club (see figure 19). In the inaugural issue, the editor said that the publication was "designed to keep all owners closer in touch with project affairs and to foster the spirit of progress that has advanced the community to such an enviable position in so short a time." In its short life span, the newsletter made the covenant a major focus, stumping for its acceptance. Both developers and residents wrote for the journal and lobbied readers on the need for permanent controls. Articles frequently referenced Cheney as the authority on the subject and repeated his view that the "community is entitled to preserve [its] outward characteristics . . . [and] needs protection from disfigurement."[73] The concept of protection governed the idea. Instead of losing control over one's own property, the homeowner was gaining control over others', thus protecting his or her investment and the advertised community.

In the January 1928 issue of the *Progress*, Cheney explained the proposition in detail, offering rationales for each category of regulations. This review, "Guarding Beauty and Investment By Protective Restrictions," presented Cheney's fundamental belief in the value of such a community agreement.

> Rancho Santa Fe has already become known as one of the finest country places in the West. The careful supervision that has been given to all improvements and the high character of people who have been drawn here by the enlightened scheme of development are building a community of remarkable attractiveness, one almost unique in its charming simplicity and freedom from the terrible billboards, ugliness and bad kinds of development so unfortunately prevalent in almost all American communities of today. Yet this very progress presents a menace which must be met.[74]

Cheney's language emphasized the urgency with which residents needed to meet the menace of rapid, unregulated development. A covenant, he argued, would safeguard the permanent values of the community and institutionalize a method of enforcing them. He hoped residents would agree and "never let it be spoiled," never allow it to "be damaged by an undesirable, inappropriate or unsightly structure." Cheney proposed installing the regulations for an initial duration of forty-five years (until 1973), with automatic twenty-year extensions, unless overturned by a two-thirds vote.[75] Together with the concept of protection, this provision constructed the covenant as a bulwark against change. As drafted and presented to residents for signature in January 1928, the covenant detailed residents' desires to protect Spanish style, investment, homes, and homogeneity. The campaign in the *Progress* revealed the way in which residents tallied these features as part of their community ideal.[76]

Advertisements had shown Spanish style to be a meaningful container for the community, as its residents relished the inheritance of the dons, and the covenant did the same. It laid out complicated building and zoning regulations, with a clear mandate to control architecture. It bound the community to the rule of a three-member art jury, which would judge architectural plans to "insure a uniform and reasonably high standard of artistic result and attractiveness." On the one hand, the jury, composed of one resident and two architects, wielded considerable power to define what was or was not attractive. The only statement the covenant made on the matter of beauty was that "a design must be reasonably good in order to be approved by the Art Jury. A poorly designed example of architecture, regardless of its proposed cost, shall not be approved." On the other hand, the covenant bound the jury to a strict interpretation of style. Architecture must always conform to "that distinctive type of architecture which for several decades has been successfully developing in California, deriving its chief inspiration directly or indirectly from Latin types, which developed under similar climatic conditions along the Mediterranean or at points in California, such as Monterey."[77] The regulations even specified the typical characteristics buildings ought to display and the handling of certain variances, such as exceptions to the tile-roof rule.

Architectural control, according to Rancho Santa Fe designers, performed several key tasks in suburban planning. Cheney believed that the art jury's most important function was to save homeowners from their neighbors' potential bad taste. A covenant operated as a "protective barrier" against too much stylistic diversity, which he and other architects believed could ruin a city, community, or block. A 1927 feature in *Southland* echoed his opinion, as did many architects. "The property owner who disregards what his neighbor has built and erects a Southern Colonial mansion hard by a Norman French Chateau detracts from both his own and his neighbor's property."[78] Rancho Santa Fe's resident architect, Lilian Rice, likely shared this view but believed that architectural control served a higher purpose. She likened the "acceptance of the new idea of city planning and protective restrictions" to the "natural result of civilization's progress." For this reason, she believed that Rancho Santa Fe manifested "true important values, aesthetically, commercially, and in every other way" and prohibited "shacks, buildings of inferior design, unsightly grounds and all other influences which might depreciate values or the opportunity to enjoy life fully." Moreover, she argued, the covenant would help maintain the community's historic integrity.

> Since the natural antecedents of present day California were Latin-blooded, those who were responsible for this covenant have recognized the suitability of requiring here architecture of the Mediterranean type. With this requirement, all buildings at Rancho Santa Fe will not only complement each other, but will conform to the landscape, climate and general California conditions.[79]

In her defense of control and Spanish style, Rice linked the community's architecture with its values and with the progress of civilization in general. Preserving the compulsory Spanish style became a proxy for guarding the community's character.

The *Progress* indicated that residents embraced the Spanish idiom in architecture and beyond. Rancho Santa Fe homeowners used the newsletter to declare the names of their estates. According to the *Progress,* the names "Rancheros" selected "for their various estates indicate a faithful adherence on the part of owners to the Spanish tradition of the community." So popular did this activity become that residents used the *Progress* as an informal way of registering their names (see table 1). "It has been suggested that publication of an estate name in the *Progress* be considered as a sort of registration. In order to establish prior claim and to avoid confusion, owners who have not yet given expression to their estate names in a public way are urged to do so."[80] This community use of the *Progress* reveals how residents considered Spanish style, and the lifestyle they believed it denoted, to be a significant expression of the community.

The *Progress* frequently catered to residents' affinity for Spanish motifs. The cover illustration for the June 1928 issue featured an impressionistic sketch of a Spanish don at rest. The caption declared that the image captured "the days when Spanish overlords ruled this and neighboring domains. It conjures up pictures of bespangled vaqueros, smiling señoritas and happy carefree days." The magazine also printed photographs of residents' houses and their decoration. Describing a montage of one home in 1927, S. R. Nelson noted "how charming effects are created in the Spanish homes of Rancho Santa Fe by the careful selection of furnishings, tapestries, and drapes." He further asserted the advantages of the prevailing Spanish style. "The fact that Rancho Santa Fe homes are all of Spanish architectural design, gives the owner an opportunity to delve deeply into the romantic past for bits of authentic detail of this interesting motif."[81] Such tributes to the Spanishness of

TABLE I. RANCHO SANTA FE ESTATE NAMES
September 1927–November 1928

Family Name	Estate Name	Translation
Bishop	Etcheonda (Basque)	"The home to which the family belongs to whose shelter every member of the family has his right and to which all pay tribute" (owner's translation)
Campbell	Casa de Reposo	House of repose or rest
Carothers	Quinta Argentina	Argentine Villa, after the owner, Argenta, whose family owned silver mines
Christiancy	Los Altos	The Hills
Christiancy	La Valenciana (apartment building)	Native of Valencia, Spain, or type of orange tree
Consigny	Cielito Lindo	Pretty little sky, a term of endearment for boys; also a Mexican folk song
Cushman	Fin del Camino	The end of the road
Delany	Agua Azul	Blue water
Fairbanks/Pickford	Rancho Zorro	Zorro's ranch, after a film character that Fairbanks played
Keck	Las Planideras	The flats
Loomis	Rancho San Dieguito	Original land-grant name for the tract that became Rancho Santa Fe
McDonald	Glengary (Scottish)	A place name in Scotland
Millard	La Casita	The little house
Neff	Olvidar	To forget
Richards	Miraflores	To look at flowers
Shore	Suma Paz	Total peace
Smillie	Bienvenido	Welcome
Tabor	La Mariposa	The butterfly
Terwilliger	La Floresta	The grove
Tomlinson	Rancho del Oso	Ranch of the bear (in recognition of owner's pet bear cub)
White	Lago Vista	Lake view

SOURCES: [Untitled], *Rancho Santa Fe Progress* 1, no. 3 (September 1927): 5; "Rancheros Name Their Estates," *Rancho Santa Fe Progress* 2, no. 2 (August 1928): 6–7; "Anent Ranch Names," *Rancho Santa Fe Progress* 2, no. 3 (September 1928): 6; "Register New Names for Rancho Estates," *Rancho Santa Fe Progress* 2, no. 5 (November 1928): 2.

NOTE: These terms all have Spanish origins, and the translations are mine, unless otherwise indicated.

Rancho Santa Fe appeared in nearly every issue of the *Progress,* praising homeowners for their attempts to reconstitute the life of the dons.

Controlling the style of building was only the residents' first step in
maintaining this atmosphere. Lilian Rice explained in the *Progress* in
1928 that the Spanish homes were integrally related to the larger project
of creating the model Southern California neighborhood. "As each new
home becomes a part of the landscape, a new unit is added to complete
the great vision that inspired the men who planned Rancho Santa Fe.
Each building is another step toward the goal—a perfect community."
Indeed, developers had been billing Rancho Santa Fe not only as a good
place to build a home but also as "California's Community Masterpiece."
Residents highlighted the same features that advertisers touted about
community at Rancho Santa Fe. In a speech at an SFLIC-hosted dinner in
1927, one man listed his most important reason for locating there as his
desire to "move his family away from the congested city life." The
Progress pinpointed the quality that this resident shared with his neighbors: "those who have chosen this spot as the seat of their permanent
home have almost without exception entered into the spirit of the community's upbuilding with a splendid eagerness. All are inspired by a
mutual desire to make this the loveliest place in America to live."[82] The
Protective Covenant reflected residents' belief that to secure a perfect
community, the most important factors to control were their neighbors.

The first order was to maintain the dominant residential character of
the suburb. Though little industry threatened the Rancho Santa Fe area
of San Diego County, the covenant still prohibited nonresidential uses
and users. In addition to barring the construction of oil refineries,
processors of animal products, foundries, smelting, or any type of factory, the covenant disallowed "nuisance businesses." Examples included
saloons; cemeteries; asylums and sanitariums, whether for disease,
mental illness, or addiction; reform schools; detention facilities; fruit
stands; and automobile camps.[83] Excluding many of the necessities of
modern society meant that Rancho Santa Fe would be strictly for residence; little commerce was allowed. Businesses that could find a home
in the community should not draw workers or customers from outside
but should provide services to the residents. Moreover, the covenant
stipulated that those retail businesses that were permitted had to conceal their commercial character; store signs had to be approved by the
art jury, and billboards were strictly prohibited.

This control of commercial expression embodied a general restriction
on use of public space in Rancho Santa Fe. Including in its jurisdiction

murals, stained glass, sculptures, fountains, and entryways visible from the street, the covenant established community control over public and private works of art. As one *Progress* article said, the art jury would prevent anything "that smacks of the bizarre" from appearing in public view.[84] These physical restrictions suggested a deeper anxiety about the character of the person who would live at a sanitarium, patronize a saloon, or erect a bizarre statue in his or her front yard. The prohibition of fruit stands appears strange given that many residents grew fruit. Yet the division between presiding over an orchard and peddling fruit from a roadside shack testifies to the types of residents Rancho Santa Fe wanted to alternately encourage and exclude.

Rancho Santa Fe denizens made sure the *Protective Covenant* would keep the financial barriers high and thus retain the community's class character. Not only did they remain committed to fast-track building schedules and cost minimums for the unsold portion of the tract, they created new investment levels for improvements to existing homes, scaled to the character of each block and the wishes of neighbors. For example, the covenant established a price floor for landscaping expenses. Owners could spend no less than 3 percent of the cost of their homes on decorative gardens, which included ornamental plants, trees, shrubs, lawns, and flowers—over and above the cost of functioning orchards. Again, Rancho Santa Fe residents wanted to gain some measure of control over their neighbors' activities. By making sure that their neighbors planted flowers, residents believed they could control who those neighbors would be. SFLIC administrator L. G. Sinnard raised the familiar specter of the boorish neighbor in promoting these new restrictions. "Restricting the minimum cost of a residence is a wise measure employed to preserve values. It means that a man who has expended ten or fifteen thousand dollars in a home may be assured that his investment will not be depreciated by a cheap or unsightly structure erected by his next door neighbor."[85]

If the covenant declared a definite preference for a particular class of residents, it also revealed a clear definition of the ideal homes to house these residents. At their most basic, restrictions established the concept of the detached single-family house as the archetypal home for the development. Except in the Civic Center area, residents could build only a "single family dwelling." The idea of the single-family dwelling was not a novel concept, either in the United States or in the Southern California region, nor was the increasingly popular view that equated the single-family home with higher standards in value and community. Developers and residents saw Southern California as an ideal terrain on which to express this philosophy, and they spread single-family houses over the landscape. By 1930 Los Angeles contained a higher percentage of single-family dwellings than any other city of comparable size in the country. Remarkably, better than nine of ten dwellings were designed to house only one family.[86] At Rancho Santa Fe, this trend complemented the emphasis on family estates. The covenant sought to ensure that residents would have similar family arrangements and goals. This vision melded and altered typical conceptions of public and private spaces. Rancho Santa Fe homeowners vouched their commitment to the private family home and their dislike of an unrestrained public realm, yet their solution called for them to yield private property rights and to trust each other to preserve the common public good. In a sense, this approach allowed for joint private ownership of public space and culture.

"THERE WERE A LOT OF RATTLESNAKES IN RANCHO SANTA FE"

The *Protective Covenant*'s definition of a single family was less straightforward than it might seem. A home was a "dwelling for one family alone, having but one kitchen and within which not more than five persons may be lodged for hire at one time, provided that reasonable quarters may be built and maintained in connection therewith for the use and occupancy of servants or guests of said family."[87] This presumption that families needed servants was hardly novel among the upper class, but it complicated both the definition of a single family and the racial restrictions the covenant put in place, though the race clause itself begged little comment from residents. In the lengthy article for the *Progress* in which Cheney explained the covenant to residents, the race proscription received a brief, obligatory mention: "the existing restrictions are to be continued prohibiting Negroes, Asiatics, or people of other than the white or Caucasian races, except in the capacity of domestic servants."[88] Inclusion of this clause seemed so commonplace as not to merit serious discussion, despite the irony palpable today.

The racial restriction reflected common practice in Southern California at the time. Widespread deed restrictions forbade any non-Caucasian from purchasing property; typically these regulations enumerated African-Americans, Asian-Americans, Jews, and sometimes foreign-born people for exclusion. Mexicans and Mexican-Americans constituted a gray area; many covenants did not indicate on which side of the racial divide these groups stood. Historian Albert Camarillo has found evidence, however, that the number of housing developments that excluded Mexicans rose dramatically in Los Angeles between 1920 and 1946, increasing from less than one-quarter to more than three-quarters of the neighborhoods. In addition, the U.S. Census Bureau in 1930 reclassified Mexicans, no longer enumerating them as part of the white category and creating a separate "Mexican" category that belonged neither to the white nor the black designations. In so doing, the bureau aligned its racial categorization to Anglo perceptions in the Southwest, though neither the government nor most restrictions used the most common ethnic denomination in Southern California itself: Anglo.[89] Rancho Santa Fe's clause did not mention Mexicans one way or another, but the fact that no Spanish-surnamed homeowner surfaced in my research of the tract's first two decades suggests that the clause barred them informally, if not technically.

On the heels of a massive influx of Mexican immigrants in the 1920s, Anglos confronted a confusing prospect: how to clearly separate these Mexican laborers from the region's Spanish heritage that Anglos admired so much. Yet if Rancho Santa Fe residents had difficulty justifying their relentless pursuit of Spanish motifs in architecture and atmosphere despite the barriers they erected to Mexican people, no note of such discomfort appears in the *Progress*. On the one hand, Rancho Santa Fe residents assigned Spanish dons membership in the white category. With the dons safely ensconced in an ideal world, Anglos emphasized these Spanish speakers' European origins and saw them as far removed from Mexican immigrants. On the other hand were numerous subtle ways in which Rancho Santa Fe established whiteness as the racial norm, removing it even from the dons. Editors extolled the health of the children at the elementary school, claiming, "Peaches-and-cream complexions such as come only from plenty of sunshine, air and exercise are everywhere."[90] The *Progress*'s review of a school play presented the history of the Rancho Santa Fe land as an instance of Anglo triumph.

> The story begins with the life of the Indians. Then came the Spanish Osuna family. Then came the Dreamer. From the earliest days, an Indian legend had it that Black Mountain, familiar eminence on what is now the Fairbanks-Pickford estate, contained great treasure. Not until the Dreamer came and showed the way was the nature of the treasure revealed. He showed that the treasure, and this was the denouement, was the prosperity and happiness produced by the bright sunshine and rich soil of modern Rancho Santa Fe.[91]

The children playacted a kind of Manifest Destiny, with the Dreamer making possible "prosperity and happiness," proving the superiority of present-day civilization. While the Dreamer has no individual identity, he clearly stands in for Anglo development and gains credit for the ability to make use of the indigenous treasure.

However, the vision of the Southern California good life that Anglos definitively associated with the life of the Spanish dons rested squarely on the labor of others, mainly Indians.[92] Rancho Santa Fe was no exception to this rule. If anything, the existence and control of nonwhite "peasant" labor only added to the residents' fantasy that Spanish rancho days ruled again, yet now with Mexicans in the mudsills. The assumption that the presence of domestic servants such as maids, gardeners, or chauffeurs required a racial loophole reflected the broader structures of labor and community in the region. The Mexican presence in the domestic labor force increased during this era as Anglo demand for domestic services rose, just as immigration restrictions shrank the supply of Asian and European laborers and black migration remained low.[93] Mexicans were present in large numbers to perform all the types of labor that Rancho Santa Fe required. Surveys during the late 1920s reveal that ethnic Mexicans accounted for the overwhelming portion of the labor force in agriculture; they also filled many of the jobs in the construction and service sectors. In San Diego alone, ethnic Mexicans constituted 90 percent of road and street laborers. The leading type of employment for Mexican women across the state was in the domestic services; these women worked as maids, laundresses, and cooks and accounted for one-quarter to two-thirds of the work force in each of these occupations.[94]

Most evidence suggests that this ethnic picture held true for Rancho Santa Fe's servant and labor population. Some indication exists that California Indians filled some of these roles as well. The *Progress* issue in September 1927 noted the seasonal departure of "the Indian boys from the Sherman Institute of Riverside who have been spending their vacation working" in the orchards. The editor of the *Progress* found them to be "especially good workers" who are "always welcomed at Rancho Santa Fe each spring." Ethnic Mexicans, however, filled most of the laboring positions in the orchard-maintenance service and the irrigation district, worked in a service capacity at the inn as well as in private homes, and completed much of the unskilled work in housing construction.[95]

Jesus Gonzalez, an immigrant from Mexico, was one of the workers who provided the muscle and know-how in building Rancho Santa Fe.

He began as a road builder and later dug and tended the tract's irrigation ditches. Gonzalez had established his own farm in Santa Paula, but
a flood wiped his family out, and in 1927 he and his family came south
to Rancho Santa Fe to answer the call for labor. As his son Frank later
recalled, the work was difficult outdoor labor that allowed his father to
get to know the land almost too well. Jesus wore tough leather leggings
to deter snakes and other perils of the chaparral. "There were a lot of
rattlesnakes in Rancho Santa Fe where he worked making roads and
grading for orchards." Road making was heavy work, requiring equal
parts strength, patience, and skill. He worked with a team of four
horses, putting "the reins over his head and control[ling] the team by
pulling back with his neck while he adjusted the blade height with a
lever by hand. Manually. There were no hydraulics. . . . He was a strong
man. He walked behind that team all week."[96] This was a different
view of the life available at Rancho Santa Fe, if not an entirely terrible
one. Jesus Gonzalez made a living for his family, and in the early years,
the family found added features in the land itself. Frank remembered
feasting on Rancho Santa Fe venison, Pacific lobster, San Dieguito River
ducks, and Lake Hodges bass. Nonetheless, families like the Gonzalezes
made possible with their labor the leisured life of Rancho Santa Fe residents. One wonders if Anglo homeowners noticed the rattlesnakes.

Where these workers were to live became an issue for the SFLIC as
the community developed. During initial phases of construction and
planting, the development company housed Mexican laborers in camps
on-site. As homeowners began to move in to Rancho Santa Fe, however,
the SFLIC transferred Mexican workers to undeveloped land due west
of the tract. Sandwiched between Rancho Santa Fe and the coastal town
of Solana Beach, this land became a permanent Mexican community
known first just as *la colonia* and later as Eden Gardens. The Gonzalez
family moved in there and remained for several generations. Evidently,
Gonzalez and other early residents built the Eden Gardens neighborhood themselves with significantly less assistance from the Santa Fe
Railway than Rancho Santa Fe residents received; the railway had neither cleared roads nor installed running water. Along with his friends in
the community, Frank Gonzalez attended the segregated Mexican
school set up in Eden Gardens in 1928. The students' parents, who
worked in the groves and homes of Rancho Santa Fe, also found segregation in the barbershops and movie theaters in the areas surrounding
the small *colonia*. Neither could they purchase land in Solana Beach,
where deeds forbade their presence even more explicitly than the ones

at Rancho Santa Fe. With these restrictions in place, Mexicans of necessity concentrated in Eden Gardens, and there established a lasting base for Mexican community and entrepreneurship.[97]

While this segregation offers a picture of clear geographic separation between Anglos and Mexicans in the area, the covenant suggested that Mexican labor would be necessary in more areas than the orchards. The fact that families were likely to employ Mexicans as private help complicated the idea of simple segregation. Mexican people would not only be present within the community on a daily basis but living in residents' homes. Rancho Santa Fe homeowners thus manipulated their architectural designs to manage this racial diversity within their homes. They required Mexican labor but needed to incorporate it into both their image of "one family alone" and their reenactment of the Spanish dons' lifestyle. As reported in the *Progress,* the plans for most homes included servants' quarters, carefully laid out to reflect the separate types of residents. One house, approvingly called "one of the most pretentious planned for Rancho Santa Fe," gained praise not only for its harmony with surrounding topography but also for its intelligent segregation of residence and service functions. "Off the dining room on the far side of the house is another patio with high walls, which serve to cut it off from still another court or service yard opposite the kitchen and servants' quarters." Douglas Fairbanks earned high marks as well for his plan to split off service areas from the home entirely; the *Progress* called his creation "a Spanish village for workers."[98] At Rancho Santa Fe, even Mexican laborers became picturesque Spanish peasants. By reminding residents of the manorial privilege of the dons, this arrangement suggested a relationship between homeowners and servants—between Anglos and Mexicans—that did not threaten the perfect community. Nevertheless, no matter how much Rancho Santa Fe residents attempted to screen themselves off from the Mexicans in their employ, Mexicans were essential to the community and remained highly visible throughout the tract.

Owners agreed readily on policies such as architectural uniformity and racial exclusivity, but Rancho Santa Fe residents fretted over the mechanisms for enforcing these restrictions. Would restrictions be secure enough? Who would retain control over the terms? Who had a right to vote on local issues? Both the *Progress* and planner Charles Cheney worked to reassure residents that local power was vested exclusively in the hands of homeowners. The covenant, Cheney explained, functioned as "a medium of self-government." The Rancho Santa Fe

Association, as the governing body, was a "non-stock, non-profit association in which every property owner who signs the protective covenant will have one vote." The homeowners' association would fulfill the normal functions of town government, maintaining streets, regulating parking, coordinating garbage collection, and cooperating with the county on matters of fire and police protection. With five resident directors elected by property owners, the association would finance these activities through annual property assessments. The key "advantage of a homeowners association over the formation of a municipality of the 6th class," Cheney argued, was that "only property owners are allowed a voice, whereas in the latter case voters without financial responsibility might conceivably dominate the situation adversely. In the case of a proposal to modify restrictions in any way this might become exceedingly important."[99] Neither the residents of Eden Gardens nor the servants living in Rancho Santa Fe could have a vote in the government of local affairs.

The language of the argument in favor of vesting the vote in home ownership bore political resemblance to some of the more exclusionary aspects of republican ideology from another era. Representing "voters without financial responsibility" as a threat to the community was reminiscent of arguments against extending suffrage throughout the nineteenth century. Allowing the propertyless a "voice" was a dangerous prospect. The rule of one home, one vote thus suggested antidemocratic tendencies, not to mention retrograde gender implications.[100] The choice to create a homeowners' association instead of a city embodied an attempt to recapture a style of local control that emulated the privilege of the dons to the extent one could in twentieth-century America. Rancho Santa Fe referenced both the American idea of the independent republican homestead and the image of the Spanish California manorial rancho; in both cases, land was the basis of wealth and suffrage, excluding by implication women, children, and workers. This older political organization was another way in which Rancho Santa Fe asserted traditionalist class privileges as a feature of the ideal community.

The backers of the *Protective Covenant* and the editors of the *Rancho Santa Fe Progress* had made a clear case to the residents on the merits of such a scheme of control. The covenant went into effect by late 1928, and owners continued to place their properties under its legal jurisdiction until only a few parcels remained outside the document's protection. The *Progress* exulted that the covenant, "by which owners secure to themselves advantages of the most advanced type of community planning and protect their property against the encroachment of undesirable influences, has now become a fact."[101] Enacting the covenant allowed Rancho Santa Fe residents to simultaneously protect and define the ideal neighborhood they wanted. They shared an affinity for Spanish-colonial architecture and an atmosphere of exclusivity, as well as a healthy fear of recalcitrant neighbors, ugly shacks, and propertyless votes. In designing the covenant to control all these factors, Rancho Santa Fe residents engineered a community that excluded Mexicans from its Spanish-styled ideal yet relied upon them to produce it. Mexicans built the structures that housed this idyllic Anglo community, maintained the groves that supplemented it, and provided the services that enabled it. That Rancho Santa Fe was a place of labor for Mexicans and leisure for Anglos symbolized a pattern that would prevail in Southern California's red-tile–roofed suburbs for decades.

CONCLUSION

By the end of the 1920s Rancho Santa Fe had seemingly not only secured itself against architectural or human encroachments, but it had also achieved some fame in the region. Observers at the time more than hinted that all subdividers and residents should aspire to its example. When San Diego newspaper art columnist Hazel Boyer accepted an invitation to view and write about the community, she found it "a model to inspire all of rural California" and the champion of "the true home." It exemplified the ideal suburb to many Southern California buyers, a tidy land of pretty Spanish-colonial houses filled with elite Anglo families. Boyer hoped that Rancho Santa Fe would have a broad effect on the countless new subdivisions still to be built in the region. "Since it is true that one person with an orderly mind may set at ease a room full of people and inspire their best thoughts, and a group of people striving to understand the higher realities of life may stem the tide of thought of a whole community, what may this far visioned plan of Rancho Santa Fe do in its influence on the untouched, treasure filled hills of California?"[102] If Rancho Santa Fe could not single-handedly remake all Southern California in its image, as architects may have wished, it epitomized the main features Anglos wanted to see in their suburbs.

The feature that many people thought Rancho Santa Fe modeled best for the region was its Spanish style. One *Sunset Magazine* writer reviewed the growing popularity of Spanish architecture and the development of

Rancho Santa Fe in the same article in 1927, suggesting that "perhaps Rancho Santa Fe, California, is digging deeper into the wells of Spanish inspiration than any other community." The laudatory piece hailed Spanish-colonial style as the most appropriate one for the region and asked the question "isn't it a shame that there aren't more places like Rancho Santa Fe where you can't build anything else?" Rancho Santa Fe's architect agreed. After working at Rancho Santa Fe for nearly a decade, Rice mounted her own rationale for the applicability of Spanish idioms to the Southern California landscape with a not-so-subtle bid for regional superiority. As she wrote in *The Architect and Engineer,* the style is "made more logical by the fact that Spain planted the seed of Christianity on our shores and brought to the new world many characteristics of the old. The modern architect, far from throwing tradition overboard, as did the Babbitts of the middle west, gladly accepts California's early Spanish background as the richest source of inspiration."[103] Though Rice would never receive the level of acclaim personally that Rancho Santa Fe did regionally, her buildings had far-reaching influence in establishing the dominance of Spanish-colonial style in Southern California.

By the late 1920s one was hard-pressed to find an architect that would argue against Spanish-colonial style. The *Architect and Engineer* reported in 1928 that there was "a definite feeling among architects that out of this Spanish-Italian-Mediterranean-Mexican mixture there is growing a true California type." This architect believed that the style was more than "a passing fad" and that "here at last was a fitting and typical California style which was destined to endure." By the end of the decade, one Los Angeles architect spoke for the region in stating his belief that "we have arrived at a distinctive architecture which is our own and which is a real expression of our culture and civilization." Another judged the style "Spanish and yet there is nothing like it in Spain. It is Mexican Colonial and yet again it is American."[104] Southern Californians, whose number grew markedly during the decade, clamored for Spanish-colonial homes and matched architects' eagerness to show off the newly acclaimed regional ideal as their own. Together they began to build Southern California with Spanish blueprints.

What made Spanish style so convincingly right, true, and American to Southern California Anglos in the 1920s? Had Rancho Santa Fe managed to fuse Spanish architecture thoroughly with Anglo family homes? Had the community successfully melded the memory of the dons with affluent modern lifestyles? However one might have felt about red tile as a design element or roofing material, the Spanish-colonial style gave residents an investment in the region as well as in their finite parcels of land. The purchase of a Spanish home seemed to offer more than a roof over one's head: it offered access to a unique regional ambiance. It recognized, in the words of scholar William McClung, that "this landscape was four-dimensional, reinventing in the present the terrain and climate of a sequence of vanished and imagined pasts."[105] Rancho Santa Fe perhaps best exhibited this imagined proprietorship of time and space, but material expression of the good life in Spanish terms abounded throughout the region. Construction of Spanish-colonial homes by the thousands testified to people's desire to own a private share of a publicly traded Spanish past. Yet with luxurious places like Rancho Santa Fe headlining Southern California's suburban dreams, powerful markers of exclusion came to encumber the Spanish style. While the 1920s had yet to see the "armed response" security signs, alarm systems, and gated communities evident in today's suburbs, Rancho Santa Fe nonetheless envisioned a divided landscape. Neither proprietorship nor an exclusive ambiance could be entirely shared, lest Southern California Anglos lose their sense of entitlement, both to the region's past and to its present.

CHAPTER 5

The Market

Olvera Street and Urban Space

In the 1920s Anglo leaders of Los Angeles were keen to declare their city the most modern metropolis in the land. They pointed with pride to the amazing speed of its growth and development—its rise from a sleepy cow town of some ten thousand people in 1880 to an upstart city of one hundred thousand in 1900 and then to the bustling urban capital of the region in 1920, with upward of half a million residents. That number would double by decade's end. Everything was new in Los Angeles; the city seemingly contained little cultural or architectural baggage tying it to old ways of life. The extraordinary popularity of automobiles and suburbs testified to the novel lifestyles Los Angeles Anglos were swiftly establishing as the regional norm. In 1928 a brand-new City Hall opened as fitting testament to all this forward thinking. Standing almost five hundred feet tall, the building may not have rivaled the skyscrapers of New York or Chicago, but its sleek white tower atop Bunker Hill soared above Los Angeles. Its modern art-deco–inspired style, brilliantly illuminated at night by the "Lindbergh beacon" that topped it, easily ascended as a visual status symbol for the metropolis.

In the early 1930s an entirely different reference came to epitomize Los Angeles. In image after image, the city was personified by an alluring young Mexican woman, whose traditional dress included a lace mantilla and tall comb upon which was printed *Los Angeles*. As one local writer explained the allusion, "Los Angeles is symbolized by a dark señorita with a high comb, this is the second largest Mexican city in the world, [and] our advertising promises the prospective visitor Spanish atmosphere."[1] The idea of Los Angeles as señorita found a home not at City Hall but nearby in the heart of the old Mexican pueblo. She lived on Olvera Street. Less than five years after City Hall's debut, this narrow lane in the hall's shadow became the essential Los Angeles landmark. In 1930 Anglo city boosters and a tireless female promoter cast in the mold of El Camino Real's Harrie Forbes transformed a back alley into Olvera Street, a theme-park–style Mexican marketplace. Five hundred feet long rather than tall, the street's tiled sidewalks, canopied curio booths, displays of folk crafts, tamale stands, wandering guitarists, and lovely young señoritas in fanciful Mexican costumes quickly made it a favorite of locals and tourists. More, Anglos came to view Olvera Street as the public face of Los Angeles. How in such a short time had Los Angeles Anglos merged these two seemingly contradictory civic self-images—modern metropolitan tower and quaint Mexican street?

Despite, or perhaps because of, the two spaces' physical and symbolic differences, they came to embody ideal urban bookends. The way in which Anglos created, adopted, and understood Olvera Street made the street not only compatible with City Hall but put the two sites in a fitting historical relationship. They anchored opposite ends of a regional historical story line that was by then familiar to Southern California Anglos, a move from humble ethnic beginnings to ultimate American triumph. Designed not just in but for the modern metropolis, Olvera Street simultaneously celebrated the Mexican character of Los Angeles and segregated it, relegating it to the past. In the most telling and oft-repeated description, it was "A Mexican Street of Yesterday in a City of Today" (see figure 20).[2] Moreover, Anglos chose as the site of yesterday the city's Plaza. The economic and cultural center of Los Angeles for its first century, the Plaza was a place of history to be sure, but it remained a space of continuing use and a social and symbolic focus of Los Angeles' Mexican life. Nevertheless, in Anglo public rhetoric, City Hall and Olvera Street came to be more than two spaces among many on the urban landscape; they came to signify entirely separate worlds. How Anglos and Mexicans in Los Angeles inhabited, traversed, and merged these worlds reveals much about the status of the romantic Spanish past some half a century into its public career.

However much Olvera Street drew upon the success of Spanish memories at other venues, it also measured their ongoing adaptation. Here nostalgia and romance came to rest squarely in the center of Southern

Figure 20. "A Mexican Street of Yesterday in a City of Today." In this *Los Angeles Times* model of the plan for Olvera Street, published before it was built, all elements of the modern city in the lower "before" image—telephone poles, automobiles, smokestacks—are eliminated, with the notable exception of City Hall. Charles H. Owens, artist. Copyright 1929, *Los Angeles Times*. Reprinted with permission. Courtesy of Mandeville Special Collections Library, University of California, San Diego.

California's most modern of cities in a self-consciously modern age. Amid the change and misfortunes of the 1930s, Anglos fine-tuned their Spanish ambiance to include greater commercial possibilities, as well as emphasizing common folk in a Hollywood-style setting, complete with a cast of Mexican people playing various roles. For all the sophistication of this production, the Anglos who built the street struggled to define and control the images they loosed on the city. Olvera Street occasioned as much contestation about the meaning of the region's past, among Anglos as well as between Anglos and Mexicans, as had four decades of developing Southern California's Spanish idioms. That the street had the potential to symbolize the region's premiere metropolis made it a more powerful and contentious issue than a tourist highway, temporary fair, or secluded subdivision. Olvera Street's meteoric rise to public acclaim and its first ten years in the city spotlight heralded the increasing centrality of the romantic Spanish past, variously construed, to the region's public self-image. Yet the street's early history also suggested the eventual end to this narrative's monopolistic grip on Southern California's cultural memory. As an important urban landmark, the "street of yesterday" prompted questions about the nature of public space and community in Los Angeles and who would share them in the "city of today."

"TO CAPITALIZE THE SPANISH AND MEXICAN INFLUENCE"

While references to the Spanish past abounded in Southern California by the 1920s, visitors in search of such sites in the heart of the region's largest city would not have found much to see. El Camino Real merely brushed central Los Angeles. No baroque castles graced its Griffith Park. Surprisingly, much of the new downtown architecture, with a few notable exceptions, reflected modern trends more than the craze for Spanish-colonial homes, which were easily found in the surrounding neighborhoods. The city preferred to advertise its spectacular urban and industrial growth, the new City Hall, or even the recreational possibilities along its beaches and highways than to highlight its historic landmarks. If literature from Los Angeles booster organizations trotted out many Spanish references, they boasted few definitive destinations where tourists could witness old California in action.

The Plaza, the original center of the Mexican pueblo of Los Angeles, suffered no lack of history but failed to deliver its past in an appealing tourist package. In its present location since the 1820s, the Plaza had been a common ground for business, politics, and social life, around which were arrayed the homes of leading citizens. Though by the end of the nineteenth century it was no longer the city center, it remained a key site for Los Angeles' Mexican community and a magnet for new immigrants from several nations. By 1920 the rapid pace of urban development had left it on the northern fringes of the city's bustling downtown. When the multiethnic immigrant neighborhood surrounding the Plaza found mention in the *Los Angeles Times,* it did so typically as a vice or health problem or as an obstacle to urban development; it lay outside the everyday paths of Anglo residents and was not on tourist itineraries.[3]

San Francisco–born Christine Sterling was among the newcomers to Los Angeles in the mid-1920s who expected to find Spanish romance around every corner, only to suffer disappointment. Sterling, née Chastina Rix, arrived in Los Angeles as Mrs. Jerome Hough, an identity that concealed her aspirations to public prominence. When her marriage to Hough, an attorney who worked in the film industry, faltered, she struggled to make ends meet for her two children and to make a place for herself among the glamorous crowd. Borrowing a tactic from Hollywood, she reinvented herself with a stage name, adopting the moniker of Christine Sterling for its catchy ring.[4] For all the name's star quality, the profession she chose—historic-preservation activist—was by that time perhaps a bit conventional for public-minded women, but she was one of the few who dared to operate without the Mrs. prefix. Following in the footsteps of numerous Anglo women in California and across the nation, Sterling fashioned herself as the savior of a particular historic spot and spent her whole career promoting and protecting it. She expanded upon her forebears' legacies, using preservation as a platform not only to develop new forms of commercial entertainment but also to make herself a key local figure, an independent woman almost as famous as the site she shepherded.

Sterling's initial foray to the Plaza produced only dismay. Where were the "colors of Spanish, Mexican romance" she had read about in booster literature? She reported that "the sunshine, mountains, beaches, palm trees were here, but where was the romance of the Past?" Where she had hoped to see a "beautiful little Spanish Village complete with balconies and señoritas with roses in their hair," she found the Plaza "forsaken and forgotten," full of filth and decay, and "suffocated in a cheap, sordid atmosphere." In her memoirs, Sterling recalled that fateful first visit to the Plaza as the moment when inspiration struck: she would rebuild that lost village. According to her narrative of redemption, she took a narrow alley of warehouses, loading docks, and one condemned old adobe in the shadow of the wrecking ball and turned it into a living diorama of old Los Angeles, where life "before the Americans came was almost an ideal existence. The men owned and rode magnificent horses. The women were flower-like in silk and laces. There were picnics into the hills, dancing at night, moonlight serenades, romance and real happiness."[5] Olvera Street, the embodiment of Sterling's vision, opened on Easter 1930 to an enthusiastic Anglo public, and her story of urban heroism became legend. Olvera Street rose to the status of civic icon, becoming a fount of local pride and entertainment for Los Angeles Anglos to an extent she could not have imagined.

This deceptively simple genesis of Olvera Street ignores a long history of discussion of the Plaza's fate as well as contemporary Anglo dissonance about the street's creation and the commercial interest that ultimately brought the marketplace to fruition. Proposals to beautify the Plaza first appeared in the late nineteenth century, not coincidentally as the business of the increasingly Anglo city began to move away from the site. By the 1880s city boosters had managed to remake the functional design of the Mexican Plaza into a ceremonial garden, along the lines of an Olmstedian urban greensward. Anglos then watched in dismay as their pleasure ground became a haven for transients. Boosters shifted gears, proposing ways to return the Plaza to a functional space—namely, a produce market. None other than Charles Lummis entered these turn-of-the-century debates, hoping to retain the open-air parklike feeling of the Plaza, even including the fruit vendors that others had suggested.[6] When Sterling proposed her plan to restore the Plaza to a romanticized version of its past, city leaders remained divided. Not all Anglos were ready to exchange their commitment to downtown progress for a quaint vision of Mexican village life. Spanish romance for tourists and architectural flourishes were one thing; installing them in the heart of a city dedicated to growth and modernity was something else entirely. The most vocal adherent of this view was Constance Simpson, who fought the development of Olvera Street all the way to the California Supreme Court.

As Simpson's lawsuit wound a convoluted path through the courts and the press, it exposed a complicated story of Olvera Street's establishment. The suit, and thus the street, became a key venue for negotiating the terms of public space and memory. Simpson, whose family had owned land in the Plaza area for several generations, was a major property holder on the street and controlled a large building with several small businesses and light manufacturers as lessees.[7] Unsympathetic to Christine Sterling's sentiments and critical of her methods, Simpson sued both the city of Los Angeles and Sterling for undue interference with her property rights. Simpson's complaint stemmed from the initial proposal to close the street to automobile traffic in 1929. With manufacturing and distribution businesses to run, Simpson and her tenants were upset that the city was blocking access to their loading docks. She sent a formal petition to the Los Angeles City Council, protesting that it would be "grossly unfair to my tenants if they are not permitted to park as they have been accustomed to in all the years past."[8] Administrators paid Simpson little heed, preferring Sterling's plan for a pedestrian mall for which she had mercilessly lobbied them for three years by that point.

Though Olvera Street's potential commercial appeal was not part of its origin myth, Sterling's case to local leaders was stronger for highlighting this feature. Sterling had first targeted a group predisposed to listen to such propositions—the Los Angeles Chamber of Commerce—which had fostered El Camino Real some twenty years before. In May 1926 Sterling asked the chamber to endorse her plan to transform the Plaza area into "a great attraction to the tourists and also a permanent attraction" for local citizens. She offered to make it "very gay with the bright costumes and customs of the people—Music in the afternoon, Spanish dancers, . . . [and] a continual round each year of 'fiestas' and the things which go to make the latin [sic] race so appealing to the American." Strangers, she wrote, already think "of us in terms of Sunny Patios, Mission Arches, Spanish costumes, etc., . . . but aside from a few Spanish homes and our old Missions we have nothing to show." The historic Plaza district, a natural tourist focus, stood in disrepair, even "squalor." Imagine the "untold possibilities," she exhorted the chamber, "if a real Spanish-Mexican quarter was created in this section."[9] Beyond tourism, she dangled new opportunities in real estate and development in this neglected area of downtown.

The chamber's board of directors seemed inclined to agree. Several voiced their desire to join her attempt to "turn a semi-slum district into a very attractive spot and . . . to capitalize the Spanish and Mexican influence into what seems to be a good thing." Many of the directors liked that the project would be "a profit-making and private enterprise outside of its artistic features" and would financially benefit both local property owners and the city at large.[10] The Plaza area was already, of course, a real Mexican quarter, as many ethnic Mexicans lived in its

orbit; the chamber of commerce understood Sterling's plan not so much
as a blueprint for creating the district but as a way to make it more profitable for Anglos. Sterling's own disappointing Plaza experience represented to the chamber a tragic failure to capture potential tourist dollars
and push downtown development.

Yet not everyone joined in the acclamation. Board member William
Lacy's memory of the Los Angeles in which he had arrived fifty years
earlier differed significantly from Sterling's ongoing fiesta. He remembered it as "a very filthy place" and described the Plaza area as "about
two or three feet deep in dust and dogs ran around in there and Mexicans
and that sort of thing." To his mind, Mexican adobes with their hanging strings of chilies and garlic were repulsive rather than picturesque,
infested, he recalled, with flies and smallpox. This place was, he argued,
representative of the true condition of early Los Angeles, a vision he
hoped never to see again. Lacy invoked personal experience to challenge the fanciful version of the past, which he declared to be "an awful
lot of bunk" made up by easterners. If Lacy's memory was as subjective
as Sterling's, in the mid-1920s he was one of the few to challenge the
official romance openly. While Lacy begrudgingly supported the venture as a tourist billboard, fake though it might be, he did not share the
rest of the chamber's enthusiasm for the plan to resurrect a Mexican
legacy in the middle of the modern city.[11]

Despite the chamber's verbal endorsement, it relied on Sterling to
bring the proposal to fruition. To do so, Sterling needed to catch the
attention of a wider audience. She found this audience in 1928, achieving local fame for her rather dramatic intervention to save the Avila
Adobe from destruction. Built in 1818 and one of the only original
Spanish adobes extant in the city, the Avila home came under threat of
condemnation soon after Sterling discovered it. When her plan
foundered for lack of funds, she despaired that some of the key historic
raw material for her plan would be razed. With the approval of the
adobe's owners, descendants of the Avila family, she posted a giant
handmade sign protesting the impending destruction. She pleaded
atop the ten-by-twelve-foot billboard, "SHALL WE CONDEMN"
this building through which so much history had passed? She offered a
litany of reasons for preserving the decaying structure, from its
reminder of the "peaceful happy days of early California" to its minor
role in the American conquest of Los Angeles in 1847. She rebuked
Anglos for their disgraceful mistreatment of this history. "If this old
landmark is not worthy of preservation, then there is no Sentiment,

no Patriotism, no Country, no Flag. Los Angeles will be forever marked
a transient, Orphan city, if she allows her Roots to rot in a soil impoverished by neglect."[12] She alerted several major newspapers of her
indictment, and the resulting stories about the building and her efforts
netted not only key donations to repair the building but some valuable
personal publicity and allies. Sterling played a well-rehearsed preservation script, effectively combining narratives of Anglos' patriotic duty,
imminent doom, female historical housekeeping, and civic attruism in
order to amplify her cause. This campaign would not be the last time
she put forth these themes.

Sterling's public success influenced the chamber to move more
actively on her behalf in 1929, sponsoring her bid before the city council. She now sought not a stay of architectural execution but an ordinance banning automobile traffic on the street so that she might
construct her pedestrian promenade. "At no expense to the city," she
offered to make an alley adjacent to the Plaza into "a clean, picturesque
Latin-American show place—a spot of beauty for all of us to enjoy—a
romantic place in which to preserve our history." Indeed, she promised
to "convert it into the greatest tourist attraction this city ever had."
Council members thought the idea "splendid": An enterprising citizen
would take a site that they saw as "more or less of a dumping place for
rubbish" and transform it into a picturesque and profitable tourist
mart.[13] Sterling coupled her abject pleas for preservation with an appeal
to boosters' business sense. Her expert use of the now–long-standing
booster formula that linked the Spanish past to urban growth, the
tourist industry, and real estate persuaded Anglo elites to join her effort.

The council did instruct Sterling to "obtain the written consent of *all*
the owners of property" along the alley before it would approve any
street closure. Sterling reported later that she had a "*majority* of property owners . . . favorable to the plan."[14] The council decided not to
press her on the remaining signatures and so passed the ordinance and
sent it on to the mayor for signature. Hearing of Simpson's and others'
objections, however, Mayor John Porter vetoed it, urging the council to
consider more carefully the property owners' divided opinions. The
council dutifully held a hearing, negotiated compromises with a few of
the objecting property owners—though not Simpson—and then sum-
marily overrode the veto.[15] Unsatisfied, Simpson attempted to bring an
injunction against Sterling's construction crews. Simpson's complaint
accused the city council of abusing its power by intending "to convert a
street from its primary use and purpose" at the behest of private interests.[16]

Her plea was rejected in February 1930, allowing the unfettered transformation of the street. Simpson was undaunted and pursued her claim,
but by the time it was heard again in open court, the marketplace had
been open for business for months.

After defeating the injunction, Sterling immediately took charge of
the tasks of readying the street and buildings over the first winter of the
Great Depression, though the stock-market crash appeared to have little
immediate effect on the project.[17] She enlisted assistance from both
public and private agencies. The city engineer's office drew up the plans,
and the police chief supplied the manual laborers from the Lincoln
Heights jail. Contractors donated equipment and materials, while social
clubs and individuals responded to her call to contribute by purchasing
decorative paving tiles at a dime apiece. Sterling spruced up the buildings that fronted the street and restored a few historic structures, including the Avila Adobe and the Pelanconi house, built in 1850 and known
as the first red-brick building in Los Angeles.[18] Sterling had a fountain
built at one end of the street, a large cross at the other, and lamps
installed in between. To create the final piece, she directed the construction of small wooden and canvas booths, which she called *puestos,* to
line the middle of the street and offer Mexican foods and trinkets for
sale.[19] In a remarkably short time, Sterling supervised a dramatic visual
and physical transformation of the alley. Nearly as quickly, area Anglo
residents adopted the street as a favorite place for an afternoon shopping stroll or an evening sampling of ethnic delights. Promotional
engines wasted little time in advertising these features to both the touring and local publics.

Simpson remained unconvinced that the transformation was an
improvement. Despite the quick popularity of Olvera Street, Simpson
alleged that the city had not backed the project for public benefit at all but
had done so solely to encourage private downtown interests. As evidence
she offered Plaza de Los Angeles, Incorporated, which had not only
underwritten the construction of the marketplace but also planned to
exploit the resultant rising real-estate values. The city of Los Angeles, she
argued, had no business supporting a private venture. Yet exactly these
financial and development aims enamored the city council and attracted
city leaders to the project, not least of them Christine Sterling's most powerful backer, Harry Chandler. Publisher of the *Los Angeles Times,* leading
conservative, real-estate mogul, and general power broker with a wide
reach into the regional economy and politics, Chandler took notice of
Sterling's plan due largely to its proximity to real-estate interests of his

own in the Plaza area. He praised Sterling for her insistence that "in this day and age romance can live only if it can be made to pay."[20]

Using such logic, Chandler recruited close associates and like-minded investors to form Plaza de Los Angeles, Inc., in 1928. A for-profit corporation that was capitalized at one million dollars and offered stock, Plaza, Inc., developed Olvera Street as a key piece of a larger real-estate venture. With the immediate goal of leasing available property on Olvera Street to build Sterling's Mexican marketplace, the corporation also planned to do some speculative investment in land around the Plaza area, developing other properties both within and outside of the theme.[21] The investors in Plaza, Inc., were engaged in a tug-of-war with other downtown developers, and Olvera Street added a little muscle to their side. Though the center of downtown had been moving steadily southward for several decades, as map 5 shows, Chandler and his colleagues hoped to pull it back north. A few victories had already been registered, like the new City Hall building, and plans called for a civic center surrounding it. Across North Main to the west from the Plaza, the city's model predicted courthouses, administrative offices, and trade buildings. Chandler's own plans for a new *Los Angeles Times* building located it just to the south of the civic center, at First and Main.[22] The prize, however, was the site for a Union Station railroad terminal. A Plaza site proposed just east of the Plaza across Alameda Street remained in heavy competition with a southerly spot for the depot. The disposition of this site, developers believed, would definitively affect the destinies of the two sectors. The development of the Plaza area with tourist amenities could only help the cause of the Plaza site, and Chandler promoted the connection early and often; a *Times* editorial claimed that newcomers would thrill to Olvera Street's presentation of "the spirit and romance of old Los Angeles" as they stepped off the trains.[23] In 1928 the decision could still go either way.

Chandler induced five interested investors to prime the pump and advance money for initial construction of the Olvera Street plan. Thirty-nine thousand dollars, including a large share from Chandler himself, came from the pockets of Henry O'Melveny, General M. H. Sherman, Lucien N. Brunswig, James R. Martin, and Rodolfo Montes. Sterling later called these key benefactors the "fairy godfathers" of Olvera Street. Each had a different motive for joining the effort, though all had vested interests in seeing the Plaza site chosen for the railroad terminal and either held interests in the Union Terminal Company itself or owned sizable properties in the area. For Montes, a Mexican businessman in

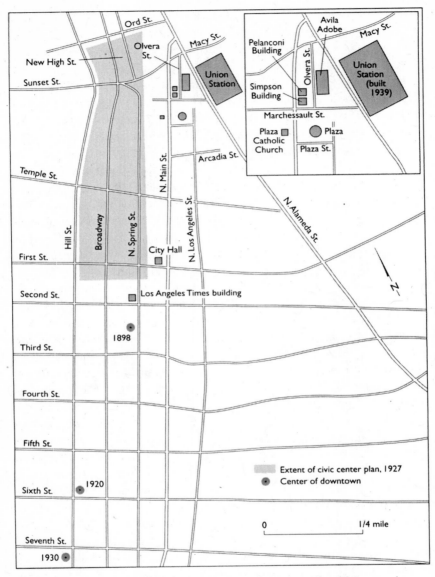

Map 5. Downtown Los Angeles and the Plaza area, ca. 1930. This map shows the relationship of Olvera Street to the southward-moving center of downtown, the proposed civic-center zone, and the location of Union Station. Adapted from a James Munson map.

exile, the project also offered a chance to re-create a bit of the home to which he could not return.[24] When the city of Los Angeles selected the Plaza site in 1929, with Olvera Street construction fast on its heels, Plaza, Inc.'s plans began to bear fruit. The *Los Angeles Examiner,* the *Times*'s rival daily, understood the connection. For the financiers who had "tethered" their "limousines" to the Olvera Street hitching post, the editors argued, the Plaza site promised "golden dividends."[25] Sterling remained the public spokesperson for the project, and an officer in Plaza, Inc., perhaps buffering any profit motives with her historical housekeeping pose. However, Chandler and his associates wielded the influence that could sway the city council and raise the necessary funds. They were the ones who made Sterling's vision a reality, and this private investment in a place of public history was significant, if not unusual.

"LONG LIVE OLVERA STREET!"

However scandalous this private involvement might appear, Southern California boosters had thrived upon a winning recipe that combined public and private interests for decades. Moreover, interpretations of the public interest in the alley had shifted nearly overnight. In the pursuit of principle, Simpson underestimated the appeal of Olvera Street's product—the performance of a lively Spanish past—to her fellow Anglos in Southern California. For many Anglos, such an image had become more than a publicity stunt or cover for baser motives. By this time, old-timers like Simpson and William Lacy, who could claim personal memories of nineteenth-century California that diverged from the romantic narrative, found themselves suddenly outnumbered by newcomers, who had come to dominate the region's demographics.

Los Angeles' population growth, already steady since the turn of the century, was spectacular during the 1920s, as city residents passed the one million mark.[26] Though Los Angeles did not need to develop special attractions or themed architecture to become a destination for home seekers and workers alike, its growth only increased the Anglo audience for the Spanish past. While the 1920s surge of migrants included people of all backgrounds and ethnicities, Los Angeles continued to attract native-born Anglo-Americans from the Midwest and East in great numbers, a group that had previously evinced great popular interest in this memory.[27] Years of deliberate boosting that identified Southern California with a romantic atmosphere primed Anglo migrants, like Sterling, to expect a perpetual fiesta. For these many thousands of new

Los Angeles residents whose local histories recorded but a few years, the advertised Spanish nostalgia was the only regional past they knew. Thus, when Simpson's lawsuit arrived at Los Angeles Superior Court in January 1931, many of them had already come to see Olvera Street as the symbolic center of the city's urban heritage. Christine Sterling easily rallied the press and the public behind her marketplace. She successfully drew upon these migrants' desires to attach a common regional past to a brand-new place. As at Rancho Santa Fe, the Spanish past as enacted on Olvera Street became, in Sterling's widely adopted logic, an essential local amenity and thus a public investment in need of protection.

The defense of the street focused on the supposedly glaring contrast between the prior condition of the alley and the uniquely historic landmark it had become. Both in her testimony and in the newspaper, Sterling eschewed discussion of the private motives behind the development and worked to discredit Simpson by alleging that the previous state of the alley was a threat to public health and welfare. She implored the court to compare her construction of a "clean picturesque Latin-American street" with the alley, which had been "a filthy eyesore."[28] Harry Chandler's Los Angeles Times backed her view with before-and-after photographs and captions that contrasted the old street, full of "rubbish heaps and broken walls," with the later "gay clean Paseo." The images were hardly cause for hyperbole; they revealed an unpaved street, with some run-down buildings, parked cars, and a few trash cans (see figure 21). Yet the Times injected them with melodrama, subtitling one article "Historic Street Strewn with Dead Dogs and Cats." Sterling furthered her assault by connecting garbage to disease, calling the former street not just dirty but "a filthy disease-breeding alley."[29]

Connecting the street with disease was an explosive association. In 1924 an outbreak of pneumonic plague in the Plaza area had killed thirty people, primarily ethnic Mexicans. The city's ensuing quarantine roped off the area, including the Plaza itself, and health officials traced disease's origin to Clara Street, just three blocks east of Olvera. The attempt to disinfect the neighborhood included use of a militarized team to kill stray animals, eradicate rats, spray chemicals, and destroy structures. This process did little to disabuse the Anglo public of the assumption that the dread disease and Mexicanness were intimately connected. Sterling's commentary recalled this association when she described the alley as "overrun by rats and other vermin, two-legged as well as fourand six-legged."[30] She lumped together the plague-carrying rat, the condition of the neighborhood, and its Mexican residents.

Figure 21. Olvera Street's previous life as an alley behind North Main Street, ca. 1929. This image was entered into evidence as exhibit A of Sterling's affidavit in the case of *Simpson v. Los Angeles*. Courtesy University of Southern California, on behalf of the USC Specialized Libraries and Archival Collections.

Moreover, Sterling charged, dirt and disease only led to criminality. The alley was "dark, dirty, filthy, a crime menace and a health menace." As evidence, the defense offered the police record for the alley before Sterling's takeover. Over a fourteen-month period, the report listed fifty-two arrests for an assortment of nonviolent petty offenses: most common were charges for the possession or sale of small amounts of alcohol, gambling, or vagrancy. From this document, Sterling sensationalized the alley as "a filthy 'crime hole' bringing shame and unhappiness to hundreds of unfortunate people."[31] Essentially, Sterling asked, which public would Olvera Street cultivate—in her terms, a leisured Anglo crowd or a group of germ-infested criminals? How could one defend the latter at the expense of the former?

Though in nonplague years the city paid little attention to the sanitary needs of the immigrant neighborhood, at the trial Constance Simpson received the blame. Sterling argued that "Mrs. Simpson never protested against this condition." Instead of admitting its own negligence,

Figure 22. Visitors strolling on Olvera Street, ca. 1935. This photograph shows the popular lane the Anglo public had come to adore, in contrast to the alley in figure 21. In addition to showing ambling patrons, the image features a row of *puestos* on the right, the American flag on the left, and City Hall in the background. Photograph by Dick Whittington. Courtesy University of Southern California, on behalf of the USC Specialized Libraries and Archival Collections.

the city offered testimony that Simpson fostered this criminal activity because she leased space to "a pool hall on the ground floor and a 'flop house' upstairs" that put "ladies of ill-repute . . . in good supply."[32] Though Simpson was the plaintiff in this case, she had to defend her management of the property. She claimed that she had paid to cart garbage away and had even asked the city to pave the street. The alley was, as one of her tenants testified, no dirtier and no different from any other unpaved street in Los Angeles.[33]

While the Plaza had been the focus of myriad local designs, the plan for Olvera Street was the first plan to sustain Anglo visitation in the area (see figure 22). For leading city boosters, the danger that "the worst kind of slums were engulfing the area around the Plaza" appeared problematic less for the residents who lived there than for their downtown neighbors, and not least for "City Hall gleaming and new and a few blocks north."[34] The plan to decorate Olvera Street addressed this latter desire for downtown beautification more than it attended to the quality of life in the neighborhood. It sought to draw the Plaza and Olvera Street into the downtown orbit, cutting the area off from the adjacent Mexican community. Sterling reported that she had lifted these jewels out of their "ugly and dirty surroundings."[35] Anglos rose to defend Olvera Street because it had become a fun destination, part of their city, not because it improved Mexican neighborhoods.

Sterling and the city, with no small help from the press, defeated Simpson in superior court largely because of Olvera Street's commercial possibilities and popularity with Anglos.[36] Sterling's tactic worked. She successfully shunted attention away from the street's financial origins and focused it on the attractiveness of the street for Anglo visitors. In an amazing scene, befitting Los Angeles' future reputation for sensational trials, Judge Caryl Sheldon even broke away from the courtroom to tour Olvera Street. In his robes and with Sterling as guide, Sheldon hoped to ascertain how the "present smart lane" contrasted with the old alley. Moreover, when Simpson's attorney subpoenaed Olvera Street vendors, Sterling directed them to appear in costume. Twenty-five of them were present, and though they were not allowed to testify, their arrival in costume created a spectacle.[37] Though Sheldon grounded his decision in the validity of the city's ordinance, the tremendous popular support for Olvera Street clearly played a decisive role in the public understanding of the case.

Undaunted, Simpson appealed and after several years managed a victory outside of the local arena. The California Court of Appeals overruled Sheldon's decision in 1934 on the basis that the judge had inappropriately taken the popularity of Olvera Street into account. The Anglo attachment to the marketplace, the justices argued, was irrelevant; it had formed subsequent to the city's ordinance and thus had no bearing on its original validity. Indeed, the appellate court ruled, none of the facts about Olvera Street's new condition had a bearing on the case. Instead, the justices understood the crucial issue to be whether the city acted in the public's interest in the decision to close the street to traffic. What was the purpose of closing the street, they asked?[38] In forcing this issue, Simpson successfully articulated a version of the public interest that countered Sterling's. The appellate court agreed with Simpson's claim that the city closed the street at a private citizen's request. The judges called the city on the breach in its logic, concluding that no evidence existed to support the claim that the city council passed the ordinance "to prevent any manifest evil" or to preserve "public health, safety, morals or general welfare." Furthermore, they said that the city "did not intend, and never has taken any action to eradicate the so-called evils existing on Olvera Street. That was left entirely to the action of private parties." Rather, the court believed that the city closed the street "simply to enable the defendants Christine Sterling and Plaza de Los Angeles [Inc.] to beautify Olvera Street."[39] The opinion stated that such aesthetic purposes alone do not define a public interest that might limit private property. As persuasive as this argument was, Simpson had little time to savor her victory.

While the appeals court clearly defined the development of Olvera Street as a private endeavor, the justices, like Simpson, misjudged the power of the market's wide public support. Anglo reactions to the reversal demonstrated that many people did see aesthetic concerns as part of a public interest, though they would use different terms to define it. The local press reported public outrage at the ruling, and city officials decided to appeal to the California Supreme Court. Newspapers applauded their determination and printed photographs showing a group of costumed señoritas kissing the councilmen in thanks.[40] Los Angeles Anglos, as well as a few prominent Californio descendants such as Florence Dodson Schoneman, joined the shower of support. Throughout the trial, pioneer societies and historical groups had petitioned the city council in support of Olvera Street.[41] After the appellate-court decision, the council received piles of correspondence urging it to defend Olvera Street. Many of these letters suggested the deep attachment that Anglo residents felt to the place. Louise Watkins of the Friday Morning Club averred that her organization "consider[ed] Olvera Street one of the greatest civic assets and certainly the most interesting attraction historically" that Los Angeles possessed. A schoolteacher sent a postcard stating, "personally, I feel this is one of the historic spots of the city and do not want to see a change."[42] Beyond their concern for aesthetics, these Angelinos considered Olvera Street a cherished possession, a keepsake from the past that they were loath to relinquish.

The *Times*, unsurprisingly, printed numerous letters to the editor from local citizens who voiced similar feelings. One woman from Altadena wrote that "Olvera Street takes one back to those early days with its delightful Mexican atmosphere and charm, and to obliterate it would be to erase from Los Angeles one of the . . . community's real assets." Another Los Angeles woman wrote, "having been born in unromantic Chicago of American parents, I found Olvera Street a romantic

bit of color. . . . I consider the street a gem artistically and historically."
She concluded her letter, "Long Live Olvera Street!"[43] For these concerned citizens, Olvera Street made Los Angeles distinctive and was a
defining public endowment of which they claimed a share. Though the
marketplace was a private development, as determined by the appeals
justices, these residents endowed the city with the responsibility to protect it as public space. Moreover, the words these residents used to make
their case suggest how thoroughly they had accepted Olvera Street as a
historic site and how little they seemed to care about its recent invention
as a business venture.

The consistency of the Olvera Street defense in Chandler's *Times*
during the Simpson case both reflected and influenced popular opinion.
It reran the previous series of before-and-after photographs for three
days in a row in December 1934. The captions invited readers once
again to compare the former "city eyesore" with the current "oasis of
beauty" in the "midst of a turbulent industrial neighborhood."
Repeated editorials argued that public sentiment would help the city
carry the day and save Olvera Street from "the hands of the despoilers."[44] The *Times*'s coverage of the case helped solidify Sterling's valiant
preservation story and keep it at the forefront of the experience of the
street itself. The trope of the new saving the old retained its clout. Once
again, Constance Simpson found herself the archvillain of this civic
drama. In one of the *Times*'s milder editorials, the paper argued that
"no single property owner should be permitted to destroy [Olvera
Street] . . . which has won the acclaim of visitors from all parts of the
world and has been the pride of all who value art, history, poetry and
culture as a city's finest heritage." In angrier tones, columnist Harry
Carr said, "whoever Mrs. Constance D. Simpson is, I hope she is satisfied. For years she has been eaten up with a desire to wreck our little
Mexican street and wipe out El Paseo."[45] Writers made scant rhetorical
room in these missives to place Simpson in the Los Angeles business
community. Though not as exceptional as her business and property
interests might have seemed, they fit uncomfortably with her gender.

Instead, the role of urban heroine went to Christine Sterling. Many
writers in the press coronated her as the model businesswoman, admir-
ing her ability to express her economic instincts in terms of beauty and
charity. They always reported that her "untiring energy and cultured
care," not her business acumen, had "nurtured" Olvera Street. "The
Mother of Olvera Street" so successfully filled the well-established roles of
female volunteer, historical housekeeper, and maternal preservationist

that her economic plans seemed uncannily smart rather than unnaturally cold. Simpson had few similar public models to rely upon, and thus her business interests appeared to lack redeeming motives. As a reporter from a San Bernardino County paper saw the situation, "the splendid Mrs. Sterling and her life-work are menaced by another woman, one without the eye for beauty and color, who would have this typical Calle de Mexico opened again to trucks and traffic." Simpson leased space and collected profits with apparent disregard for sentiment. At no time did the press imagine her as a representative for business, protecting its interests against the encroachment of government; she was instead a "selfish" woman who rejected the pursuit of beauty and romance supposed to be her nature.[46] The story that the press missed was the remarkable instance of two independent women in the political spotlight.

Constance Simpson finally lost her fight in the California Supreme Court in 1935, though not for these reasons. The justices reversed the appellate decision on the straightforward argument that civic power to regulate public streets can be arbitrary. Another round of kisses from Olvera Street señoritas descended upon the councilmen, as the press and the Anglo public celebrated the decision.[47] Simpson's case revealed the extent to which Anglo Los Angeles had come to identify Olvera Street with the city's public memory. Along the way, her case made Olvera Street a crucible for debating the definition of public interest in the city and the meaning of the Spanish past for its Anglo residents. While one could easily view the debate over Olvera Street as a battle between two women with disparate commercial interests in the street, their conflict represented much more. Constance Simpson represented old-guard Los Angeles, and she tended to see urban growth and progress in terms of the freedom of private enterprise from government intrusion; she ran up against not only Harry Chandler's steamroller but an increasingly popular vision, fostered by Hollywood but begun earlier in the century, that envisioned city dwellers as lifestyle- and leisure-oriented citizens who demanded public protection of their common interest and investment in the local ambiance. Simpson fell short at the supreme court, and her understanding of civic identity lost out as well, yielding to a more complex booster formula that elided the public and the private. While Simpson quietly sold her building on North Main Street, Anglos continued their celebration of Olvera Street, an alley of shops and cafes that had become a venerable historic landmark less than four years after its debut.

"SPANISH COLONIAL—IS THAT
THE SAME THING AS MEXICAN?"

However swiftly Los Angeles adopted Olvera Street as its own, the process by which the place assumed its identity in Anglo imaginations was in no way natural or automatic. The street meant a great deal to many Los Angelinos, but what did it mean? Perhaps most surprising about Anglos' affinity for the street was their unprecedented embrace of its explicitly "Mexican" character. Why did Olvera Street not employ the long-standing technique of claiming a Spanish, and thus European, origin rather than a Mexican one? During the three decades before Olvera Street's 1930 opening, most Anglo representations of the California past had made a point of withholding their admiration for the Spanish era from present-day Mexicans. For most Southern Californians, the terms *Spanish* and *Mexican* were not interchangeable. Christine Sterling had initially expressed a desire to build a "Spanish Village." She ended up with a "Mexican Marketplace."[48] What happened?

Sterling's early proposals for the street sparked a debate over this issue that illustrates the way in which Anglos grappled with the apparent shift in ethnic perception. In Sterling's early letters, her references to Mexico did not assign it blame for the fall of the missions, as did many El Camino Real narratives. Mexican lands did not appear exclusively as an open field for imperial ambitions, as San Diego's fair had pictured them. Nor did Sterling bypass Mexican independence to glorify the Spanish dons, as did the allusions at Rancho Santa Fe. She even implied that Olvera Street could be a place for the Mexicans of Los Angeles, especially those who lived around the Plaza, to celebrate their heritage. "[I]t might be well to really take our Mexican people seriously and allow them to put a little of the romance and picturesqueness into our city, which we so freely advertise. . . . Make the Plaza Section into a true representation of Mexico, give the Mexican people one place which is really and rightfully their own."[49] Though Sterling never detailed how she would include Mexican people in the planning or operation of Olvera Street, her seeming willingness to allow them to fashion their own presentation broke markedly from the traditions established by her forerunners and caused concern among her potential Anglo supporters.

Some members of the chamber of commerce board of directors even found her use of the word *Mexican* objectionable. One stated, "I believe the title of this should be changed instead of Mexican to Latin and should include Italian. It would be unfortunate at the present time if we should use the term Mexican. . . . Practically all in Mexico that has any value is essentially Spanish." He argued in favor of Santa Barbara's strategy to "take a stand very definitely that their development is a Spanish development and not Mexican." Others concurred; they urged the chamber not to "swallow . . . the word Mexican" and to word its endorsement of Olvera Street in exclusively Spanish terms.[50] Another group disagreed, arguing that the total exclusion of Mexican references from the project was offensive. The problem was becoming a complex dilemma, as this 1927 exchange between a member of the board, John Austin, and chamber president Arthur S. Bent illustrates:

> *Bent*: You refer to Spanish Colonial. Is that the same thing as Mexican?
>
> *Austin*: Mexican is Spanish Colonial.
>
> *Bent*: Might it not be well to put it just simply or refer to it as Spanish Colonial?
>
> *Austin*: I think you would make a great big mistake. The Mexicans are very proud of being Mexicans and they somewhat resent the bringing in of the word Spanish. They prefer Mexican. I got that from the Mexican consul and several others. I think Senator Del Valle also voiced that sentiment. The word Mexican should be used and not Spanish.
>
> *Bent*: Would Latin American cover it?[51]

Austin apparently based his defense of the term *Mexican* on the preferences of Mexican people as he understood them, as well as on the views of prominent Californio Reginaldo del Valle, and in doing so he made a rather contentious political argument. Calling Mexican culture by the name of the colonial power it overthrew, he argued, would be neither truthful nor respectful. Bent's awkward attempt to compromise on *Latin American* skirted the issue, and in the end the chamber followed his lead using any and all terms except *Mexican—Latin American, Pan-American, old Californian, Spanish,* or *Mediterranean.*

Though the chamber could reach no clear consensus, under Sterling's direction the street began to take shape definitively as Mexican. But it was Mexican according to Sterling's conception of the term—that is, a conception rooted firmly in conventions developed at other popular representations of the Spanish past. For all her claims to give the space over to Mexicans, she assumed that in taking over Olvera Street, Mexicans would largely display a version of this popular romance. Sterling did not misrepresent her motives, however. Though her perspectives on the Spanish-Mexican debate and the sources of her understanding of Mexican culture will probably forever remain unclear, her publicly expressed beliefs about Mexican people never wavered. She voiced a genuine fondness and pleasure in their company. In fact, she represents them as almost impossibly perfect types. As she wrote in a guidebook shortly after the street's opening, "the Mexican people are the most lovable people on the face of the earth. They have fine characters, are honest, industrious, well-mannered and loyal." Looking back on her accomplishment, she later recalled, "Olvera Street holds for me all of the charm and beauty which I dreamed for it, because out of the hearts of the Mexican people is spun the gold of Romance and Contentment." Was she being patronizing, or was she a true believer in Southern California's Spanish fantasy? Her descriptions seem drawn more from stock characters than from daily life, yet she lived for many years among Mexican people in the Chavez Ravine neighborhood.[52] Perhaps she marshaled the romantic caricature to improve Anglo judgments of Mexicans, or maybe she combined all three approaches: maternalistic, sentimental, and supportive. Sterling herself remains a puzzle, but her peculiar brand of ethnic delight clearly resonated with Anglos in Los Angeles.

Despite Sterling's inconsistencies, Olvera Street became Mexican in more than name. Mexican people made the street intriguing to Anglo visitors; they animated the romantic vision of the past in a way that mere buildings could not. Olvera Street did not invent this appeal; observers in the 1920s noticed that Mexican restaurants and the taco carts and tamale vendors that did a thriving business in the Plaza area had begun to attract curious Anglo diners. The container of Olvera Street, however, drew even more Anglo patrons, who marveled at the Mexican ambiance seemingly created explicitly for them. A convention advertisement enticed visiting newspaper reporters, promising that "Here are beautiful señoritas and gallant caballeros whose sole wish it is to entertain you with music, with singing, and with dancing." One reviewer recalled one of the street's opening galas with similar awe: "Mexican food and señoritas conjured up an atmosphere of the days of the dons while strolling Mexican troubadours strummed airs of a romantic California day."[53] These singing, strolling, living Mexicans offered observers a rare chance to immerse themselves in the theme, to surrender totally to Spanish reveries.[54] The little alley had become "El Paseo de Los Angeles," where "beautiful coloring; soft guitar music; pungent odors from the open-air cooking of tamales, tacos and enchiladas; cries of vendors of native wares and the constant stream of visitors all blend into a fabric." No static diorama, the street was a living

tableau where one could see "quaintly-clad señoritas" and hear the
street filled "with their native cries."[55] For Anglo visitors and commentators, real, live Mexicans were the draw; these players brought Southern
California's past to life.

   That the street explicitly relied upon Mexican participation and facil-
itated Anglo encounters with Mexican people made the enterprise
largely new to the Spanish romance genre, if it was not alone. Following its lead was the Padua Hills Theater, a hybrid historical pageant and
ethnic theater begun in 1931 in the citrus and college town of Claremont.
Mexicans acted in the Spanish-language plays, although the target audience was an Anglo one. The Anglo producers stated their intentions to
promote greater intercultural understanding, yet relied on romanticized
narratives and stereotypes to create positive images of Mexican people
in Anglo minds. Like Sterling and Olvera Street, Padua Hills plays both
replayed popular tropes of the Spanish past and clearly applied their
positive images to Mexicans. Both venues focused less upon mission
nostalgia or aristocratic privilege than upon the festive moments of the
Mexican era, and they reenacted them for purposes of pleasure, diver-
sion, and consumption.[56] In the darkened theater, Anglo audiences
watched this narrative, but on Olvera Street they relished the opportunity to step on the stage and play a role. These 1930s variations on the
ethnic theme showed once again the malleability of Anglos' pursuit of
the Spanish past. Olvera Street allowed for new Anglo-Mexican inter-
actions, spoke to Southern California Anglos' desires for a local history,
affirmed Anglos' ascendance in the present, and measured the region's
shifting racial patterns in terms of an exotic and colorful past. If the
street offered an opening for Mexicans to claim some historical space,
the Anglo expectations—and dollars—that drove Olvera Street's development placed clear limits on Mexicans' ability to influence the city
beyond it.

   Yet Mexican people lived outside of Olvera Street too, and not only
as phantoms from a fantasy past. As the nervous chamber directors
hinted, Los Angeles Mexicans were touchy subjects, and more and more
of them came to the city with each passing year. While the population
of Los Angeles had merely doubled in the 1920s, the Mexican population tripled, growing to nearly one hundred thousand, according to
conservative estimates. With the building industry in full swing, agriculture on the upswing in the city's backcountry, and labor in great
demand, employers welcomed Mexican immigrants and successfully
fought Congress to exempt them from the restrictive nationality quotas

implemented in immigration acts of the 1920s. When the Great Depression descended upon the region, this welcome was abruptly rescinded as new residents, Mexican and Anglo alike, overwhelmed public-relief programs. Agencies that in early 1931 listed thirty-five hundred applicants three years later had to assist over six hundred thousand. Approximately 10 percent were Mexican families, of both Mexican and U.S. citizenship. Despite the fact that Mexican families received monthly grants of twenty dollars while Anglo families got thirty dollars per month, reports circulated widely throughout the region that Mexican immigrants were taking the lion's share of public relief. City leaders convinced the Anglo public that expunging these foreign citizens might ease their economic hardships. Beginning in 1931 and throughout the decade, the city carried out a plan of repatriation that would send up to seventy-five thousand Mexican nationals from Southern California alone back to Mexico. Local press measured the success of the program by the number of rail departures, citing weekly counts of "aliens sent home" and thus presumably excised from welfare rolls.[57]

It remains a startling irony that the repatriation campaign to remove portions of the region's Mexican community began within a few months of Olvera Street's opening. Indeed, the two came closer than one might imagine. On the afternoon of February 26, 1931, a squad of immigration agents and uniformed police descended upon the Plaza. The officers guarded the exits, lined up the panicked crowd, and demanded proof of citizenship. Those who could not produce satisfactory documents were held for questioning and possible deportation. The agents detained thirty Mexican people, and fear spread rapidly throughout the surrounding neighborhood. The Plaza was a particularly brazen target in the broader plan of repatriation.[58] Less than a year into its ballyhooed existence, Olvera Street witnessed an interruption of its daily fiesta that must have been disturbing to many people. How could the street celebrate Mexican Los Angeles at the same time that and nearly in the same place where Los Angeles was attempting to rid itself of Mexicans?

"MAKE THEM WEAR COLORFUL COSTUMES"

Olvera Street director Christine Sterling's response to repatriation was complicated but suggestive of the ways in which her Anglo patrons negotiated this problematic moment. On the one hand, though she remained worried that "our Spanish speaking population numbers many thousands . . . yet lies dormant and unproductive," she rejected repatriation as a solution. She claimed that the street's booths "given to the poor people justify the entire activity and constitute its greatest attraction. Olvera Street is making self-supporting five hundred Mexican people who would otherwise be on relief or struggling with poverty."[59] This assertion, that the street reduced the public-relief burden, was one Sterling repeated often. Moreover, she proposed that the city take this formula one step further and set aside Chavez Ravine, the largely Mexican neighborhood in nearby Elysian Park, "for the manufacture of Mexican pottery, glassware, weaving and the other arts and crafts in which the Mexicans are so skilled." She believed that by putting them to work in presumably "natural" or appropriate occupations, "Los Angeles could make every Mexican on relief self-supporting and at the same time attract thousands of tourists."[60]

On the other hand, Sterling favored managing the Plaza more carefully. The repatriation raid offered a telling example of coercive politics, but it was not the only one. Since 1909 the Plaza had been practically the only legal outlet for free speech and protest in the city. At that time, in response to fears of radical unionism, the city council banned free speech in all public streets and private property except the Plaza. Thus, in the notoriously open-shop city of Los Angeles, the Plaza hosted regular gatherings of the Industrial Workers of the World, a vigil in protest of the execution of accused anarchists Sacco and Vanzetti, annual rallies by the Communist Party, and as the Depression began, demonstrations by unemployed workers and World War I veterans' "Bonus Army."[61] City leaders began to worry that perhaps even this space gave leftism too much latitude. When a series of activities that the Los Angeles Times termed "red riots" broke out in the Plaza area in 1930, authorities moved to control people and political expression there. According to the Times, preventing the "Red sympathizers" who "thronged Main Street" from reaching the Plaza was a focus of "unusual" concern. While in February the police held back a crowd of three thousand with tear gas, in August they were foiled. The protestors reached the Plaza by "a Trojan horse plan," where a "large cattle truck was driven through the police cordon, its high sides concealing the Communists."[62] Los Angeles police began to obstruct most organized demonstrations and potentially controversial gatherings at the Plaza.

Because the Plaza had been an important pocket of toleration in a tightly controlled city, it thus became a key symbolic site at which to assert authority. Sterling concurred with the city's efforts. In her opinion, all "the soap box orators should be removed from the Plaza and a band of Spanish Musicians play there at frequent intervals. All the feast and saint days should be celebrated and Mexican vendors be allowed to occupy the space." Replacing soapbox speakers with entertainers and souvenir shops would represent a significant transformation. But she had to be careful. Under certain circumstances, even the colorful tamale vendors could appear menacing. At the police-instigated "Christmas Day Riot" at a 1913 IWW rally, which the press blamed on Mexicans, even the street vendors seemed culpable. As the *Times* insinuated, "The tamale wagons were present in force during the early afternoon all expecting a huge business. At these places, much of the revolutionary flub-tub of that portion of the city is hatched."[63] The ability to minimize such risks thus relied less on the presence of Mexicans than on the romantic expectations in which Olvera Street entangled them. Though Sterling never converted the Plaza as completely as she did the alley, her creation exerted as much control as did police actions, helping transform a center of protest into a commercialized attraction.[64]

Sterling had no intention of letting Mexican expression run free, and little in the Olvera Street experience was left to chance. Her backers in the chamber of commerce had insisted that she keep a tight rein on the Mexicans in her marketplace. The board directed her to "make them wear colorful costumes"; Mexican vendors could then "purvey their tortillas and Mexican wares controlled," not only by regular licenses but also "under control by the way they conduct themselves."[65] That chamber directors assumed that the costumes would exert a kind of control suggests their belief in the veracity of the romantic version of California history—that wearing traditional Mexican clothing somehow rendered one incapable of thinking radical thoughts. Yet if this reading was accurate, then how might we account for Mexican independence, the Mexican Revolution? The chamber preferred not to contemplate these possibilities, instead imagining and keeping the Olvera Street populace fundamentally apolitical. Sterling's key benefactor, Harry Chandler, warned her in 1932 to keep the radical threat at bay: "this is poison and will eventually wreck El Paseo."[66] She heeded their counsels, decreed regulation costumes, and employed both subtle and overt methods to maintain social order on the street (see figure 23).

The street's romantic world was thus a highly ordered landscape. The segregated geography Sterling imposed upon it conveyed a sense of ethnic control. Sterling described the scene this way: "We have made little awning stands or 'puestos' for the street. Each one will be given to a Mexican family and they will sell all things typical of Mexico. Lovely

Figure 23. Costumed vendors at a pottery *puesto*, ca. 1935. Photograph by
Dick Whittington. Courtesy University of Southern California, on behalf of
the USC Specialized Libraries and Archival Collections.

little shops and studios are being taken by American people and these
will add greater interest to the whole." The "shops" opened their doors
from the permanent buildings that lined the sides of the street, while
the *puestos* ran down the middle of the former roadway (see map 6).
While a few Mexican-American merchants leased shops, the majority
of the lessees were Anglos, and their businesses often had little to do
with the fact that their address was on Olvera Street. These "American"
enterprises included bookstores, interior-decorating businesses, European
and Asian import businesses, antique shops, art galleries, sculpture studios, a puppet theater, attorney's offices, stationery marts, palmistry
parlors, and Italian restaurants (see table 2). The *puestos* and their proprietors were solely Mexican (see table 3).[67]

Moreover, Sterling's rhetoric of charity clearly established the hierarchy. *Puesto* merchants (*puesteros*) paid no rent per se, but they owed
Sterling the same monthly membership and maintenance fees that shop
owners did and had to purchase vending licenses from the city and pay
all their own operating expenses. Yet Sterling was fond of claiming that
puestos were to be given to the "very colorful and very needy" Mexican

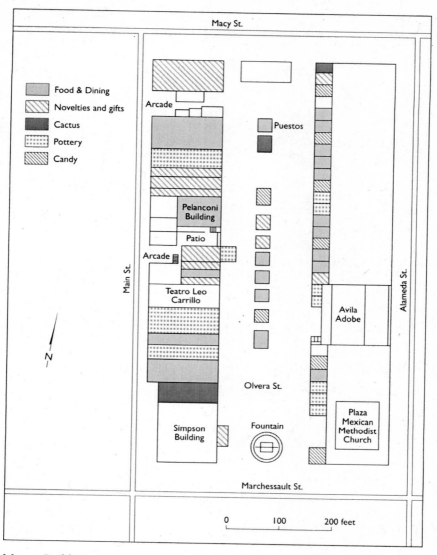

Macy St.

Food & Dining

Novelties and gifts

Cactus

Pottery

Candy

Arcade

Puestos

Main St.

Pelanconi Building

Patio

Arcade

Teatro Leo Carrillo

Alameda St.

Avila Adobe

Olvera St.

Simpson Building

Fountain

Plaza Mexican Methodist Church

N

Marchessault St.

0   100   200 feet

Map 6. Buildings and businesses on Olvera Street, ca. 1932. Though this representation does not include all shops and *puestos* on the street, it sketches the geography of the marketplace. See tables 2 and 3 for details about specific vendors. Adapted from a James Munson map.

TABLE 2. OLVERA STREET SHOPS, 1930-32

Type of Business	Shop	Proprietor(s)	Other Merchandise or Specialty
Art shops	Casa Gisela	—	
	Casa de Moro	—	Moroccan art, leather
	—	Alice Longyear, Jeanne Darling	
Bookstores	Dobe Dollar Bookstore	George F. Brown	
	La Cueva	Salvador Banuelos	
	—	Marjory Kay	Stationery
Curio shops	Adrian's	—	European antiques
	Ah Wane-U Sharon	—	Indian novelties
	Aztec Curio Shop	L. Mayo	Mexican curios
	Casa de Indios Americanos	E. G. Johnson	
	Duff's Treasure House	Helen Duff	Antiques
	El Navajo	Clare Stratton	Indian rugs
	—	B. A. Whalen	Imports from Mexico
	—	Mrs. Wheadon	Mexican novelties
Jewelry/gift shops	La Amapola	—	Mexican gifts
	La Bolsa Shop	Flo Nathan, Lina Burrows	Gifts and jewelry
	Mexican Gift Shop	Mrs. J. H. Decker	
	—	Nell Henvis	Oriental gifts
	—	Alberto Navarro	Gifts and jewelry
Offices	—	Frederick R. Burrows	Legal services
	—	Genevieve Rix Burrows	Cottage furnishings
	—	Bertram Grassby	Interior decorating
	—	Harmen Koops	Furniture decorating
	—	B. R. Magoffin	Imports
	—	Ken Rendahl, Marion Nelson	
Pottery and glass shops	Casa de Loza	—	Italian novelties
	Cup Shop	Alicia Morrows	
	Tienda de Alfereria	—	Catalina pottery
	Tlaquepaque	J. A. Pacheco	Mexican glass
	—	M. Garcia	Glass, wrought iron
	—	Guillermo Ocampo	Mexican glassware
	—	Charles Panza	Lanterns

TABLE 2 (continued)

Type of Business	Shop	Proprietor(s)	Other Merchandise or Specialty
Restaurants	Café La Golondrina	Sra. Consuelo Castillo de Bonzo	Mexican food
	Cafe du Tom	—	Refreshments
	Casa de la Morena	Mary W. Brown	American food
	El Aliso	Norval Munroe	American food
	El Balcon de Flores	—	Tea and gifts
	Peluffo's Casa di Pranza	—	Italian food
	—	Mrs. Brooks	Sweets
Studios	Plaza Art Center	F. K. Ferenz	
	—	Carmelo Barbara	Sculpture
	—	Virginia Gardener	"Atelier"
	—	Jeannette Johns	
	—	F. L. Moreno	Leatherwork
	—	Ernest M. Pratt, Viroque Baker	Photography
	—	Estelle Robbins, Frances Woods	Leather
	—	Jose Saldivar	Clay
Theaters	Teatro Leo Carillo	—	Theater
	Teatro Torito	Yale Puppeteers	Puppet theater
Miscellaneous shops	Estrella del Destino	Raquel and George de Sulerzyski	Tarot reading and palmistry
	La Nopalera de Roque Wolo	—	Rare cacti
	—	—	Caricatures
	—	Genie Lovell	Children's items
	—	Dolores de Roma	Flowers

SOURCES: Forman Brown, *Olvera Street and the Avila Adobe* (Los Angeles: Dobe Dollar Bookstore, 1930); *El Paseo: Olvera Guide* (Los Angeles: Clyde Brown's Abbey Print Shop, 1932).

people at no charge and that she occasionally lent them the money to get started.[68] Her claims showed who held the purse strings, on Olvera Street and in the region at large. If Señora Sterling, as she liked to be called on the street, could give, she could also take away. She wielded the threat of eviction openly and acted upon it frequently enough to make an impact. However long a *puestero* might remain in business— and several of today's *puestos* have operated on the street for multiple

TABLE 3. OLVERA STREET *PUESTO* BUSINESSES, 1930–32

Merchandise	Proprietor(s)	Other Merchandise or Specialty
Cacti	Fidel Anaya	
	Baltasar Flores	
	Salvador Valensuelo	
Candy	Luis Bianes	Ice cream
	Rita Galinda	Curios
	Jose Garcia	Ice cream
	Francisco Gonzales	Magazines
	Sacrias Hernandez	Mexican candy
	Ana Ledesma	
	Alexander Mendez	
	Josefina Ocampo	Ice cream
Curios	Manuel Balsalde	Mexican curios
	Jose Barber	Mexican curios and cigarettes
	Catalina Daniels	Mexican curios
	Baltasar Flores	Mexican curios
	Angel Gutiérrez	
	Jose Hinojasa	
	Victoria de Mesa	
	Lucia Velasquez	
Jewelry/gifts	Andres Alonzo	
	Carlos Flores	Jewelry repair
Mexican foods	Maria Cajedo	
	Antonia Escobar	Mexican cooking
	Margarita Gonzales	
	Florentino Jimenez	
	Nicolosa Juarez	
	Librada Martinez	
	Antonio Silva	Tamales
	Raul Vargas	Fruit
Pottery	"Cresencio the Potter"	
	Baltasar Flores	
	Jesus Gonzalez, L. Pacheco	
	Juan Lopez	
	Luis Olmos	
	Julio Rueda, Francisco Gonzalez	
	Luis Valverde	
Miscellany	"La Cruz Azul"	Mexican novelties
	Jose Herrera	Handmade candles
	Francisco Perez	Photo tinting
	Martin Rivera	Souvenirs

SOURCES: Forman Brown, *Olvera Street and the Avila Adobe* (Los Angeles: Dobe Dollar Bookstore, 1930); *El Paseo: Olvera Guide* (Los Angeles: Clyde Brown's Abbey Print Shop, 1932).

generations—from a physical standpoint, his *puesto* always appeared impermanent. The assumption that Mexicans were temporary regional residents, to be welcomed and rebuffed depending upon economic circumstance, thus aligned Olvera Street with the beliefs underlying repatriation, whatever Sterling's personal reaction to the policy.

Olvera Street's Anglo commentators and patrons preferred to imagine that the Mexicans on the street were happy poor people. For example, *Los Angeles Times* pundit Lee Shippey enjoyed his frequent visits to the marketplace, where he could see "the smiling faces of people who can be happy for very little." He noted that the Mexican vendors, rather than fret about financial hardships, "merely draw out their guitars and begin strumming tunes." In the volatile context of the Depression, repatriation, and labor agitation, such images held significant political implications. One has to wonder if Anglos like Shippey wished that the increasingly militant Mexican laborers in the fields and factories would only do the same as the Mexican vendors on Olvera Street.[69] Anglo observers of Olvera Street saw a harmonious, quiescent labor force that remained content in picturesque poverty, singing instead of striking.

Characterizing Mexicans as quaint but oblivious craftspeople made them appear anomalous within the larger economy. A reporter attributed to potter Julio Rueda "an intense dislike for economics which force him to sell his beloved ollas." Another observer claimed that Cresencio the potter fired his pots in the kiln behind the Avila Adobe every day, "but once they are complete he cares little about them, whether they sell or not. His joy is in his work, not his profits."[70] This naive image elided the fact that the potter might need profits in order to live. Such commentaries imagined that the street existed outside the bounds of modern economic woes. According to a *Los Angeles Examiner* writer, it was a place "where a fellow can savor careless gayety and forget taxes and business."[71] Olvera Street gave Anglos a respite from money problems. The marketplace represented an idealized economic landscape, where the apparently carefree vendors offered a less fearful picture of poverty than the mounting Depression suggested. Yet, for the Mexicans whose labor produced this illusion, the assumption that they were to earn a living by appearing not to care, offered not respite but poverty, as a self-fulfilling prophecy. Presuming that Mexicans could be happy for very little, for example, rationalized lower wages, a routine part of the Southwest's ethnically based dual-wage system.

Olvera Street figured the region's emerging ethnic-class system as the natural order, enshrining the common Anglo belief that Mexicans were particularly suited to the place of laborers. A 1920s chamber of commerce publication for potential migrants described Los Angeles as "The Home of Contented Labor," in large part due to the city's Mexican residents: "We have a Mexican population in this section in excess of 50,000 people and these people make excellent workers," the men as common laborers and the women as workers who were naturally adept at hand labor and textiles. Because they "come from a race of people who have been workers . . . for centuries, . . . they make splendid employees." Olvera Street sponsor Harry Chandler himself voiced his partiality for the supposedly compliant Mexican laborer before the House Immigration and Naturalization Committee as late as 1930: "the peon who comes here is an innocent, friendly, kindly individual. . . . They [sic] are not enterprising, of course, like other races, but they are more desirable from our standpoint than any other class of labor that comes, and they create fewer problems."[72] This image of docility was clearly more enforced than natural. Chandler, a large employer himself, employed vigilantes to quell union activities for decades both in Imperial Valley fields and the *Times*'s plants. During the 1930s, when Mexican-labor organizing reached new heights in agricultural areas, growers used repatriation as a strikebreaking strategy, deporting leaders at will.[73] Despite such tactics, the belief that Mexicans were racially predisposed to working-class status persisted.

Christine Sterling also went to great lengths to prove to Anglo visitors that Mexicans on Olvera Street were docile rather than dangerous. She tried to portray the street as a place where "a woman wearing diamonds and furs, with an escort as finely dressed will be seen eating tamales in a little cabana, sitting beside a Mexican laborer out of a job."[74] Such a picture of class mixing posed no threat, as Olvera Street rendered unemployed Mexicans content. In one 1932 guidebook, Sterling reassured tourists that

> There are no arrests, no disturbances, no crime, and yet Mexicans in great numbers are upon the street. Visitors comment upon the courtesy shown them by the Mexicans. The Police comment upon the few disorders on Olvera Street. In a little street shrine before the Virgin of Guadalupe money is placed and is not stolen by the Mexicans. The Mexican laborer shovels dirt all day, but in the evening he brings his guitar to the Paseo and sings with the voice of an artist.[75]

Sterling's characterization of Mexicans made them seem humble yet delightful inferiors. The affability of the race-class divide within the Olvera Street container made her praise possible. Outside Olvera Street, as Sterling had suggested at the Simpson trial, Mexicans endangered public health and safety. In the confines of a colorful past, they were safe and lovable. Moreover, if the picture of insouciant poverty on the street was Mexicans' natural predisposition, then Mexican economic complaint or political expression appeared unnatural, something to be controlled.

Olvera Street, while officially repudiating repatriation, thus embodied its larger regional lessons. As Carey McWilliams deftly argued, the repatriation project was in part an effort to "deradicalize" the Mexican population. There was a fear in Los Angeles, he wrote, that Mexicans on relief turned to radical politics. The Plaza protests seemed to furnish ample evidence of that effect. Repatriation deradicalized Mexicans with the threat of removal or actual deportation.[76] Turning Mexicans into Olvera Street tourist attractions appeared to deradicalize Mexicans as well; wedding their economic survival to the perpetuation of a fantasy past that tolerated them only as the happy poor allowed precious little space for contestation, let alone radical critique. The street portrayed an instructive social relationship for the repatriation era, wherein Mexicans might earn a living by being quietly picturesque but not so great a living as to betray their assigned place in the peasantry. In essence, Olvera Street presented Mexicans as "sights rather than social problems."[77] This perspective not only made ethnicity a kind of commodity but also prompted Anglos to evaluate the social issues facing Mexican people—poverty, labor organization, repatriation—according to romantic standards.

"COSTUMING OURSELVES INTO THE PAST"

Olvera Street was more explicitly and positively Mexican than previous Anglo representations of California's past had been. But Sterling and her Anglo patrons established definite guidelines for the Mexican culture on display there. Los Angeles Anglos understood Olvera Street as a slice of Mexican life pulled from California's past. If Rancho Santa Fe projected the genteel world of leisured dons, Olvera Street offered the colorful crafts and lively fiestas of the common people. The picture of a festive folk contributed to the street's image of isolation amid the troubling Depression beyond its confines. Anglo visitors imagined that the street not only was exempt from economic problems but also was lifted bodily from the past, creating an island of nostalgic pleasure in the modern city. One bulletin invited patrons to "pay no heed to the noise,

the turmoil and the trouble of the outside world which you have quit-
ted for a time—a world which lies more than a century ahead of you."
The street's recent creation notwithstanding, observers rendered it a
surviving piece of the past, "a living memory of the romantic days of El
Pueblo." *Times* writer Harry Carr called it "this bit of old California,
sheltered from modernity like some lovely princess who has slept
through the ages."[78] As at previous venues, much of what drove Anglo
fascination here was a desire to experience the past of and in a particular place. The physical environment allowed visitors to engage in a bit
of time travel. Here they could measure the progress—and the loss—
wrought by their own transformation of Los Angeles into the most
modern of cities.

To sustain the illusion of the street as a relic, Sterling had to sever
most of the street's connections with the modern city, in terms of both
time and space. Her development set off the street, and perhaps the
Plaza too, as historic space, separate from the nonhistoric spaces that
adjoined it, the future-oriented downtown, and the downtrodden Sono-
ratown. The street also marked time in a selective way, emphasizing the
distant over the immediate past, a technique often used in validating
"historic" environments and landmarks of various sorts.[79] Signs of the
street's relation to present-day uses were masked. For example, at the
Simpson trial, Sterling listed the standing water and sewage in the alley
as one of the problems her attraction solved. Yet, upon discovering
during excavation the Zanja Madre, one of the key flumes that brought
water to the pueblo in early days, Sterling decided to revive the street's
little canal, "the Mother ditch." Sterling directed laborers to cement
rows of pebbles zigzagging down the street not only to represent the
Zanja but also to serve as a useful drain for the street's daily scrub
down. Her original proposals and testimony against Simpson had
decried the alley's condition as "the gutter of the city," yet she literally
rebuilt and celebrated the original gutter of the city.[80] The "restored"
street and buildings thus avoided references to the space as a site of continuing social use, other than via the heroic act of salvaging it from
modernity. The street thus not only preserved history but also preserved
the history of its own preservation, putting Sterling and Anglos at the
center of the story.[81]

Such choices lent the street a structure of time that further marked the
Mexicans who worked in this landscape as part of the past and
obscured their presence in the modern social world. Sterling supported
the association by urging vendors to do more than just sell Mexican

souvenirs; she wanted them to demonstrate traditional crafts in action. She encouraged the *puesteros* to throw pots, fashion wrought-iron objects, weave baskets and blankets, and embroider clothing where visitors could observe them. The display of hand labor, as it had done with Indians, linked the craftsperson to an older, preindustrial way of life.[82] Guidebooks and observers took every opportunity to praise the apparent authenticity and antiquity of these crafts. One *Times* reporter typified the scene as follows: "Craftsmen of Olvera Street [are] leisurely following the arts of Old Mexico, . . . the trade of their Mexican forefathers. . . . Unhurried, these craftsmen work day by day, happily absorbed in their labor and not too conscious of the future." Another description singled out Jose Herrera, who made candles "just as candles were made 2,000 years ago. Jose is a descendent of an old candlemaking family of Mexico and makes his candles the way his ancestors used to."[83] Connecting Herrera to his ancestors in this way rendered him outside the march of progress, presenting him less as a merchant in a commercial economy than like the candles themselves, latter-day representations of the ancient past.[84]

Sterling orchestrated the Mexican imagery on the street to display an obliging traditional peasantry. The street's display of Mexican culture could not be separated from its definitive interpretation as both part of the past and representation of an impoverished class. Olvera Street seemed to focus on a distinctly different segment of people than had previous venues for representing the Spanish past. These "little peons of El Paseo" were not the Spanish dons who lorded over vast ranchos but rather their servants.[85] Like the dons, peons were supposed to be picturesque, romantic, indolent, content, and simple, but they were also explicitly poor. In the 1930s the popular fascination with folk and peasant cultures of various origins increased the audience for representations of the nonelite.[86] Yet the portrayal of Mexicans as "picturesque urban peasants" suggested a regional hierarchy of both race and time— the ethnic premodern as a counterpoint to the Anglo modern. Moreover, it transformed their poverty into an aesthetic object, a sight to see rather than part of an economic structure.[87]

If for Mexicans these images were debilitating, for Anglos the display of an idealized folk offered liberating possibilities. Olvera Street provided an opening for Anglos to express dissatisfaction with some elements of modernity. But they did so obliquely, in the guise of wistful longing for the supposed simplicity of life in this past. Sterling nurtured this perspective, hoping that the street would allow Anglos to reclaim some of the

"romance and picturesqueness" from the Mexican past and to rehabilitate the "cold mechanical age." Others picked up this refrain, using the
quaint street to escape the city: "To step aside from a rushing, commercial age and wander about this lazy, sunny little street is to find in life a
new joy as fragrant as the flowers which bloomed in the old pueblo days."
The street's appealing vision of a past where even the flowers smelled
sweeter lent Anglos a language in which to voice their frustrations with
modern life. Yet this nostalgia was unlikely to blossom into social critique; the constructed isolation of the street and the insistence that the
past, in the end, was irretrievable, quashed any potential for broader
protest. As Lee Shippey noted, "in all those old places, between songs and
music, there is a note of sadness—a realization that much of this quaintness is doomed and must soon pass." If the picturesque world of Olvera
Street could not survive beyond its own confines, then it offered few
usable blueprints with which to remake the city, other than the effort to
encourage nostalgia tourism, which was a modern invention.[88] Time and
again, Anglos' stated desires to rehabilitate modern life with Spanish
romance became merely plans to redecorate. The experience of the street
encouraged visitors to see this romance as doomed from the start, a self-
contained world severed from its urban surroundings.

Re-creation of the bygone Mexican past gave Anglos outlets for vicarious experience. The popularity of dressing in Spanish costumes
exemplified this desire. Southern California Anglos costumed themselves with the accouterments of a romantic Spanish past with frequency
and apparent zest. Elite clubs held fiestas and attended them in Spanish-
colonial finery, sometimes participating in costume contests. The street
hosted charity fund-raising events where "society girls of Los Angeles
[sold] flowers on the Street in señorita costume." One announcement
invited attendees to "dust off the sombrero and mantilla and bring out
the guitar. . . . Dignified citizens will don costumic splendor which dates
to early days of the city when Mexican rule held sway."[89] By dressing in
Spanish costume, visitors temporarily joined the fiesta atmosphere they
claimed for the past. The term *to go Spanish* reveals the deliberateness
of this activity. A city bus schedule encouraged the city "native [to]
exercise your weekly pass and go Spanish for an evening or a Sunday
afternoon" by visiting Olvera Street. Lee Shippey reported in 1934 that
"Don Charlie Adams, Don Harry Carr, Señora Sterling . . . and other of
us went Spanish in a big way" at a street fiesta. An advertisement for the
Western Costume Company marketed Spanish costumes with exactly
this appeal (see figure 24). It pictured a dancing woman, wearing the

Figure 24. "Costuming Ourselves into the Past" with the help of the Western Costume Company, 1931. This advertisement appeared in the program for the city's sesquicentennial celebration, La Fiesta de Los Angeles. Several key events in the week-long festival took place on Olvera Street. Courtesy of Western Costume Company, North Hollywood, California, and Department of Special Collections, University Research Library, University of California, Los Angeles.

obligatory lace mantilla but in a decidedly modern dress, with a plunging neckline and revealing skirt. She had roses in her hair and castanets on her fingers. The title was "Costuming Ourselves into the Past."[90] The image does not depict a picturesque urban peasant but rather a glamorous, modern woman, primed to party by the merest of allusions to a festive past.

If not quite ready to go Mexican, for Anglos going Spanish still represented an aberration, a vacation from everyday life even as it became a typical leisure activity. The act of putting on a costume implied that the costume could (and would) also be taken off. The more license a Spanish dress or Mexican sombrero suggested, the more it proved the converse: the Anglo identity of the person underneath.[91] On the street, Anglos found various opportunities to opt out of the immersion. One guidebook, for example, assured visitors that at No. 33, "Mary W. Brown serves American food in the Southern manner—lunches, teas, and dinners—for those who like Mexican atmosphere better than Mexican food."[92] As a whole, the street offered a consistent place for Anglos to take a temporary leave of absence from the city and partake of this past, gastronomically or otherwise.

On one level, the thoroughly Mexican Olvera Street was a place for Anglos; they produced, patronized, and consumed its ambiance. If many failed to recognize the ways in which they shared the space with Mexican people, Anglo references to the street clearly understood it as Anglo historic territory. Possessive pronouns marked the space in a good deal of Anglo press, and Christine Sterling's publicity was no exception. She proclaimed it a place to "preserve *our* history," an opportunity to "keep alive *our* patriotism and sentiment." While her broadest audience was all Southern Californians, the way in which she and others used these words was self-referential and implied a much narrower definition of "we." "*We* could have all the 'fiestas' as *they* have them in Spain and Mexico"; "*We* thrill to its rhythm and beauty"; "*our* lost inheritance." This phrasing clearly separated "we" and "they" along ethnic lines. An article entitled "Bringing Back *Our* Yesterdays" applauded Olvera Street for its revival of "the romance and glamour which surrounds the city's beginnings, . . . [for] building and rehabilitating *our* culture."[93] Sterling and her Anglo supporters envisioned the street as part of their own past. They owned rather than shared the space and its memory. Classifying the street as a historic site gave Southern California Anglos a way to reassert their presence in an urban space that had begun to seem altogether foreign and thus lost to their city.[94] Olvera Street projected a dual personality, managing to appear to be both an exotic ethnic place and a proud Anglo possession.

"THE MIGHTY CITY'S WOMB"

If Anglo visitors could shed their costumes, they saw Mexicans on Olvera Street as not wearing costumes at all. While Mexican *puesteros* were the only people required to wear costumes on the street, commentary on Mexican dress emphasized its natural appropriateness. Lee Shippey, for one, believed them to be "just as they came from their homes." He imagined that Mexicans were involuntarily drawn to Olvera Street "by the music, the manners, the tortillas, the frijoles, the cigarros and something of the atmosphere of their native land." In fact, in a later column Shippey suggested that "people living in the towns just across the Mexican border ought to visit Olvera Street to get a little genuine Mexican atmosphere. . . . There you can find the best and most genuine Mexican food, Mexican entertainment, Mexican ways."[95] When Anglos rendered Olvera Street a truer evocation of Mexico than Mexico itself, they questioned the legitimacy of a Mexican cultural identity other than one consigned to the past. If Olvera Street was the measuring stick for Mexicanness, it left precious little ground for understanding those who diverged from its illusion. Anglos could always revert to the normal, the American, while Mexicans were rendered in terms similar to those for Olvera Street: exotic, poor, and stuck in the past.

The female counterpart to craftsmen and peons on Olvera Street, the sultry señorita, furnished the most compelling example of the ways in which Anglos constructed their complex images of Mexicanness. Not only had the señorita become Los Angeles' mascot, but she had long stood at the center of Anglo yearnings for Spanish romance. Promoters advertised the possibility of encountering real señoritas every day on Olvera Street. One guidebook set the scene this way: A man strolls down the street and finds himself in front an appealing young lady selling flowers. "'Flores, señor?' And who could resist buying a fragrant gardenia when such an appealing brown-eyed señorita is the vendor?"[96] For Anglo visitors, that Olvera Street contained a significant concentration of so-called señoritas increased its appeal, its distance from the everyday world, and its possibilities for extraordinary experiences.

Among the most common activities for an Olvera Street señorita was dancing. Typical was a report about Señorita Costello, a dancer at the

Cafe La Golondrina, who gave performances three nights a week. She "wears a red flounced dress, a red rose in her hair, a Spanish shawl, red, high-heeled slippers, and is young and very beautiful. She plays the castanets till the candles flicker wildly in excitement. She dances the jota till the diners bound on the tables."[97] With no disrespect for her apparent talent, the frenzy that Señorita Costello caused on a regular basis had roots in a long-standing association of Mexican women and dancing in Anglo narratives of Mexican California, both contemporary and historical. By the 1920s the dancing señorita was an obligatory symbol of Mexican life, past and present. Yet dancers of the fandango had not always inspired the devotion of Anglo spectators, who had in the nineteenth century often considered it evidence of Mexican moral depravity. As Arnoldo de León has explained, dancing fed the idea that Mexican women were too sensual, voluptuous, and brazen, a description that seemed to measure at once an Anglo estimation of Mexican morality and an Anglo sexual desire for Mexican women. In the twentieth century's more romantic interpretation, dancing retained its erotic associations but with less overt disapproval. When one magazine writer explained, for example, that on Olvera Street one might see "obsidian-eyed señoritas flirt coquettishly with their lithe partners" as they danced, the emphasis was on the suggestive appeal, not the immorality, of the scene.[98] The Anglo view of Mexican women had perhaps shifted little, but the cultural context allowed for a change; one could now respectably desire or envy señoritas for their assumed sensual nature.

Still, remnants of earlier contempt for the fandango remained. While Sterling understood dancing señoritas to be important ingredients in the production of the romantic past, she and other reformers led campaigns to shut down Mexican dance halls in the Plaza area, which largely catered to immigrant Mexican men who paid dimes to dance with Mexican women. In imagining a similar scene in the past, however, *Times* columnist Harry Carr could freely admit his longing: "if the señoritas of the old days looked like the present daughters . . . , I don't wonder that the young caballeros spent most of their time tinkling serenades. Some of them are so beautiful that they fairly take our breath away."[99] So-called sultry señoritas trying to make a living outside of Olvera Street found themselves targeted as a purveyors of vice. Within the street's nostalgic past, and for Anglo consumers, however, they formed an indispensable draw.

Olvera Street commentary often contained strong undertones of such desire. Even ordinary news items described the Mexican women of the street in these terms. "Señoritas, with tresses like midnight and flashing eyes that never have been taught to hide behind their fringed veils, sawed with sinuous grace to the cadence of native melodies." Both alluring and immodest, the physical presence of the señorita seemed to quicken the pulses of many an Anglo observer. In one guide, the whole atmosphere of the street seemed to suggest a sensual experience, where "each twisting stairway promises adventure, each doorway hints of pleasures within." Some renditions even wrote the street itself into a sexualized metaphor:

Its way is narrow and its passage brief;
Around it throbs a clamoring pulsing beat
Its crumbling fronts stand out in quaint relief—
The mighty city's womb. . . . Olvera Street![100]

If Olvera Street was the womb of the modern city to come, who else could be the parents but a sultry señorita and an Anglo-American conqueror? In this metaphor, the nature of the Anglo possession of this exotic beauty is made explicit. Anglo commentary construed the figure of the señorita as welcoming both territorial and sexual advances, whether in the name of romance or of progress.[101]

Though these fantasies obliquely approved Anglo regional dominance, the street also hosted less subtle approvals of the American conquest of Mexican California. A focal point for this celebration was the Avila Adobe, a building that gained fame as much for its brief use as headquarters for the American military occupation of Los Angeles in 1847 as for its position as the oldest-standing adobe of Spanish construction within the city limits. Indeed, Sterling had staked her first claims to the Avila Adobe on the legacy of several American patriots who played a role in the brief battle for California: Commodore Robert Stockton, mountain man Kit Carson, and Army adventurer John C. Frémont. Her colossal handwritten sign protesting the condemnation of the house appealed more to American patriotism than to Spanish romance. In a well-worn preservationist plea, she argued that if the sites of Plymouth Rock, Lexington Green, and Bunker Hill, and "the homes of Washington, Lincoln, and Jefferson have become truly American shrines," then why not this house, through which had passed such notable heroes of the nation? "This old adobe belongs to the history of Los Angeles. It is not ours to destroy but an entrusted heritage left to us to preserve and pass on to future generations." Though Sterling denied possession—"it is not ours"—she also suggested that this Spanish-Mexican place belonged to the American nation. It was, after all, the "spot where the city of Los Angeles was born," not in 1781 by a small party of Spanish soldiers and mestizo colonists but in 1847 by the fact of conquest.[102]

Sterling celebrated the anniversaries of Mexican War battles and patriotic dates like the Fourth of July at the Avila Adobe, often by lavishly draping the building with American flags, ritually recapturing it several times a year. About one such fête commemorating the American invasion of Los Angeles, the *Times* ran a photograph of the red-white-and-blue spectacle with the caption "City Captured by Americans!" Soon after the street opened, local historical clubs chose it as the most appropriate location to erect a permanent monument explicitly honoring only the American veterans of the Mexican-American War. As Eric Lott has written about blackface minstrelsy, such an act "flaunted as much as it hid the fact of expropriation."[103] Not only did Anglos take possession of the Mexican past on Olvera Street, they celebrated the act of taking possession of Mexican California.

How could Anglos simultaneously celebrate their own victory and the cherished romantic past that it necessarily doomed? The practice presents a paradox. Unlike earlier narratives blaming Mexican secularization, Olvera Street descriptions typically did not shy away from admitting that the American arrival had destroyed the golden age. *Times* columnist Harry Carr verily lamented the destruction: Olvera Street, he wrote, was a happy display of "California before we gringos came and spoiled everything." John McGroarty shared Carr's sentiments: the "Mexican handicraft on view, the luring Latin shops, the Spanish theatricals, the tamales and enchiladas in the cafes, the fiestas and bailes, the four sides of the Square bright with serapes and gay vestidos, the tinkle of guitars and the click of castanets—all this that once was *ours* but of which the Gringo years have robbed *us*."[104] This seemingly remorseful longing among Anglos suggests a type of imperialist nostalgia, in which the commitment to progress generates a sense of loss for what has been destroyed along the way.[105] Yet Olvera Street gave Los Angeles Anglos a place in history other than the role of modern despoilers. Anglos could simultaneously impersonate the victorious conquerors, the happy-go-lucky peons and señoritas, and the latter-day redeemers of their quaint past.

As much as the nostalgia, the process of possession fascinated Anglo Olvera Street visitors, as evidenced by the continual commemorations and reenactments of various phases of conquest. The passage between modern life and fantasy past was enthralling, in a way replicating the conquest on an individual level. One description of day's end on Olvera Street suggests this viewpoint:

> And the prominent citizens marched back to the *real* city, to the clamoring clangor of the life of today, the churlish chase for livelihoods, the rivalries of commerce while still tingled in our ears the dulcet strains of La Golondrina. . . . The gallant wraiths that had filled the old adobe, scurried back to their graves and we stepped from yesterday, to today.[106]

This narrative made Anglos into citizens and Mexicans into wraiths. The egress determined the difference between the two groups: while Anglos shed their costumes after an afternoon of going Spanish and returned to the real city, perhaps with a few souvenirs to remind them of their dalliance in the past, Mexicans remained trapped in an exotic history and landscape and could but fall back into their graves.

"THIS IS OUR FIESTA, A MEXICAN FIESTA"

Olvera Street may have been designed as a Mexican place by and for Anglos, but it was never solely that. Mexican people, whether *puesteros,* residents, or activists, made their presence felt from the moment of the street's opening. Mexican uses of the street and challenges to its memory were neither consistent nor continuous, but their claims on the space were clear. The Mexican community of Los Angeles began renegotiating the cultural memories on Olvera Street upon its opening and in many ways is still doing so.[107] Several episodes in the 1930s illustrate this fact; taken together, they document a clear pattern of Mexican uses of the place, both in the course of daily life and as a site for their own interpretation of the past. Olvera Street offered Mexicans a venue to maintain an ongoing if submerged dialogue with the Anglo memories that so dominated Southern California's public imagery.

The physical and symbolic transformation of Olvera Street may have been on the edge of the Anglo downtown, but it took place in the heart of the Mexican community. As their initial responses to the project demonstrate, local residents understood Olvera Street to be part of their neighborhood. Members of the Plaza Mexican Methodist Episcopal Church, on the corner of Olvera and Marchessault streets, objected to the city's initial attempt to close the alley to traffic in 1929, saying that the barrier would greatly inconvenience church members by denying them adequate space for parking. This petition had over one hundred signatures, all but a few with Spanish surnames and local residences.[108]

Affiliated with the Methodist Church, the Plaza Community Center
also petitioned the city council, backed by the signatures of fifty-five
people, again most of whom had Spanish surnames, some of whom
worked in the businesses on the alley. The resolution declared "a space
for us to park is vital to our needs and in the process of earning for ourselves and our families a livelihood."[109] Olvera Street portrayed Mexicans as primitive, humble craftspeople, but many Mexicans expressed a
thoroughly modern and quintessentially Southern Californian concern:
Where will I park? Elsewhere a subject of great concern, this need for
parking caused little concern in city-council chambers. Without Constance Simpson's wherewithal to take the city to court, Mexican neighborhood residents could do little to halt the developers' plans to put the
alley to more picturesque uses.

That Mexicans did not win public recognition of their interests on
Olvera Street did not make them cede the space to Anglos. Nor did they
vocally join Simpson in her attempt to dismantle the street. Instead, they
asserted claims on the space and its representations, demonstrating that
they still regarded the street as their own. For them, Olvera Street was not
a world apart from the modern city. If not all ethnic Mexicans agreed on
its meanings, the street remained a part of the neighborhood, a place to
work, eat, shop, and meet. Mexican people used Olvera Street not only as
costumed employees, despite the Anglo control and clientele. In fact, they
drew on the Anglo memory as well as the space, using the popular appeal
of the romantic past to develop their businesses. The street thus contained
a complicated social landscape, as both Anglos and Mexicans used the
street and its various representations for their own purposes.[110]

An early point of conflict over costumes reveals the diversity of Mexican claims and uses of memory. Costumes were key to the Olvera Street
illusion, and Sterling used them as a contract. While shopkeepers were
not required to wear them, *puesteros* could work on the street only if
they wore the regulation costumes. A story in Los Angeles' leading
Spanish-language newspaper, *La Opinión* (but absent from the *Times*
and other dailies), reported a dispute between some Olvera Street vendors and Sterling about these required costumes. Many Mexicans
resisted wearing them, and within a few weeks of the street's opening,
"a group of puesteros deserted" the street, judging that "Mexican culture
was denigrated" there. Sterling decided to evict another set of vendors
who tried to stay and operate their stalls without costumes; this group
subsequently "demanded compensation from her." Yet another set
decided to stay; "other tenants remain loyal and report they will continue

having shops there and dressing in picturesque costumes."[111] The diversity of these responses demonstrates that Mexican people did not passively accept the Anglo control that the costumes represented. They fashioned their own interpretations and acted upon them, whether they walked out or decided to stay and profit from Anglos' fascination with the fiesta atmosphere.

Moreover, Mexican people, in or out of costume, clearly established their own social life on the street apart from the tourist illusion that Sterling mandated. The plain fact that vendors sold copies of La Opinión on the street meant that not everything was for Anglos' benefit (see figure 25). Though La Opinión disparaged Olvera as a "pseudo-Mexican street" and initially ignored it as a site for Mexican celebrations, there is evidence that street businesses retained a Mexican clientele.[112] Consuelo Castillo de Bonzo's café, Casa La Golondrina, for example, immediately established a significant presence on the street. One of the few Mexican operators of a shop, De Bonzo opened her café in the historic Pelanconi Building. Though she and La Golondrina played host to Anglo gatherings, including a glittering Hollywood nightlife, she also sponsored parties for the Mexican community, which were advertised in La Opinión's society columns.[113] De Bonzo told the Anglo press that her goals for opening this restaurant on Olvera Street included "anything to make for a better understanding with Mexico." Her efforts to improve ethnic relations simultaneously used and undermined romantic imagery. Though she drew many Anglo customers by hiring the expected "dancing señoritas," she used her resulting stature on the street to sustain an independent Mexican agenda there.[114]

In addition to catering parties, De Bonzo sponsored meetings of community leaders at La Golondrina. One such assembly debated the course of "moral, social and economic improvements of the Mexicans that live in the county." This program included a discussion of "the relationship between the different Mexican colonias and Spanish speaking peoples in the county" and explored how to create "more solidarity and search for their well-being."[115] If not always overtly political, Mexican vendors followed De Bonzo's lead in organizing activities for Mexican benefit. In October 1933, puesteros coordinated a fund-raising effort for the victims of severe flooding in Tampico, Mexico. Setting aside a portion of their profits on a particular day, they donated nearly seven hundred dollars to the Tampico Emergency Relief Committee, which was supported largely by the Mexican community of Los Angeles. Ethnic Mexicans also continued to use the Plaza for various functions, despite

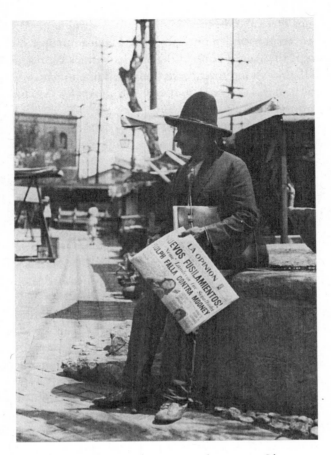

Figure 25. *La Opinión* newspaper salesman on Olvera
Street, ca. 1935. Courtesy Seaver Center for Western
History Research, Los Angeles County Museum of
Natural History.

the police crackdown. The Mexican Relief Society, for example, distrib-
uted food, clothing, and toys there on Christmas Eve 1933.[116] These
uses of the street outlined a sphere of activity that paralleled Anglo
patronage. The two spheres intersected but rarely, as the Anglo rhetoric
preferred the Mexican past to the present, and Mexican *puesteros* knew
that continued Anglo business depended upon some maintenance of
illusion. Anglos and Mexicans might have purchased similar items and
dined at the same cafés, but they did so for different purposes.

A notable early clash of these interpretations came in 1932, when the
Plaza Art Center commissioned a mural from radical Mexican artist

David Alfaro Siqueiros. With Diego Rivera and Jose Clemente Orozco, Siqueiros completed Mexico's renowned circle of modernist muralists. He arrived in Los Angeles after his release from jail in Mexico City, incarcerated there for Communist activities. While in Los Angeles, he had the chance to observe and discuss the ongoing repatriation activities and violent strikebreaking there. He reportedly attended several gatherings of the Mexican community and heard their view of Southern California's ethnic relations. The Plaza Art Center's mercurial director, F. K. Ferenz, asked him to paint a large mural on the upper wall of the Pelanconi Building, partially visible from the street. While Siqueiros would later express his disdain for the kind of Mexican culture that Olvera Street peddled—"the Mexican curios, the tourist-oriented souvenirs that so distorted North American visions of Mexico"—he accepted the commission.[117] The artist saw the street as an opportune place to put public art in the center of political discourse. By its divergence from the vision of the Mexican past enacted on the street, the mural—*America Tropical*—ignited his hoped-for public controversy.

In Siqueiros's words, instead of painting "a continent of happy men, surrounded by palms and parrots where the fruit voluntarily detached itself to fall into the mouths of happy mortals, I painted a man . . . crucified on a double cross, which had, proudly perched on the top, the eagle of North American coins." As figure 26 shows, the setting included a stepped pyramid, twisted trees, jumbled stone blocks, and fallen pre-Columbian sculptures. The peon on the cross wore a loincloth, while the crouching riflemen appeared to be soldiers of the Mexican Revolution, taking aim at the eagle. This mural inspired a host of interpretations, from sorrow about the conquest of Indian civilizations and Mexico's own tumultuous past, to a critique of the imperialism of the United States, the exploitation of Mexican labor, and a possible communist revolution waiting in the wings. A great crowd gathered for the unveiling of the sixteen-by-eighty-foot mural. *Los Angeles Times* art critic Arthur Millier attested that "when the scaffolding finally came down . . . onlookers gasped."[118]

Some gasped in awe, finding inspiration "for the coming revolution in art and life that says, out of the way, old-timers, here comes the future!" In fact, much of the Los Angeles art community hailed Siqueiros's Southern California sojourn and praised his few works there.[119] Christine Sterling, unsurprisingly, was among the horrified. She would not tolerate this indictment of American society. The sharp leftist criticism represented a brand of politics that Sterling had tried to expunge from Olvera

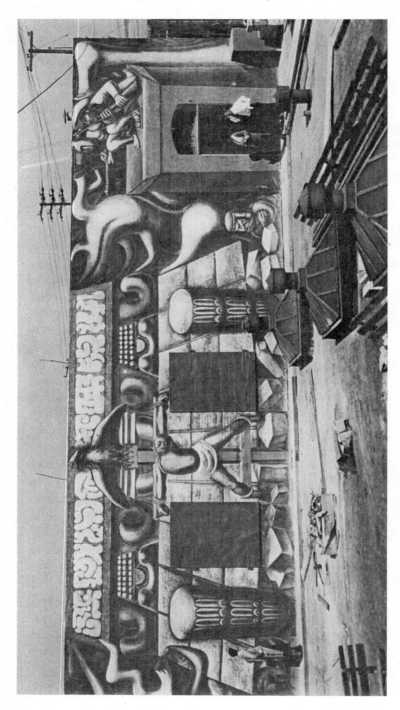

Figure 26. David Alfaro Siqueiros, *America Tropical*, 1932, fresco, sixteen by eighty feet, Olvera Street, Los Angeles. Several people inspect the mural from the roof. The section to the right of the figure on the cross, the only portion visible from the street below, was whitewashed shortly after this photo was taken. From the *Los Angeles Examiner* Collection. Courtesy University of Southern California, on behalf of the USC Specialized Libraries and Archival Collections.

Street. She continued her control over such expression by having the visible portion of the mural whitewashed and incorporating into the lease for the upstairs club at the Pelanconi Building a requirement that Siqueiros's work remain covered.[120] Though the mural swiftly vanished and Siqueiros was soon deported, the momentary rupture in the street's imaginary landscape demonstrated that Olvera Street and its memory would become increasingly contested ground.

In 1939 the Congress of Spanish-Speaking Peoples made a dramatic and radical attempt to reclaim the space politically. El Congreso de Pueblos de Hablan Espanola, it was known in Spanish, held an ebullient rally in the Plaza on the night of April 30 to celebrate the successful conclusion of its first national convention. Organizers of this gathering included key Southern California labor activists such as Luisa Moreno, representative and later vice president of the United Cannery, Agricultural, Packing, and Allied Workers of America. El Congreso's convention platform demanded political rights, unionization, and an end to discrimination. The leaders chose young Josefina Fierro—a Los Angeles resident; former student at the University of California, Los Angeles; and enthusiastic El Congreso participant—to give a speech to kick off the rally.[121] Her speech not only reiterated the political platform but also openly challenged the Anglo understanding of Olvera Street: "I'm going to say a few words in English first, to explain to the Americans here what this is all about. Then I'll continue in Spanish, because this is *our* fiesta, a Mexican fiesta. It's a kind of birthday party, a different kind of celebration than Olvera Street has ever seen before. An awakening of the Mexican people in the United States!" Fierro's words and the rally itself did indeed celebrate something different; instead of heralding a romantic past, she declared that "our fiesta" was a celebration of the fact that Mexican people had "gathered together for unified action against the abuses of discrimination and poverty which have embittered and paralyzed them for so many years."[122]

This strident tone signified the increasingly vocal political presence of Mexican-Americans on the street and in the city. Historian George Sánchez and others have shown that the 1930s witnessed a rise in Mexican-American activism in Los Angeles. The timing was the result of a major demographic transformation, hastened by repatriation, in which the ethnic Mexican community in Los Angeles decreased by at least a third during the decade. This population decline quickened the trend toward dominance by the second generation, children who had been born or, like Fierro, educated in the United States. As Sánchez said, these "children made it much harder for the Anglo American community to designate Mexicans as relics of the past." Younger Mexican-Americans proved both willing and able to use American political institutions to demand inclusion in the city.[123]

This turn to oppositional politics offered an outlet for Mexican people's feelings about Anglos' infatuation with everything Spanish. As David Gutiérrez has noted, "Mexican Americans have long been aware [that] . . . the seemingly harmless celebration of Spanish fiestas masked the disdain so many Americans felt about the actual remaining representatives of Hispanic culture in the West." From intimations in La Opinión, Mexicans in Los Angeles understood that Olvera Street's celebration was a double-edged sword. The paper knew in 1929 that the "Los Angeles millionaires" who planned to build a "pretend Mexican barrio" in the Plaza district were developing the site for their own benefit, not for the Mexicans who lived in the real barrio. An article about the opening of Olvera Street the following year remarked that the street illustrated "the success of the Saxon race" and specifically, Christine Sterling's personal "labor of conquest." Moreover, the author described the "daily procession of 800 curious" tourists as her militia, coming "armed with cameras."[124] El Congreso activists broadcast these interpretations to an Anglo audience, articulating the ethnic contradictions within Anglo fantasies.

Just as immigration agents found the Plaza a good target for repatriation, El Congreso perhaps deliberately chose the Plaza as a venue to highlight enduring ethnic ironies. By establishing a claim to the space of the Plaza and Olvera Street, El Congreso both asserted the Mexican presence in Los Angeles and claimed a stake in its memory. While the group's platform spoke to the present and future, the fiesta referenced a memory apart from Olvera Street's narrative of American conquest. Fierro predicted that "this night will eventually take its place alongside all the other holidays of the Mexican people in the celebration of liberty."[125] If El Congreso could not carry its plan to fruition, hampered by the onset of wartime and postwar crackdowns on radicalism, continued Mexican use of the space established, as Fierro indicated, a different kind of celebration on Olvera Street.

CONCLUSION

The active Mexican presence that El Congreso's rally announced on Olvera Street projected a different vision of Mexican people and culture than did Anglo interpretations of the street. On Christine Sterling's street, Anglo visitors marveled at the invented Mexican marketplace, complete with antiquated artisans in fanciful costumes. This memory of a romantic regional past became for Anglo visitors a central community asset of modern-day life in Los Angeles. Like sunshine and palm trees, it defined the Southern California good life. In the process, it envisioned Mexicans in this landscape as inhabitants of the city's past. In this view, Mexicans were not fellow citizens who could share the dividends of Spanish romance; they were to produce the romance. As such, they were artifacts of a bygone era—of their own culture even—anomalous and potentially dangerous outside their assigned space on the street of yesterday. By cleaving regional history and urban space along racial lines, the street's celebration of an imagined Mexican past supported the denial and denigration of Mexicans in the present. More than a tourist attraction and theme park, Olvera Street became a crucial venue for enacting both a public memory and a microcosm of the ideal public that codified concepts of citizenship around racialized categories.

For all their burdens of memory, both Olvera Street and the Plaza are often hailed as the last truly public spaces in Los Angeles. According to Plaza historian William Estrada, the Plaza's public restrooms, perhaps the only ones in the downtown area, underscore the place's civic character and authenticity amid the "placelessness of globalization." Scholar Mary Ryan suggests that in all the controversy these spaces have spawned, and for all the control that Sterling and the city tried to assert, they have never been claimed as private domains and thus serve as an enduring venue for public culture in a city that seems to have none. Yet, if both street and plaza constitute that postmodern rarity of traditionally defined public spaces, then the fact that the space remains deeply embedded in its romantic roots is all the more significant. That a place understood as truly public can also be ethnically bifurcated calls into question the meaning of *public*. Ryan asks this question as well, suggesting that public culture is rarely inclusive, even if it is not overtly divisive, given that it rests on hidden or assumed exclusions, such as gender or race.[126] Olvera Street cultivated this fractional public but at the same time appeared to represent the whole of Southern California. This is why the acclamation of it as pure public space is troubling.

A more significant fact about the residual openness of Olvera Street is that, for all its chronological sleights of hand, it has remained a distinctly Mexican place. By relying upon the participation of Mexican people, Anglo leaders could never fully realize a more restricted notion of the public, within either time or space. The costumed Mexican people of Olvera Street made the past come to life for Anglo visitors. At the same time, their presence challenged the notion that Mexicans existed only as a memory. Whether on the street or in the city, Mexicans in Los Angles refused to become simply part of the city's colorful atmosphere. They expressed their regional citizenship in myriad ways, often in how they used the city's landscape. In doing so, they nourished an alternative interpretation of public space and challenged the romantic fantasy that was increasingly becoming the region's official memory.

By the eve of World War II, the Spanish past had proven to be a malleable tool by which Anglos dictated the terms of regional discourse, and Olvera Street was no exception, even as the ability of developers to manipulate public space and define cultural citizenship came upon new limits. Olvera Street inscribed ethnic difference upon the physical and temporal landscape and thus stood both as a bulwark against change and a lightning rod for it. The battles for place and past on Olvera Street thus did not end in 1939. Today the street remains a contentious urban space. The marketplace continues to harbor an independent Mexican social life, with fewer costumes and more individual control over *puestos*. However, schoolchildren on field trips still come to the street to see California's past.[127] Such persistent ethnic divergence in an otherwise open public place shows the degree to which space and memory, Spanish pasts and future plans, and Mexicans and Anglos have become entwined in Southern California. As both a source and a stage for debates about regional identity, Olvera Street continues to shape its public.

Conclusion

The Trouble with Red-Tile Roofs

The red-tile roof, if not unique to Southern California, has become a significant regional icon. More than a mere architectural feature, red tile is visual shorthand both for the whole Spanish look of the region and for a still-resonant vision of the California good life. For roughly the first half of the twentieth century, Southern California seemed to offer not just a place to live but a newly expansive lifestyle. Rich or humble, all Southern Californians appeared to share in the region's Edenic landscape and community, and this common possession came to include a romantic ambiance. A particular set of images spun around the region's Spanish past—gallant conquerors and ruined arches, serenades and sun-drenched patios—became evocative metaphors for these aspirations. More than public history, these allusions became public property, a basic amenity that residents considered to be a regional entitlement. The acres of red tile that came to top homes, offices, shopping malls, and service stations offered visual testimony to the region's civic investment in the Spanish-inspired good life. Indeed, this distinctive regional cap seems to have proliferated in recent decades, even as public faith in the availability of the good life wanes and Southern California appears to be tragically bereft of its former magic in the popular imagination. What should we make of the continuing fascination—and trouble—with the red-tile roof? What does Southern California's sea of red roofs say about the fortunes and future of the Spanish past?

By 1940 red-tile roofs and a host of more elaborate visual references to the Spanish past could be found throughout Southern California. Four decades of earnest promotion and concerted imagination combined to produce a landscape that teemed with reminders of bygone romance amid the otherwise overwhelming evidence of the present. The venues I discuss here were only a few among many, but they were important catalysts, both for Anglo investment in particular memories of the Spanish past and for the attendant transformation of the region's built environment. In the first two decades of the century, Anglos experimented with versions of the Spanish past that might simultaneously give the region a distinctive identity and anchor it more securely within national culture. El Camino Real not only proved that nostalgia for the Spanish era could generate profit, it also allowed Southern California Anglos to claim a romantic heritage equal to eastern or even European legacies. The Panama-California Exposition painted regional ambitions in imperial terms. At the same time, it transformed the Spanish inheritance into one of national glory. These efforts at locating an appropriate regional past aligned Anglos with conquistadors and padres while distancing them from the uncomfortably near, apparently primitive Indian past. The stories of racial succession enacted at each of these venues lent Southern California a logic of history that was attuned to contemporary national rhetoric.

By the 1920s and 1930s Southern California Anglos were largely confident in their regional image and national belonging. They began to integrate their adopted Spanish metaphors into life at home. Rancho Santa Fe exemplified the desire for Spanish-colonial homes and the affluent suburban lifestyle the architecture stood for. Moreover, the tract merged private possession of a Spanish fantasy with collective ownership of the Spanish past. Olvera Street brought the past to center stage, occupying significant urban space—both physical and symbolic—in the heart of metropolitan Los Angeles. Its performance of a now explicitly Mexican past made it a key site for negotiating who would share in this public endowment, this good life. Anglo developers of suburbs and cities alike relied upon Mexicans to produce this landscape and culture yet did not envision them as participants in its bounty. During the Great Depression, questions about what the public was entitled to expect from the state and which citizens would find inclusion in the national community were under active debate. In this context, Southern California's articulations of space and memory rose to central importance. The various Anglo versions of a romantic Spanish past, even when under fire, served as measures of regional citizenship and carried significant weight in determining the shape of public culture for years to come.

The Spanish look of Southern California persists. The missions of El Camino Real and the marketplace at Olvera Street continue to be highly promoted tourist destinations. Recent commentaries about them recall those from nearly a century ago. A *New York Times Magazine* feature, for example, describes an easterner's 2002 driving tour of El Camino Real in terms not far removed from those in the travel diaries of earlier days. The author of this travelogue revels in her rental car and the coastal highway as she discovers the region's exotic ambiance: "Driving through Southern California was akin to visiting a foreign country." Although she is far more careful than were her predecessors to note Indian roles and deaths at the missions, she still strikes a romantic tone. "I stood next to a moss-covered Moorish fountain, shaded by pepper trees, and admired the regal façade of Mission Santa Barbara, with its tall pink columns. . . . When I entered the empty church, tears came to my eyes. The interior glowed. Golden-hued *faux marbre* had been painted on the walls and arches and pilasters."[1] The missions are ruins no longer, but El Camino Real still has the power to enrapture tourists.

El Camino Real even continues to attract the allegiance of locals. Californians are still marking the road with mission-bell guideposts. The California Federation of Women's Clubs, a booster of the original project, undertook a campaign in the late 1990s to restore many of the missing bells in honor of the state's sesquicentennial. So trusted are these bells that accounts often imply that Harrie Forbes's project was one of restoration rather than creation—that she was responsible merely for replacing the mythical "original bells" the padres had erected themselves. Whether because of the bells or the mandatory year of state history in elementary school, narratives crafted in the early twentieth century endure. "Every fourth-grader knows [that] El Camino Real is the footpath Father Junípero Serra trod," just as they all know that Olvera Street is "the oldest street in Los Angeles," despite its relatively recent transformation.[2]

For local residents, Spanish style has never had more cachet, with Rancho Santa Fe only the most striking example. The luxurious Spanish-colonial homes have held their value remarkably well, with a median value of $1.7 million, and the small enclave continues to house the uppermost class of Southern California. In fact, the 2000 census calculated that Rancho Santa Fe was the wealthiest neighborhood in the nation, with an annual income of over $113,000 for each of its five thousand residents. Yet Rancho Santa Fe homeowners did not revel in the designation when it appeared. As the vice president of the Rancho Santa Fe Garden Club claimed, "The last thing in this world we want is to be known as the richest town in America. We're just a pretty, quaint community full of everyday people." The idea of the perfect community remains, with the quaint atmosphere buffering elite pretensions. A reporter found that inhabitants "show no signs of wanting to throw off their splendid isolation, consistently turning down the idea of becoming a city. . . . Cityhood, residents concluded, might mean opening up Art Jury meetings to the public and lifting the residents-only restrictions on the soccer fields."[3] Rancho Santa Feans still prefer their controlled privacy to the uncertainty that comes with cities and uncontrolled public spaces, believing that isolation and the good life, not to mention Spanish style and property values, go hand in hand.

Despite outward appearances of this unbroken faith, the Spanish romance began to unravel even at the height of its popularity in the 1920s and 1930s. A number of vocal skeptics, Anglo and otherwise, took aim at both its frivolities and contradictions. Hard times in the 1930s led some people to categorize Spanish celebrations, such as Los Angeles' 1931 sesquicentennial celebration, as pointless municipal waste. The local African-American press protested that during "a winter in which hundreds of poor and destitute men, women and children will go without adequate food, clothing, and shelter, . . . it is little short of criminal to waste money on Fiestas which serve no purpose except to cram money into the pockets of the promoters and the sellers of gew-gaws."[4] Among the crowd of writers that gathered in Los Angeles during this era, more than a few came to see evidence of the city's predilection for fakery in the Spanish atmosphere. Acerbic commentator Louis Adamic, mystery novelist Raymond Chandler, and others of their cohort attempted to expose the Spanish looks and advertised good life of the region as a perverse sham, signs of a place gone absurdly wrong. If their boulevard-of-broken-dreams style was an invented genre too, this noir vision of California acquired an appeal all its own, in part due to its conspicuous contrast with the romantic view.[5]

Social reformers, critics, and academics began to join the chorus and to discredit Southern California's vaunted good life. Carey McWilliams appeared on the scene in the 1930s and 1940s, scrutinizing the region's reputation, history, and culture, particularly its penchant for Spanish romance. Along with John Steinbeck's oeuvre and Dorothea Lange's photographs, his *Factories in the Field* helped publicize the atrocious conditions of migrant agricultural laborers in the state, showing the region to be a far cry from the promised Arcadia. In the 1940s, however, McWilliams went on to study not the famous Okies but the less-visible problems of prejudice in California, not least the dynamics of Mexican-Anglo relations. As a good muckraker should, he revealed the many distortions upon which Anglos had built the "schizoid" Spanish legacy and judged this view of the past to be a major contributor to ethnic discrimination. Along the way, he argued that ethnic Mexican residents and immigrants would be pivotal to the economic fortunes and cultural evolution of Southern California.[6]

Although many regional residents followed these leads in later decades, historian Mike Davis has likely made the biggest recent waves in debunking Southern California's culture. Sharing both McWilliams's indignation and Chandler's cynicism, Davis has become a controversial public figure for his rejection of the region's booster ethos. The romantic version of the Spanish past was but one of several local shams, according to Davis. He excoriates the "specious historicism" in the region's memory, culture, and architecture—particularly the latter, characterizing it as "sprinkled like cheap perfume over hundreds of instant subdivisions." Laments Davis, "The nadir . . . is probably southern Orange County where the endlessly regimented rows of identical red-tiled townhouses (an affluent version of architectural Stalinism) are located on cul-de-sacs with names like Avenida Sevilla or Via Capri."[7] Whether or not one accepts Davis's characterizations and conspiracy theories, he is merely the latest in a long line of skeptics who have progressively undermined early champions' faith in the possibilities of the Southern California good life and the Spanish metaphor for it.

More difficult to dismiss than the critics, whose pessimism makes them the targets of Southern California's still-vociferous boosters, have been California Indian and Mexican-American activists. While a comprehensive history of these ethnic movements is beyond the scope of this book, their increasing appearance on the regional scene in the 1940s and 1950s and their rising demands for public recognition from the 1960s to the present have impeded efforts to sustain a hegemony of romance.[8] Some tribal groups, for example, have made definite claims on the presentation of mission history, pressing for on-site public acknowledgement of their ancestors' contributions to the building, decoration, and productive efforts of the missions and, perhaps most important, of the many Indian deaths there. If acknowledgment of the tragic consequences of the mission era for Indian populations has been

increasing in school texts, recognition of this fact at the missions themselves remains scarce. Although paid for not by the state but by individual donations, the Mission Indian Memorial, installed at Sonoma
Mission in 1999, represents one notable success for Indian activists.
Etched into slabs of granite are the names of approximately nine hundred Coast Miwok, Pomo, Patwin, and Wappo men, women, and children who died while living at the mission between 1824 and 1839—their
unmarked graves currently covered by parking lots, sidewalks, and gardens. This group represents a small percentage of the tens of thousands
of Indians who died at the missions. But the memorial's style, deliberately reminiscent of the Vietnam Veterans Memorial in Washington,
D.C., marks a significant departure for mission remembrance.[9]

Ethnic Mexican people have pressed for greater inclusion as well.
The political activism of Mexicans in Southern California and the
Southwest in the 1960s and 1970s not only introduced a new youth
movement but also signaled a new cultural agenda. Various elements of
the Chicano movement vigorously pursued civic and economic rights as
well as ethnic pride and history. Their desire to be acknowledged as
prior, and thus more rightful, inhabitants of the region ironically relied
on the very landscape Anglos had created—as it also echoed Californios'
nineteenth-century appeals for recognition and inclusion. Anglo development of Spanish architecture and historic places had already associated Southern California with a particular image of the Spanish past;
Mexican activists hoped to gain recognition as this past's legitimate
heirs, wresting ownership from Anglos. Olvera Street has continued to
be a key symbolic site at which to make such statements. The longtime
presence of ethnic Mexicans as proprietors, *puesteros,* and entertainers
has sustained both its tourist business and its sotto voce Mexican auton-
omy. Not only have Mexican groups insisted upon representation in the
leadership of the street and the state historic district that now contains
it, but their persistent pressure has also led to the restoration and celebration of the Siqueiros mural. The street's function as a meeting place
for Spanish speakers has continued and expanded, catering in part to
the growing Latino immigrant population that frequents the Plaza area,
although not all of the immigrants are of Mexican origin. Merchants
report that local Mexican-American residents come to Olvera Street
too, sometimes to learn about parts of traditional Mexican culture or to
ask merchants for help in selecting costumes to wear for ethnic demonstrations. Activists can even come there for "T-shirts emblazoned with
Emiliano Zapata or Che Guevara." As shopkeeper Teresa Velez suggests,

"This street represents the not-forgetting, from the *guarache* to the *molcajete*. When we're here, we're closer to Mexico."[10] Whether Olvera Street represents the Mexico of traditional food and clothing or of revolutionary and activist leanings, Southern California Mexicans have made the street and other venues of regional history work for them, even as their labor still helps create a romantic vision of Mexico for tourists and locals.

The Spanish past thus has offered a vehicle for Southern Californians of various origins to create spaces and memories for themselves, if in different ways. For decades, a romantic vision of this history offered Anglo women an avenue to public prominence, a way to influence the creation and use of built environments. Harrie Forbes, Lilian Rice, and Christine Sterling used Spanish memories to preside over key public and private spaces in the region. In so doing, they joined women in other parts of the nation who strategically fashioned the role of the historical housekeeper, opening up avenues to local politics and in some cases furthering women's causes. Although this role may offer fewer rewards today, we know that non-Anglo women never had true access either to the role or to the benefits it granted in the venues I describe in this book. Alongside their male counterparts, Mexican and Indian women endeavored in their own ways to shape public space and memory, and in the process they demanded rights to equal space and representation. Yet the prior establishment and physical presence of Anglo memories on the landscape—an impulse for which the historical housekeepers had received great public acclaim—made these efforts appear defensive rather than charitable.

For example, some observers have characterized the resistance of some Mexican-Americans to recent efforts to expand Olvera Street's mission—to encompass a multiethnic, specifically Chinese and Italian, influence—as a decidedly intolerant reaction. Yet Mexican-Americans' desires to protect the street as Mexican space are not so different from Anglos' earlier attempts to control place through memory. The two groups may not share tactics or public personae, but historical housekeepers and Mexican advocates have both understood that space and memory offer key symbolic venues for gaining a public voice about present-day society. Loath to give up what they worked so hard to reclaim, Los Angeles Mexicans see that Olvera Street, in part because of its largely Anglo genesis, is an important place to reaffirm their presence in the city.[11] Whether for romance, women's advancement, or ethnic representation, challenging the use of spaces and defending the preservation

of memories continue to create inroads into local politics and public culture for people who lack ready access to traditional channels.

The Spanish past thus confers upon the region an ambiguous legacy.
On the one hand, Spanish style remains a dominant decorative expression of a still-profitable regional appeal. As long as Rancho Santa Fe
remains sought-after property, allusions to Spanish romance will remain
a part of Southern California's cultural fabric. As the venues in this
book show, the Anglo memories set in place in the first half of the twentieth century placed ethnic division at the center of regional identity and
thus established the context for a bifurcated public. The fact that ethnic
Mexicans and California Indians alike have continued to feel the need
to challenge official narratives testifies to the lasting impact of these cultural memories on race relations. On the other hand, for all the historical quagmires of the region's long regional romance, the commitment to
the romantic past both saved and created a built environment for future
generations to see, interpret, and reclaim. While Anglos deliberately
marked Spanish Southern California as past, they did not obliterate it.
The places they preserved were a hedge against forgetting and indeed
allowed the "not forgetting" that meant so much to Olvera Street merchant Teresa Velez. Many Anglos have come to join this new consensus,
acknowledging the romance as a counterproductive fiction and working
to create more multiethnic spaces.

How then have red-tile roofs survived the many years of debunking
Southern California's Spanish romance? Consider the material presence of
memories, in California and beyond, in historic preservations, theme
districts, and domestic architecture. A visual presence on the landscape
helps preserve the interpretations that fostered such sites' creation or
restoration. Though, as recent events demonstrate, such installations do
not preclude the evolution of new interpretations over time, built memories often prove to be quite resistant to transformation. The physical
remnants of historical sites themselves can be obstacles to cultural
change. Romance, race, and region have come to inhabit the landscape
together, not as discrete elements that can be exchanged at will. Of
course, razing red-tile roofs would not erase the region's legacy of racial
exclusion, since the built environment is clearly only one factor influencing racial understandings in the region. More important, perhaps, is
the fact that Southern California's landscape has so thoroughly imbibed
this romantic Spanish past that the memory appears to be almost a natural feature, an innate regional quality that eludes interpretation instead
of a historical development that demands it. The issue that many people

have overlooked is not the Spanish metaphor itself but the reasons and process by which it came to be so emblematic.[12] The trouble with the red-tile roof is that it appears to be merely an ornamental commodity, but it is more important than that. Its instinctive, habitual consumption elevates rather than diminishes its cultural influence. As a popular abbreviation for the region's Spanish character, it both inspires remembrance and obscures it.

This paradox lies at the heart of the relationship between memory and place. Historic spaces can enshrine certain cultural narratives of race, citizenship, or nation, and at the same time, by providing an impetus for resistance, contain the seeds of those narratives' transformation. That memories can be ambiguous and that places can be reclaimed only confirms the ability of the past—or a particular vision of it—to set the stage on which we enact and contest public culture.

Notes

INTRODUCTION

1. Frank Lloyd Wright quoted in Carey McWilliams, *Southern California Country: An Island on the Land* (New York: Duell, Sloan & Pearce, 1946), 359. I use the terms *region* and *regional* to denote specifically Southern California, not the broader West or Southwest, which I reference separately. My capitalization of *Southern California* runs counter to standard usage but indicates my view of the region as a self-consciously coherent whole—a unified image that the memory boosters I study sought to produce. Geographically, I delimit the region along the lines of Carey McWilliams, as the land "South of the Tehachapi" range of mountains. This area takes in the cities, suburbs, and towns along the coast as well as their hinterlands, focusing primarily on Los Angeles, San Diego, and points in between but including the counties of San Diego, Imperial, Orange, San Bernardino, Los Angeles, Ventura, and Santa Barbara. This area has historically formed a coherent subregion of California, partially defined by its rivalry with Northern California. McWilliams, *Southern California Country*, 2–17. For a discussion of subregions within the West, see David M. Wrobel and Michael C. Steiner, eds., *Many Wests: Place, Culture and Regional Identity* (Lawrence: University Press of Kansas, 1997).

2. Scholars in the field of memory studies have widely varied opinions about the proper terminology for memories. There are collective, social, public, historical, and cultural memories, to name a few of the most popular terms. The term I prefer is *cultural memory,* because it links memories with an array of cultural products and practices. As Mieke Bal has written, contrasting memories to invented tradition, "that memories are cultural does not make them lies. Instead it ties them to other images produced and circulated within the culture." Moreover, to my mind, *cultural memory* does a better job of conveying the materiality of remembrance and while not denying its political nature, does not reduce

it to "an indice of power," suggesting rather its operation as "as a framework of meaning," as Barry Schwartz has offered. When on occasion I use the alternate term of *public memory,* my intention is to indicate the semiofficial nature that some cultural memories come to assume. Bal, "Introduction," in Mieke Bal, Jonathan Crewe, and Leo Spitzer, eds., *Acts of Memory: Cultural Recall in the Present* (Hanover, N.H.: Dartmouth College, University Press of New England, 1999), xvii; Schwartz, *Abraham Lincoln and the Forge of National Memory* (Chicago: University of Chicago Press, 2002), xi; Wulf Kansteiner, "Finding Meaning in Memory: A Methodological Critique of Collective Memory Studies," *History and Theory* 41 (2002): 183; Marita Sturken, *Tangled Memories: The Vietnam War, the AIDS Epidemic, and the Politics of Remembering* (Berkeley: University of California Press, 1997), 5; Jan Assmann, "Collective Memory and Cultural Identity," *New German Critique* 65 (1995): 125–33; John Bodnar, *Remaking America: Public Memory, Commemoration, and Patriotism in the Twentieth Century* (Princeton, N.J.: Princeton University Press, 1992).

3. The discourse on the role of place in history is vast and varied. My emphasis on place draws less from the study of how people develop affective ties with particular pieces of geography than on the way certain places and spaces set the physical and symbolic context for enacting both memory and culture. A good overview of the historiography of place appears in David Glassberg, "Place and Placelessness in American History," ch.5, in *Sense of History: The Place of the Past in American Life* (Amherst: University of Massachusetts Press, 2001), 109–27. Other works in memory studies that offer helpful readings of place include Katharine Hodgkin and Susannah Radstone, "Introduction: Contested Pasts," in Katharine Hodgkin and Susannah Radstone, eds., *Contested Pasts: The Politics of Memory* (London: Routledge, 2003); Paul A. Shackel, *Memory in Black and White: Race, Commemoration, and the Post-Bellum Landscape* (New York: Altamira Press, 2003); Bonnie Christensen, *Red Lodge and the Mythic West: Coal Miners to Cowboys* (Lawrence: University Press of Kansas, 2002); Yoshikuni Igarashi, *Bodies of Memory: Narratives of War in Postwar Japanese Culture, 1945–1970* (Princeton, N.J.: Princeton University Press, 2000); Edward T. Linenthal, *Sacred Ground: Americans and Their Battlefields* (Urbana: University of Illinois Press, 1991). My understanding has also been influenced by works on place in both environmental and urban history. For the former see, for example, Wallace Stegner, "The Sense of Place," in *Where the Bluebird Sings to the Lemonade Springs: Living and Writing in the West* (New York: Random House, 1992), 199–206; and William Cronon, "A Place for Stories: Nature, History, and Narrative," *Journal of American History* 78 (March 1992): 1347–76. For the latter, consult Max Page, *The Creative Destruction of Manhattan* (Chicago: University of Chicago Press, 2001); Michael Sorkin, ed., *Variations on a Theme Park: The New American City and the End of Public Space* (New York: Noonday Press, 1992); and, Edward Soja, *Postmodern Geographies: The Reassertion of Space in Critical Society Theory* (New York: Verso, 1989).

4. Michael Kammen, *Mystic Chords of Memory: The Transformation of Tradition in American Culture* (New York: Knopf, 1991), 93–100. This flurry of social interest in the past has been matched perhaps only by the recent

academic interest in studying public memory itself. See, for example, several review essays documenting the increasing scholarship in this field: Patrick Hutton, "Recent Scholarship on History and Memory," *The History Teacher* 33 (August 2000): 533–48; Casey Blake, "The Usable Past, the Comfortable Past, and the Civic Past: Memory in Contemporary America," *Cultural Anthropology* 14 (1999): 423–35; and "American Historical Review Forum: History and Memory," *American Historical Review* 102 (December 1997): 1372–1412.

5. For a discussion of the gold rush and its remembrance, see Kevin Starr, *Americans and the California Dream, 1850–1915* (New York: Oxford University Press, 1973); Malcolm J. Rohrbough, *Days of Gold: The California Gold Rush and the American Nation* (Berkeley: University of California Press, 1997); Susan Lee Johnson, *Roaring Camp: The Social World of the California Gold Rush* (New York: Norton, 2000); and Glassberg, "Making Places in California," Chapter 7 in *Sense of History*. For a discussion of regional rivalry within California, see Glen Gendzel, "Pioneers and Padres: Competing Mythologies in Northern and Southern California, 1850–1930," *Western Historical Quarterly* 32 (Spring 2001): 55–82; and Richard Rice, William Bullough, and Richard Orsi, *The Elusive Eden: A New History of California* (New York: McGraw-Hill, 1996).

6. Christine Sterling, *Olvera Street: Its History and Restoration* (Los Angeles: Old Mission Printing Shop, 1933), 7. Boosters in the late nineteenth and early twentieth centuries were urban promoters of many professions, but typically they were real-estate speculators, investors in other growth-oriented businesses, tourist entrepreneurs, and press agents, whose penchant for exaggeration earned them the reputation of shysters. But boosters were also respectable folk who joined together in coalitions for growth. In California and other parts of the West, they were not only perenially bullish on the region's future, but they became leaders of society, culture, economy, and state. Useful treatments of California boosters appear in William Deverell, *Whitewashed Adobe: The Rise of Los Angeles and the Remaking of Its Mexican Past* (Berkeley: University of California Press, 2004); Kevin Starr, *Material Dreams: Southern California Through the 1920s* (New York: Oxford University Press, 1990); Robert M. Fogelson, *The Fragmented Metropolis: Los Angeles, 1850–1930* (Cambridge, Mass.: Harvard University Press, 1967; Berkeley: University of California Press, 1993). David Wrobel has done the best recent study of western boosters in general. See his *Promised Lands: Promotion, Memory, and the Creation of the American West* (Lawrence: University Press of Kansas, 2002).

7. The anxiety model has numerous adherents and has inspired a good deal of historical inquiry, a large proportion of which draws significant inspiration from T. J. Jackson Lears's analysis of "antimodernism" among elite intellectuals in the late nineteenth century. Where Lears, however, draws his circle of antimodernists narrowly, many students of memory suggest that antimodernism was a typical impulse among many upper-class Americans and that the desire to retain control was a key motive for nostalgia during the turn-of-the-century era. The belief that motives for memory were thus on some level disingenuous—the invention of tradition in order to consolidate power—has been a springboard for memory studies in the past several decades. Lears, *No Place of Grace:*

Antimodernism and the Transformation of American Culture (New York: Pantheon, 1981); Eric Hobsbawm and Terence Ranger, eds., *The Invention of Tradition* (Cambridge: Cambridge University Press, 1983); Jeffrey K. Olnick and Joyce Robbins, "Social Memory Studies: From 'Collective Memory' to the Historical Sociology of Mnemonic Practices," *Annual Review of Sociology* 24 (1998): 108; Dan Ben-Amos, "Introduction," in Dan Ben-Amos and Liliane Weissberg, eds., *Cultural Memory and the Construction of Identity* (Detroit: Wayne State University Press, 1999), 10–11.

8. My reading of the myth of the Old South here condenses a number of complex studies. For the full story, see David W. Blight, *Race and Reunion: The Civil War in American Memory* (Cambridge, Mass.: The Belknap Press of Harvard University Press, 2001), esp. 216–31; Tony Horwitz, *Confederates in the Attic: Dispatches from the Unfinished Civil War* (New York: Pantheon, 1998); Catherine Clinton, *Tara Revisited: Women, War, and the Plantation Legend* (New York: Abbeville Press, 1995); Nina Silber, *The Romance of Reunion: Northerners and the South, 1865–1900* (Chapel Hill: University of North Carolina Press, 1993); and Gaines M. Foster, *Ghosts of the Confederacy: Defeat, the Lost Cause, and the Emergence of the New South* (New York: Oxford University Press, 1987).

9. Instead of taking modernity to be entirely about material progress and labeling anything that looks backwards as antimodern, I take the nostalgic impulse to be an integral part of modernity itself. To paraphrase Marshall Berman, to be fully modern is to desire a premodern past on some level. Or, as Alon Confino has noted about Germans during this same turn-of-the-century era, people "yearned for the past not because it was antimodern but because it originated from modernity." And they appreciated the past not only for "the origins it bestowed upon the present" but also for "its modern application, namely for profit," and especially through tourism. Marshall Berman, *All That Is Solid Melts Into Air: The Experience of Modernity* (New York: Simon & Schuster, 1982), 13–14; Alon Confino, *The Nation as a Local Metaphor: Württemburg, Imperial Germany, and National Memory, 1871–1918* (Chapel Hill: University of North Carolina Press, 1997), 98, 119–22, 156, 241.

10. As Paul Grainge suggested in his study of the black-and-white image in contemporary culture, nostalgia operates at two levels: (1) a mood, typified by feelings of longing and loss, anxiety about discontinuity, desire for stability and authenticity; and (2) a mode, a consumable, aesthetic style, a commodified representation not always derivative of mood. He sees nostalgia "as a political and commercial investment in 'pastness' rather than a content-specific experiencing of loss" and focuses on "historicizing the popularity of 'pastness' in a culture that is not so much reeling from discontinuity . . . as able to transmit, store, retrieve, reconfigure, and invoke the past in specific ways." While I would argue that both are at work here and elsewhere in cultural memories, Grainge's observations are quite useful in thinking about the currency of the past in novel ways. Grainge, *Monochrome Memories: Nostalgia and Style in Retro America* (Westport, Conn.: Praeger, 2002), 6–13, 19–27, 43–57.

11. Max Page sees a similar speculative paradigm, drawn from the real-estate market, at work in the making of Manhattan as both place and memory.

Historic preservation, he argues, is not a movement composed entirely of "grumpy elites" but is a form of memory entrepreneurship, a creative business class "firmly engaged in designing, building and reforming the future city, not those reveling in nostalgic reveries for 'old New York.'" Whether in New York or Southern California, there was a solid link between the pursuit of profit (especially through development of space) and the search for the past. Page, *Creative Destruction of Manhattan*, 113–16, 252.

12. Outside of Orwellian worlds, one cannot entirely invent a believable past to suit one's desires, but nor does one find the past a ready-made refuge for present-day woes. A past that speaks to the present must be improvised using materials drawn from both eras. As Michel-Rolph Trouillot has said, we are contemporaries of the past we remember, not its heirs. Trouillot, *Silencing the Past: Power and the Production of History* (Boston: Beacon Press, 1995), 16. See also Schwartz, *Abraham Lincoln*, 17; Michael Schudson, *Watergate in American Memory: How We Remember, Forget, and Reconstruct the Past* (New York: Basic Books, 1992), 5, 206–18; and Arjun Appadurai, "The Past is a Scarce Resource," *Man* (New Series) 16 (1981): 201–19.

13. This relationship echoes Johannes Fabian's landmark study of anthropological methodology in which the creation of the "ethnographic present" places scholars and readers in a privileged, historical time, while the objects of study sit in an atemporal culture. Fabian calls this phenomenon the "denial of coevalness," and in a different form, cultural rather than academic, I see this process at work in Anglo memories. Fabian, *Time and the Other: How Anthropology Makes Its Object* (New York: Columbia University Press, 1983).

14. This process of Anglo-American ascendancy and Indian and Mexican dispossession in nineteenth-century California is covered in chapter 1. For a fuller treatment, see also Deverell, *Whitewashed Adobe*, ch. 1; Virginia M. Bouvier, *Women and the Conquest of California, 1542–1840* (Phoenix: University of Arizona Press, 2001); Ramón A. Gutiérrez and Richard Orsi, *Contested Eden: California Before the Gold Rush* (Berkeley: University of California Press, 1998); Leonard Pitt, *Decline of the Californios: A Social History of the Spanish-speaking Californians, 1846–1890* (1966; Berkeley: University of California Press, 1998); W. W. Robinson, *Land in California: The Story of Mission Lands, Ranchos, Squatters, Mining Claims, Railroad Grants, Land Scrip, Homesteads* (1948; Berkeley: University of California Press, 1979).

15. McWilliams, *Southern California Country*, 70–83. While Kevin Starr sees the Anglo fascination with the Spanish past largely as the result of a search for local identities and a desire for rootedness, Mike Davis follows upon McWilliams's suspicion of mercenary booster interests at work to find a conspiracy among the Los Angeles elite to manipulate history as a means of maintaining power over the Anglo and Mexican city. Douglas Monroy weighs in on the identity side but sees less a migrant's isolation than a desire for authenticity amid the stultifying effects of industrial capitalism. Leonard Pitt looks at the issue from the Californios' perspective and marvels at the irony of the Anglo appropriation of their heritage. Dydia DeLyser calls for scholars to avoid characterizing tourists of Southern California's romantic Spanish attractions as dupes and to envision them instead as important social actors who helped create

a uniquely compelling regional memory. Starr, *Material Dreams,* chs. 6, 10; Starr, *Inventing the Dream: California Through the Progressive Era* (New York: Oxford University Press, 1986), chs. 2, 3; Davis, *City of Quartz: Excavating the Future in Los Angeles* (London: Verso, 1990), chs. 1, 2; Monroy, *Thrown Among Strangers: The Making of Mexican Culture in Frontier California* (Berkeley: University of California Press, 1990), 261–280; Monroy, *Rebirth: Mexican Los Angeles from the Great Migration to the Great Depression* (Berkeley: University of California Press, 1999); Pitt, *Decline of the Californios,* ch. 16; Dydia DeLyser, *Ramona Memories: Tourism and the Shaping of Southern California* (Minneapolis: University of Minnesota Press, 2005), 181. In addition, two recent studies analyzing the commodification of the Spanish past in New Mexico are useful for comparison. See Charles Montgomery, *The Spanish Redemption: Heritage, Power, and Loss on New Mexico's Upper Rio Grande* (Berkeley: University of California Press, 2002); and, Chris Wilson, *The Myth of Santa Fe: Creating a Modern Regional Tradition* (Albuquerque: University of New Mexico Press, 1997).

16. Deverell, *Whitewashed Adobe,* 62. For another view that highlights the dissonance, see William A. McClung, *Landscapes of Desire: Anglo Mythologies of Los Angeles* (Berkeley: University of California Press, 2000), 41–48, 84–405.

17. For a discussion of the broadly popular nineteenth-century cultural production of blackface and the twentieth-century consumption of Navajo blankets, respectively, see Eric Lott, *Love and Theft: Blackface Minstrelsy and the American Working Class* (New York: Oxford University Press, 1993); and Erika M. Bsumek, "Making 'Indian-Made': The Production, Consumption, and Construction of Navajo Ethnic Identity, 1880–1935," Ph.D. diss., Rutgers University, 2000). While there are many scholarly analyses of cultural appropriations, the following have been the most helpful to me: Philip J. Deloria, *Playing Indian* (New Haven, Conn.: Yale University Press, 1999); Barbara Kirshenblatt-Gimblett, *Destination Culture: Tourisms, Museums, and Heritage* (Berkeley: University of California Press, 1998); Alexander Saxton, *The Rise and Fall of the White Republic: Class Politics and Mass Culture in Nineteenth-Century America* (London: Verso, 1990); George Lipsitz, *Time Passages: Collective Memory and American Popular Culture* (Minneapolis: University of Minnesota Press, 1990); Robert W. Rydell, *All the World's a Fair: Visions of Empire at American International Expositions, 1876–1916* (Chicago: University of Chicago Press, 1987); Richard Handler, "Authenticity," *Anthropology Today* 2 (1986): 6–9; James Clifford and George E. Marcus, *Writing Culture: The Politics and Poetics of Ethnography* (Berkeley: University of California Press, 1986).

18. My understanding of nationalism draws on several sources but specifically on historian Alon Confino's exploration of "the nation as a local metaphor." In showing how the abstract concept of nation in late nineteenth-century Germany became manifest in response to specific local contexts and was forged out of local materials, Confino tries to illuminate the process by which a nation becomes an "imagined community." Benedict Anderson introduced this term to explain how, since citizens can never know every member of a nation individually, nations must be forged from discourse that unites them in common bonds of sentiment and loyalty. His idea that citizens experience the nation primarily as

an "imagined community" has become the starting line for many scholarly interpretations of nationalism, although many scholars have come to take this view
as a given rather than investigate the process as Confino does. My analysis has
similar goals, but I see the relationship somewhat reversed; that is, in Southern
California people sought to turn the local into a national metaphor. In studying
place and nation, Confino and others follow Anderson's lead in assuming that
the local experience is more intimate, immediate, and genuine than that of the
national world, which is more remote, intangible, and abstract. Yet for many
Anglos, the local experience of Southern California was more alienating than
was their connection to national narratives. Only as they began to imagine the
region in national terms did the local experience begin to feel genuine. Confino,
The Nation as a Local Metaphor; Benedict Anderson, *Imagined Communities:
Reflections on the Origin and Spread of Nationalism* (London: Verso, 1983; rev.
ed., 1991). For other seminal works on nationalism, see John R. Gillis, ed., *Commemorations: The Politics of National Identity* (Princeton, N.J.: Princeton University Press, 1994); Bodnar, *Remaking America;* Homi K. Bhabha, ed., *Nation
and Narration,* (London: Routledge, 1990); Pierre Nora, "Between Memory and
History: *Les Lieux de Mémoire,*" trans. Marc Roudebush, *Representations* 26,
Special Issue: Memory and Countermemory (Spring 1989): 7–25; Hobsbawm
and Ranger, *The Invention of Tradition.*

19. The study of urban tourism led Catherine Cocks to conclude that cities
often sought to "brand" themselves, packaging their personalities as a "salable
commodity for a national clientele." While a city could do so more easily than
a larger region could, the cultivation of a distinctive look or personality, often
tied to a place's past or folklife, became a key object of regional boosters in the
West and elsewhere. Cocks, *Doing the Town: The Rise of Urban Tourism in the
United States, 1850–1915* (Berkeley: University of California Press, 2001), 145.
For similar trends in Germany see Confino, *Nation as a Local Metaphor,* 50; for
the creation of New England's signature village look, see Glassberg, *Sense of
History,* ch. 6; for the marketing of New York City as place, see Page, *Creative
Destruction of Manhattan,* 66.

20. This version of sectional pride and national reunion is nowhere more
evident than in Ken Burns's blockbuster documentary *The Civil War;* this and
many other of the show's arguments have been the subject of animated scholarly debates since its initial airing in 1990. See, for example, Robert Brent
Toplin, ed., *Ken Burns's Civil War: Historians Respond* (New York: Oxford
University Press, 1996), especially Eric Foner's piece in that volume, "Ken Burns
and the Romance of Reunion." For the historical development of this perspective, see Blight, *Race and Reunion;* Foster, *Ghosts of the Confederacy;* C. Vann
Woodward, *The Burden of Southern History* (Baton Rouge: Louisiana State
University Press, 1968); C. Vann Woodward, *Origins of the New South,
1877–1913* (Baton Rouge: Louisiana State University Press, 1951).

21. The mythology of the West has a thick historiography. A few excellent
examples that relate it directly to national culture include Richard Slotkin, *The
Fatal Environment: The Myth of the Frontier in the Age of Industrialization,
1800–1890* (New York: Atheneum, 1985); Richard Slotkin, *Gunfighter Nation: The
Myth of the Frontier in Twentieth-Century America* (New York: Atheneum, 1992);

Joy S. Kasson, *Buffalo Bill's Wild West: Celebrity, Memory, and Popular History* (New York: Hill and Wang, 2000); Henry Nash Smith, *Virgin Land: The American West as Symbol and Myth* (Cambridge, Mass.: Harvard University Press, 1971); Richard Aquila, *Wanted Dead or Alive: The American West in Popular Culture* (Urbana: University of Illinois Press, 1996); Richard White, "When Frederick Jackson Turner and Buffalo Bill Both Played Chicago in 1893," in Robert C. Ritchie and Paul A. Hutton, eds., *Frontier and Region: Essays in Honor of Martin Ridge* (Albuquerque: University of New Mexico Press, 1997), 201–12.

22. Blight discusses the remarkable absence of African-Americans from white Civil War memories, despite their central roles during the conflict and their continuing social and political presence in public culture afterward. About Los Angeles, Deverell noted this effect in passing, even though the point runs counter to his theme of whitewashing. Anglos were not attempting to make Mexicans disappear by confining them to the past; instead "borders created from discriminatory wage systems, from public memory, and from political exclusion all had to do with rendering Mexicans *expressly visible*, lest they disappear into the polity, into the neighborhoods, into the city of the future." This relationship of visibility to marginalization is the issue that begs additional analysis. Blight, *Race and Reunion*, 209, 383; Deverell, *Whitewashed Adobe*, 10, emphasis added.

23. In this study, I use the term *Anglo* to refer to white, non-Hispanic Californians, although people in this category may be of various ethnicities or national origins. I use *Mexicans* or *ethnic Mexicans*, unless otherwise specified, to refer to, as David Gutiérrez has offered, the "total Mexican-origin population." According to many Indian peoples' preferences, whenever possible, I refer to individuals by tribal identification, such as San Ildefonso Pueblo or Luiseño. When a more general ascription is required, I use *California Indians* or *Indian people*. I use this Anglo/Mexican/Indian system of terminology not for its ideological clarity but because of its cultural dominance and the important roles these labels played in the history I seek to tell. David G. Gutiérrez, *Walls and Mirrors: Mexican Americans, Mexican Immigration, and the Politics of Ethnicity* (Berkeley: University of California Press, 1995), 218, n. 3. For the nineteenth-century history of derogatory views of Mexicans, see David J. Weber, "'Scarce More than Apes': Historical Roots of Anglo Stereotypes of Mexicans in the Border Region," in David J. Weber, ed., *New Spain's Far Northern Frontier: Essays on Spain in the American West, 1540–1821* (Albuquerque: University of New Mexico Press, 1979); Reginald Horsman, *Race and Manifest Destiny: The Origins of American Racial Anglo-Saxonism* (Cambridge, Mass.: Harvard University Press, 1981); and Arnoldo De León, *They Called Them Greasers: Anglo Attitudes toward Mexicans in Texas, 1821–1900* (Austin: University of Texas Press, 1983).

24. Simon's work brings to the fore substantial evidence of the way in which Americans build their conceptions of the public on exclusion. As he writes, "Access to public space was, in the eyes of middle-class America, never supposed to be inclusive. Only through exclusion could the public take shape." Bryant Simon, *Boardwalk of Dreams: Atlantic City and the Fate of Urban America* (New York: Oxford University Press, 2004), 16.

25. The phrase "festive deployment of ethnicity" belongs to Catherine Cocks. See her *Doing the Town*, 176, 194.

26. For women's role in historic preservation and memory entrepreneurship during this era, see Kammen, *Mystic Chords of Memory,* 266–69; Patricia West, *Domesticating History: The Political Origins of America's House Museums* (Washington, D.C.: Smithsonian Institution Press, 1999); and Julie Des Jardins, *Women and the Historical Enterprise in America: Gender, Race, and the Politics of Memory* (Chapel Hill: University of North Carolina Press, 2003), 4–5, 67–68. For a discussion of California women and their strategies for public participation and suffrage, including public history, see Gayle Gullett, *Becoming Citizens: The Emergence and Development of the California Women's Movement, 1880–1911* (Urbana: University of Illinois Press, 2000), esp. 130, 175–85.

27. David G. Gutiérrez, "Significant to Whom?: Mexican Americans and the History of the American West," *Western Historical Quarterly* 24 (November 1993): 519–39.

28. Lisbeth Haas's work was a major effort to document the ways in which Indians, Californios, and Mexicans continually pursued claims to California places, persisted in cultural resistance, and participated in "a larger debate over the meaning of being an American which was ongoing, if muted, and where non-white ethnic minorities were the most faithful champions of a more inclusive vision of America." The concept of these "submerged dialogues" is one that many scholars owe to George Lipsitz. Lisbeth Haas, *Conquests and Historical Identities in California, 1769–1936* (Berkeley: University of California Press, 1995), 126; Lipsitz, *Time Passages.*

29. The terminology people use to describe the relationship between dominant and alternative memories often poses them as oppositional: hegemonic memory versus countermemory, as some theorists have called it, or public memory versus vernacular memory, according to several American historians. This perspective risks reducing the workings of cultural memory to a competition for power and downplays the traffic between dominant and alternative forms of memory. Moreover, it dismisses the possibility that counterhegemonic memories can be conservative and fails to capture the ways in which the development of memories at several points on a power continuum can be dynamic and conflictual. Memory is not simply a projection of a political standpoint or social position, although it sometimes can include this feature; it makes meaning in far more complex ways. Ann Burlein, "Countermemory of the Right: The Case of Focus on the Family," in Bal, Crewe, and Spitzer, eds., *Acts of Memory,* 208–17; Roberta Pearson, "Custer Loses Again: The Contestation over Commodified Public Memory," in Ben-Amos and Weissberg, eds., *Cultural Memory,* 180–81; Natalie Zemon-Davis and Randolph Starn, "Introduction," *Representations* 26, Special Issue: Memory and Counter Memory (Spring 1989): 1–6.

30. Matt Garcia, *A World of Its Own: Race, Labor, and Citrus in the Making of Greater Los Angeles, 1900–1970* (Chapel Hill: University of North Carolina Press, 2001), ch. 4.

31. This nineteenth-century precursor to Anglo nostalgia is explored in chapter 1. See also Rosaura Sánchez, *Telling Identities: The* Californio *Testimonios* (Minneapolis: University of Minnesota Press, 1995); Genaro Padilla, *My History, Not*

Yours: The Formation of Mexican American Autobiography (Madison: University of Wisconsin Press, 1993); Pitt, *Decline of the Californios,* ch. 16.

32. David Blight has written about the standard vision of white Civil War valor that reunified the sections in brotherly bonds while dividing whites and blacks into separate societies and histories: "it [this vision] would always be out there as a set of images that emancipationist memory of the Civil War would have to counter." Still, nurtured within that separate society, publicly "beleaguered, but hardly invisible, emancipationist memory lived on to fight another day." As with alternative formations of the Spanish past and Anglo narratives, this emancipationist version of the Civil War still has to contend with the authority of whites' memories, which have over the years acquired the imprimatur of official history. This establishment does not preclude the formation of counternarratives, but it both defines them as "counter" and impedes their public acceptance. Blight, *Race and Reunion,* 397.

33. Memory studies often trace the origins of the field to French sociologist Maurice Halbwachs, whose work in the 1920s suggested that memory was fundamentally social rather than personal. He argued that we are only able to recollect the past by locating it and ourselves within a social framework, or as he said, "with the help of landmarks that we always carry within ourselves." Though these landmarks need not always be physical, if a belief, a past, or "a truth is to be settled in the memory of a group, it needs to be presented in the concrete form of an event, of a personality, or of a locality." Maurice Halbwachs, *On Collective Memory* (Chicago: University of Chicago Press, 1992), 175, 200.

34. The installation of a building or monument does not halt the interpretive process but commemorates a particular moment within the evolution of a given memory. Debate about buildings' symbols or meanings will obviously continue, but they are material objects, not empty vessels; as Michael Schudson has written, "Architecture, to take the most solid example, embraces not only aesthetic values of a given age, but social values and social relations." The concept that remembrance of buildings tends to focus on the more pure or decorous moments in their pasts comes from Charlene Mires's study of Independence Hall. Schudson, *Watergate in American Memory,* 218; Charlene Mires, *Independence Hall in American Memory* (Philadelphia: University of Pennsylvania Press, 2002), 181, 241. Helpful studies of memory, monuments, and architecture include Matthew Levinger, "Memory and Forgetting: Reinventing the Past in Twentieth-Century Germany," *The Public Historian* 24, no. 4 (Fall 2002): 117–26; Andreas Huyssen, "Monumental Seduction," in Bal, Crewe, and Spitzer, eds., *Acts of Memory,* 191–207; Kirk Savage, *Standing Soldiers, Kneeling Slaves: Race, War, and Monuments in Nineteenth-Century America* (Princeton, N.J.: Princeton University Press, 1997); M. Christine Boyer, *The City of Collective Memory: Its Historical Imagery and Architectural Entertainments* (Cambridge, Mass.: MIT Press, 1994); James E. Young, *The Texture of Memory: Holocaust Memorials and Meaning* (New Haven, Conn.: Yale University Press, 1993).

35. This idea of places as stages draws upon Robin D. G. Kelley's discussion of public buses in the South as "moving theaters" for race and civil rights. They played this role both in the climatic moments of the early civil rights movement

and in the decades leading up to it. I refer also to Karen Till's explication of "landscapes as duplicitous, because on the one hand they are materially experienced . . . while on the other they can simultaneously function as social symbols." I seek to capture this duality by analyzing these places as venues. Kelley, *Race Rebels: Culture, Politics, and the Black Working Class* (New York: Free Press, 1994), 57–76; Till, "Staging the Past: Landscape Designs, Cultural Identity and Erinnerungspolitik at Berlin's Neue Wache," *Ecumene* 6, no. 3 (1999): 255.

36. I see these texts not simply as the language of a set of memories but as ways of accessing a set of social practices governing the production, experience, and reception of cultural memories. Nor is memory, material or otherwise, all about representation. As Confino reminds us, "the representation of a past, say, in a museum, becomes a social mode of action . . . through books, museums, organizations, and associations." DeLyser also suggests that "fictional places"—those that evoke or celebrate an explicitly invented occurrence or past—can become "real" in the social world of the present. As people incorporate these places into their own networks of everyday life and sets of personal memories, the places cease to be purely fiction and become social facts. Confino, *Nation as a Local Metaphor*, 157; DeLyser, *Ramona Memories*, xii.

37. For a discussion of the "spatialization of time," see McClung, *Landscapes of Desire*, 85, 105–6. My reference to reenactment here is metaphorical rather than specific; although Southern Californians had more than a few opportunities to reenact particular scenes of local Spanish history, these performances compare only in the most general sense to the growing hobby of, for example, Civil War–battle reenactments. Nevertheless, the desire to "experience the past," whether by immersing oneself bodily in another time or simply by standing in a physical or memorial space with echoes of a past moment or people, binds the two activities. Both are thus social practices that make meaning for participants and observers in the present even as they try to recapture an authentic feeling of the past. For a discussion of desires to experience the past in contemporary society, see Roy Rosenzweig and David Thelen, *Presence of the Past: Popular Uses of History in American Life* (New York: Columbia University Press, 1998). For more about reenactment, see Horwitz, *Confederates in the Attic*. For a description of theme-park presentations of the past, see Kirshenblatt-Gimblett, *Destination Culture;* Richard Handler and Eric Gable, *The New History in an Old Museum: Creating the Past at Colonial Williamsburg* (Durham, N.C.: Duke University Press, 1997); Mike Wallace, *Mickey Mouse History and Other Essays on American Memory* (Philadelphia: Temple University Press, 1996).

1. LOS DÍAS PASADOS

1. *Ramona* was first published in serial form in the *Christian Union* in May 1884 and appeared in book form in November. Since that time, the novel has never been out of print and has gone through three hundred reprintings. By 1946 the book had sold well over half a million copies. An ongoing outdoor pageant and four film versions of the story appeared between 1910 and 1938, the first by D. W. Griffith starring Mary Pickford in the title role. A later version cast Mexican actress Dolores Del Rio as Ramona. Valerie Sherer Mathes, *Helen*

Hunt Jackson and her Indian Reform Legacy (Austin: University of Texas Press, 1990), 81; Carey McWilliams, *Southern California Country: An Island on the Land* (New York: Duell, Sloan & Pearce, 1946), 74; Errol Wayne Stevens, "Helen Hunt Jackson's *Ramona*: Social Problem Novel as Tourist Guide," *California History* 77, no. 3 (Fall 1998): 197, n. 5.

2. Discussions of Ramona's influence upon Southern California are available in many locations, including Dydia DeLyser, *Ramona Memories: Tourism and the Shaping of Southern California* (Minneapolis: University of Minnesota Press, 2005); McWilliams, *Southern California Country,* 71–77; Kevin Starr, *Inventing the Dream: California Through the Progressive Era* (New York: Oxford University Press, 1985), 55–63; Douglas Monroy, *Thrown Among Strangers: The Making of Mexican Culture in Frontier California* (Berkeley: University of California Press, 1990), 281–86; Mathes, *Helen Hunt Jackson,* ch. 5; Roberto R. Lint-Sagarena, "Inheriting the Land: Defining Place in Southern California from the Mexican American War to the Plan Espiritual de Aztlán," Ph.D. diss., Princeton University, 2000; William A. McClung, *Landscapes of Desire: Anglo Mythologies of Los Angeles* (Berkeley: University of California Press, 2000), 41–48, 74–81, 94–96.

3. I borrow the phrase *los días pasados* to reference the Spanish/Mexican origins of romantic Southern California pasts from Genaro M. Padilla, *My History, Not Yours: The Formation of Mexican American Autobiography* (Madison: University of Wisconsin Press, 1993), 11.

4. Helen Hunt Jackson, *Ramona: A Story* (1884; New York: Signet Classic, 1988), 12. For literary analysis of *Ramona,* see Michael Dorris, introduction to *Ramona: A Story,* by Helen Hunt Jackson (New York: Signet Classic, 1988); John R. Byers, "Helen Hunt Jackson," *American Literary Realism: 1870–1910* 2 (Summer 1969): 143–48; John R. Byers, "The Indian Matter of Helen Hunt Jackson's *Ramona*: From Fact to Fiction," *American Indian Quarterly* 2 (Winter 1975–76): 331–46; Rosemary Whitaker, *Helen Hunt Jackson,* Western Writers Series (Boise, Idaho: Boise State University, 1987); David Luis-Brown, "'White Slaves' and the 'Arrogant Mestiza': Reconfiguring Whiteness in *The Squatter and the Don* and *Ramona,*" *American Literature* 69, no. 4 (December 1997): 813–40; Michele Moylan, "Reading the Indians: The Ramona Myth in American Culture," *Prospects* 28 (1993): 153–87; Lawrence Clark Powell, *Land of Fiction: Thirty-Two Novels and Stories about Southern California from* Ramona *to* The Loved One: *A Bibliographical Essay* (Los Angeles: Historical Society of Southern California, 1991).

5. Leonard Pitt, *The Decline of the Californios: A Social History of the Spanish-speaking Californians, 1846–1890* (1966; Berkeley: University of California Press, 1998); Reginald Horsman, *Race and Manifest Destiny: The Origin of American Racial Anglo-Saxonism* (Cambridge, Mass.: Harvard University Press, 1981), ch. 11; David J. Weber, "'Scarce More Than Apes': Historical Roots of Anglo American Stereotypes of Mexicans in the Border Region," in *Myth and the History of the Hispanic Southwest* (Albuquerque: University of New Mexico Press, 1987).

6. Jackson, *Ramona,* 88. For details on this complex racial diversity in the nineteenth century, see Lisbeth Haas, *Conquests and Historical Identities in*

California, 1769–1936 (Berkeley: University of California Press, 1995); Tomás Almaguer, *Racial Faultlines: The Historical Origins of White Supremacy in California* (Berkeley: University of California Press, 1990); Monroy, *Thrown Among Strangers;* James J. Rawls, *Indians of California: The Changing Image* (Norman: University of Oklahoma Press, 1984); Albert Camarillo, *Chicanos in a Changing Society: From Mexican Pueblos to American Barrios in Santa Barbara and Southern California, 1848–1930* (Cambridge, Mass.: Harvard University Press, 1979); Pitt, *Decline of the Californios.*

7. Albion Tourgée, "Study in Civilization," *North American Review* (September 1886): 246–49. Tourgée's view of *Ramona* is odd, given his consistent critique of the late nineteenth-century Southern literary offensive that sought to hide the horrors of the war, as well as its causes and consequences, under a blanket of sentiment. Tourgée was a Union veteran, prisoner of war, and Reconstruction judge in North Carolina and remained deeply committed to the rights of freed people. David Blight argues that "As a novelist, and especially in much of his journalism and nonfictions, Tourgée sustained a one-man counterattack on the emerging 'plantation school' of Southern literature while appealing for an emancipationist view of the war." Ironically, the part of Jackson's novel he admired, its public indictment of Americans' treatment of Indian people and Californios, was buried as well beneath another regional romance. Blight, *Race and Reunion: The Civil War in American Memory* (Cambridge, Mass.: Belknap Press of Harvard University Press, 2001), 216–21.

8. This figure represents about 12% of the Indian population then living in the area that is now the state of California. The number is interesting in light of the fact that nearly 50% of California Indians now reside in Southern California. George Harwood Phillips, *Chiefs and Challengers: Indian Resistance and Cooperation in Southern California* (Berkeley: University of California Press, 1975), 6–19; Sherburne F. Cook, *The Population of the California Indians, 1769–1970* (Berkeley: University of California Press, 1976), 34–43.

9. For work on California history before the gold rush, see David J. Weber, ed., *New Spain's Far Northern Frontier: Essays on Spain in the American West, 1540–1821* (Albuquerque : University of New Mexico Press, 1979); David J. Weber, *The Spanish Frontier in North America* (New Haven, Conn.: Yale University Press, 1994); Richard B. Rice, William A. Bullough, and Richard J. Orsi, *The Elusive Eden: A New History of California* (New York: Knopf, 1988), 84–85; Ramón A. Gutiérrez and Richard J. Orsi, eds., *Contested Eden: California Before the Gold Rush* (Berkeley: University of California Press, 1998).

10. Albert L. Hurtado, *Indian Survival on the California Frontier* (New Haven, Conn.: Yale University Press, 1988), 10–13, Phillips, *Chiefs and Challengers,* 5, 22–34. For more on social organization, Spanish-Indian relations, and life at the missions, see, in addition to the above, Virginia M. Bouvier, *Women and the Conquest of California, 1542–1840: Codes of Silence* (Phoenix: University of Arizona Press, 2001); Haas, *Conquests and Historical Identities,* ch. 1; Rose Marie Beebe and Robert Senkewicz, *Lands of Promise and Despair: Chronicles of Early California, 1535–1846* (Berkeley, Calif.: Heyday Books, 2001).

11. Hurtado, *Indian Survival*, 10–13; Haas, *Conquests and Historical Identities*, 209; Rice, Bullough, and Orsi, *Elusive Eden*, 84–87, 89–94.

12. Robert M. Fogelson, *The Fragmented Metropolis: Los Angeles, 1850–1930* (Cambridge, Mass.: Harvard University Press, 1967; Berkeley: University of California Press, 1993), ch. 1; Rice, Bullough, and Orsi, *Elusive Eden*, 95, 115–123; Walton Bean and James J. Rawls, *California: An Interpretive History*, 5th ed. (New York: McGraw-Hill, 1988), 44–55.

13. Pitt, *Decline of the Californios*, ch. 1; María Raquél Casas, "'In Consideration of His Being Married to a Daughter of the Land': Interethnic Marriages in California from 1825–1875," Ph.D. diss., Yale University, 1998, 113. For analyses of Mexican independence, secularization politics, and rancho culture, see, in addition to the above, David J. Weber, *The Mexican Frontier, 1821–1846: The American Southwest Under Mexico* (Albuquerque: University of New Mexico Press, 1982); Albert L. Hurtado, *Intimate Frontiers: Sex, Gender, and Culture in Old California* (Albuquerque: University of New Mexico Press, 1999); Monroy, *Thrown Among Strangers*.

14. Casas, "In Consideration," 4, 260–61; Hurtado, *Intimate Frontiers*, ch. 2.

15. Dana quoted in Deena J. Gonzalez, "La Tules of Image and Reality: Euro-American Attitudes and Legend Formation on a Spanish Mexican Frontier," in Adela de la Torre and Beatriz Pesquera, eds., *Building With Our Hands: New Directions in Chicana Studies* (Berkeley: University of California Press, 1993), 86.

16. Robert Glass Cleland, *The Cattle on a Thousand Hills: Southern California 1850–1870* (San Marino, Calif.: The Huntington Library, 1941); Fogelson, *Fragmented Metropolis*, 15; Bean and Rawls, *California*, 96–100. For an insightful reading on the legend of Murieta, see Bruce Thornton's *Searching for Joaquín: Myth, Murieta, and History in California* (San Francisco: Encounter Books, 2003). The best recent study of the social history of the gold rush is Susan Johnson, *Roaring Camp: The Social World of the Gold Rush* (New York: Norton, 2001).

17. Padilla, *My History*, 78; Cleland, *Cattle on a Thousand Hills*; Fogelson, *Fragmented Metropolis*, 15–23; Elias Lopez, "Major Demographic Shifts Occurring in California," *California Research Bureau Note* 6, no. 5 (October 1999).

18. Vallejo quoted in Padilla, *My History*, 98; see also Padilla, *My History, Not Yours*, 27–34; Rosaura Sánchez, *Telling Identities: The* California *Testimonios* (Minneapolis: University of Minnesota Press), x, 4. Of course, not all Californios had the same reaction. As Sánchez writes, some who had lost everything were deeply resentful, and others were resigned and nostalgic; still more tried to accommodate themselves to the new society.

19. Padilla, *My History*, 26–27.

20. Sánchez, *Telling Identities*, 6; see also Padilla, *My History*, 103.

21. Padilla, *My History*, 27, 91; see also Sánchez, *Telling Identities*, 24–28. Sánchez and Padilla provide detailed studies of the narratives and Bancroft's collection process. Certainly not all the Californios whom Bancroft's team approached decided to participate; a number, especially women apparently, "were so angry with the Americans that they simply refused to collaborate in giving their life stories." Padilla, *My History*, 25; Pitt, *Decline of the Californios*, 281.

22. Padilla, *My History,* x, 11–16, 21–28.

23. Sánchez, *Telling Identities,* 168; see also Haas, *Conquests and Historical Identities,* 127–37; Casas, "In Consideration," 280–81.

24. For the postwar history of landless Californios and barrio formation, see Camarillo, *Chicanos in a Changing Society*; Richard Griswold del Castillo, *The Los Angeles Barrio, 1850–1890: A Social History* (Berkeley: University of California Press, 1979).

25. Padilla, *My History,* 110; Antonia Castañeda, "The Political Economy of Nineteenth Century Stereotypes of Californianas," in *Between Borders: Essays on Mexicana/Chicana History,* ed. Adelaida R. Del Castillo (Encino, Calif.: Floricanto Press, 1990): 215–25.

26. Sánchez, *Telling Identities,* 70.

27. For treatment of Indian fortunes in the latter half of the nineteenth century, see Hurtado, *Indian Survival*; Florence Shipek, *Pushed Into the Rocks: Southern California Indian Land Tenure, 1769–1986* (Lincoln: University of Nebraska Press, 1988); Richard Carrico, *Strangers in a Stolen Land: American Indians in San Diego, 1850–1880* (Sacramento, Calif.: Sierra Oaks Publishing Co., 1987); Haas, *Conquests and Historical Identities.* Philip Deloria points to this turn-of-the-twentieth-century era as a nadir for Indian people in general, although the period offered unique opportunities for cultural production. See his *Indians in Unexpected Places* (Lawrence: University Press of Kansas, 2004), 225–26.

28. For biographical details of Jackson's life and career, see Ruth Odell, *Helen Hunt Jackson* (New York: Appleton-Century, 1939); Evelyn I. Banning, *Helen Hunt Jackson* (New York: Vanguard Press, 1973); Mathes, *Helen Hunt Jackson*; DeLyser, *Ramona Memories,* ch. 1; Kate Phillips, *Helen Hunt Jackson: A Literary Life* (Berkeley: University of California Press, 2003).

29. Jackson quoted in Wallace E. Smith, *This Land Was Ours: The Del Valles and Camulos* (Ventura, Calif.: Ventura County Historical Society, 1977), 187; see also Smith, *This Land,* 177–188; Mathes, *Helen Hunt Jackson,* x; Anne E. Goldman, "'I Think Our Romance is Spoiled,' or, Crossing Genres: California History in Helen Hunt Jackson's *Ramona* and María Amparo Ruiz de Burton's *The Squatter and the Don*," in *Over the Edge: Remapping the American West,* eds. Valerie J. Matsumoto and Blake Allmendinger (Berkeley: University of California Press, 1999), 70; McWilliams, *Southern California Country,* 70–83; Monroy, *Thrown Among Strangers,* 264.

30. DeLyser, *Ramona Memories,* 17.

31. DeLyser, *Ramona Memories,* 27–30.

32. Ronald C. Woolsey, *Migrants West: Toward the Southern California Frontier* (Sebastopol, Calif.: Grizzly Bear Publishing Co., 1996).

33. Coronel quoted in Auguste Wey, [Anna Picher] "Side-Lights on 'Ramona,'" *Land of Sunshine* 3, no. 1 (June 1895): 20. See also Smith, *This Land was Ours,* 177–80.

34. Jackson quoted in Smith, *This Land was Ours,* 179. For a history of Rancho Camulos as well as Jackson's involvement with it, see Smith, *This Land was Ours,* passim, and DeLyser, *Ramona Memories,* ch. 3.

35. Those who recount Jackson's visit to Guajome include Smith, *This Land was Ours,* 186–88; Iris H. W. Engstrand and Mary F. Ward, "Rancho Guajome:

An Architectural Legacy Preserved," *Journal of San Diego History* 41, no. 4 (Fall 1995): 251–83. Kate Phillips throws doubt on the evidence; see her *Helen Hunt Jackson,* 320 n. 53. For full treatment of the Guajome controversy, see DeLyser, *Ramona Memories,* ch. 4.

36. Engstrand and Ward, "Rancho Guajome"; Smith, *This Land was Ours,* 186–87. Couts had a reputation for both generosity and violence; he stood twice accused of murder, once for beating an Indian servant to death. Jackson supposedly quarreled with Señora Couts about this incident. For more on Couts's involvement in California's system of virtual Indian enslavement, see Michael Magliari, "Free Soil, Unfree Labor: Cave Johnson Couts and the Binding of Indian Workers in California, 1850–1867," *Pacific Historical Review* 73, no. 3 (August 2004): 349–90.

37. Pitt, *Decline of the Californios,* 253; see also 271–72; DeLyser, *Ramona Memories,* 67–69; Engstrand and Ward, "Rancho Guajome."

38. Casas, "In Consideration," 264, 266.

39. Pitt, *Decline of the Californios,* 269.

40. [John Edmund Poingdestre], "Souvenir Hotel Ramona, H. W. Lake, Manager, San Luis Obispo, Cal." (San Francisco: W. M. Patterson, ca. 1890); Smith, *This Land Was Ours,* 196. Physically, the Moreno rancho in the book exhibited characteristics of both Camulos and Guajome, although Camulos was the more commonly acknowledged home.

41. Thomas P. Getz, *The Story of Ramona's Marriage Place: Old San Diego, California* (T. P. Getz: North San Diego, ca. 1900), 7–10. Ramona's Marriage Place receives extended treatment in DeLyser, *Ramona Memories,* ch. 5.

42. Getz, *Ramona's Marriage Place,* 12.

43. McWilliams, *Southern California Country,* 73; DeLyser, *Ramona Memories,* 111.

44. A. C. Vroman and C. F. Barnes, *The Genesis of the Story of Ramona* (Los Angeles: Press of Kingsley-Barnes & Neuner Co., 1899), 1. The list of Ramona guides is nearly endless. The following is a partial listing of articles, guides, commentaries, and travelogues published before 1915. Charles F. Lummis, *The Home of Ramona* (Los Angeles: Chas. F. Lummis, 1888); Taber Photographic Company, *Ramona* (San Francisco: The Company, ca. 1890); Owen Capelle, "A Field for Fiction," *Land of Sunshine* 1, no. 3 (August 1894): 49–51; Wey, [Picher], "Side Lights on Ramona"; Eleanor F. Wiseman, "Hacienda de Ramona," *Overland* 33 (February 1899): 112–21; B. D. A. Hufford, *The Real Ramona of Helen Hunt Jackson's Famous Novel* (Los Angeles: B.D.A. Hufford, 1900); "House of Ramona," *Chataquan* 31 (1900): 297–98; Carlyle C. Davis, "Ramona, the Ideal and the Real," *Out West* 19, no. 6 (December 1903): 575–96; E. M. Streider, "Illustrations of Ramona's Home," *Sunset* 16, no. 1 (January 1906): 292; "The Man who Inspired Ramona," *Overland Monthly,* 2nd. ser., 50 (September 1907): 252–55; George Wharton James, *Through Ramona's Country* (Boston: The Tudor Press, 1908); Alfred K. Glover, "In Ramona's Footsteps," *Overland Monthly,* 2nd. ser., 56 (October 1910): 406–10; Margaret V. Allen, *Ramona's Homeland* (Chula Vista, Calif.: Denrich Press, 1914); Carlyle C. Davis and William A. Alderson, *The True Story of "Ramona": Its Facts and Fictions, Inspiration and Purpose* (New York: Dodge

Publishing Co., 1914); A. C. Vroman, "The Story of Ramona," *Out West* 40, no. 1 (January 1914): 17–45.

45. Hufford, *The Real Ramona*, emphasis from the original. McWilliams, *Southern California Country*, 76. See also DeLyser, *Ramona Memories*, ch. 7.

46. Monroy argued that whatever Ramona's influence in Southern California's "nostalgia market," it still "called forth a storm of protest." There was some increased activity. Perhaps the Sequoyah League, founded in 1902 by Charles F. Lummis to aid the cause of the mission Indians, was the novel's most direct result. In the context of *Ramona* mania, however, I would characterize the protest as a minor squall rather than a "storm." Monroy, *Thrown Among Strangers*, 263–64.

47. The article was by Edwards Roberts, "Ramona's Home: A Visit to the Camulos Ranch, and to the Scenes Described by 'H. H.,'" *San Francisco Chronicle*, May 9, 1886. See DeLyser, *Ramona Memories*, 70.

48. Reginaldo del Valle to Ysabel del Valle, October 1, 1888, Reginaldo del Valle Papers, Henry E. Huntington Library; Ulpiano del Valle quoted in *Ventura Democrat*, February 28, 1896; James, *Through Ramona's Country*, 97; Smith, *This Land Was Ours*, 180–98.

49. Couts quoted in James, *Through Ramona's Country*, 97; see also Smith, *This Land Was Ours*, 180–98; Engstrand and Ward, "Rancho Guajome"; Wey, "Side-Lights on 'Ramona,'" 20–22. For other evidence of tourist impoliteness and Californio annoyance with *Ramona* mania, see Wiseman, "Hacienda de Ramona," 112–21; [Charles F. Saunders], "Rancho Camulos, Literary Landmark of Southern California," *Los Angeles Times*, October 9, 1910.

50. "Ramona," *Overland Monthly*, V, no. 27 (March 1885): 331; "Real Ramona and Ramona of Romance," *The Oceanside Blade*, November 26, 1898; Charles F. Lummis, "Comment on 'Ramona,'" in *San Gabriel Mission, The Birthplace of Ramona and Fifth Station on El Camino Real* (Los Angeles: Edward Hilton, 1905).

51. See William Deverell, *Whitewashed Adobe: The Rise of Los Angeles and the Remaking of its Mexican Past* (Berkeley: University of California Press, 2004), ch. 1.

52. *Tours De Luxe: California Personally Directed* (Boston: The Nippon-California Tour Co., 1900), 16; *Tourists' Guide and Directory to the Hotels, Boarding and Rooming Places of Los Angeles and Pasadena*, (Los Angeles: Home Comforts/Downing & Mertz, 1894), 5. For discussion of both modern and nostalgic promotion of the West, see Anne Farrar Hyde, *An American Vision: Far Western Landscape and National Culture, 1820–1920* (New York: New York University Press, 1990).

53. John S. Hittell, *A History of the City of San Francisco and Incidentally of the State of California* (San Francisco: A. L. Bancroft & Co., 1878), 206; see also Glen Gendzel, "Pioneers and Padres: Competing Mythologies in Northern and Southern California, 1850–1930," *Western Historical Quarterly* 32, no. 1 (Spring 2001): 59–61.

54. Hubert Howe Bancroft, *California Pastoral* (San Francisco: The History Company Publishers, 1888), 260, 262, 263; Hubert Howe Bancroft, from *History of California*, quoted in Padilla, *My History*, 106; Padilla, *My History*, 107.

55. Bancroft, *California Pastoral*, 260; see also Lint-Sagarena, "Inheriting the Land," 58–62; Kevin Starr, *Americans and the California Dream, 1850–1915* (New York: Oxford University Press, 1972), 115–17.

56. Major Horace Bell, *Reminiscences of a Ranger; or, Early Times in Southern California* (Los Angeles: Yarnell, Caystile & Mathes, Printers, 1881), 242, 446, 455, 456; Starr, *Inventing the Dream*, 30.

57. Dana quoted in Padilla, *My History*, 120.

58. Casas, "In Consideration," 290; Engstrand and Ward, "Rancho Guajome"; Lint-Sagarena, "Inheriting the Land," 67.

59. Charles Dudley Warner, *Our Italy* (New York: Harper & Brothers, 1891), 147; see also Starr, *Inventing the Dream*, 44–46. Warner was a New England essayist and journalist who wrote on diverse subjects in the 1870s, 1880s, and 1890s; the work that made him famous at the time was a collection of humorous essays about his farm, though now he is often known for his collaboration with Mark Twain on *The Gilded Age* (1873). Though *Our Italy* was his sole contribution to Southern California booster literature, the book held great influence in forming a national image of the region.

60. DeLyser claims that Ramona was "the most important woman in the history and geography of southern California." De Lyser, *Ramona Memories*, 188. See also, for example, McClung, *Landscapes of Desire*, 47–48, 94–95; Starr, *Inventing the Dream*, 58–63. Lint-Sagarena does show that *Ramona* has some interpretive precedents and perhaps was not the only text to transform Southern California Anglos' imagination of the Spanish past. Yet he, as others, still envisions Southern California of this period as "Ramonaland." Lint-Sagarena, "Inheriting the Land," 94.

61. Sánchez, *Telling Identities*, 28; Vallejo quoted in Pitt, *Decline of the Californios*, 284.

62. For the original Spanish text and analysis of this example, see Padilla, *My History*, 149–50.

63. Auguste Wey, "The Camino Real," *Land of Sunshine* 3, no. 4 (September 1895): 156–61; Wey, "Side-Lights on 'Ramona'"; Davis and Alderson, *True Story of Ramona*; Vroman and Barnes, *Genesis of the Story*; Don Antonio Francisco Coronel, "Things Past: Remembrances of sports, dances, diversions and other domestic and social customs of old California," trans. Nellie Van der Grift Sanchez, *Touring Topics* 21, no. 9 (September 1929): 18–23, 51–52. As both Padilla and Sánchez have suggested, however, one has to read such statements as if Mexicans were "speaking out of both sides of their mouths"; seemingly "ideologically subordinate speech" may turn out to be a feat of "rhetorical duplicity" that appropriates a public voice for oppositional purposes. While this statement is likely true, few Anglo readers at the time were likely to pick up on this "multiaddressed utterance." Padilla, *My History*, 34.

2. THE ROAD

1. Leonard Pitt, *Decline of the Californios: A Social History of the Spanish-speaking Californians, 1846–1890* (1966; Berkeley: University of California Press, 1998), 285.

2. "Mission Dolores," stereograph #1703 in *Watkins' Pacific Coast* series (San Francisco, ca. 1885).

3. After the secularization of the missions under Mexican policy in the 1830s, many of the buildings were sold. Some remained in private hands after the Mexican-American War, and others were claimed by the American government as public domain. In his presidency, Abraham Lincoln began to return the missions to the Catholic Church, but few were then in good enough repair to support congregations. Except for a few of the best-preserved and functioning missions, such as Dolores in San Francisco and Santa Barbara, the Catholic Church was slow to take over their care.

4. N. W. Griswold, *Beauties of California* (San Francisco: H. S. Crocker & Co., 1883); *Souvenir of California*, (n.p., ca. 1880). Neither of these two typical guides from the 1880s included a single image of missions or referenced the Spanish past in any way. They largely showed urban sites, as was typical of nineteenth-century tourism in the American West. For a discussion of western railroad tourism, see Marguerite Shaffer, *See America First: Tourism and National Identity, 1880–1940* (Washington, D.C.: Smithsonian Institution Press, 2001); Anne Farrar Hyde, *An American Vision: Far Western Landscape and National Culture, 1820–1920* (New York: New York University Press, 1990); Earl Pomeroy, *In Search of the Golden West: The Tourist in Western America* (New York: Knopf, 1957); and John A. Jakle, *The Tourist: Travel in Twentieth-Century North America* (Lincoln: University of Nebraska Press, 1985).

5. Southern Pacific Railway, "El Camino Real," advertisement, *Sunset* 1, no. 6 (October 1898): 87–88, 94.

6. Typical of 1890s mission representations were the following albums: "Views of Europe, California, and Scenes along the Denver & Rio Grande R.R.," ca. 1890, Album 397; "California and the Pacific Coast," ca. 1890s, Album 94; "California," ca. 1890s, Album 93; "San Gabriel Mission, June 7th, 1896," Park Photo #337, in "California and the West, 1900–1910," Album 49, Henry E. Huntington Library (hereafter Huntington Library); *Tours De Luxe: California Personally Directed* (Boston: The Nippon-California Tour Co., 1900); Edward H. Mitchell, pub., *Southern California View Book* (San Francisco: n.p., ca. 1900); and, *California: Burlington Route, Personally Conducted Excursions* (Boston: C. B. & Q. R. R., 1902).

7. Edwards Roberts, "All About Santa Barbara," *Outing Magazine* 9 (March 1887): 563–68.

8. Charles F. Carter, *Some By-Ways of California* (San Francisco: Whitaker & Ray-Wiggin Co., 1902), 187. Tourist inquiries printed in the *Los Angeles Record*, February 11, 1896. See William Deverell, *Whitewashed Adobe: The Rise of Los Angeles and the Remaking of its Mexican Past* (Berkeley: University of California Press, 2004), 73.

9. James Steele, *Old Californian Days* (Chicago: Morrill, Higgins & Co., 1892), 11–12. Steele authored more than two dozen books, mostly travelogues and tourist guides to the American West and Latin America, several of them published by Rand-McNally. He was also a Civil War–era veteran who wrote a semifictional account of his army days in the West.

10. Charles Dudley Warner, "Race and Climate," *Land of Sunshine* 4, no. 3 (February 1896): 103–6

11. Warner, "Race and Climate," 103–6.

12. Gertrude K. Stoughton, *The Books of California* (Los Angeles: Ward Ritchie Press, 1968), 109–113; Mrs. A. S. C. Forbes to Caroline M. Severance, November 22, 1904, Caroline M. Severance Papers, Huntington Library (hereafter Severance Papers); [Charles F. Lummis], "The Camino Real," *Out West* 19, no. 6 (December 1903): 671; Anna Picher to Horatio N. Rust, August 14, 1892, Horatio N. Rust Papers, Huntington Library (hereafter Rust Papers); John D. Bruckman, *The City Librarians of Los Angeles* (Los Angeles: Los Angeles Library Association, 1973), 22–24; Landmarks Club, *The Landmarks Club: What it Has Done, What it Has to Do* (Los Angeles: Out West Co., 1903).

13. A decade earlier, Lummis arrived in Southern California as one of the multitude of health seekers, though his transportation was more unusual than most: he walked three thousand miles from Ohio to get there. After a stint with the *Los Angeles Times* and a recuperative interlude in New Mexico, Lummis threw himself into promoting Southern California and its unique heritage. He published books and photographs on the Spanish past and landscape, founded the Southwest Museum to collect Spanish and Indian artifacts, became the city librarian, and campaigned for the preservation of all manner of historic landmarks. For detailed looks at Lummis's transformation from Harvard invalid to Los Angeles impresario, see Kevin Starr, *Inventing the Dream: California through the Progressive Era* (New York: Oxford University Press, 1985), 75–86; Martin Padget, *Indian Country: Travels in the American Southwest, 1840–1935* (Albuquerque: University of New Mexico Press, 2004), ch. 4; Mark Thompson, *American Character: The Curious Life of Charles Fletcher Lummis and the Rediscovery of the Southwest* (New York: Arcade Publishing, 2001); Sherry Smith, *Reimagining Indians: Native Americans through Anglo Eyes, 1880–1940* (New York: Oxford University Press, 2000), ch. 4; Edwin R. Bingham, *Charles F. Lummis, Editor of the Southwest* (San Marino, Calif.: Huntington Library, 1955).

14. Auguste Wey [pseud., Anna Picher], "The Camino Real," *Land of Sunshine* 3, no. 4 (September 1895): 157; Philip Mills Jones, M. D., "Mission San Antonio—A Plea for its Restoration and Preservation," *Sunset* 5, no. 6 (October 1900): 303.

15. John E. Bennett, "Missions of California: Should they Be Restored?" *Overland Monthly,* 2nd. ser., 29, no. 179 (February 1897): 156, 160. For details on the *La Fiesta* cancellation and analysis of its general, if brief, impact on Los Angeles in the last years of the century, see Deverell, *Whitewashed Adobe,* ch. 2. The festival was one of several early influences generating local understanding of the salience and marketability of the region's Spanish past.

16. Charles Augustus Keeler, *Southern California* (Los Angeles: n.p., 1899), 90; F. A. Ober, "Picturesque Ruins," *The Evening Star* [Los Angeles], 1899. Discourse on Indian slavery and Indians' place in mission history seemed to parallel the rhetoric of the Spanish-American War that disparaged Spain's colonial policies past and present. The suggestion that Indians were like slaves failed to sustain the analogy to American plantation slavery and faded as the romantic

version of mission memories rose. Even critics of the missions became less likely to make this accusation as the years progressed. For analysis of southwestern Indians and slavery, see James Brooks, *Captives and Cousins: Slavery, Kinship and Community in the Southwest Borderlands* (Chapel Hill: University of North Carolina Press, 2002).

17. Evaleen Srein, "A December Morning at Santa Barbara Mission," *Sunset* 7, no. 4 (August 1901): 92.

18. Harrie Rebecca Piper Smith Forbes was born in Everett, Pennsylvania, in 1861. She later moved to Kansas, where she attended Episcopal College and met Armitage S. C. Forbes, an Englishman. Once in Los Angeles, Armitage invested in the gold- and gypsum-mining industry while Harrie quickly took an interest in her new community, joining several local organizations, including the Friday Morning Club, the Landmarks Club, the Historical Society of Southern California, the California Federation of Women's Clubs, the Los Angeles Camera Club, and the Ruskin Art Club. Max Binheim, ed., *Women of the West* (Los Angeles: Publishers Press, 1928), 43; Don Snyder, "The Bells of El Camino Real," *Los Angeles Corral Westerners Branding Iron*, no. 175 (Spring 1989): 17; "Mrs. Armitage Forbes, Head of California Landmarks Club, Dies," *Los Angeles Herald*, September 18, 1951; Justice B. Detwiler, ed., *Who's Who in California: A Biographical Dictionary, 1928–29* (Who's Who Publishing Co.: San Francisco, 1929); Perry Worden, Charles Yale, and Lillian A. Williamson, "Armitage S. C. Forbes, a Biographical Sketch," *Annual Publications* (Historical Society of Southern California), 14 (1928): 80–83.

19. Harrie Forbes, quoted in "Mrs. A. S. C. Forbes," *Los Angeles Examiner*, May 8, 1904.

20. The Native Sons and Daughters of the Golden West required members to be of California birth. Representing a fraternal order that operated much as other such groups, the local clubs spoke out on a variety of issues; their campaign against state division was a passionate cause around the turn of the century. For a look at the clubs' early efforts to mark historical landmarks, see David Glassberg, *Sense of History: The Place of the Past in American Life* (Amherst: University of Massachusetts Press, 2001), ch. 7.

21. "El Camino Real Association," *San Diego Union*, June 14, 1904; Max R. Kurillo, "Marking the Past: A History of the Road Called El Camino Real, El Camino Real Association and the Bells," *The Ventura County Historical Society Quarterly* 37, nos. 3–4 (Spring/Summer 1992): 15; Mrs. A. S. C. [Harrie] Forbes, *California Missions and Landmarks: El Camino Real* (3rd ed., Los Angeles: n.p., 1915), 270; Mrs. A. S. C. Forbes, *California Missions and Landmark*, 8th ed. (Los Angeles: n.p., 1925), 355; "El Camino Real Association."

22. Clara Burdette, "President's Address," California Federation of Women's Clubs, San Francisco, 4–7 February 1902, typescript, Clara Burdette Collection, Huntington Library; see also *A Book for Club Women* (Los Angeles: Federation of Women's Clubs, 1902), 15; Binheim, ed., *Women of the West*, 43; "The Ruskin Art Club Directs Display," *Los Angeles Times*, March 12, 1904; Gayle Gullett, *Becoming Citizens: The Emergence and Development of the California Women's Movement, 1880–1911* (Urbana: University of Illinois Press, 2000), 117–18.

23. Patricia West, *Domesticating History: The Political Origins of America's House Museums* (Washington, D.C.: Smithsonian Institution Press, 1999), 56. For analysis of California women in the Progressive movement, see Gullett, *Becoming Citizens*, and Judith Raftery, "Los Angeles Clubwomen and Progressive Reform, in *California Progressivism Revisited*, eds. William Deverell and Tom Sitton (Berkeley: University of California Press, 1995).

24. Gullett, *Becoming Citizens*, 107–9.

25. Gullett, *Becoming Citizens*, 124–26.

26. Gullett, *Becoming Citizens*, 118, 130. The Ebell Club built an elaborate Spanish-renaissance home in 1897; the Friday Morning Club answered with an imposing mission-style structure in 1900.

27. "The Good Roads Movement and the California Bureau of Highways," *Overland Monthly*, 2nd. ser., 28, no. 165 (September 1896): 247; Roy Stone, "Good Roads: How to Add $300,000,000 to the Taxable Property of the State," *Overland Monthly*, 2nd ser., 25, no. 147 (March 1895): 234; see also Ben Blow, *California Highways: A Descriptive Record of Road Development by the State and by Such Counties as have Paved Highways* (San Francisco: [California State Automobile Association], 1920), 1–27; *Biennial Report of the Department of Highways of the State of California* (Sacramento: State Printing, 1902), 5.

28. Before 1910 automobiles were custom-made machines that cost thousands of dollars and were expensive and unreliable to operate. Farmers often intensely opposed automobiles, and small towns imposed extremely low speed limits, three to five miles per hour, to discourage motorists from speeding through their main streets. The ACSC organized to combat these regulations, which they considered unreasonable, as well as to provide more general support for the minority of automobile owners. They produced road maps, posted directional signs, held races, and offered a strong public defense of the machine on many occasions. Anne Farrar Hyde, "From Stagecoach to Packard Twin Six: Yosemite and the Changing Face of Tourism, 1880–1930," *California History* 69, no. 2 (Summer 1990): 160. For a history of the Automobile Club of Southern California see J. Allen Davis, *The Friend to All Motorists: The Story of the Automobile Club of Southern California Through 65 Years, 1900–1965* (Los Angeles: Anderson, Ritchie & Simon, 1967). For a general history of early automobiles and their owners, see, among others, Warren James Belasco, *Americans on the Road: From Autocamp to Motel, 1910–1945* (Cambridge, Mass.: The MIT Press, 1979); James J. Flink, *America Adopts the Automobile, 1895–1910* (Cambridge, Mass.: The MIT Press, 1970).

29. There were approximately 90 attendees, with 72 official delegates. Notable attendees included Harrie Forbes, Charles Lummis, Anna Picher, A. P. Fleming (Los Angeles Chamber of Commerce chairman), Benjamin Hahn (state senator from Pasadena), Milbank Johnson (president of the ACSC), Eliza Keith (past president of the Native Daughters), J. R. Knowland (state senator from Alameda). "Names Associated with the El Camino Real Association of California," *The Morning Press* [Santa Barbara], April 20, 1904; Forbes, *California Missions* (1915), 264, 272; "Camino Real Convention Opens with Unbound Enthusiasm," *The Morning Press* [Santa Barbara], April 20, 1904.

30. Women accounted for 26% of attendees; thirteen of these attendees were affiliated with women's clubs. "Names Associated," *The Morning Press;* Forbes, *California Missions* (1915), 264, 272; "Camino Real Convention Opens," *The Morning Press.*

31. Charles F. Lummis, "The Camino Real," *Out West* 20, no. 1 (January 1904): 79; Lummis's own Landmarks Club drew largely from women for its staffing and support. The *Land of Sunshine,* as Kevin Starr has characterized it, was "a highly female magazine, written in the main by women for women under Lummis' guidance." Tension between male and female organizations in the Progressive Era remained one of the "changing challenges clubwomen faced in the late 19th and early 20th centuries as they moved from the world of female reform to mainstream political activities." Starr, *Inventing the Dream,* 95; Raftery, "Los Angeles Clubwomen," 144–46; see also Karen Blair, *The Clubwoman as Feminist: True Womanhood Redefined, 1868–1914* (New York: Holmes and Meier, 1980), 34.

32. C. F. Lummis to Caroline M. Severance, January 15, 1904, Severance Papers; C. F. Lummis to Major E. W. Jones, March 17, 1904; C. F. Lummis to Mary Stilson, April 7, 1905; C. F. Lummis to Major E. W. Jones, March 8, 1904; Major E. W. Jones to C. F. Lummis, March 11, 1904, C. F. Lummis Manuscripts Collection, Braun Research Library, Southwest Museum (hereafter Lummis Collection).

33. Mrs. A. S. C. Forbes, *California Missions and Landmarks and How to Get There* (Los Angeles: Official Guide, 1903); "Mrs. A. S. C. Forbes," *Los Angeles Examiner,* May 8, 1904; Forbes, *California Missions,* (1915), 271–72; "Camino Real Convention," *Los Angeles Times,* April 17, 1904; The Board of Directors of the Los Angeles Chamber of Commerce, Minutes (hereafter LACOC Minutes), February 24, 1904, Los Angeles Chamber of Commerce Collection, Regional History Center, University of Southern California (hereafter USC Chamber Collection).

34. Eliza D. Keith, *Report of the Historical Landmarks Committee, Native Daughters of the Golden West* (San Francisco: Walter N. Brunt, 1902), 28. See West, *Domesticating History,* 47–48, for a discussion of the gender dynamics of the preservation movement.

35. "Camino Real Convention," *Los Angeles Times.*

36. LACOC Minutes, January 27, 1904, USC Chamber Collection; "Camino Real Convention," *Los Angeles Times;* Charles F. Lummis, "The Camino Real," *Out West* 20, no. 3 (March 1904): 280.

37. George R. Lawson and George Wharton James, "Over 'Camino Real' Route: Historic Highway's Boundaries are Lost," *Los Angeles Examiner,* June 26, 1904; George Wharton James, [notes], ca. 1905, George Wharton James Papers, Huntington Library (hereafter James Papers). James was an English migrant to Southern California, a former Methodist minister, a prolific writer of light regional narratives, and a consistent adherent of the romantic vision of the region's past. He acquired some of his initial fame from a divorce scandal that defrocked him and continued to be viewed as a bit of an oddball despite his wide popularity. He took over the editorship of *Out West* between 1912 and 1914. See Starr, *Inventing the Dream,* 109–12; Smith, *Reimagining Indians,* ch. 5.

38. [Editorial], *San Francisco Chronicle,* quoted in Charles F. Lummis, "In the Lion's Den: In the Vacuous Summer-Time," *Out West* 21, no. 3 (September 1904): 295.

39. James Miller Guinn, *El Camino Real: an address read before the Historical Society of Southern California, 16 April 1906* ([Los Angeles: The Society, 1906]) 3; Guinn, "To the Editor," emphasis added.

40. Guinn, *El Camino Real,* 5; Wey [Picher], "The Camino Real," 156–58; Mrs. M. E. Dudley, "The True 'Camino Real,'" *Ventura Free Press,* October 4, 1907.

41. James, [notes], ca. 1905, James Papers. See also George Wharton James, *In and Out of the Old Missions of California* (1905; New York: Grosset and Dunlap, 1927), pp. 379–80.

42. Mrs. A. S. C. Forbes to Mrs. [Harriet Williams Russell] Strong, August 24, 1909 [letter typed on pictorial brochure of Camino Real Association, Los Angeles Section, 618 Laughlin Building, Los Angeles], Harriet Williams Strong Papers, Huntington Library (hereafter Strong Papers)..

43. Charles F. Lummis, "In the Lion's Den: The Turn of the Road," *Out West* 20, no. 5 (May 1904): 471; Charles F. Lummis, "In the Lion's Den: Turn to the Right," *Out West* 20, no. 4 (April 1904): 389–90.

44. Lillian Ferguson, "El Camino Real Plans Pledge Prompt Action," *San Francisco Examiner,* April 26, 1904.

45. Mrs. A. S. C. Forbes, "Good Roads Means Restoration of El Camino Real," *Grizzly Bear* 5, no. 3 (July 1909): 5.

46. Mrs. A. S. C. Forbes to C. F. Lummis, March 30, 1909; Mrs. A. S. C. Forbes to C. F. Lummis, May 20, 1909, Lummis Collection. To the latter, Lummis responded, "Glad the work is going so well. Power to your elbow." C. F. Lummis to Mrs. A. S. C. Forbes, May 22, 1909, Lummis Collection. See also Blow, California Highways, 1, 28–32, 81.

47. Blow, *California Highways,* 33.

48. Blow, *California Highways,* 83–84, 125–27; "Expenditure of Highway Funds in California," *American Motorist* 4, no. 12 (December 1912): 963.

49. Forbes, *California Missions,* (1915), 266, 275; LACOC Minutes, August 8, 1906, USC Chamber Collection.

50. Mrs. A. S. C. Forbes, "The Bells of El Camino Real," *Grizzly Bear* 5, no. 5 (September 1909): 9; see also Mrs. A. S. C. Forbes, "El Camino Real: Interesting Record of the Old Historical Road Reaching from San Diego to Sonomo [sic] Counties," *Grizzly Bear* 2, no. 3 (January 1908): 36–37; Mrs. A. S. C. Forbes to Ida Blaine, May 15, 1914, Vertical File Collection, Los Angeles Public Library; "Ninetieth Mission Bell Erected by Native Sons," *Grizzly Bear* 6, no. 4 (February 1910): 16; Native Sons of the Golden West, Los Angeles Parlor #45, Minute Book, February 7, 1910 and February 14, 1910, Huntington Library.

51. "A Fountain for El Camino Real," *Sunset* 28, no. 6 (June 1912): 765; Forbes, *California Missions* (1915), 267–79; Marjorie Driscoll, "Mission Bells Maker Mrs. Forbes Dies," *Los Angeles Examiner,* September 19, 1951.

52. E. E. Hamilton, *Thorpe's Automobile Road Maps* (Los Angeles: Thorpe Engraving Co., 1911), 51; Eleanor Gates, "Motoring Among the Missions," *Sunset* 28, no. 3 (March 1912): 314.

53. Mrs. A. S. C. Forbes to Caroline M. Severance, October 1, 1906, Severance Papers; Kurillo, "Marking the Past," 23–24; Snyder, "The Bells of El Camino Real," 17–21; Worden, Yale, and Williamson, "Armitage," 82; Frank Rolfe, "In Memory," *The Historical Society of Southern California Quarterly* 33, no. 3 (September 1951): 270; Detwiler, ed., *Who's Who in California,* 448. Though evidence that an item commands avid buyer interest on eBay (where people will buy virtually anything) is hardly significant, the traffic in these Forbes-produced souvenir bells remains both busy and lucrative today. As many as a dozen of her ten-inch souvenir mission-bell guideposts go on the block per month, selling at times for close to one hundred dollars to a select group of avid bell collections.

54. Forbes, "Good Roads Means Restoration," 5; Detwiler, ed., *Who's Who in California,* 448.

55. "Mrs. A.S.C. Forbes."

56. John S. Mitchell, speech at San Fernando roof-restoration ceremony, quoted in Charles F. Lummis, *Stand Fast, Santa Barbara!* (Santa Barbara: Plans and Planting Committee of the Community Arts Association, 1927).

57. These participants included, among others: from the real-estate industry, Charles W. Allen, Abbot Kinney, various realty companies, and architects, including Myron Hunt; from the tourist industry, Frank A. Miller, owner of the Mission Inn in Riverside; C. C. Pierce and Co., photographer; and miscellaneous businesses like the Pacific Sign and Enameling Co., the Southern California Music Co., and the Out West Company. [El Camino Real Association], Roster, June 6, 1910, Lummis Collection.

58. A. L. Westgard, "The Path of the Mission Fathers: California's Scenic Coast Route," *American Motorist* 4, no. 12 (March 1912): 203; Los Angeles Chamber of Commerce, *California's Old Mission Scenic Tour, By Motor or Rail* ([Los Angeles: The Chamber], 1916); Effie Price Gladding, *Across the Continent by the Lincoln Highway* (New York: Brentano's, 1915), 64; see also Thomas D. Murphy, *On Sunset Highways: A Book of Motor Rambles in California* (Boston: The Page Company, 1915), 226; Spencer Kingman, "An Inn from the Middle Ages," *Touring Topics* 24, no. 11 (November 1932): 18–20; John S. McGroarty, "At the Sign of the Poinsettia," *Sunset* 29, no. 6 (December 1912): 622–23; George Frederick Kunz, "The Spanish Missions in California," *17th Annual Report* (American Scenic and Preservation Society), 1912.

59. Hamilton, *Thorpe's,* 215; *Paso Robles Hot Springs, Sunshine, Sulphur, Mud* (San Francisco, Sunset Press, ca. 1920); see also Hugo A. Taussig, *Retracing the Pioneers: From West to East in an Automobile* (San Francisco: privately printed, 1910), 2; Ruth Kedzie Wood, *The Tourist's California* (New York: Dodd, Mead, 1914), 269; Caroline Rittenberg, *Motor West* (New York: Harold Vinal, 1926).

60. Starr, *Inventing the Dream,* 86; see also, for *The Mission Play,* Deverell, *Whitewashed Adobe,* ch. 6.

61. Automobile Club of Southern California [ACSC], *California's Mission Tour* (Los Angeles: The Club, 1915), 10.

62. Not all travelers wrote diaries and fewer still published them, yet early automobile tourists were particularly prolific in writing about their experiences,

and a variety of publication outlets existed for their narratives. Carey S. Bliss, *Autos Across America: A Bibliography of Transcontinental Automobile Travel: 1903–1940* (Los Angeles: Dawson's Book Shop, 1972); Hyde, "From Stagecoach to Packard," 160; Flink, *Automobile Age,* 37–38, 169.

63. The work of Marguerite Shaffer—on tourist experiences, diaries, scrapbooks, and the relationship between individual and promotional accounts—has been influential in my understanding here. I have drawn upon her book *See America Firs,* as well as her article "Southwestern Scrapbooks: The Travels of Mildred E. Baker," *The Culture of Tourism, the Tourism of Culture* (Albuquerque: University of New Mexico Press, 2004).

64. Murphy, *On Sunset Highways,* 3; Walter V. Woehlke, "San Diego, the City of Dreams Come True," *Sunset* 26, no. 2 (February 1911): 139; Lloyd Osbourne, "Motoring Through California," *Sunset* 26, no. 4 (April 1911): 366; Henry F. McNair, "Following the Spanish Padres by Motor," *Travel* 30, no. 3 (January 1918): 12. For the history of Southern California's great affinity for the automobile, see Flink, *The Automobile Age;* and Richard Longstreth, *City Center to Regional Mall: Architecture, the Automobile, and Retailing in Los Angeles, 1920–1950* (Cambridge, Mass.: The MIT Press, 1997).

65. J. B. Scofield, ed., *The Land of Living Color* (San Francisco: Sunset Publishing House, 1915), 22; "Alice" to "Mother," New York, September 3, 1920, "Santa Barbara Mission, Cal.," postcard, Carte De Luxe, 1920. One cannot easily measure the increasing pace of automobile tourists in California in numerical terms, despite the overwhelming evidence in personal observations like those cited here. Writers frequently mentioned Southern California's weather and its ambitious paving program as key factors in its high rate of automobile ownership; these factors could only have encouraged visiting automobilists as well. For accounts of the general increase in U.S. auto tourism and California's particular appeal, see Shaffer, *See America First,* 148–61; Jakle, *The Tourist,* 117–22, 169, 225; Pomeroy, *In Search of the Golden West;* Belasco, *Americans on the Road;* and Cindy Aron, *Working at Play: A History of Vacations in the United States* (New York: Oxford University Press, 1999).

66. *The Sightseer* (Los Angeles: Pacific Tours), 1, no. 1 (January 1907).

67. Murphy, *On Sunset Highways,* 159; Thomas J. O'Shaughnessy, *Rambles on Overland Trails* (Chicago: privately printed, 1915), 123–24.

68. For evidence of such disappointment, see, for example, Trowbridge Hall, *Californian Trails: Intimate Guide to the Old Missions* (New York: Macmillan, 1920), 61; W. C. Scott, *Westward, Ho! A Story of an Auto Trip to the Pacific Country* (privately printed, 1921), 21.

69. For the development of the Southwest as a tourist destination full of romance and exotic peoples, see Chris Wilson, *The Myth of Santa Fe: Creating a Modern Regional Tradition* (Albuquerque: University of New Mexico Press, 1997); Leah Dilworth, *Imagining Indians in the Southwest: Persistent Visions of a Primitive Past* (Washington, D.C.: Smithsonian Institution Press, 1998); Barbara Babcock and Marta Weigle, eds., *The Great Southwest of the Fred Harvey Company and the Santa Fe Railway* (Tucson: University of Arizona Press and The Heard Museum, 1996); Charles Montgomery, *The Spanish Redemption: Heritage, Power, and Loss on New Mexico's Upper Rio Grande*

(Berkeley: University of California Press, 2002); and, Erika M. Bsumĕk, "Making 'Indian-Made': The Production, Consumption, and Legal Construction of Navajo Identity, 1880–1935," Ph.D. diss., Rutgers University, 2000.

70. T. J. Jackson Lears, *No Place of Grace: Antimodernism and the Transformation of American Culture, 1890–1920* (Chicago: University of Chicago Press, 1981), 103–7; Wilson, *Myth of Santa Fe*, 5–6, 110–13; Starr, *Inventing the Dream*, 44–46.

71. O'Shaughnessy, *Rambles*, 60.

72. Southern Pacific Railway, "El Camino Real," 88; Wood, *The Tourist's California*, 281. Wood wrote half a dozen guidebooks for the New York publisher Dodd, Mead & Co. between 1912 and 1919, the most famous of which was *Honeymooning in Russia*.

73. Maria Antonia Field, *Chimes of Mission Bells: An Historical Sketch of California and Her Missions*(San Francisco: The Philopolis Press, 1914), 16; McGroarty, "At the Sign," 623; Laura Bride Powers, *The Missions of California: Their Establishment, Progress and Decay* (San Francisco: Doxey Press, 1897), 10; Steele, *Old Californian Days*, 49.

74. Alice I. Anson, "Mountain and Mission," *Overland Monthly*, 2nd ser., 25, no. 149 (May 1895): 490; see also Aimee Tourgée "Mission Ruins," *Out West* 21, no. 6 (December 1904): 533.

75. Vernon J. Selfridge, *The Miracle Missions* (Los Angeles: Grafton Publishing Co., 1915), n.p.

76. Eleanor Gates, "Motoring Among the Missions: Concluding Chapter of a Gasoline Pilgrimage in the Footsteps of the Padres," *Sunset* 28, no. 6 (June 1912): 704; Hi Sibley, "Byways of El Camino Real," *Westways* 26, no. 9 (September 1934): 37. For other suggestions of ghosts at the missions, see McGroarty, "At the Sign," 624; John S. McGroarty, *The King's Highway* (Los Angeles: Grafton Publishing Co., 1909). Eleanor Gates authored numerous works of fiction, many of which she transposed for the stage; the most famous dramatization was *Poor Little Rich Girl*, which popularized the phrase. Gates was an Episcopalian, married twice but briefly, and lived in Los Angeles in the latter part of her working life, which included some early screen credits. Whether her *Sunset* travel diaries were completed on assignment or were submitted on a freelance basis after undertaking the trip as a tourist remains unclear. Durward Howes, ed., *American Women* (Los Angeles: Richard Blank, 1935–36).

77. Charles Francis Saunders and J. Smeaton Chase, *The California Padres and their Missions* (Boston: Houghton Mifflin, 1915), 213; John Brinckerhoff Jackson, *The Necessity for Ruins and Other Topics* (Amherst: University of Massachusetts Press, 1980), 102; Murphy, *On Sunset Highways*, 160.

78. Sibley, "Byways of El Camino Real," 37; Saunders and Chase, *The California Padres;* Hall, *Californian Trails*, 116. Among the other restorations that tourists criticized were San Buenaventura and San Luis Rey and by 1934, a "fake reconstruction" near Mission San Antonio de Padua. Woodcraft aficionado Hi Sibley published various schema for his "teardrop" home trailers in the 1930s and 1940s in magazines such as *Popular Homecraft* and *Mechanix Illustrated;* he also authored a still-used handbook on building birdhouses.

79. Murphy, *On Sunset Highways,* 232; Charles Francis Saunders, *A Little Book of California Missions* (New York: McBride and Co., 1925), 35. Murphy penned several such "auto-rambles" in various parts of the United States and Europe for Page and Co. in the 1910s.

80. Irwin W. Delp, *The Santa Fe Trail to California* (Boston: The Christopher Publishing House, 1933), 157–58; David M. Steele, *Going Abroad Overland: Studies of Places and Peoples in the Far West* (New York: Putnam's, 1917), 49. For a discussion of how World War I affected tourism in particular to accelerate domestic travel during and after the war, see Hyde, *An American Vision,* 296; Jakle, *The Tourist,* 225–26.

81. Westgard, "Path of the Mission Fathers," 203; Murphy, *On Sunset Highways,* 67; Sibley, "Byways of El Camino Real," 37.

82. ACSC, *California's Mission Tour,* 3.

83. Eleanor Gates, "Motoring Among the Missions—Second Chapter of an Auto Journey," *Sunset* 28, no. 4 (April 1912): 445.

84. Murphy, *On Sunset Highways,* 80; Selfridge, *The Miracle Missions.* Philip Deloria's discussion of the role of "expectations" in contextualizing white encounters with native people is illuminating. See Philip J. Deloria, *Indians in Unexpected Places* (Lawrence: University Press of Kansas, 2004).

85. ACSC, *California's Mission Tour,* 4.

86. After 1900 the native population began to climb, slowly, reaching twenty thousand during the 1950s and expanding more rapidly since. James J. Rawls, *Indians of California: The Changing Image* (Norman: University of Oklahoma Press, 1984), 171, 214.

87. Edith Wagner, "The Oldest Californian," *Land of Sunshine* 5, no. 6 (November 1896): 234–35. See also, for example, the following images: C. C. Pierce, "Mission Indian women," 1890, photograph #3307, C. C. Pierce Collection, Huntington Library (hereafter Pierce Collection); [Taber Co.], "The Oldest Indians of San Diego Co.," in "California and the West, 1900–1910," Album 49, Huntington Library; Lee Bernard McConville, "El Camino Real—A California Pilgrimage," *The Tidings* 1, no. 51 (December 16, 1910): 29. My understanding of these images owes much to Jennifer Watts's interpretation of the photography of "old Indians" in the region and Indians' relationship to the constructions of nature. Jennifer Watts, "Nature's Workshop: Photography and the Creation of Semi-Tropic Southern California, 1880–1930" (paper presented at the Southern California Environment and History Conference II, September 1997, Northridge, California).

88. C. C. Pierce, "Ancient Belles of San Luis Rey," 1893, photograph #2870, Pierce Collection. Placing Indians amid ruins increased the appearance that Indians were "living relics," as Leah Dilworth has noted, "simultaneously appearing from the past and disappearing from the present." These images stand in great contrast to the photography of Pueblo Indians, which most often showcased women with young girls and children. Dilworth, *Imagining Indians,* 3, 80; Barbara Babcock "'A New Mexican Rebecca': Imaging Pueblo Women," *Journal of the Southwest* 32, no. 4 (Winter 1990): 400–437.

89. Alfred V. LaMotte, "The California Indian," *Overland Monthly,* 2nd. ser., 37, no. 4 (April 1901): 831.

90. Murphy, *On Sunset Highways*, 165; Nolan Davis, *The Old Missions of California: The Story behind the Peaceful Conquest of the State* (Oakland, Calif.: The Claremont Press, 1926), 70–71.

91. Hall, *Californian Trails*, 8; Davis, *The Old Missions*, 70. For more about how the rhetoric of degradation rationalized the view that Indian extinction was inevitable, see Rawls, *Indians of California*, 200–201 and Dilworth, *Imagining Indians*, 3, 80.

92. Powers, *The Missions of California*, 104–5; Mary Crehore Bedell, *Modern Gypsies: The Story of a Twelve Thousand Mile Motor Camping Trip Encircling the United States* (New York: Brentano's, 1924), 124; Davis, *The Old Missions*, 70; Clifton Johnson, *Highways and Byways of the Pacific Coast* (New York: Macmillan, 1908), 34. Bedell, the wife of renowned physicist Frederick Bedell, recalled their journey across the country, leaving New York to retire in Southern California, where her husband would perform research at the California Institute of Technology. This book was Bedell's only foray into publishing. On the common derogatory reference to California native peoples as "Digger" Indians, see Rawls, *Indians of California*, 49–51, 97–99, 187–99.

93. Though the preference for European heritage may seem to be inevitable, it was not the only choice available. As Charles Montgomery discovered about New Mexico, Anglo-Americans chose to emphasize the native role over the Spanish one in building the Mission Church at Acoma. Stylistically, the church's resemblance to Pueblo Indian architecture made this approach understandable, but Spanish-Americans in New Mexico objected heartily to both this emphasis and the society it represented, believing that the project minimized the role of Spanish missionaries. See Montgomery, *Spanish Redemption*, ch. 3.

94. Studies of the conditions and treatment of native people at missions are burgeoning. See Virginia Bouvier, *Women and the Conquest of California, 1542–1840: Codes of Silence* (Tucson: University of Arizona Press, 2001); Lisbeth Haas, *Conquests and Historical Identities in California, 1769–1936* (Berkeley: University of California Press, 1995); George Harwood Phillips, *Indians and Intruders in Central California, 1769–1849* (Norman: University of Oklahoma Press, 1993); Edward D. Castillo, ed., *Native American Perspectives on the Hispanic Colonization of Alta California* (New York: Garland, 1991); Albert L. Hurtado, *Indian Survival on the California Frontier* (New Haven, Conn.: Yale University Press, 1988).

95. Gates, "Motoring Among the Missions," 703; Murphy, *On Sunset Highways*, 159; Letitia Stockett, *America: First, Fast & Furious* (Baltimore: Norman-Remington, 1930), 200. For a discussion of tourists' use of the language of pilgrimage in narrating their tours, see John F. Sears, *Sacred Places: American Tourist Attractions in the Nineteenth Century* (New York: Oxford University Press, 1989), 5–6. Stockett taught English and English history at the Friends School in Baltimore and also authored a whimsical history of the city that remains in print. Born in 1884, she was a member of the growing cohort of college-educated, never-married women at the turn of the century, and she undertook her trip with an all-women group of travelers.

96. Forbes, *California Missions*, (1915), 280; Selfridge, *Miracle Missions*; "Native Daughters"; Alice Harriman, "California's Camino Real," *Los Angeles*

Times, June 4, 1923. Harriman was a Christian Scientist, a native of Maine who traveled to the West, particularly to Montana, as a magazine writer. Landing in Seattle she formed the only female-owned publishing company in the nation in 1907, though the company lasted only a brief time and published few books. Upon moving to Los Angeles, she became fascinated by bells and was working on a history of bells in California at the time of her death in 1925.

97. Carey McWilliams, *Southern California Country: An Island on the Land* (New York: Duell, Sloan and Pearce, 1945), 79–80.

98. McConville, "El Camino Real."

99. Eliza D. Keith, "California Our State," speech at the San Francisco mission-bell–guidepost dedication, quoted in "Native Daughters and Native Sons Erect Bell Posts," *Grizzly Bear* 6, no. 2 (December 1909): 8.

100. Field, *Chimes of Mission Bells,* 27, 70; Starr, *Inventing the Dream,* 89. Field was a descendant of Esteban Munras, a Spanish-born diplomat to California who lived in Monterey. Field's book, *Chimes of Mission Bells,* was widely sold. Jackson Lears noted Protestants' growing fascination with Catholic forms of art and ritual during the period. American Protestants, particularly Episcopalians, envied the "sensuous luxury" of European cathedrals, their incense and medieval artifacts. The phrase "sensuous luxury" comes from a Nathaniel Hawthorne quotation that Lears includes in his narrative, the full text of which is "Oh that we had cathedrals in America, were it only for the sensuous luxury." For discussion of the latent desires for Catholic luxury among the antimodernist set, see Lears, *No Place of Grace,* 185–215, ch. 4, and passim; Hawthorne quoted in Lears, *No Place of Grace,* 186.

101. Steele, *Old Californian Days,* 31; Saunders and Chase, *The California Padres,* 233, 360.

102. Keeler, *Southern California,* 89–90, 132; Forbes, *California Missions* (1903), 95–96; H.E. Booth, speech quoted in Ferguson, "El Camino Real Plans"; Landmarks Club, *The Landmarks Club,* 9; Hall, *Californian Trails,* 12; Murphy, *On Sunset Highways,* 165; Johnson, *Highways and Byways,* 42; Field, *Chimes of Mission Bells,* 43.

103. For a discussion of the purposes of demonizing reconstruction, see David Blight, *Race and Reunion: The Civil War in American Memory* (Cambridge, Mass.: The Belknap Press of Harvard University Press, 2001), 139.

104. Sarah Keppel Vickery, "The Missions of California," in *The Spanish Missions of Alta California: with descriptive notes* (San Francisco: W.K. Vickery, ca. 1905). Earl Pomeroy has also noted that the confluence of rhetoric about the antiquity and the religion of the missions connotes a similar desire for Christian unity: "The golden age of Spanish California extended . . . perhaps in some senses back to the Middle Ages, before the Protestant revolt, since there was no sense of alienation among the pious sons and daughters of the Middle West who venerated Fathers Serra and Lausen." Pomeroy, *In Search of the Golden West,* 45.

105. Mrs. M.E. Dudley, "Uncle Nathan Talks about the Camino Real," *Ventura Daily Democrat,* June 23, 1904.

106. Gregory H. Singleton, *Religion in the City of Angels: American Protestant Culture and Urbanization, Los Angeles, 1850–1930,* (UMI Research Press,

1979), xxiv, 121; see also Robert Fogelson, *Fragmented Metropolis: Los Angeles, 1850–1930* (1967; Berkeley: University of California Press, 1993), 63–84; McWilliams, *Southern California Country*, 113–82; Dana W. Bartlett, *The Christian City* (Los Angeles: n.p., 1923), 18–27; Starr, *Inventing the Dream*, 57–58. Singleton reports that although Los Angeles was never more than 30% Protestant, between 1899 and 1920 Protestants from voluntaristic denominations held 91% of all elective and appointive city offices. According to Singleton, the voluntaristic Protestant denominations are Baptist, Methodist, Congregational, Episcopal, Presbyterian, and Disciples of Christ. Harrie and A. S. C. Forbes were Episcopalian. Detwiler, ed., *Who's Who in California*, 448; Durward Howes, ed., *American Women* (Los Angeles: Richard Blank, 1935–36).

107. Emphases added in all the following: Davis, *The Old Missions*, 9; Murphy, *On Sunset Highways*, 118; Alfred Roncovieri, speech quoted in "Native Daughters," 8; Bishop Thomas Conaty quoted in Selfridge, *The Miracle Missions;* see also "Father Serra Memorial Tablet at Riverside, Gift of Frank Miller," Pierce photo #3983; "Father Junípero Serra Monument, Golden Gate Park, San Francisco," Pierce photo #3993; "Mission Capistrano and Father Serra Monument," Pierce photo #3988, Pierce Collection; "Native Daughters and Native Sons Erect Bell Posts," *Grizzly Bear* 6, no. 2 (December 1909): 8. Roberto Lint Sagarena has found that Southern Californians also likened the padres to the Puritans. Roberto Lint Sagarena, "Inheriting the Land: Defining Place in Southern California From the Mexican American War to the Plan Espiritual de Aztlán," Ph.D. diss., Princeton University, 2000, 3.

108. Powers, *Missions of California*, 105–6; Harriet Russell Strong, "Europeans on the Pacific," typescript, ca. 1920, Strong Papers. On the eighteenth-century politics of the California Franciscans, see Lint-Sagarena, "Inheriting the Land," 89.

109. I refer here to the idea that William Appleman Williams identified as the logic of imperial anticolonialism, which allowed Americans to incorporate their growing empire into the rhetoric of liberty. William Appleman Williams, *The Tragedy of American Diplomacy* (1959; New York: Norton, 1972), 28–30, 45–58. On the domestic implications of the Spanish-American War, see also Gail Bederman, *Manliness and Civilization: A Cultural History of Gender and Race in the United States, 1880–1917* (Chicago: University of Chicago Press, 1996); Alexander Saxton, *Rise and Fall of the White Republic: Class Politics and Mass Culture in 19th Century America,* (London: Verso, 1990), 369–76; Michael Hunt, *Ideology and U.S. Foreign Policy* (New Haven, Conn.: Yale University Press, 1987), 40, 52–54, 126; C. Vann Woodward, *Origins of the New South, 1877–1913* (1951; Baton Rouge: Louisiana State University Press, 1971), 325–26.

110. George Wharton James, *Picturesque Pala: The Story of the Mission Chapel of San Antonio de Padua, Connected with Mission San Luis Rey* (Pasadena, Calif.: Radiant Life Press, 1916), 7.

111. *Missions of California: Historic Monuments of California's Early Civilization,* postcard folder ([San Francisco]: Edward H. Mitchell, ca. 1908); see also Saunders and Chase, *The California Padres,* 112; Anna F. Lacy, "Dedicate

Mission Bell as Sequel to Celebration," *Grizzly Bear* 7, no. 6 (October 1910): 7; Steele, *Going Abroad*, 192.

112. Gates, "Second Chapter," 438;

113. McGroarty, "At the Sign," 624; Ernest McGaffey, "Building a Country by Building Good Roads," *Southern California Business* 5, no. 1 (February 1926): 15; Scofield, *Land of Living Color*, 22.

114. Examples of this image are nearly ubiquitous in the mission imagery of the period. Gates, "Motoring Among the Missions," 307; Gates, "Second Chapter," 439; McNair, "Following the Spanish Padres," 12; Touring Information Bureau of America, *TIB Automobile Route Book, Coast-to-Coast* (Kansas City, Mo.: The Bureau, 1915), 257; Charles Hamilton Owens, "The Bell Tower, Pala Mission, San Diego County, California," *Touring Topics* 15, no. 2 (February 1923): cover; drawing, *Touring Topics* 17, no. 8 (August 1925): cover; "California Missions: Souvenir Folder," postcards, ca. 1915, Warshaw Collection of Business Americana, Archives Center, National Museum of American History, Smithsonian Institution; "Mission San Fernando, Californi[a]," postcard, no. 5316 (San Francisco: Pacific Novelty Co., ca. 1910); Gladding, *Across the Continent*, 32; *California: Winter's Summer Garden* (Chicago: Chicago, Milwaukee & St. Paul Railway, ca. 1910), cover.

115. Belasco, *Americans on the Road*, 30–31.

116. "Main Roads Traveled in the Sunset Country," *Sunset* 39, no. 7 (July 1917): 82. See also Shaffer, *See America First*, 148.

117. Horatio Nelson Rust, "Memorandum on Indian matters," 1890, Rust Papers.

118. Charles A. Keeler, "At Pala Mission," *Overland Monthly*, 2nd. ser., 33, no. 197 (May 1899): 400.

119. Besides Lummis, the other two Anglo members of the committee were Russell C. Allen and Charles L. Partridge. The villages forced to relocate included Cupa, San Jose, Puerta La Cruz, Puerta Ignoria (Noria), Tawhee, Mataguay, Puerta de San Felipe, and San Felipe. Warner's Ranch Indian Advisory Commission, "Preliminary Report," July 23, 1902, Charles F. Lummis Collection, Huntington Library; Florence Connolly Shipek, *Pushed Into the Rocks: Southern California Indian Land Tenure, 1769–1986* (Lincoln: University of Nebraska Press, 1987), 44.

120. James, *Picturesque Pala*, 49. James offered a brief counterpoint to the romantic vision, yet he titled the book in which he registered this small objection in a footnote *Picturesque Pala* and devoted most of its pages to romantic descriptions of its setting and history. Only a few others joined James in his minor protest.

121. Warner's Commission, "Preliminary Report"; Forbes, "El Camino Real," 36; "Mrs. A. S. C. Forbes"; Kunz, "The Spanish Missions," 407; James, *Picturesque Pala*, 42.

122. Anglos eagerly seized upon this remissionizing rhetoric on at least one other occasion in this era. The Simons Brick Company built a company town in Montebello to house workers for its brickyards. These workers were almost entirely Mexican, and when the local press discovered the town of Simons in 1907, the village became in reporters' imagination a virtual mission. Though

Mexican laborers replaced Indian neophytes and Anglo capitalists succeeded the Spanish padres, the metaphor worked for Southern California Anglos as a model for labor and racial control. See Deverell, *Whitewashed Adobe,* ch. 4.

123. [C.E. Kelsey], *Report of the Special Agent for California Indians to the Commissioner of Indian Affairs, March 21, 1906,* (Carlisle, Pa.: Indian School Print, 1906), 26; Murphy, *On Sunset Highways,* 111; Smith, "The Scattered Sheep," 3.

124. Wood, *The Tourist's California,* 339; Saunders and Chase, *The California Padres,* 55; see also Shipek, *Pushed Into the Rocks,* 44; James, *Picturesque Pala,* 49; McConville, "El Camino Real," 30; Saunders and Chase, *The California Padres,* 60–61.

125. James, *Picturesque Pala,* 43.

126. Blacktooth quoted in Warner's Commission, "Preliminary Report," 30–31; Shipek, *Pushed Into the Rocks,* 44.

127. [Kelsey], "Report of the Special Agent"; "Death of Indian Chief," *The Tidings* (September 15, 1911); Shipek, *Pushed Into the Rocks,* 45; James, *Picturesque Pala,* 43. The reservations at Santa Ysabel, Mesa Grande, La Jolla, Los Coyotes, and Morongo accepted such refugees, according to Shipek.

128. Eleanor Gates, "Motoring to Mass," *Sunset Magazine* 31, no. 4 (October 1913): 730–36, emphasis from the original.

129. Pala Indian School and Agency, "Annual Report, 1913"; Pala Indian School and Agency, "Annual Report, 1918," June 30, 1918; Department of the Interior, Office of Indian Affairs, "Dancing," Education-Administration Circular No. 331, August 19, 1909; Department of the Interior, U.S. Indian Service, "To Superintendents and Others in Chare *[sic]* of Indians," Circular No. 548: Methods-Statistics, July 3, 1911; Francis A. Swayne, Cahuilla School to Supt. Phil T. Loregan, Pala Agency, June 27, 1910; F. H. Abbot, Acting Commissioner, Office of Indian Affairs, Department of the Interior, to William J. Davis, Superintendent Rincon Indian School, October 28, 1909; F. M. Garnes, Volcan Indian School, to Phil T. Lonergan, Superintendent, Pala Agency, June 3, 1910, Records of the Pala Superintendency, Records of the Bureau of Indian Affairs, RG75, National Archives and Records Administration, Pacific Region, Laguna Niguel Office (hereafter Pala Superintendency Records).

130. Pala Indian School, "Annual Report, 1913"; "Annual Report, 1916," June 30, 1916; Pala Indian School and Agency, "Annual Report, 1915," June 30, 1915, Pala Superintendency Records. For more on the Pala Indian fiesta and its transformation, see ch. 3.

131. Murphy, *On Sunset Highways,* 111; James, *Picturesque Pala,* 61.

132. "Pala Indians Forsake Chase for Quiet Farm Life; Kindness Makes Aborigines Thrifty Ranchers," *San Diego Union,* January 1, 1916; Haas, *Conquests and Historical Identities,* 125–6. Haas tells of the restoration of San Juan Capistrano at the hands of Father John O'Sullivan. The project sought to promote tourism but involved the entire community, including native people. This new prominence of the mission, she argued, fostered new articulations of local history and identity among Californio and Indian residents.

133. Arthur A. Turney, from *Los Angeles Tribune,* quoted in "Centennial Celebration," *Indian Sentinel* (October 1917).

134. G. B. Betts, "The Rediscovery of America by the Automobile," *Outing* 42 (May 1903): 167, 175. For discussion of the patriotic and pioneering stances of early automobilists, see Shaffer, *See America First*, ch. 4; Belasco, *Americans on the Road,*3; Bliss, *Autos Across America*, xiii-xiv.

135. ACSC, *California's Mission Tour,* 8.

136. Glen Gendzel, "Pioneers and Padres: Competing Mythologies in Northern and Southern California, 1850–1930," *Western Historical Quarterly* 32, no. 1 (Spring 2001); U.S. House of Representatives National Statuary Hall Law (section 1814 of the Revised Statutes), July 2, 1864. The law allowed each state to designate two "deceased persons who have been citizens thereof, and illustrious for their historic renown or for distinguished civic or military services such as each State may deem to be worthy of this national commemoration." Initial discussion about California's representatives began in the 1920s; the statues were erected in 1931.

137. C. F. Lummis to G. W. Marston, November 27, 1916, Lummis Collection.

3. THE FAIR

1. San Francisco registered the first bid to host an exposition in honor of the projected opening of the Panama Canal in 1915, but the plan was waylaid after the 1906 earthquake and fire. In 1909 San Diegans offered to stand in as host. After a year of San Diego fund-raising and advertisement, San Franciscans announced their intention to go ahead with plans to hold the fair and easily won the official national bid. Nevertheless, the southern city's stubborn boosters refused to withdraw and decided to stage their own exposition.

2. W. L. Frevert, "Planning to Make the City Beautiful," *San Diego Union,* October 10, 1903; see also Abraham Shragge, "Boosters and Bluejackets: The Culture of Civic Militarism in San Diego, California, 1900–1945," Ph.D. diss., University of California, San Diego, 1999, 95–100; Robert Fogelson, *The Fragmented Metropolis: Los Angeles, 1850–1930* (1967; Berkeley: University of California Press, 1993), 190–91.

3. See, for example, the chamber's advertisement in the 1907 City Directory, which listed its primary goals for the city: "cleaner streets; encouraging desirable immigration; making San Diego a great naval rendezvous; the annual distribution of 400,000 pieces of advertising . . . the general recognition that we have the finest climate on earth, that San Diego is indeed an Ideal Home Land." *San Diego City and County Directory 1907* (San Diego: San Diego Directory Co., 1907). For more about San Diego's growth strategy in general, see Shragge, "Boosters and Bluejackets"; and Fogelson, *Fragmented Metropolis.*

4. Shragge, "Boosters and Bluejackets," 80–83; Gregg Hennessey, "George White Marston and Conservative Reform in San Diego," *Journal of San Diego History* 32 (Fall 1986): 237.

5. Dana A. Basney, "The Role of the Spreckels Business Interests in the Development of San Diego," master's thesis, San Diego State University, 1975, 16–28; Gilbert A. Davidson, *Makers of the San Diego Panama-California Exposition, 1915, and Southern California* (San Diego: Arthur H. Gaebel, 1915);

Rufus Choate, interview, San Diego Historical Society (hereafter SDHS) Oral History Program, 1957, 6–8; Ed Fletcher, *Memoirs of Ed Fletcher* (San Diego: privately printed, 1952), 205; Richard V. Dodge, *Rails of the Silver Gate: The Spreckels San Diego Empire* (San Marino, Calif.: Pacific Railway Journal, 1960), 23–50; "Direct Railroad to East Assures Future of City," *San Diego Union*, January 1, 1907.

6. *San Diego Union* 1900–1915, passim; Fogelson, *The Fragmented Metropolis*, 190–91; Roger W. Lotchin, "The Darwinian City: The Politics of Urbanization in San Francisco Between the World Wars," *Pacific Historical Review* 48 (1979): 359–62.

7. "Committee Named to Boost for World's Fair," *San Diego Union*, September 2, 1909; "Plan World's Exposition for San Diego in Year 1915," *San Diego Union*, August 28, 1909; "The San Diego Exposition Assured," *San Diego Union*, September, 6 1909; "$1,000,000 Corporation Organized to Hold Panama Canal Exposition," *San Diego Union*, September 6, 1909; Gilbert A. Davidson, "History of the Panama-California Exposition of 1915 and the Panama-California International Exposition of 1916," in Carl Heilbron, ed., *History of San Diego County* (San Diego: San Diego Publishing Co., 1936), 401–2.

8. D. C. Collier, developer of some of the most successful real-estate subdivisions in the city, was named president; Davidson, chairman at the Southern Bank and Trust, accepted the position of second vice president. Other officers included L. S. McLure, a financier and colleague of Davidson's at the Southern Trust; bankers George Burnham, J. W. Sefton, Jr., Julius Wangenheim, Lucien A. Blochman, D. F. Garrettson and Fred W. Jackson; Albert G. Spalding, sports-product magnate and Burnham's partner in a securities venture; William Clayton, manager of the Spreckels-owned San Diego Electric Railway Co.; Charles L. Williams, police commissioner and cashier at Sefton's American National Bank; Arthur Marston, vice president of The Marston Store; Lyman Gage, former secretary of the treasury; real-estate developers Charles W. Fox and Percy Goodwin; and insurance-company owner William F. Ludington. "Exposition Assured," *Exposition News* 1, no. 1 (December 1911): 5; "Organization," *Exposition News* 1, no. 1 (December 1911): 5; "D. C. Collier San Diego's Biggest Asset," *Exposition News* 1, no. 1 (December 1911): 5–6; Davidson, *Makers of San Diego;* "Businessmen Approve of Exposition," *San Diego Union*, September 7, 1909; *San Diego Directory 1907; San Diego City and County Directory 1910* (San Diego: San Diego Directory Co., 1910); Robert Rydell, *All the World's a Fair: Visions of Empire at American International Expositions, 1876–1916* (Chicago: University of Chicago Press, 1984), 213.

9. "Exposition Notice No. 4," *San Diego Union*, November 24, 1909; L. A. Blochman and Fred Jewell quoted in "Businessmen Approve"; editorial, *San Diego Union*, August 10, 1910.

10. "Eastern Architect is Here to Plan Grounds for Exposition," *San Diego Union*, November 6, 1910; "Committee Selects Olmsted to Plan Park and Fair Improvements," *San Diego Union*, November 10, 1910; "Olmsted Outlines Plan for Park Improvement," *San Diego Union*, November 11, 1910. The two Olmsteds, John C. and Frederick L., Jr., had their hands in the design of the 1893

World's Columbian Exposition, the 1905 Lewis and Clark Centennial Exposition in Portland, and the 1909 Alaska-Yukon-Pacific Exposition in Seattle.

11. Bertram G. Goodhue to F. L. Olmsted, Jr., March 28, 1911, and John C. Olmsted to Bertram G. Goodhue, March 27, 1911, Bertram G. Goodhue Papers, Avery Library of Art and Architecture, Columbia University (hereafter Goodhue Papers); "Magnificent Exposition Site Laid Out," *San Diego Union,* September 6, 1911.

12. John C. Olmsted to Julius Wangenheim, telegram, June 6, 1911, George White Marston Papers, SDHS (hereafter Marston Papers); "Hotel Men Favor Bay Front as Fair Site," *San Diego Union,* November 8, 1909; Mary Gilman Marston, *George White Marston: A Family Chronicle,* (San Diego: Ward Ritchie Press, 1956) v. 2: 35–36; "Sehon Reiterates his Criticisms of the Panama Exposition Plans," *San Diego Union,* September 30, 1909; Gregory Montes, "Balboa Park, 1909–1911: The Rise and Fall of the Olmsted Plan," *Journal of San Diego History* 28, no. 1 (Winter 1982): 18.

13. Montes, "Olmsted Plan," 53; John C. Olmsted to Julius Wangenheim, August 30, 1911, Marston Papers.

14. "Exposition Officials Change Site of Fair, Choose Higher Ground," *San Diego Union,* September 3, 1911; Olmsted Brothers Co. to Julius Wangenheim, September 2, 1911, Julius Wangenheim to John C. Olmsted, September 5, 1911, and John C. Olmsted to Julius Wangenheim, September 8, 1911, letters reprinted in *San Diego Union,* September 10, 1911; "Olmsted Resigns; Opposed to New Site Chosen for Exposition," *San Diego Union,* September 10, 1911; "Exposition Plans," *San Diego Union,* January 1, 1913; Carleton M. Winslow, "Descriptive Notes of the Architecture and Gardens," in C. M. Winslow, ed., *The Architecture and the Gardens of the San Diego Exposition* (San Francisco: Paul Elder & Co., 1916), 37; Montes, "Olmsted Plan," 61–62.

15. "Labor Back Faith in Fair with Coin," *San Diego Union,* September 21, 1909; William Clayton, "Outlines Plan for Fair and Defines its Scope," *San Diego Union,* September 16, 1909; Edwin H. Clough, "Boosters, Knockers and the Cities They Build," *San Diego Union,* July 29, 1910; "The Chamber of Commerce's Stand," editorial, *San Diego Union,* September 30, 1909.

16. Leroy Harris, "The Other Side of the Freeway: A Study of Settlement Patterns of Negroes and Mexican Americans in San Diego, California," Ph.D. diss., Carnegie Mellon University, 1974, 8; Richard F. Pourade, *Gold in the Sun* (San Diego: The Union-Tribune Publishing Company, 1965), 34, 41–42, 113; Rydell, *All the World's,* 216. The 1910 census listed the San Diego population as 39,578 and the Los Angeles population as 319,198.

17. Emma Goldman, "Leaders of Murderous Vigilantes Pilloried," *Mother Earth* 7, no. 4 (June 1912): 108; Robert Warren Diehl, "To Speak or Not to Speak: San Diego 1912," master's thesis, University of California, San Diego, 1976. Panama-California Exposition Company (PCEC) directors listed as members of the "vigilance committee" were J. F. Forward, George Burnham, Percy Goodwin, W. F. Ludington, Fred Jewell, and Carl Ferris. Though John Spreckels was not a member, almost all *Union* articles supported the vigilantes and denounced the IWW.

18. James A. Sandos, *Rebellion in the Borderlands: Anarchism and the Plan of San Diego, 1904–1923* (Norman: University of Oklahoma Press, 1992), xv-xvii, 17–18; Friedrich Katz, "From Alliance to Dependency: The Formation and Deformation of an Alliance between Francisco Villa and the United States," in *Rural Revolt in Mexico and US Intervention,* ed. Daniel Nugent (San Diego: Center for US-Mexican Studies, 1988), 233; Alan Knight, *The Mexican Revolution* (Cambridge, England: Cambridge University Press, 1986), I: 45–47.

19. Catherine Cocks says that this idea of encouraging citizens to see with tourist eyes was common to urban promoters during this era. As she notes, "tourist itineraries embodied a way of seeing and moving through a city that enabled the journeyer to perceive it as an integrated whole, not a patchwork of antagonistic regions. Ideal urban citizens, tourists modeled a kind of vicarious, collective ownership that promised to obviate conflicts rooted in work and the division of wealth. Now visitors would teach city dwellers how to live in the city rather than learn local customs." Cocks, *Doing the Town: The Rise of Urban Tourism in the United States, 1850–1915* (Berkeley: University of California Press, 2001), 108, 131–32. For another look at the relationship between residents and visitors in the development of twentieth-century tourism, see Hal Rothman, *Devil's Bargains: Tourism in the Twentieth-Century American West* (Lawrence: University Press of Kansas, 1998).

20. Walter V. Woehlke, "Staging the Big Show," *Sunset* 33, no. 2 (August 1914), 337; see also Publicity Department, Panama-California Exposition, "Character of the Exposition," *Exposition News* 1, no. 1 (December 1911): 7; Rufus Choate, "Why San Diego Will Hold a Great International Exposition in 1915," *Sunset* 26, no. 4 (April 1911): 465–68; Rydell, *All the World's,* 219.

21. D. C. Collier, "What an Exposition is For," *Sunset* 31, no. 1 (July 1913): 146–47.

22. Panama-California Exposition Company, *Fore-Glance at Panama-California Exposition, San Diego 1915; Unique International Year 'Round, Jan. 1- Dec. 31* (San Diego: Panama-California Exposition Company, 1910).

23. "Balboa Park Chosen as Name of City's Big Pleasure Ground," *San Diego Union,* October 28, 1910.

24. Winfield Hogaboom, "Breaking Ground for the San Diego Fair," *Sunset* 27, no. 3 (September 1911): 340; John S. McGroarty, "San Diego Pageant: Exposition Ground-Breaking Beautifully Illustrated," *West Coast Magazine* 11, no. 1 (October 1911): 16, 19; "Ground Breaking Exercises: Cabrillo"; "Ground Breaking Exercises: Coronation of Queen," Panama-California Exposition Miscellaneous File, C. F. Lummis MSS Collection, Braun Research Library, Southwest Museum (hereafter Lummis Collection).

25. Panama-California Exposition Company, *Official Program Four Days' Celebration: during which ground will be broken for the first building of the Panama-California Exposition, July 19, 20, 21, and 22, 1911, San Diego, California* (San Diego: PCEC, 1911) 15.

26. "Ground Breaking Exercises: Mission Floats," Panama-California Exposition Miscellaneous File, Lummis Collection; McGroarty, "San Diego Pageant," 16, 19, 23; see also Panama-California Exposition postcards, Southwest

Postcard Collection, Mandeville Special Collections Library, University of California, San Diego; PCEC, *Official Program Four Days'*, 49–53.

27. Santa Fe Railroad Co., *Ground Breaking Ceremonies, Panama-California Exposition, San Diego, July 19–22, 1911* (Chicago: Santa Fe Railroad Co., 1911), 7; PCEC, *Official Program Four Days'*, 57.

28. "Exposition Grounds Broken Amid Pomp," *San Diego Union*, July 20, 1911.

29. David Glassberg, *Sense of History: The Place of the Past in American Life* (Amherst: University of Massachusetts Press, 2001), 85. San Francisco's 1909 Portolá Festival, which is a major focus of Glassberg's study of urban festivals, clearly was an inspiration for the ground breaking at San Diego. Glassberg argues that this "cultivation of an irrational attachment to 'the city' and the channeling of that attachment into particular political allegiances" was an important political development and that urban festivals, by converting "city streets that were ordinarily arenas for social conflict into elaborate stage sets for dazzling spectacle" were key to this transformation. Glassberg perhaps downplays the structuring of social conflict into the displays themselves, not least in terms of race, but his contention that their significance lies more in the shared experiences of the audience than in specific content dictated by city leaders is useful. Though gauging how local attendees consumed the messages of the pageants or the carnival is difficult, the repetition and official aura of the histories that these events presented equally complicate efforts to mount an alternative explanation. See also Glassberg's previous work, *American Historical Pageantry: The Uses of Tradition in the Early Twentieth Century* (Chapel Hill: University of North Carolina Press, 1990); for a look at celebratory uses of the streets in another era, see Susan G. Davis's helpful *Parades and Power: Street Theatre in Nineteenth-Century Philadelphia* (Berkeley: University of California Press, 1986).

30. E. M. Roorbach, "The Garden Apartments of California: Irving J. Gill, Architect," *The Architectural Record* 34, no. 6 (December 1913): 523; Sally B. Woodbridge, *California Architecture* (San Francisco: Chronicle Books, 1988), 84–87; Richard Oliver, *Bertram Grosvenor Goodhue* (New York and Cambridge, Mass.: The Architectural History Foundation and the MIT Press, 1983), 110; Karen J. Weitze, *California's Mission Revival* (Los Angeles: Hennessey & Ingalls, 1984).

31. Collier, "What an Exposition is For," 148, emphasis added; Elmer Grey to George Wharton James, December 16, 1914, Goodhue Papers; see also Harold Kirker, *Old Forms on a New Land: California Architecture in Perspective* (Niwot, Colo.: Roberts Rinehard Publishers, 1991), 60–62.

32. C. Matlack Price, "The Panama-California Exposition, San Diego, California: Bertram G. Goodhue and the Renaissance of Spanish-Colonial Architecture," *The Architectural Record* 37, no. 3 (March 1915): 240, 242; Kirker, *Old Forms*, 82–84. For a discussion of Goodhue's earlier designs, see Oliver, *Bertram Grosvenor Goodhue*. The two books Goodhue had already authored by 1910 were *Mexican Memories: The Record of a Slight Sojourn below the Yellow Rio Grande* (New York: G. M. Alten, 1892); and, with Sylvester Baxter and Henry G. Peabody, *Spanish-colonial Architecture in Mexico* (Boston: J. B.

Millet, 1901). Before the fair opened, he would also publish his definitive work, *A Book of Architectural and Decorative Drawings* (New York: The Architectural Book Pub. Co., 1914).

33. Bertram G. Goodhue to F. L. Olmsted, Jr., December 28, 1910, and F. L. Olmsted, Jr., to Bertram G. Goodhue, December 24, 1910, Goodhue Papers; see also in the Goodhue Papers, Olmsted Brothers to Bertram G. Goodhue, January 4, 1911; Bertram G. Goodhue to F. L. Olmsted, Jr., January 5, 1911; Bertram G. Goodhue to Wells Goodhue, January 11, 1911; Bertram G. Goodhue to Elmer Grey, December 29, 1911; Elmer Grey to Bertram G. Goodhue, January 4, 1911; Myron Hunt to Bertram G. Goodhue, telegram, January 8, 1911; and John C. Olmsted to Bertram G. Goodhue, telegram, January 9, 1911. Goodhue hoped to increase the number of his California commissions and to gain greater exposure in the state through participation in the San Diego fair.

34. Bertram G. Goodhue to Wells Goodhue, February 20, 1911, Goodhue Papers; architectural contract between Bertram G. Goodhue and U. S. Grant, Jr., representative of the Panama-California Exposition Company, January 30, 1911, Panama-California Exposition Papers, California Room, San Diego Public Library; "Noted Architect is Engaged to Design Exposition Buildings," *San Diego Union,* January 28, 1911; see also in the Goodhue Papers: Bertram G. Goodhue to Archdeacon Madden of Liverpool, England, March 1, 1911; and Bertram G. Goodhue to J. W. Gillespie, February 15, 1911; "San Diego's Mission City Destined to be Standard of Californian Architecture," *San Diego Union,* February 19, 1911, 9–10.

35. *Fore-Glance;* Walter V. Woehlke, "San Diego, the City of Dreams Come True," *Sunset* 26, no. 2 (February 1911): 136.

36. "Hotel Men Favor"; PCEC, *Official Program Four Days' Celebration,* 15.

37. Goodhue, "The Architecture and the Gardens," in *The Architecture and the Gardens,* 5.

38. *Fore-Glance;* G. Aubrey Davidson, *Official Opening Address of Gilbert Aubrey Davidson, Panama-California Exposition,* [San Diego]: n.p., 1915.

39. Emily Post, *By Motor to the Golden Gate* (New York: D. Appleton, 1916), 193; see also "What and Where the San Diego Exposition Is," *San Diego Union,* January 1, 1915; Panama-California Exposition Company, *Official Guide Book of the Panama-California Exposition,* (San Diego: PCEC, 1915); Rydell, *All the World's,* 2. Admission fees for the fair were fifty cents per day and twenty-five cents for children, on Sundays and after 6:00 P.M. Annual passes went for five dollars. The exposition was open 7:00 A.M. to midnight, seven days a week. Unlike many world's fairs during this era, the Panama-California Exposition stayed open for an additional year. After closing on December 31, 1915, it reopened on March 1, 1916, incorporating some of the international exhibits from San Francisco's now-ended Panama-Pacific Exposition. For the history of this decision and the differences between the 1915 and 1916 fairs, see Matthew F. Bokovoy, *The San Diego World's Fairs and Southwestern Memory, 1880–1940* (Albuquerque: University of New Mexico Press, 2005).

40. *San Diego 1915: International Panama-California Exposition,* (Chicago: Santa Fe Railway, 1915); David M. Steele, *Going Abroad Overland : Studies of Places and Peoples in the Far West* (New York: Putnam's, 1917); Dorothy Sears

to Bertram G. Goodhue, July 16, 1915, Goodhue Papers; Goodhue, "The Architecture and Gardens," 6; Bensel Smythe, "The Fair at San Diego," *Review of Reviews* (May 1915): 88. For a different treatment of the relationship between San Diego growth and the Panama-California Exposition's display of Spanish themes, see Bokovoy, *San Diego World's Fairs.*

41. Price, "The Panama-California Exposition," 238–39; Walter V. Woehlke, "Nueva España by the Silver Gate," *Sunset* 33, no. 6 (December 1914): 1120; John Bakewell, Jr., "The Santa Fe Station, San Diego," *The Architect and Engineer* 41, no. 1 (April 1915); Cliff May, interview, University of California, Los Angeles, Oral History Program, 1982, Oral History Collection, University of California, Los Angeles; Miller quoted in Ellen Van Kleeck to Bertram G. Goodhue, June 26, 1915, Goodhue Papers. For a rare negative review of the architecture, which judged it "heavy" and on "an exaggerated scale with no studied refinement," see W. B. Faville, "The Panama-California Exposition, San Diego, California," *The American Architect* 107, no. 2047 (March 17; 1915): 178–79.

42. *San Diego 1915,* n.p.; William Templeton Johnson, "Architecture of the Exposition" typescript, Edgar L. Hewett Papers, Fray Angelico Chavez History Library, Santa Fe, New Mexico (hereafter Hewett Papers); J. P. Harrington, "The Indians Living Along the Santa Fe Railroad in New Mexico, Arizona, and California," typescript, n.d, Hewett Papers; George Ellery Hale quoted in Gloria Martyn, "The 1915 Panama-California Exposition: San Diego's Dreamland," unpublished paper, San Diego Historical Society, 1974; Panama-California Exposition Company, *San Diego, All the Year 1915, Panama California Exposition* (San Diego: PCEC, 1914).

43. *San Diego 1915.*

44. Richard W. Amero, "Fairy City or Country Park," unpublished paper, San Diego Historical Society, 1984.

45. Ruth Townsend, "The City of the Sun: Sketches of the San Diego Exposition," typescript, Atchison, Topeka and Santa Fe Railway Publicity Dept., 1914, Hewett Papers; George W. Marston, Address at the Dedication of the California Building, December 31, 1914, Hewett Papers.

46. [PCEC], *San Diego, All the Year.*

47. *The Exposition Beautiful: Over One Hundred Views: The Panama-California Exposition and San Diego, the Exposition City* (San Diego: The Pictorial Publishing Co., 1915); "Official Views: In a Tropical Garden," postcard (San Diego: PCEC, 1914); untitled postcard (n.p., [1915]), 4418; "The Isthmus Amusement Street," postcard ([San Diego]: n.p., 1915); "Looking West on Prado from East Gate, Panama-California Exposition, San Diego, 1915," postcard (San Diego: I. L. Eno, 1915), Seaver Center for Western History Research, Natural History Museum of Los Angeles County (hereafter Seaver Center).

48. George W. James, *Exposition Memories: Panama-California Exposition, San Diego, 1916* (Pasadena, Calif.: The Radiant Life Press, 1917), 19; "San Diego's Exposition is Marvel of Beauty," *Los Angeles Record,* March 8, 1916; Hogaboom, "Looking," 336; Woehlke, "Staging," 336–37. Woehlke's text on the "sloe-eyed, nimble-footed senoritas" was reproduced on an exposition postcard: "Looking down the Prado," (San Diego: PCEC, 1914), Seaver Center.

49. "Turkish Harem Must Go Says Marsh," *San Diego Tribune,* April 21, 1916; "Exposition Board Will Visit the Harem," *San Diego Sun,* April 26, 1916; "Hoochie Kooch Show Not Allowed in Court; Many People Disappointed," *San Diego Sun,* April 29, 1916.

50. "Exposition Beautiful; Balboa Guards," postcard (San Diego: PCEC, 1915), Seaver Center; "On the Puente Cabrillo," stereograph no. 17663, Keystone View Company, 1915, Seaver Center; Joseph M. Grady, "San Diego Exposition a Marvel of Building and Nature Beauty," *The Denver Post,* February 24, 1915.

51. Winslow, "Descriptive Notes," in *The Architecture and The Gardens,* 126–27. For the provocative discussion of Columbus as Yankee hero in Chicago, see Michel-Rolph Trouillot, *Silencing the Past: Power and the Production of History* (Boston: Beacon Press, 1995), ch. 4.

52. "Exposition Beautiful Triumphantly Closes First Successful Year," *San Diego Union,* January 1, 1916, 7.

53. Post, *By Motor,* 193–94; Woehlke, "San Diego," 136; Woehlke, "Staging," 336–37; Woehlke, "Nueva España," 1129.

54. [PCEC], *San Diego, All the Year;* Woehlke, "Staging," 334; Woehlke, "Nueva España," 1126, 1128; Collier, "What an Exposition is For," 150; E. L. Hubbard, "A Little Journey to San Diego," *The Philistine,* 39, no. 6 (November 1914), n.p.

55. Lillie to Miss M. Barnes, "Reflections in Lily Pond," postcard ([San Diego]: I. L. Eno, 1915), Seaver Center; M. Carey Thomas to Lockwood DeForest, September 10, 1915, Lockwood DeForest Papers, Archives of American Art; Post, *By Motor,* 193; Bertram G. Goodhue to Ruth A. Baldwin, February 5, 1915, Goodhue Papers.

56. Mark Watson, "Permanent Buildings of Rare Architectural Beauty Will Mark Coming Exposition at San Diego," *The Architect and Engineer* 39, no. 1 (November 1914): 48; "The Mirror Pool," stereograph no. 17710 (n.p.: Keystone View Co., 1915), Seaver Center. For discussion of the consistent desire, even obsession, of many Americans to make the deserts of the West bloom, see Marc Reisner, *Cadillac Desert: The American West and Its Disappearing Water* (New York: Viking, 1986).

57. "International Harvester Company's Building," stereograph no. 17659 (n.p.: Keystone View Co., 1915); "In the Grape Fruit Orchard Looking Toward Isthmus, Panama-California Exposition," stereograph no. 17694 (n.p.: Keystone View Company, 1915), Seaver Center; Winslow, "Descriptive Notes," in *The Architecture and The Gardens,* 154–55; Post, *By Motor,* 193–94; Woehlke, "Staging," 336–37, 342–43; "Government Motion Picture Films," 1916, Exposition Records of the Smithsonian Institution and the U.S. National Museum, Smithsonian Institution Archives (hereafter Smithsonian Exposition Records); PCEC, *Official Guide Book,* 14–15.

58. Winslow, "Descriptive Notes," in *The Architecture and The Gardens,* 154–55; "Exposition Beautiful Triumphantly"; Harlan D. Smith, "As California Would Farm," *The Country Gentleman,* June 5, 1915; *The Exposition Beautiful;* "Resources Shown by Southland's Model Farm," *San Diego Union,* January 1, 1916.

59. Carey McWilliams, with his 1939 publication of *Factories in the Field,* and University of California, Berkeley, economist Paul Taylor, who published a three-volume study of *Mexican Labor in the United States,* between 1928 and 1934, were among the first writers to report on California's industrial approach to farming and its effects on Mexican immigrants. Later, historian Donald Worster argued that the primary motivation for this form of agricultural development was the need for wide-scale irrigation in arid conditions, such as that which literally conjured Imperial Valley from the desert. See Worster's *Rivers of Empire: Water, Aridity, and the Growth of the American West* (New York: Oxford University Press, 1992), as well as the following, for a more general history of California agriculture and migrant labor during this era: Lawrence J. Jelinek, *Harvest Empire: A History of California Agriculture* (San Francisco: Boyd & Fraser, 1979); Donald J. Pisani, *From the Family Farm to Agribusiness: The Irrigation Crusade in California, 1850–1931* (Berkeley: University of California Press, 1984); Devra Weber, *Dark Sweat, White Gold: California Farm Workers, Cotton, and the New Deal* (Berkeley: University of California Press, 1994); David Vaught, *Cultivating California: Growers, Specialty Crops, and Labor, 1875–1920* (Baltimore, Md.: Johns Hopkins University Press, 2002).

60. Steele, *Going Abroad Overland,* 153; "Virgin Soil Calls Willing Toilers Westward," *San Diego Union,* January 1, 1916, 4; "In San Diego's Back Country: Valleys of Orange, Grape and Olive," postcard, (Los Angeles: Panama-California Exposition Company and George Rice & Sons, 1914), Seaver Center; Davidson, *Makers of San Diego; At the San Diego Panama-California Exposition All the Year 1915.*

61. Panama-California Exposition Company, "Prospectus of the 1915 San Diego Exposition," typescript, San Diego Historical Society, 152; PCEC, *Fore-Glance;* Rydell, *All the World's,* 230–31.

62. For discussion of the presentation of Indians at world's fairs, see Robert A. Trennert, "Fairs, Expositions, and the Changing Image of Southwestern Indians, 1876–1904," *New Mexico Historical Review* 62, no. 2 (Spring 1987): 127–50; Curtis M. Hinsley, *Savages and Scientists: The Smithsonian Institution and the Development of American Anthropology, 1846–1910* (Washington, D.C.: Smithsonian Institution Press, 1981), 116–20, 180; Paul Greenhalgh, *Ephemeral Vistas: The Exposition Universelles, Great Exhibitions and World's Fairs 1851–1939* (Manchester, England: Manchester University Press, 1988), 82–94; and Rydell, *All the World's,* 23–29, 57–66, 99–100, 111–22, 228–30.

63. This interpretation of the ideological shift from viewing Indians as violent but vanishing to viewing them as pacified and primitive is best articulated by Philip J. Deloria, *Indians in Unexpected Places* (Lawrence: University Press of Kansas, 2004), 50.

64. PCEC, *Fore-Glance;* C. F. Lummis, to editor, *Hearst's Magazine,* April 10, 1912; C. F. Lummis, "Letter sent by me to all my associates in the Executive Committee of the School of American Archaeology, In Confidence," November 26, 1911; C. F. Lummis, to D. C. Collier, [ca. January 1912], Lummis Collection. For discussion of the use of anthropology at world's fairs, see Curtis M. Hinsley, "The World as Marketplace: Commodification of the Exotic at the World's Columbian Exposition," in *Exhibiting Cultures: The Poetics and*

Politics of Museum Display, eds. Ivan Karp and Steven D. Lavine, (Washington, D.C.: Smithsonian Institution Press, 1991), 346–48; Rydell, *All the World's,* 55–69, 162–67, 219–23.

65. Aleš Hrdlička to W. H. Holmes, Head Curator, Department of Anthropology, U.S. National Museum, March 29, 1912; Aleš Hrdlička "Advantages to the National Museum," typescript, ca. January 1912; D. C. Collier to Charles D. Walcott, Secretary, Smithsonian Institution, January 24, 1912; Aleš Hrdlička to W. H. Holmes, January 31, 1912; W. H. Holmes to Richard Rathbun, Assistant Secretary, Smithsonian Institution, January 31, 1912; Charles D. Walcott to D. C. Collier, February 12, 1912; D. C. Collier to Charles D. Walcott, March 20, 1912, Office of the Secretary, Records, Record Unit 45, Smithsonian Institution Archives, (hereafter Smithsonian Records). For greater detail about the effort to win Smithsonian participation and about Hrdlička's involvement at the fair, see Rydell, *All the World's,* 219–23; and Phoebe S. Kropp, "'All Our Yesterdays': The Spanish Fantasy Past and the Politics of Public Memory, 1884–1939," Ph.D. diss., University of California, San Diego, 1999, 213–17, 265–74.

66. Aleš Hrdlička to W. H. Holmes, October 19, 1912, Smithsonian Records; see also in the Smithsonian Records: Aleš Hrdlička to W. H. Holmes, March 29, 1912; Aleš Hrdlička to W. H. Holmes, April 27, 1912; Aleš Hrdlička to W. H. Holmes, October 6, 1914; and Aleš Hrdlička, "San Diego (& S.I.) Field Work: Results and Distribution," Aleš Hrdlička Papers, National Anthropological Archives, National Museum of Natural History, Smithsonian Institution (hereafter Hrdlička Papers).

67. D. C. Collier to Charles D. Wolcott, January 24, 1912, Smithsonian Records; PCEC, *Official Guide Book,* 20–21; *Exposition Beautiful.*

68. "The Beautiful Front of the California Building, Panama-California Exposition," stereograph no. 17687 (n.p.: Keystone View Company, 1915), Seaver Center.

69. Aleš Hrdlička, "The Division of Physical Anthropology at the Panama-California Exposition, San Diego," typescript, 1915, Hrdlička Papers; Aleš Hrdlička, *A Descriptive Catalog of the Section of Physical Anthropology, Panama-California Exposition, 1915* (San Diego: National Views Co., 1914), 7–10; Rydell, *All the World's,* 222–23.

70. "Savage Surgeons Fix Skulls," *San Diego Union,* April 11, 1915; *Exposition Beautiful.*

71. James W. Wilkinson, "Exposition Excursions: Number Fourteen: Man's Evolution," *San Diego Union,* May 16, 1915; Hrdlička quoted in Rydell, *All the World's,* 223; see also Rydell, *All the World's,* 222–23; Greenhalgh, *Ephemeral Vistas,* 104.

72. Edgar L. Hewett and William T. Johnson, "Architecture of the Exposition," *Papers of the School of American Archaeology* 40 (1916); Hector Alliot, Curator of the Southwest Museum, to J. L. Nusbaum, October 27, 1915, Jesse L. Nusbaum Papers, Talley Collection, Museum of Indian Arts and Culture/Laboratory of Anthropology, Museum of New Mexico (hereafter Nusbaum Papers).

73. Along with food and souvenir hawkers, roller coasters, and a Ferris wheel, as well as the concessions mentioned in the text, the Isthmus visitor

might also encounter an ostrich farm; a model Panama Canal; a movie theater; a ride through a gem mine; a tea plantation where East Indian laborers tended several acres and served Lipton tea; a forty-niner camp complete with saloon and dance-hall girls; camel and donkey rides; California and the Missions, a diorama and theater for productions of *The Mission Play*; the Sultan's Harem; a Hawaiian village; a shooting gallery; "Captain, the horse with the human brain"; Madam Ellis, telepathist; Ernest Darling, the nature man; Lilliputian Kingdom; Motordrome; and Sop-O-Zon.

74. Davidson, *Makers of San Diego*, emphasis added. This visual and ideological split between exposition zones has been well studied by world's-fair scholars. See, for example, Rydell, *World's a Fair*, 88; Hinsley, "The World as Marketplace," 351, 354–55; Burton Benedict, "The Anthropology of World's Fairs," in *The Anthropology of World's Fairs: San Francisco's Panama Pacific International Exposition of 1915*, Burton Benedict et. al. (London and Berkeley: The Lowie Museum of Anthropology and Scolar Press, 1983), 43–45; Greenhalgh, *Ephemeral Vistas*, 54.

75. "The Underground World," advertisement, in Earl W. Hill and Harry G. Seber, *Panama-Canal Extravaganza: Panama-California International Exposition: Souvenir 1916* (East San Diego: The Moyer Printing Co., 1916), inside back cover; see also PCEC, "Prospectus," 125, 267, 457; Woehlke, "Nueva España," 1124. For a discussion of the evolution of the Chinatown "slumming" tour, see Cocks, *Doing the Town*, ch. 6.

76. "The War of the Worlds," advertisement, in *Panama-Canal Extravaganza*, inside back cover; see also PCEC, "Prospectus," 427.

77. For analyses of this Santa Fe/Harvey Company agenda, see Rothman, *Devil's Bargains*, chs. 3 and 4; Leah Dilworth, *Imagining Indians in the Southwest: Persistent Visions of a Primitive Past* (Washington, D.C.: Smithsonian Institution Press, 1996); Barbara Babcock and Marta Weigle, eds., *The Great Southwest of the Fred Harvey Company and the Santa Fe Railway* (Tucson and Phoenix: University of Arizona Press and The Heard Museum, 1996); Marta Weigle, "Exposition and Mediation: Mary Colter, Erna Fergusson and the Santa Fe/Harvey Popularization of the Native Southwest, 1902–1940," *Frontiers* 12, no. 1 (Fall 1992): 117–50; Marta Weigle, "From Desert to Disney World: The Santa Fe Railway and the Fred Harvey Company Display the Indian Southwest," *Journal of Anthropological Research* 45, no. 1 (Spring 1989): 115–38; Lesley Poling-Kempes, *The Harvey Girls: Women Who Opened the West* (New York: Paragon House, 1989); T. C. McLuhan, *Dream Tracks: The Railroad and the American Indian, 1890–1930* (New York: Abrams, 1985); and, D. H. Thomas, *The Southwestern Indian Detours: The Story of the Fred Harvey/Santa Fe Railway Experiment in 'Detourism'* (Phoenix: Hunter Publishing, 1978).

78. [Santa Fe Railway], "The Santa Fe is the only line to *both* expositions," advertisement, 1914, Warshaw Collection of Business Americana, Archives Center, National Museum of American History, Smithsonian Institution (hereafter Warshaw Collection).

79. J. L. Nusbaum to Herman Schweizer, February 28, 1914, Nusbaum Papers; T. Harmon Parkhurst and John P. Harrington, "Suggestions for Exhibiting the Indians of the Southwest at the Panama-California Exposition"

typescript, n.d., Hewett Papers; Application for Building Permit, Division of Works, Panama-California Exposition, [1914], Nusbaum Papers; Herman Schweizer to J.L. Nusbaum, November 15, 1914, Nusbaum Papers; Lynn Adkins, "Jesse L. Nusbaum and the Painted Desert in San Diego," *Journal of San Diego History* 29, no. 2 (Spring 1983): 87; "Indians at Work on Exhibit For Exposition," *San Diego Union,* October 6, 1914. The total cost of the exhibit was about $150,000. Some structures were made of adobe mixed on-site, while others applied cement and plaster to a wooden and wire frame.

80. Philip J. Deloria, *Playing Indian* (New Haven, Conn.: Yale University Press, 1998), 93–94, 100–1. Scholars have shown that the idea of authenticity was as socially and historically constructed as the Santa Fe's presentation of it. As Deloria argues, "the quest for such an authentic Other is a characteristically modern phenomenon, one that has often been played out in the contradictions surrounding America's long and ambivalent engagement with Indianness." My own interpretation of the concept of authenticity and of the fascination with primitiveness takes much from discussions in Deloria, *Indians in Unexpected Places;* Marguerite S. Shaffer, *See America First: Tourism and National Identity, 1880–1940* (Washington, D.C.: Smithsonian Institution Press, 2001); Erika Bsumek, "Making 'Indian-Made': The Production, Consumption, and Legal Construction of Navajo Identity, 1880–1935," Ph.D. diss., Rutgers University 2000; Dilworth, *Imagining Indians;* Richard Handler and Eric Gable, *The New History in an Old Museum: Creating the Past at Colonial Williamsburg,* (Durham: Duke University Press, 1997); James Clifford, *The Predicament of Culture: Twentieth Century Ethnography, Literature and Art* (Cambridge, Mass.: Harvard University Press, 1988); James Clifford and George E. Marcus, eds., *Writing Culture: The Poetics and Politics of Ethnography* (Berkeley: University of California Press, 1986); Richard Handler, "Authenticity," *Anthropology Today* 2, no. 1 (1986): 6–9; and, T.J. Jackson Lears, *No Place of Grace: Antimodernism and the Transformation of American Culture, 1880–1920* (Chicago: University of Chicago Press, 1983).

81. Parkhurst and Harrington, "Suggestions for Exhibiting the Indians"; "'Injun' Band is Coming Here to Make Bow July 4," [*San Diego Tribune*], July 1914, San Diego Exposition: Painted Desert clippings, Nusbaum Papers; "Indian Tribes Will Be Brought to Exposition to Live and Work in Replicas of Their Real Homes," *San Diego Union,* August 21, 1913. The first set of rail passes issued for work in the exhibit went to Cresencio Martinez, Dionicio Sanchez, Florentine Martinez, Alfonso Roibal, Julian Martinez, Juan Cruz Roibal, and Atelano Montoya. J.J. Byrne to Julian Martinez, April 30, 1914, Nusbaum Papers.

82. Nusbaum had apprenticed in archaeology under Hewett at the Museum of New Mexico. Though the design team included other Santa Fe associates— Herman Schweizer, John F. Huckel, Mary Colter, and Edgar Hewett—Nusbaum collected the lion's share of the credit. According to Schweizer and Huckel, Nusbaum did nothing to disabuse the media of its assumption that he was solely responsible for the Painted Desert's success. Rosemary Nusbaum, *Tierra Dulce: Reminiscences from the Jesse Nusbaum Papers* (Santa Fe: The Sunstone Press, 1980), 8; Herman Schweizer to [?], July 19, 1921, Fred Harvey Papers, Heard Museum (hereafter Harvey Papers); Adkins, "Jesse L. Nusbaum," 88–90.

83. "'Painted Desert' Excels all Similar Fair Exhibits," *San Diego Union,* August 2, 1914.

84. "Santa Fe Railroad's Indian Pueblo Marvel of Primitive Craft," *San Diego Union,* January 1, 1915; Mark Watson, "San Diego's Panama-California Exposition," in *Semi-Tropic California: The Garden of the World,* ed. F. W. Benton (Los Angeles: Benton & Co., 1914), 182.

85. Jesse L. Nusbaum, "Zuni Pueblo for the Painted Desert," photograph and manuscript notes, 1914, Nusbaum Papers.

86. Parkhurst and Harrington, "Suggestions for Exhibiting the Indians"; PCEC, *Official Guide Book,* 14; "Santa Fe Railroad's."

87. Erika Bsumek demonstrates convincingly the ways in which this label was a talisman for white understanding of authentic Indianness. My understanding of whites' consumption of both Indian crafts and Indianness has been greatly influenced by her work. See Bsumek, "Making 'Indian-Made.'"

88. "Santa Fe Railroad's." Leah Dilworth found that Harvey arranged its Indian displays "along an implicit evolutionary scale, . . . which rated Indian groups 'good' or 'bad' according to their hostility to civilized life." In this scheme, Apaches represented the bottom, uncivilized rung, while Pueblos appeared on a higher plane that presented them as more pastoral, stable, and cultured. Dilworth, *Imagining Indians,* 95.

89. Steele, *Going Abroad Overland,* 152; Post, *By Motor,* 275, 194.

90. "Santa Fe Railroad's"; "Santa Fe is the only Line"; Mark S. Watson, "The Exposition at San Diego," *Pacific Mutual News* (1914): 177; Hubbard, "A Little Journey."

91. Watson, "San Diego's," 186; Jesse Nusbaum in Nusbaum, *Tierra Dulce,* 38.

92. ["Pueblo Indians in Electriquette"], postcard (n.p.: Csko Publishing, 1915), Seaver Center; "Indian Drives Car," *[San Diego Tribune],* 1914, San Diego Exposition: Painted Desert clippings, Nusbaum Papers. See next section for more interpretation of these images.

93. "Santa Fe Railroad's"; Watson, "The Exposition," 177. For a discussion of the relationship between the Fred Harvey Company and its Indian artisans, see Diana F. Pardue and Kathleen L. Howard, "Making Art, Making Money: The Fred Harvey Company and the Indian Artisan," in *The Great Southwest,* 171; Dilworth, *Imagining Indians,* 87.

94. "An Old Indian Woman at Work," postcard (n.p.: Azo, 1915); "Apache Pounding Silver," postcard (n.p.: Noko, 1915); "Making Pottery," postcard (n.p.: Azo, 1915); "Dancing," postcard (n.p.: Azo, 1915); "Firing Pottery," postcard H-1029 ([Chicago]: Fred Harvey Co., 1915); "Blanket Weavers," postcard H-1033 ([Chicago: Fred Harvey Co., 1915); "Pueblo Indian Firing Pottery," postcard H-876 ([Chicago]: Fred Harvey Co., 1915); "Pueblo Indians Baking Pottery," postcard H-877 ([Chicago]: Fred Harvey Co., 1915), Seaver Center; Bsumek, "Making 'Indian-Made'"; Barbara A. Babcock, "'A New Mexican Rebecca': Imaging Pueblo Women," *Journal of the Southwest* 32, no. 4 (Winter 1990): 400–37.

95. Hubbard, "A Little Journey"; Harrington, "Indians Living Along." For a discussion of "salvage ethnography," see Deloria, *Playing Indian,* and Hinsley, *Savages and Scientists.*

96. Deloria, *Indians in Unexpected Places*, 67–68; Johannes Fabian, *Time and the Other: How Anthropology Makes its Object* (New York: Columbia University Press, 1983). I borrow the analysis of the three storylines—Indians as vanishing, primitive, and modern—from Philip Deloria's discussion of the repeated clash of white expectations of Indianness with native participation in modern life. See especially his treatment of Buffalo Bill's Wild West and his detailed look at Indians in cars in ch. 4, "I want to Ride in Geronimo's Cadillac: Technology," in *Indians in Unexpected Places*.

97. María Martinez quoted in Susan Peterson, *The Living Tradition of María Martinez* (1977; Tokyo and New York: Kodansha International, 1989), 109; Alice Marriott, *María: The Potter of San Ildefonso* (Norman: University of Oklahoma Press, 1948), 215 n. 95.

98. Tuyo ____ (San Ildefonso Pueblo) to Charles Lummis, February 24, 1915, Nusbaum Papers, emphasis from the original. For an extended treatment of this episode, see Bokovoy, *San Diego World's Fairs*.

99. Deloria, *Indians in Unexpected Places*, 55–56, 69; Joy S. Kasson, *Buffalo Bill's Wild West: Celebrity, Memory, and Popular History* (New York: Hill and Wang, 2000), 163–76; L. G. Moses, *Wild West Shows and the Images of American Indians, 1883–1933* (Albuquerque: University of New Mexico Press, 1996); Vine Deloria, Jr., "The Indians," in Brooklyn Museum, ed., *Buffalo Bill and the Wild West* (Brooklyn: The Brooklyn Museum, 1981): 45–56. For a discussion of the changing social, ethnic, and economic context in the Southwest and its effects in Pueblo and Navajo communities, see Charles Montgomery, *The Spanish Redemption: Heritage, Power, and Loss on New Mexico's Upper Rio Grande* (Berkeley: University of California Press, 2002), ch. 1; and, Bsumek, "Making 'Indian-Made.'"

100. Marriott, *María*, 213–15; María Martinez, interview by Alice Marriott, n.d., University of Oklahoma, Western History Collections, Alice Marriott Papers. Thanks to Matt Bokovoy for the latter.

101. Dionicio Sanchez quoted in "Painted Desert Excels."

102. J. L. Nusbaum to Herman Schweizer, February 28, 1914, Nusbaum Papers; Edgar K. Miller, memorandum, 1935, Harvey Papers.

103. Harvey supervisor Herman Schweizer quoted in Barbara Babcock, "Pueblo Cultural Bodies," *Journal of American Folklore* 107 (1994): 47, emphasis from the original; Harrington and Parkhurst, emphasis added; Geddes Smith, "California's County Fair," *Independent Magazine* 83 (July 1915): 120.

104. Marriott, *María*, 119–20, 215–16; Rayna Green, "We Never Saw These Things Before: Southwest Indian Laughter and Resistance to the Invasion of the Tse va ho," in *The Great Southwest*, 202–6; Nora Naranjo-Morse, *Mud Woman: Poems from the Clay* (Tucson: University of Arizona Press, 1992), 54. Clowning is a long-standing tradition among Pueblos and has often been used for commentary on tourists.

105. Deloria, *Indians in Unexpected Places*, 130, 230; see also Laura Peers, "'Playing Ourselves': First Nations and Native American Interpreters at Living History Sites," *The Public Historian* 21, no. 4 (Fall 1999): 39–59.

106. Herman Schweizer to J. L. Nusbaum, November 9, 1914, Nusbaum Papers.

107. "Indian 'Rags' Style for Tonight," *San Diego Union*, August 28, 1915; Deloria, *Playing Indian*.

108. Harrington, "Indians Living Along."

109. "Indians to Open Big Powwow Tomorrow," *San Diego Union*, August 24, 1915; Richard L. Carrico, "San Diego County Indian Fiestas, 1880–1940: From Cultural Ritual to Generating Profit and Reinforcing Stereotypes." Paper presented at the Western History Association Annual Meeting, Las Vegas, Nevada, October 15, 2004.

110. Carobeth Tucker, "Pala Indian Dances Held during their Festival at the San Diego Exposition," [*San Diego Union*] clipping, Hewett Papers; "Pala Indians Forsake Chase for Quiet Farm Life; Kindness Makes Aborigines Thrifty Ranchers, " *San Diego Union*, January 1, 1916.

111. Lorraine White, interview, San Diego Historical Society Oral History Program, 1974, 8.

112. Yorick, "On the Margin," *San Diego Union*, January 10, 1915.

113. Rydell, *All the World's*, 4–6; Benedict, "The Anthropology of World's Fairs," 3–5, 34; Greenhalgh, *Ephemeral Vistas*, 50–54, 72–76, 96. Paul Greenhalgh has shown that "imperial achievement was celebrated to the full at international exhibitions. . . . Even the Americans, by the end of the [nineteenth] century, lauded the idea of empire at World's Fairs" and seemed "most eager to show off their gains" to the world.

4. THE HOME

1. Mary Pickford Fairbanks, "Spanish Architecture Ideal for the California Home," *The Architect and Engineer* 87, no. 3 (December 1926): 117–18. Thanks to Merry Ovnick for alerting me to this citation.

2. Catherine Cocks suggests this idea of "imagined proprietorship" in her book on urban tourism, analyzing how visitors at expositions of the turn-of-the-century era consumed what they saw, heard, and did there. Not only would tourists model for residents a new "kind of vicarious, collective ownership" of the city as a whole, but these "visitor-citizens . . . constituted themselves as members of a leisured public by looking. The receptive visitor identified himself or herself with the splendid commercial achievement of the fairs, conflating the republic with the market." Though ordinary citizens, as at San Diego, had scant real ownership in a fair, they were encouraged to take on this "imagined proprietorship" as a part of their experience of citizenship. I use her concept here to suggest the ways in which investing in Spanish-colonial real estate granted a seemingly broader ownership over the region as a whole, deeding buyers something beyond land. Cocks, *Doing the Town: The Rise of Urban Tourism in the United States, 1850–1915* (Berkeley: University of California Press, 2001), 108, 128–9. For a provocative look at tourism as a central experience of citizenship, and at tourists as ideal citizens, see Marguerite Shaffer, *See America First: Tourism and National Identity, 1880–1940* (Washington, D.C.: Smithsonian Institution Press, 2001).

3. The idea of the importance of ambiance in creating value in Southern California real estate comes from William Alexander McClung, *Landscapes of*

Desire: Anglo Mythologies of Los Angeles (Berkeley: University of California Press, 2000).

4. "Santa Fe Buys San Dieguito," *San Diego Union*, August 17, 1906; Constance C. Clotfelter, *Echoes of Rancho Santa Fe* ([Rancho Santa Fe]: CONREG, 1985), 9–10; Lucinda Liggett Eddy, "Lilian Jenette Rice: The Search for a Regional Ideal: The Development of Rancho Santa Fe," *Journal of San Diego History* 29, no. 4 (Fall 1983): 273, 282 n. 26. The Santa Fe Railway paid the two stock ranchers, James E. Connell and G. N. Gilbert, one hundred thousand dollars in August 1906. It purchased the Osuna share in October 1906 for an unknown amount.

5. "Santa Fe Buys"; Ed Fletcher, *Memoirs of Ed Fletcher* (San Diego: privately printed, 1952), 211–13, 221–22; Charles K. Fletcher, interview by Sylvia Arden, San Diego Historical Society, Oral History Program, 1984, (hereafter SDHS Oral History Program); Ed Fletcher to E. O. Faulkner, Manager, Tie and Timber Dept., Santa Fe Railway, July 27, 1915; Ed Fletcher to W. E. Hodges, Vice President, Santa Fe Railway, August 19, 1916, Col. Ed Fletcher Manuscript Collection (hereafter Fletcher Collection), Mandeville Special Collections Library, University of California, San Diego, (hereafter UCSD Special Collections).

6. Ed Fletcher to W. E. Hodges, December 11, 1916; see also E. O. Faulkner to Ed Fletcher, December 22, 1917; E. O. Faulkner to Ed Fletcher, November 19, 1920; Ed Fletcher to E. O. Faulkner, November 29, 1920; Ed Fletcher to E. O. Faulkner, March 29, 1922, Fletcher Collection; Fletcher, *Memoirs,* 220–26; Ruth R. Nelson, *Rancho Santa Fe: Yesterday and Today* (Encinitas, Calif.: The Coast Dispatch, 1947), 60–65.

7. W. E. Hodges to Ed Fletcher, June 22, 1922, Fletcher Collection; see also Marc Weiss, *The Rise of the Community Builders: The American Real Estate Industry and Urban Land Planning* (New York: Columbia University Press, 1987), 3; Merry Ovnick, *Los Angeles: The End of the Rainbow* (Los Angeles: Balcony Press, 1994), 165.

8. Weiss, *Rise of the Community Builders*, 2, 88, 91, 102, 111–14; Greg Hise, *Magnetic Los Angeles: Planning the Twentieth-Century Metropolis* (Baltimore, Md.: The Johns Hopkins University Press, 1997), 23–24; Roy Lubove, *Community Planning in the 1920s: The Contribution of the Regional Planning Association of America* (Pittsburgh, Pa.: University of Pittsburgh Press, 1963), 18–19. Southern California's real-estate developments paralleled national trends, only in a more concentrated fashion. Subdivisions appeared faster in the boom years between 1922 and 1929, and thus development appeared to slow more dramatically when the Great Depression began.

9. These two periodicals contained the highest density of such architectural arguments, although discussions appear in a variety of other regional publications, including *Touring Topics, Sunset Magazine, Land of Sunshine/Out West,* and the Real Estate section of the *Los Angeles Times.* Articles on the subject also appeared occasionally in national professional journals like *Architecture, The Architectural Record,* and *Architectural Review.*

10. H. Roy Kelley, "Why Have an Architect?" *California Southland* 9, no. 89 (May 1927), 30; "A Course in the Appreciation of Architecture," *California*

Southland 8, no. 78 (June 1926), 26; see also "The Merit and Fate of California Architecture," *The Architect and Engineer* 57, no. 3 (June 1919): 78; L.C. Mullgardt, "What About Local Architects?" *The Architect and Engineer* 83, no. 3 (December 1925): 85–87; editorial, *California Southland* 8, no. 74 (February 1926): 18; Robert Field, Jr., interview, University of California, Los Angeles Oral History Program, 33. For examples of architects' earlier laments about "bad building," see Arthur B. Benton, "Architecture for the Southwest," *Land of Sunshine* 4, no. 3 (February 1896): 130; and Alfred F. Rosenheim, "Los Angeles Woefully Lacking in Beautiful Municipal Buildings," *The Architect and Engineer* 37, no. 3 (July 1914): 78–79.

11. S.P. Hunt, "The Adobe in Architecture," *Land of Sunshine* 1, no. 2 (July 1894): 25; Charles F. Lummis, "The Lesson of Adobe," *Land of Sunshine* 2, no. 4 (March 1895): 65–67; Charles F. Lummis, "The Patio," *Land of Sunshine* 3, no. 1 (June 1895): 15; Charles F. Lummis, "The Grand Veranda," *Land of Sunshine* 3, no. 2 (July 1895): 63–67; Arthur B. Benton, "The Patio," *Land of Sunshine* 7, no. 3 (August 1897): 108–12. For a discussion of Lummis's influence on the mission revival, see Karen J. Weitze, *California's Mission Revival* (Los Angeles: Hennessey & Ingalls, 1984), 74–76; and Harold Kirker, *Old Forms on a New Land: California Architecture in Perspective* (Niwot, Colo.: Roberts Rinehard Publishers, 1991), 59–60.

12. See Weitze, *California's Mission Revival,* for an in-depth treatment of the various stages and many examples of the mission style. For analysis of its influence in Northern California, see Richard Longstreth, *On the Edge of the World: Four Architects in San Francisco at the Turn of the Century* (New York and Cambridge, Mass.: The Architectural History Foundation and MIT Press, 1983), 289–91.

13. Herbert D. Croly, "The Country House in California," *The Architectural Record,* Special Number on California Architecture, 34, no. 6 (December 1913): 485. This writer is the Herbert Croly of *The Promise of American Life* (1909) fame. Before he became a public intellectual and political philosopher of wide regard, Croly was (and continued to be) an architectural critic.

14. For a discussion of the shingle style, the bungalow, and the Greenes, see Kirker, *Old Forms,* 52–56; Randell L. Makinson, *Greene and Greene* (Salt Lake City: Peregrine Smith, 1977); Robert Winter, *The California Bungalow* (Los Angeles: Hennessey & Ingalls, 1980). For a discussion of the Bungalow and the English-colonial style, see Ovnick, *Los Angeles,* 123–51, 157–77. For an overview of many of these styles in Southern California, see Kevin Starr, *Material Dreams: Southern California Through the 1920s* (New York: Oxford University Press, 1990), ch. 8; for one on styles in Northern California, see Longstreth, *On the Edge,* chs. 5–11. For a contemporary's review of the stages of local architecture, see E.L. Bruner, "California Type of Architecture," *The Architect and Engineer* 87, no. 1 (October 1926): 97–99. Stratford Inn was designed by Los Angeles architect John C. Austin. The quotation about the Stratford Inn is from South Coast Land Company, *Del Mar, California* ([San Diego]: South Coast Land Company, 1912). The French-country example appears in "An Original Californian Architecture is Being Developed to Answer Our Needs," *California Southland* 8, no. 73 (January 1926): 23.

15. Croly, "The Country House," 483–88; Ellen Leech, *California Homes by California Architects* (Los Angeles: California Southland Magazine, 1922); Elmer Grey, "What a Home in California Should Mean," *The Architect and Engineer* 47, no. 3 (December 1916): 45.

16. William Winthrop Kent, "Domestic Architecture of California: Illustrating the Influence of the Spanish and Italian Renaissance, Part I," *The Architectural Forum* 32, no. 3 (March 1920): 96–98. For similar appraisals of the effect of Goodhue's designs at the Panama-California Exposition, see C. Matlack Price, "The Panama-California Exposition, San Diego, California: Bertram G. Goodhue and the Renaissance of Spanish-Colonial Architecture," *The Architectural Record* 37, no. 3 (March 1915): 238–42; and Dwight James Baum, "An Eastern Architect's Impressions of Recent Work in Southern California," *Architecture: The Professional Architectural Monthly* 38, no. 1 (July 1918): 177–78.

17. Elmer Grey, "Southern California's New Architecture," *Architecture: The Professional Architectural Monthly* 39, no. 3 (March 1919): 57. For a discussion of Grey's work in Spanish-colonial styles, see Starr, *Material Dreams*, 191–99.

18. A number of scholars have seen Spanish style as more of a "natural" outgrowth than a deliberate choice with specific catalysts. Merry Ovnick suggests that the style came to be favored over others because the Spanish colonial was somehow more "indigenous" than other "borrowed" styles. Architectural historian Reyner Banham found that the "Spanish Colonial Revival" was not a "consciously adopted style, but . . . something which is ever-present and can be taken for granted." I argue instead that people had begun to take the style for granted by the time of Banham's 1971 study of Los Angeles specifically because of the prior regional debate, not because of an inherent quality of either the Spanish style or of Southern California. The apparent indigenousness of the Spanish-colonial style was a rhetorical product of this era. Ovnick, *Los Angeles*, 180; Reyner Banham, *Los Angeles: The Architecture of the Four Ecologies* ([Harmondsworth, England]: Penguin Books, 1971), 61. For other treatments of the Spanish style in Southern California, see David Gebhard, "One Hundred Years of Architecture in California," in *Architecture in California, 1868–1968*, ed. David Gebhard and Hanette Von Breton (Santa Barbara: The Regents, University of California, 1968); and Starr, *Material Dreams*, 191–222.

19. Harwood Hewitt, "A Plea for Distinctive Architecture in Southern California," *Allied Architects Association of Los Angeles, Bulletin* 1, no. 5 (March 1, 1925); Charles Gibbs Adams, "Our Architectural Tragedy," *California Southland* 103, no. 28 (July 1928).

20. Arthur B. Benton, "The California Mission and its Influence upon Pacific Coast Architecture," *The Architect and Engineer* 24, no. 1 (February 1911): 73. For further discussion of the relationship of Spanish style to architects' professional goals in Southern California in the first thirty years of the twentieth century, see Mabel Urmy Seares, "The Use of Mission Architecture," *California Southland* 1, no. 1 (October 1919): 18; "The Merit and Fate," 78; Mullgardt, "What About Local Architects?" 85–87; Kelley, "Why Have an Architect?" 30; and Phoebe S. Kropp, "'All Our Yesterdays': The Spanish Fantasy Past and the Politics of Public Memory, 1884–1939," Ph.D. diss, University of California, San Diego, 1999, 314–19.

21. Elmer Grey, "Southern California's New Architecture—II," *Architecture: The Professional Architectural Monthly* 40, no. 1 (April 1919): 103–4. Given the inexact terminology of the day, I have chosen to use the term *Spanish colonial* to refer to the style as a whole, including Spanish, Californian, Mediterranean, Mexican, Moorish, Latin, and related styles. A multitude of alternative terms will appear in the numerous quotations in this chapter, given that each author and architect came up with his or her own term for the style.

22. Cazenove Lamar, "Mexican Influence in California Architecture," *The Architect and Engineer* 61, no. 2 (May 1921): 75; Grey, "Southern California's New Architecture—II," 103.

23. M. Urmy Seares, Introduction to Leech, *California Homes*, v.

24. Frederick Jennings, "Civic Improvement Ojai, California: How an Old, Uninteresting Town Was Made Beautiful," *The Architect and Engineer* 58, no. 2 (August 1919): 39, 42; Robert Fogelson, *The Fragmented Metropolis: Los Angeles, 1850–1930* (1967; Berkeley: University of California Press, 1993), 157; Gebhard, "One Hundred Years," 20. Requa's life typified the biography of Spanish-colonial–style architects in Southern California in that he was not native; he was born in Illinois and moved to San Diego as a child. Yet his architectural education was through practical apprenticeship rather than through formal, much less Beaux-Arts, education. Henry F. Withey and Elsie Rathburn Withey, *Biographical Dictionary of American Architects (Deceased)* (Los Angeles: New Age Publishing Co., 1956), 503; Kirker, *Old Forms*, 83–84; Milton P. Sessions, interview by Craig Carter, SDHS Oral History Program, 1990.

25. Elmer Grey noted soon after the armistice that the "progress of the style, . . . temporarily arrested by the war, has already been resumed with new vigor." A list of books on Spanish architecture in *The Architect and Engineer* in 1923 contained a wealth of newly published material, including travel books, photographic surveys, albums of plans and drawings, and practical guidebooks. Grey, "Southern California's New Architecture," 57; "Books on Spanish Architecture," *The Architect and Engineer* 72, no. 2 (February 1923): 81–82.

26. Richard S. Requa, *Architectural Details of Spain and the Mediterranean* (Los Angeles: Monolith Portland Cement Co., 1926); Richard S. Requa, *Old World Inspiration for American Architecture* (Los Angeles: Monolith Portland Cement Co., 1929). Portland cement was a key ingredient in stucco, the material that builders use most often to simulate adobe. The Monolith Portland Cement Company, a large regional supplier of the material, commissioned both works from Requa and reportedly financed some of his European travels.

27. Requa, *Architectural Details*, frontispiece. Of 141 plates, 113 were labeled as Spanish locations.

28. Requa, *Architectural Details*, i, v; Randoph Sexton, *Spanish Influence on American Architecture and Decoration* (New York: Brentano's, 1927), 11.

29. Richard S. Requa, "An Architectural Style for Southern California," *The Architect and Engineer* 89, no. 3 (June 1927): 45–47; Sumner M. Spaulding, "Southern California Chapter A.I.A. Monthly Bulletin: Impressions of Rural Spain," *California Southland* 8, no. 83 (November 1926): 25.

30. Lilian J. Rice, "Architecture—A Community Asset," *The Architect and Engineer* 94, no. 1 (July 1928): 43; Jennings, "Civic Improvement Ojai," 39; Eddy, "LJR: The Search," 71.

31. Born in 1888 in National City, near San Diego, Rice was one of only four women who graduated from the University of California, Berkeley, before 1911. Though both the University of California and the University of Southern California, the two leading schools of architecture on the West Coast, had admitted women since their inception, the numbers remained low during the first four decades of the twentieth century. Still, according to Teresa Grimes, compared to women in other regions of the country, "women in California had a high degree of accessibility to academic architectural training." Judith Paine, "Lillian [sic] Rice," in *Women in American Architecture: A Historic and Contemporary Perspective,* ed. Susana Torre (New York: Whitney Library of Design, 1977), 65, 90, 108; Teresa Grimes, "A Woman in a Man's Profession: Edla Muir and the Architectural Community of Los Angeles" master's thesis, University of California, Los Angeles, 1992, viii, 8, 46; Withey and Withey, *Biographical Dictionary,* 505; Lucinda Liggett Eddy, "Lilian Jenette Rice: The Lady as Architect," master's thesis, University of San Diego, 1985, 35–36.

32. Paine, "Lillian Rice," 108; Clotfelter, *Echoes of Rancho Santa Fe,* 33; Sessions, interview. Unfortunately, Rice's exact itinerary in Spain could not be located.

33. For a comprehensive list of Rice's built designs, at Rancho Santa Fe and beyond, see Eddy, "LJR: Lady as Architect," appendix.

34. Rice, "Architecture," 44; see also Grimes, "A Woman in a Man's Profession," viii, 8, 46; Elizabeth Grossman and Lisa Reitzes, "Caught in the Crossfire: Women and Architectural Education, 1880–1910," in *Architecture: A Place for Women,* ed. Ellen Perry Berkeley (Washington, D.C.: Smithsonian Institution Press, 1989).

35. William H. Wheeler, "Southern California's Changing Architecture," *The Architect and Engineer* 94, no. 1 (July 1928), 35–41.

36. Lilian Rice quoted in Mildred Finley Wohlford, interview by Cora Jane Jenkins, SDHS Oral History Program, 1987; see also Z.L. Parmelee Co., "Mission Fixtures," advertisement, in Mrs. A.S.C. Forbes, *California Missions and Landmarks and How to Get There* (Los Angeles: Official Guide, 1903); Dwight James Baum, "An Eastern Architect's Impressions of Recent Work in Southern California, Part Two," *Architecture: The Professional Architectural Monthly* 38, no. 2 (August 1918): 217–18; Marion Hugus Clark, "Arts and Crafts Society," *California Southland* 8, no. 69 (September 1925): 26; Edgar Harrison Wileman, "We Furnish in the Spanish Style," *Sunset* 63, no. 4 (October 1929): 26.

37. "Residence," *Southwest Builder and Contractor* (May 25, 1928), 54; Lee Shippey, *The Transformation of an Old Spanish Estate* (San Diego: The John W. Snyder Co., [1926]), n.p.; see also Eddy, "LJR: Lady as Architect," 96–97.

38. Lilian J. Rice, "More Building in 1928 than Ever Before," *Rancho Santa Fe Progress* 1, no. 7 (January 1928): 14; Lee Shippey, "Rancho Santa Fe—California's Perfectly Planned Community," *The Architect and Engineer* 76, no. 2 (February 1924): 72.

39. Shippey, "Rancho Santa Fe," 72; "Rancho Santa Fe Development," *Standard Oil Bulletin* 11, no. 6 (October 1923): 13–14; Requa, *Old World Inspiration,* plate 3.

40. Fogelson, *Fragmented Metropolis,* 145, and ch. 9; SFLIC, "15 Square Miles of Uniform Beauty," advertisement, *California Southland* 7, no. 69 (September 1925): 32.

41. Ed Fletcher to E. O. Faulkner, vice president, SFLIC, May 17, 1922; Ed Fletcher to W. E. Hodges, vice president, Santa Fe Railway, September 22, 1921; see also Ed Fletcher to W. E. Hodges, May 5, 1922; E. O. Faulkner to J. H. Keefe, vice president, Santa Fe Railway, May 20, 1922; W. E. Hodges, vice president, Santa Fe Railway, to L. G. Sinnard, manager, SFLIC, June 13, 1922, Fletcher Collection.

42. These stunts were typical of early 1920s speculative mania in Los Angeles. See Ovnick, *Los Angeles,* 164–66.

43. L. G. Sinnard to Ed Fletcher, July 15, 1922, Fletcher Collection; SFLIC, "Let Rancho Santa Fe Suggest Your Permanent Home," advertisement, *Los Angeles Times,* November 30, 1924, sec. 5. The Pacific Advertising Clubs Association judged Rancho Santa Fe ads to be the best real-estate advertising produced on the Pacific Coast in 1927, in particular because of their "dignity, conservatism, and restraint." "Rancho Santa Fe Wins First Prize in Ad Competition," *Rancho Santa Fe Progress* 2, no. 1 (July 1928): 6.

44. L. G. Sinnard to Ed Fletcher, August 15, 1922, Fletcher Collection. Fewer ads appeared in the *San Diego Union,* even though San Diego was seventy-five miles closer to Rancho Santa Fe. Los Angeles not only contained and drew more home seekers than San Diego did, but its newspaper was more regionally prominent; the *Los Angeles Times* had more local readers and was more likely to be read outside of California.

45. SFLIC, "Rancho Santa Fe, California's Greatest," advertisement, *Los Angeles Times,* January 6, 1924, sec. 5; SFLIC, "Rarest natural beauty," advertisement, *California Southland* 8, no. 75 (March 1926): 43; SFLIC, "The place to make your dreams come true!" advertisement, *California Southland* 7, no. 68 (August 1925): 31; SFLIC, "15 Square Miles."

46. Lee Shippey, "Old Spanish Estate: A Colony Where No House Can Violate the Old California Traditions of Beauty," *Los Angeles Times,* May 6, 1923, sec. 3; Shippey, *Transformation of an Old Spanish Estate.*

47. SFLIC, "Trips to Your Home in the Country," advertisement, *Touring Topics* 18, no. 6 (June 1926): 49, emphasis from the original; Hazel Boyer, "Men Who Build for the Future Perpetuate the Charm of Old Spain," *California Southland* 6, no. 59 (November 1924): 27; SFLIC, "Gentlemen's Estates," advertisement, *Touring Topics* 19, no. 7 (July 1927): 47.

48. SFLIC, "Rancho Santa Fe—Announced a Few Months Ago," advertisement, *Los Angeles Times,* April 27, 1924, sec. 5; SFLIC, "The place to make"; SFLIC, "Covered Wagons of 1927," advertisement, *Touring Topics* 19, no. 2 (February 1927): 47.

49. SFLIC, "When Your Spirit Rebels Against Too-much-city," advertisement, *Touring Topics* 19, no. 11 (November 1927): 43; SFLIC, "Covered Wagons"; SFLIC, "Who Are the Owners at Rancho Santa Fe?" advertisement, *Touring Topics* 19, no. 12 (December 1927): 47.

50. While in 1922 a 10 percent down payment was required, with ten payments allowed for the balance, by 1928 a buyer had to put down 20 percent and pay

up in only five additional payments. Early in the subdivision's development, advertised land values topped out at $450 per acre, with the price for each lot ranging from $1,300 to $7,500 during the first six years. Yet a survey of estates that were advertised in the late 1920s reveals that these estimates had steadily increased. Per-acre costs now ranged from $375 to $3,000. Despite a decidedly slowed real-estate market after 1925, the average price per acre rose to nearly $1,000, while the price for the average individual lot reached almost $12,000. For a detailed review of lot values, see Kropp, "'All Our Yesterdays,'" ch. 6.

51. SFLIC, "The Place to Make"; SFLIC, "Climate Headquarters," advertisement, *Touring Topics* 19, no. 6 (June 1927) 47; SFLIC, "Bounded Only By Your Imagination," advertisement, *California Southland* 10, no. 101 (May 1928): back cover; SFLIC, "Why Rancho Santa Fe is a Tremendous Success," advertisement, *California Southland* 10, no. 103 (July 1928): back cover.

52. SFLIC, "The Place to Make."

53. This emphasis on recreation made Rancho Santa Fe distinctly different from the "typical" Los Angeles subdivision, for which the proximity of employment centers was key to both its location and its advertising. See Hise, *Magnetic Los Angeles,* ch. 1.

54. SFLIC, "A Challenge to Creative Minds," advertisement, *Touring Topics* 20, no. 11 (November 1928): 4; Boyer, "Men Who Build," 27; SFLIC, "Rancho Santa Fe Has Sold Estates to 24 Realtors," advertisement, *Touring Topics* 20, no. 10 (October 1928): 4. The country club financed the golf course by borrowing money from the SFLIC, which subsequently planned and advertised estate lots on the fringes of the course, constituting yet another type of appeal. Nelson, *Yesterday and Today,* 78–79.

55. SFLIC, "How much longer," advertisement, *Touring Topics* 18, no. 2 (February 1926): 35; SFLIC, "You have sometimes stood," advertisement, *Touring Topics* 19, no. 3 (March 1927): 51.

56. SFLIC, "Rancho Santa Fe, Owned by the Santa Fe Land Improvement Company," advertisement, *Touring Topics* 20, no. 12 (December 1928): 52; Shippey, *Transformation of an Old Spanish Estate.*

57. E. Palmer Conner, *The Romance of the Ranchos* (Los Angeles: Title Insurance and Trust Co., 1929), 3, 39–40 (map).

58. SFLIC, "When the Franciscan Fathers," advertisement, *San Diego Union,* January 1, 1924.

59. John S. McGroarty, *The Endless Miracle of California* (Chula Vista: [Denrich Press], 1922), n.p.

60. McGroarty, *Endless Miracle.*

61. SFLIC, "The Rancho Santa Fe Plan," advertisement, *Touring Topics* 20, no. 3 (March 1928): 10; Boyer, "Men Who Build," 26; Shippey, *Transformation of an Old Spanish Estate.*

62. *Rancho Santa Fe: A Unique Community of Country Estates in a Land of Rural Beauty* ([Los Angeles]: n.p., ca. 1925); A. V. Echternach, "Spanish or Californian?" *Sunset* 58, no. 5 (May 1927): 88.

63. Shippey, *Transformation of an Old Spanish Estate;* McGroarty, *Endless Miracle;* SFLIC, "The place to make."

64. SFLIC, "For your sons," advertisement, *Touring Topics* 19, no. 4 (April 1927): 47, emphasis from the original. For use of the "Gentlemen's Estates" phrase, see SFLIC, "Unusual Progress!" advertisement, *California Southland* 10, no. 102 (June 1928): back cover; for the "Country Estates" term, see SFLIC, "Is Rancho Santa Fe a Millionaires' Colony?" advertisement, *Touring Topics* 20, no. 9 (September 1928): 4.

65. SFLIC, "When Your Spirit Rebels."

66. Shippey, *Transformation of an Old Spanish Estate*; SFLIC, "15 Square Miles"; SFLIC, "Millionaires Colony?"

67. For a revealing look at the idealization of citrus culture in Southern California and the activities behind "the orange curtain" in this era—"the labor that produced the sweet fruit, idyllic landscape, and phenomenal profits"—see Matt Garcia, *A World of Its Own: Race, Labor, and Citrus in the Making of Greater Los Angeles, 1900–1970* (Chapel Hill: University of North Carolina Press, 2001), esp. ch. 1.

68. SFLIC, "A Challenge to Creative Minds"; Boyer, "Men Who Build," 27; see also *Uncle Walt is Converted Too* (Chula Vista, Calif.: Denrich Press, [1926]), reprinted from *Los Angeles Times*, n.d..

69. SFLIC, "How much longer."

70. Fogelson, *Fragmented Metropolis*, 146; Weiss, *Rise of the Community Builders*, 68–72.

71. "Plan to Perpetuate R.S.F. Restrictions," *The Endless Miracle* 1, no. 1 (July 1927): 1, 7. Cheney was a graduate of the University of California and supplemented his studies at the École des Beaux Arts in Paris. He arrived in Los Angeles in 1920, at the behest of the Los Angeles Realty Board to advise it on zoning ordinances. He was, according to Marc Weiss, "a strong advocate of the creation of exclusive single-family residence districts to encourage home ownership and property investment. He was wedded to the notion that Los Angeles should remain a city of large and small houses, and was strenuously opposed to apartment buildings." Weiss, *Rise of the Community Builders*, 94; Henry F. Withey, "The Work of Charles Henry Cheney, Architect and City Planner," *The Architect and Engineer* 53, no. 3 (June 1918): 39.

72. "Plan to Perpetuate," 1; Nelson, *Yesterday and Today*, 73–75. Cheney's services were secured by the Rancho Santa Fe Association on June 11, 1927. The articles of incorporation were signed by five residents, including S. R. Nelson, the SFLIC manager.

73. Charles H. Cheney, "Building for Permanency: The Esthetic Considerations in a Master or City Plan," in *Planning Problems of Town, City, and Region, Papers and Discussions at the Twentieth National Conference on City Planning, Held at Dallas and Fort Worth Texas, May 7 to 10, 1928* (Philadelphia: Wm. F. Fell Co., 1928), 39; see also [editorial], *The Endless Miracle* 1, no. 1 (July 1927): 4; "Home Owners' Assn. Papers Approved," *The Endless Miracle* 1, no. 2 (August 1927): 2; Clotfelter, *Echoes*, 40.

74. Charles H. Cheney, "Guarding Beauty and Investment By Protective Restrictions," *Rancho Santa Fe Progress* 1, no. 7 (January 1928): 6.

75. Cheney, "Guarding Beauty," 6–7.

76. *Rancho Santa Fe Protective Covenant, Rancho Santa Fe, California, Adopted by Rancho Santa Fe Association, July 14th, 1927,* (San Diego: Frye & Smith, ca. 1937), 7. The covenant was dated January 21, 1928, and was recorded February 9, 1928, in Book 1412, p. 436, Official Records of San Diego County, California, in three declarations covering both the sold and unsold portions of the tract. References herein refer solely to declaration no. 1, which was signed by then-current residents and—with the two following declarations—by the corporate owner, SFLIC, accepted in full. The regulations in the two following declarations concerned only minor issues that related to initial sale and development and did not apply to the tract as a whole.

77. *Protective Covenant,* art. III, sec. 1, and art. IV, sec. 28. Specific requirements in the covenant roughly corresponded with the characteristics described in architectural journals: light-colors; use of plaster, adobe, or stucco; and low-pitched roofs of tile. Color and style both required approval.

78. Cheney, "Guarding Beauty," 7; Harold O. Sexsmith, "Los Angeles A 12% City," *California Southland* 9, no. 95 (November 1927): 22.

79. Rice, "Architecture," 43.

80. "Rancheros Name Their Estates," *Rancho Santa Fe Progress* 2, no. 2 (August 1928): 6–7; "Anent Ranch Names," *Rancho Santa Fe Progress* 2, no. 3 (September 1928): 6.

81. [The Spanish Don], *Rancho Santa Fe Progress* 1, no. 12 (June 1928): cover, 12; S. R. Nelson, "There is Much More than Golf at Rancho Santa Fe," *Rancho Santa Fe Progress* 1, no. 6 (December 1927): 4.

82. Rice, "More Building, 14; SFLIC, "Trips to Your Home"; J. F. McKitrick quoted in "Rancheros Guests at Project Dinner," *The Endless Miracle* 1, no. 2 (August 1927): 2; Editorial, *Endless Miracle* 1, no. 1 (July 1927): 4.

83. *Protective Covenant,* art. I, secs. 1, 8.

84. "Print Covenant in Booklet Form," *Rancho Santa Fe Progress* 1, no. 9 (March 1928): 3; see also Cheney, "Guarding Beauty," 7; *Protective Covenant,* art. II, sec. 1 and art. III, sec. 3.

85. *Protective Covenant,* art. I, secs. 8–10; L. G. Sinnard, *Rancho Santa Fe, California: Yesterday, Today* (Chula Vista: Denrich Press, [1928]).

86. *Protective Covenant,* art. III, sec. 1; Hise, *Magnetic Los Angeles,* 37–40;. Lee Michelle Simpson, "Selling the City: Women and the California City Growth Game," Ph.D. diss., University of California, Riverside, 1996, 242; Fogelson, *Fragmented Metropolis,* 144–46.

87. *Protective Covenant,* art. III, sec. 1.

88. Cheney, "Guarding Beauty," 7. The text of this prohibition reads as follows: "No part of said property shall be sold, conveyed, rented or leased in whole or in part to any person of an African or Asiatic race or to any person not of the white or Caucasian race. No part of said property shall be used or occupied or permitted to be used or occupied in whole or in part by any person of African or Asiatic descent or by any person not of the white or Caucasian race, except that domestic servants, chauffeurs, or gardeners who are members of a race other than the white or Caucasian race may live on or occupy the premises where their employer resides." *Protective Covenant,* art. I, sec. 2.

89. Albert Camarillo in Vicki L. Ruiz, *From Out of the Shadows: Mexican Women in Twentieth-Century America* (New York: Oxford University Press, 1998), 68; see also Hise, *Magnetic Los Angeles*, 7; George Sánchez, *Becoming Mexican American: Ethnicity, Culture, and Identity in Chicano Los Angeles, 1900–1945* (New York: Oxford University Press, 1993), 77; Fogelson, *Fragmented Metropolis*, 80. Race restrictions in housing were not struck down until a 1948 U.S. Supreme Court decision that deemed such exclusionary covenants or deed restrictions to be "unenforceable as law" (*Shelley v. Kraemer*). Kenneth T. Jackson, *Crabgrass Frontier: The Suburbanization of the United States* (New York: Oxford University Press, 1985), 178, 208. The designation of *Mexican* as a separately enumerated category of the census appeared only in the 1930 version. It disappeared again to resurface in 1970 as a separate question about Hispanic origins. The absence of *Anglo* as a legal term despite its widespread use is surprising. Perhaps the term's blanket, almost indiscriminate use made it an ineffectual legal definition in the era before justices could resort to "I know it when I see it," as Supreme Court Justice Potter Stewart was forced to define *obscenity* in 1964 (*Jacobellis v. State of Ohio*). For a discussion of Mexicans' changing racial status in legal terms, see Ian F. Haney-Lopez, *White By Law: The Legal Construction of Race* (New York: New York University Press, 1998); and Ian F. Haney-Lopez, *Racism on Trial: The Chicano Fight for Justice* (Cambridge: Belknap Press, 2003).

90. "Children Grow Like Trees Here," *Rancho Santa Fe Progress* 1, no. 4 (October 1927): 6.

91. "Children of Aliso School Make Own Costumes for Play Depicting Story of Rancho Santa Fe," *The Endless Miracle* 1, no. 1 (July 1927): 2.

92. Roberto Lint Sagarena, "Inheriting the Land: Defining Place in Southern California From the Mexican American War to the Plan Espiritual de Aztlán," Ph.D. diss., Princeton University, 2000, 82–83; Rosaura Sánchez, *Telling Identities: The* Californio *Testimonios* (Minneapolis: University of Minnesota Press, 1995), 168.

93. Sánchez, *Becoming Mexican American*, 103–4.

94. Albert Camarillo, *Chicanos in a Changing Society: From Mexican Pueblos to American Barrios in Santa Barbara and Southern California, 1848–1930* (Cambridge, Mass.: Harvard University Press, 1979), 158, 210–13, 221; Leroy E. Harris, "The Other Side of the Freeway: A Study of Settlement Patterns of Negroes and Mexican Americans in San Diego, California," Ph.D. diss., Carnegie-Mellon University, 1974, 86–88; Mary Romero, *Maid in the U.S.A.* (New York: Routledge, 1992), 79–85

95. [Untitled], *Rancho Santa Fe Progress* 1, no. 3 (September 1927): 6; Clotfelter, *Echoes*, 38–39; Tim Andre and Stephen Melton, "Separate Stories of Shared Spaces: Linking Histories of Solana Beach," unpub. paper in possession of the author, 1998, n.p.

96. Frank Gonzalez quoted in Brian Wiersema, "They Called the Valley Eden," *San Diego Union*, May 17, 1984, North County Panorama, 1.

97. Wiersema, "They Called the Valley Eden," 1,2, 4; Andre and Melton, "Separate Stories," n.p. Solana Beach was a new subdivision planned by Ed

Fletcher; the Santa Fe Railway provided land and financial helps as a reward for Fletcher's success at Rancho Santa Fe.

98. "Fitting the Home to the Homesite," *Rancho Santa Fe Progress* 1, no. 9 (March 1928): 12; Nelson, "Much More than Golf," 10.

99. "Cheney Explains Covenant at Home Owners Meeting," *Rancho Santa Fe Progress* 1, no. 11 (May 1928): 2; Cheney, "Guarding Beauty," 6; "Plan to Perpetuate."

100. "Plan to Perpetuate." In the realm of party politics, Rancho Santa Fe further congratulated itself on being anti-Democratic. The *Progress* reported that in 1928, ninety-three of the one hundred and five votes cast in Rancho Santa Fe for U.S. president were for Herbert Hoover. The article did note that many people had their main registration elsewhere. It reported the block voting in 1928 as follows: presidential votes = 105, Republican = 93, Democrat = 11, and surprisingly, Socialist = 1. "Slightly Republican!" *Rancho Santa Fe Progress* 2, no. 5 (November 1928): 4.

101. "Covenant Filed and In Operation," *Rancho Santa Fe Progress* 1, no. 8 (February 1928): 4; see also "Owners Sign Up On Covenant," *Rancho Santa Fe Progress* 1, no. 12 (June 1928): 7; "Many Sign Covenant," *Rancho Santa Fe Progress* 1, no. 10 (April 1928): 4; Clotfelter, *Echoes*, 32–33.

102. Boyer, "Men Who Build," 26, 27, emphasis from the original. Boyer was married to Maurice Braun, a Hungarian-born California impressionist painter; both resided in San Diego and were active in the Theosophy movement there.

103. Echternach, "Spanish or Californian?" 87–88; Rice, "Architecture," 43.

104. Bruner, "California Type of Architecture," 99, 97; "Los Angeles architect," quoted in Fogelson, *Fragmented Metropolis*, 157; Dwight James Baum, "Architectural Impressions of Southern California," *The American Architect* 133, no. 2537 (January 20, 1928): 71–73; Vernon B. McClurg, "How May California Adapt Mediterranean Styles," *California Southland* 10, no. 101 (May 1928): 27.

105. McClung, *Landscapes of Desire*, 227; see also Mike Davis, *City of Quartz: Excavating the Future in Los Angeles* (London: Verso, 1990), 169–70, 246–48. McClung writes that Davis, in fact, best describes how this "paradoxical desire for private property and paradisal community succumbed to its internal contradictions. . . . What has been lost, or perceived to have been lost, however, is not empty space waiting to be filled but a common ambiance, . . . the envelope of climate and nature [and history] thought to be the democratic common property of Southern California. . . . That is the 'Eden' that has been largely neutralized in the civic imagination." Neither McClung nor Davis connect this idea directly to Spanish-colonial architecture itself, but the persistence of value in Spanish-style properties and the continued use of its elements in contemporary designs suggests an attempt to maintain a connection to that golden age of the Southern California good life, though the good life was, I would argue, never entirely a "democratic common property."

5. THE MARKET

1. James H. Collins, "A One-Woman Revolution," *Southern California Business* 9, no. 6 (June 1930): 14; "Los Angeles for Short," cartoon, *Los Angeles Times,* August 2, 1934.

2. Charles H. Owens, "A Mexican Street of Yesterday in a City of Today," drawing, *Los Angeles Times,* May 26, 1929.

3. George Sánchez, *Becoming Mexican American: Ethnicity, Culture, and Identity in Chicano Los Angeles, 1900–1945* (New York: Oxford University Press, 1993), 71–72.

4. Sterling was the granddaughter of gold-rush–era New England migrants to San Francisco and the daughter of a prominent University of California scientist. She attended both Mills College and Parkington Art School, though did not graduate from either. She was married briefly and divorced before she wed Hough and moved to Los Angeles. Justice B. Detwiler, ed., *Who's Who in California: A Biographical Dictionary, 1928–29* (San Francisco: Who's Who Publishing Co., 1929), 326; McIntyre Faries, *Rememb'ring* (Glendale, Calif.: Griffin Publishing, 1993), 109; Christine Sterling, *Olvera Street: El Pueblo de Nuestra Señora Reina de Los Angeles: Its History and Restoration* (Los Angeles: Mario Valadez, 1947), 23–26; William D. Estrada, "Sacred and Contested Space: The Los Angeles Plaza," Ph.D. diss., University of California, Los Angeles, 2003, 232–33, 300 n. 67.

5. Christine Sterling, *Olvera Street: Its History and Restoration* (Los Angeles: Old Mission Printing Shop, 1933), 7–9, 20.

6. For a review of these early arguments, see Estrada, "Sacred and Contested Space," 113–30.

7. Simpson was the daughter of John Jones, one of the city's early Anglo-American arrivals and later the president of the city's common council. Born in 1866 in an adobe house facing the Plaza (later torn down to widen Main Street), Simpson iterated a historic claim on the space. J. S. McGroarty, *California of the South: A History* (Chicago: S. J. Clarke Publishing Co., 1933), V: 731–35; *Who's Who in Los Angeles 1930–31* (Los Angeles: Who's Who Publishing Co., 1930), 259; Constance D. Simpson to Board of Police Commissioners, April 2, 1929, council file (hereafter CF) 3210 (1929), Los Angeles City Council Records (hereafter Council Records), Archives of the City of Los Angeles, (hereafter City Archives).

8. "Petition," March 20, 1929, CF 2591 (1929); E. O. McLaughlin, "Petition," [August 1929], CF 4312 (1929), Council Records; "Affidavit of Paul Porta," January 20, 1930; "Affidavit of Henry Garbe," January 20, 1930, *Constance D. Simpson v. City of Los Angeles, et. al.,* Los Angeles County Court Records, case #294013 (hereafter *Simpson v. Los Angeles*). The official address of the Simpson building was 606–620 North Main Street. The tenants of the brick building at the time included a cigar shop, a shooting gallery, a cobbler, a wagon shop, a tailoring shop, an auto-repair shop, a restaurant, a machinist, a storage company, and the Main Cornice Works, in addition to several vacancies. Constance D. Simpson, [notes], Simpson Building File, El Pueblo de Los Angeles Archive, n.d. (hereafter El Pueblo Archive).

9. Christine Sterling to Clarence Matson, Trade Extension Department, Los Angeles Chamber of Commerce, March 29, 1926, El Pueblo Archive.

10. The Board of Directors of the Los Angeles Chamber of Commerce, Minutes (hereafter LACOC Minutes), November 4, 1926, December 9, 1926, March 17, 1927, Los Angeles Chamber of Commerce Collection, Regional History Center, University of Southern California (hereafter USC Chamber Collection).

11. LACOC Minutes, January 17, 1929, November 4, 1926. Lacy was a very successful Southern Californian, dabbling in banking, manufacturing, and most significantly, in development of the Puente oil fields in the 1870s. As president of the chamber in 1924, he advocated greater industrial development of Los Angeles. Detwiler, *Who's Who in California: 1928–29*, 249; McGroarty, *California of the South*, III: 45–58; Harris Newmark, *Sixty Years in Southern California* (1916; Los Angeles: Zeitlin & Ver Brugge, 1970), 377; Boyle Workman, *The City That Grew* (Los Angeles: Southland Publishing, 1936), 256; Jackson A. Graves, *California Memories, 1857–1930* (Los Angeles: Times-Mirror Press, 1930), 104.

12. Sterling, *Olvera Street* (1947), 13–14; Estrada, "Sacred and Contested Space," 257. Women preservationists often used the guise of helplessness to ask safely the same kinds of provocative questions and to prick the consciences of local citizens as Sterling did. Their self-sacrificing personae helped shield them from potential backlash from the business community, which might otherwise see them as inconvenient, amateurish meddlers, as some of the early chamber comments about Sterling suggest. See Patricia West, *Domesticating History: The Political Origins of America's House Museums* (Washington, D. C.: Smithsonian Institution Press, 1999) for analysis of women's roles and this preservationist posture, particularly at Mount Vernon and Orchard House.

13. Christine Sterling to City Council, May 16, 1929, CF 4312 (1929); Board of Police Commissioners, "Memorandum," March 5, 1929, CF 2378 (1929); John C. Shaw, City Engineer, to Public Works Committee, June 18, 1929, CF 4312 (1929), Council Records.

14. Board of Public Works to City Council, July 5, 1929, CF 4312 (1929), emphasis added; Sterling to City Council, May 16, 1929, emphasis added. Ordinance No. 64715, which added Section 17.5 to Ordinance No. 50515, passed on August 12, 1929, was returned without the mayor's approval on August 23, and was passed over the mayor's veto on September 3, 1929. John C. Porter, Mayor, to City Council, August 23, 1929, CF 4312 (1929), Council Records.

15. The council accommodated the Los Angeles Railway Company, which had operated a transformer station on the street since about 1904. This building stood at one end of Olvera Street, and the city agreed to prohibit obstructions directly in front of its egress. Public Works Committee, "Memorandum," August 28, 1929, CF 4312 (1929), Council Records; "Porter Vetoes Traffic Ban in Olivera [sic] Street," *Los Angeles Times*, August 25, 1929; "Porter Vetoes Plan to Close Up Olivera [sic] St.," *Los Angeles Examiner*, August 25, 1929; "Pair of Porter Vetoes Beaten," *Los Angeles Times*, September 4, 1929; "Pueblo Plan Foes Balked," *Los Angeles Times*, November 2, 1929; Faries, *Remembr'ing*, 107.

16. J. Wiseman MacDonald, attorney for Constance D. Simpson, "Complaint for Injunction to Restrain Enforcement of Ordinance," December 30, 1929, *Simpson v. Los Angeles;* see also "Avila Adobe Rescuing Brings Injunction Row," *Los Angeles Times,* January 3, 1930; "Olivera [sic] St. Closing Halted by Woman," *Los Angeles Examiner,* January 3, 1930; "Olvera Street Ban Attacked," *Los Angeles Examiner,* January 9, 1930; "Olvera Closing Protests Heard," *Los Angeles Examiner,* February 5, 1930; "Affidavit of Constance D. Simpson," January 29, 1930; Judge Walter E. Gates, "Judgment," February 26, 1930, *Simpson v.. Los Angeles.* For a detailed review of the city politics involved in this tussle, see Phoebe S. Kropp, "'All Our Yesterdays': The Spanish Fantasy Past and the Politics of Public Memory in Southern California, 1884–1939," Ph.D. diss, University of California, San Diego, 1999, 494–501.

17. How the October stock-market crash immediately affected the project is not clear. Work began on November 3, a scant few days after the crash, and little mention was made of the calamity.

18. "Dimes Will Pave Street," *Los Angeles Times,* October 26, 1929; "City Commences Antique Tiling of Olvera Street," *Los Angeles Examiner,* November 8, 1929; "Tractors Delve into Early History," *Los Angeles Times,* November 26, 1929; "Tiles Laid in Olvera Street," *Los Angeles Times,* January 9, 1930; Sterling, *Olvera Street* (1933), 15–18; Faries, *Rememb'ring,* 113; "Mexicans Open Cafe With Rites," *Los Angeles Times,* April 17, 1930.

19. Sterling, *Olvera Street* (1933), 11, 17; "Old Street Opens Easter," *Los Angeles Times,* April 7, 1930.

20. Chandler quoted in John S. McGroarty, "The Plaza Beautiful: Shall Our City Forfeit its Last Heritage from Old Spain?" *Los Angeles Times,* September 12, 1926. Harry Chandler was an extremely powerful Los Angeles leader who orchestrated an economic empire with an enormous reach; he had diverse holdings in oil, shipping, cattle, water projects, construction, rubber, and aviation. The newspaper was of minor financial importance among these holdings, though it allowed him an even larger share of public clout and influence. The center of his empire, however, was real estate; he owned ranches all over the Southwest, including in Baja California; controlled much of downtown Los Angeles development; and was a key member of the land syndicate helping to orchestrate the Owens Valley Aqueduct to develop real estate in the San Fernando Valley. Robert M. Fogelson, *The Fragmented Metropolis: Los Angeles, 1850–1930* (1967; Berkeley: University of California Press, 1993), 219–20. See also Robert Gottlieb and Irene Wolt, *Thinking Big: The Story of the Los Angeles Times, Its Publishers, and Their Influence on Southern California* (New York: Putnam's, 1977); Mike Davis, *City of Quartz: Excavating the Future in Los Angeles* (London: Verso, 1990), ch. 2; and, Kevin Starr, *Material Dreams: Southern California Through the 1920s* (New York: Oxford University Press, 1990), 107–109, 112–24.

21. "Realty Concern Incorporates," *Los Angeles Times,* March 3, 1928; *Plaza de Los Angeles Incorporated* ([Los Angeles]: Plaza de Los Angeles Inc., 1928); Faries, *Rememb'ring,* 110. Among other plans, Plaza Inc. anticipated developing "a fine hotel of Spanish architecture, a building for the Latin-American

consuls, display rooms for the products of South and Central America and Mexico, and a Manufacturers' Building where American goods can be exhibited to foreign buyers," as well as coffee shops, restaurants, and smaller businesses. Chandler apparently opposed suggestions to make it a nonprofit corporation. For a detailed review of the commercial aspects of Olvera Street's development, see Kropp, "'All Our Yesterdays,'" 494–500.

22. Established after a bitter fight, the official plan of 1927 showed the civic center bounded by Hill, Ord, Main, and First streets. See Fogelson, *Fragmented Metropolis*, 262–72; Starr, *Material Dreams*, 112–24; Gottlieb and Wolt, *Thinking Big*, 152–55.

23. "First Impressions," *Los Angeles Times*, September 12, 1926. For a discussion of the Union Station affair, see Gottlieb and Wolt, *Thinking Big*, 152–55; Starr, *Material Dreams*, 107–109; Estrada, "Sacred and Contested Space," 289–93; and, Robert Howard Tracy, "John Parkinson and the Beaux-Arts City Beautiful Movement in Downtown Los Angeles, 1884–1935," Ph.D. diss., University of California, Los Angeles, 1982, 367–68. The Plaza site would not alter the Plaza itself but rather displace the city's established Chinatown, which sat directly adjacent. After the construction of Union Station there, Sterling attempted to repeat her success at Olvera Street, building China City, a new Chinatown oriented to tourist business, just south of the station. The project was, however, largely a failure, as Chinese business owners moved instead onto North Broadway. See Gottlieb and Wolt, *Thinking Big*, 154–55; and, Estrada, "Sacred and Contested Space," 285–89.

24. Sterling, *Olvera Street* (1933), 15–18; see also Rockwell D. Hunt, ed., *California and the Californians* (Chicago: Lewis Publishing Co., 1926), IV: 57–59; "James R. Martin, Banker and Civic Leader Dies," *Los Angeles Times*, December 24, 1944; Gottlieb and Wolt, *Thinking Big*, 152; William W. Clary, *History of the Law Firm of O'Melveny & Myers, 1885–1965* (Los Angeles: privately printed, 1966), 1: 120–21; Detwiler, *Who's Who in California: 1928–29*, 16–17, 35, 492; McGroarty, *California of the South*, II: 39–42; "Wholesale Druggists Will Build," *Los Angeles Times*, August 1, 1930; Lucien N. Brunswig, "I Bought Los Angeles Real Estate," *Los Angeles Times*, June 18, 1933; Faries, *Rememb'ring*, 109; "Solemne Fiesto Hubo Ayer en la Placita," *La Opinión*, September 5, 1929; *The Latest City Map of Los Angeles* (Los Angeles: Bekins Fireproof Storage, 1923). Montes was exiled in 1927 due to a religious conflict with the new anticlerical administration in Mexico. See Estrada, "Sacred and Contested Space," 244–45.

25. "Pueblo Days to Live Again in Olivera [sic] St.," *Los Angeles Examiner*, July 17, 1929.

26. The following population figures indicate the pace of growth (actual figure followed by the rate of growth over the previous decade). In the city of Los Angeles, 1920: 577,000 (81 percent); 1930: 1,238,000 (115 percent). In Los Angeles County, 1920: 936,000 (86 percent); 1930: 2,208,000 (136 percent). This growth also vaulted Los Angeles to the position of fifth-largest city in the nation, behind only New York, Chicago, Philadelphia, and Detroit. Fogelson, *Fragmented Metropolis*, 78–79, tables 4 and 5.

27. Fogelson, *Fragmented Metropolis*, 74–75, 80–81, tables 6, 7, and 8.

28. "Porter Perils City Landmark," *Los Angeles Times,* August 27, 1929; "Affidavit of Christine Sterling," January 11, 1930, *Simpson v. Los Angeles.*

29. "Olvera No Rose Garden," *Los Angeles Times,* January 14, 1931; "Porter Perils"; "Photograph of the alley behind North Main Street," n.d., exhibit A, "Affidavit of Christine Sterling," January 11, 1930, *Simpson v. Los Angeles.*

30. Sterling quoted in Collins, "A One-Woman Revolution," 14–15; Faries, *Rememb'ring,* 108. For a detailed look at the plague outbreak and its ethnic politics, see William Deverell, "Plague in Los Angeles, 1924: Ethnicity and Typicality," in *Over the Edge: Remapping the American West,* eds. Valerie J. Matsumoto and Blake Allmendinger (Berkeley: University of California Press, 1999), 172–200, as well as ch. 5 of his *Whitewashed Adobe: The Rise of Los Angeles and the Remaking of its Mexican Past* (Berkeley: University of California Press, 2004).

31. "Affidavit of Christine Sterling"; "Police Record for the alley behind North Main street, August 27, 1928 through October 8, 1929," exhibit A of "Affidavit of Christine Sterling," *Simpson v. Los Angeles;* Christine Sterling, to W. J. Sanborn, President, City Council, January 19, 1930, CF 4312 (1929), Council Records. Of the 52 people arrested, 16 had Spanish surnames; the other names reveal the ethnic diversity of the area. Examples include O'Donnell, Koloski, Jordanski, Vujevich, Chorkovich, Sobel, Heilman, Van Arsdale, Danzola, Tescino, Johnson, and Adams. Most of the cases were either dismissed or prompted small fines. Only three men received jail sentences; all three men had Spanish surnames.

32. Sterling to Sanborn, January 19, 1930; "Judge to Visit Olvera Street," *Los Angeles Times,* January 10, 1931; "Historic Lane Now Clean," *Los Angeles Times,* January 15, 1931; Faries, *Rememb'ring,* 108–109. As reported by the *Times,* the testimony about the flophouse and pool hall was by Charles F. Lewis, an inspector with the city Health Department.

33. Simpson, [notes]; "Affidavit of Henry Garbe," "Affidavit of Paul Porta," "Affidavit of Constance D. Simpson," "Affidavit of Ralph T. Merchant," January 27, 1930, *Simpson v. Los Angeles.*

34. Ed Ainsworth, *Memories in the City of Dreams: A Tribute to Harry Chandler, Gran Benefactor de la Ciudad* ([Los Angeles]: n.p., 1959), 22; see also Sánchez, *Becoming Mexican American,* 71–72; Deverell, "Plague in Los Angeles," 173–74, 190–91.

35. Sterling quoted in "Porter Perils."

36. Judge Caryl M. Sheldon, "Findings of Fact and Conclusions of Law," January 21, 1931; Judge Caryl M. Sheldon, "Judgment," December 16, 1931, *Simpson v. Los Angeles;* "Olvera Street Case Nears End," *Los Angeles Times,* January 21, 1931; "Olvera Street Action Upheld," *Los Angeles Times,* May 1, 1931; "El Paseo Wins," editorial, *Los Angeles Times,* May 2, 1931; Olvera Street Law Sustained," *Los Angeles Times,* December 24, 1931; "A Diluted Victory," editorial, *Los Angeles Times,* December 28, 1931.

37. "Olvera Street Trial Brings Back Old Days," *Los Angeles Examiner,* January 20, 1931; "Old Mexico Enters Court," *Los Angeles Times,* January 20, 1931.

38. Court of Appeal, Third Appellate District, California, "Simpson v. City of Los Angeles et. al. Civ. 5254," *Pacific Reporter*, 2nd ser., 38, November 21, 1934, 177–78, 181; "Answer of Defendants, City of Los Angeles," March 4, 1930, *Simpson v. Los Angeles*. The seated appellate-court justices were John A. Plummer, who authored the opinion, John F. Pullen, Presiding Justice, Rolf L. Thompson, concurring.

39. Court of Appeal, "Simpson v. City of Los Angeles," 177–78. The right of the federal government to take property of purely historical interest by right of eminent domain had been established in the case of *United States v. Gettysburg Railway Company* at the turn of the century. In the opinion, Justice Rufus Peckham argued that this action was necessary to "enhance the respect and love of the citizen for the institutions of his country." Interestingly, the Olvera Street defendants did not rely upon this accepted argument, instead concentrating on the public service the new pedestrian mall would perform by cleaning up the alley's evils. *U.S. v. Gettysburg* was never mentioned at trial, in any of the appeals or in the decisions. For more on this legal precedent, see West, *Domesticating History*, 102–103, 132.

40. "Decision Blow to Olvera Street," *Los Angeles Evening Herald and Express*, November 21, 1934; "Olvera Street, Menaced by Ruling, Still Carefree," *Los Angeles Times*, November 23, 1934; "A Blow to Los Angeles," *Los Angeles Times*, November 23, 1934; "Besos Para El Alcalde Shaw," *La Opinión*, December 6, 1934; "Councilmen Get Compliments and Kisses," *Los Angeles Times*, December 6, 1934; "City to Appeal on Olvera Street," *Los Angeles Examiner*, December 14, 1934; "Rehearing Granted in Olvera Case," *Los Angeles Examiner*, January 22, 1935.

41. Florence Dodson Schoneman, State Chairman of the Division of California History, California Federation of Women's Clubs, to Los Angeles City Council, n.d., CF 3210 (1929); Rowland P. Fontana, John A. Schwamm, and John V. Scott, Ramona Parlor No. 109, Native Sons of the Golden West to Los Angeles City Council, August 31, 1929, CF 4312 (1929); ["In favor of Olvera Street"], typescript, [n.d.], CF 4312 (1929), Council Records. Schoneman had become a powerful ally of Sterling early in the process, and she now lent a full measure of public support, which was a consequential gift. A member of the Sepulveda family, Schoneman was influential in society circles and had become known for her zealous campaign to preserve Spanish place names. She was a leader in the Native Daughters of the Golden West, the California Federation of Women's Clubs, and the Friday Morning Club. See Estrada, "Sacred and Contested Space," 242.

42. Louise Watkins, Friday Morning Club, to City Council, December 5, 1934, CF 4947 (1934); Alice T. Mills to City Council, January 19, 1935, CF 218 (1935), Council Records; see also "Clubs Plead for Olvera," *Los Angeles Times*, December 7, 1934.

43. Mrs. F. L Whitlock, Altadena, "Letter to the Editor: A Fascinating Spot," *Los Angeles Times*, January 14, 1935; Mrs. S. L. L., Los Angeles, "Letter to the Editor: Attracts Tourists," *Los Angeles Times*, March 24, 1935.

44. "Olvera Street Transformed from City Eyesore to Spot of Picturesque Charm," *Los Angeles Times*, December 12, 1934; "Quaint and Colorful Shops

Breathing Spirit of Old Mexico Periled By Ruling," *Los Angeles Times,* December 13, 1934; "Quaint Olvera Street as it Now Stands and How it May Appear if City's Fight Fails," *Los Angeles Times,* December 14, 1934; "The Olvera Street Fight," editorial, *Los Angeles Times,* January 25, 1935; "Save Olvera Street," editorial, *Los Angeles Times,* November 2, 1934.

45. "A Blow to Los Angeles"; Harry Carr, "The Lancer," *Los Angeles Times,* November 24, 1934.

46. Crombie Allen, "Wandering and Wondering," *Ontario Daily Report,* April 5, 1935; Lopez to Council. For further comparison of these characterizations, see McGroarty, "The Plaza Beautiful"; and "Court Upholds Traffic Ban in Historic Area," *Los Angeles Examiner,* May 1, 1931.

47. Supreme Court of California, "Constance D. Simpson, Appellant, v. The City of Los Angeles (a Municipal Corporation) et. al., Respondents," *Californian,* 2nd. ser., July 1, 1935, 60–67; "Señoritas Mary Figueroa and Rosa Cgero Bestow Thankful Kisses upon Councilman Parley Christensen Celebrating Victory in Fight to Save Olvera Street," *Los Angeles Examiner,* July 17, 1935.

48. Sterling to Matson, March 29, 1926; Sterling to City Council, May 16, 1929. For a discussion of the functional differences between *Spanish* and *Mexican* in the Southwest, see Carey McWilliams, *North From Mexico: The Spanish-Speaking People of the United States* (1948; new ed., updated by Matt S. Meier, New York: Praeger, 1990), 44–47; Carey McWilliams, *Southern California Country: An Island on the Land* (New York: Duell, Sloan & Pearce, 1946), 80–82.

49. Sterling to Matson, March 29, 1926.

50. LACOC Minutes, December 9, 1926.

51. LACOC Minutes, March 17, 1927. Both Austin and Bent had made significant marks on the Los Angeles built environment. Bent Bros. was a leading general-contracting firm in the city, and Austin was an influential architect who had contributed to the design of City Hall.

52. Christine Sterling, "Viva Mejico!" in *El Paseo: Olvera Guide Book* (Los Angeles: Clyde Brown's Abbey Print Shop, 1932), 2; Sterling, *Olvera Street* (1947), 14. Though Sterling published excerpts of a diary she kept between 1930 and 1932 in multiple publications, including both 1933 and 1947 editions of her *Olvera Street,* the complete and original diary has remained unavailable. Her descendants have denied numerous requests by researchers to examine the manuscript. William Estrada reports that Jean Bruce Poole, past director of El Pueblo de Los Angeles Historical Monument, did finally secure exclusive access to the diary and plans to edit it for publication. The terms of her agreement with the family are unknown, but the public is unlikely to be able to access the diary in its original form. See Estrada, "Sacred and Contested Space," 300–301 n. 71. Sterling moved to live at the Avila Adobe on Olvera Street itself after the Chavez Ravine neighborhood was forced to make way for Dodger Stadium in the early 1950s.

53. "Señores y Señoras de la Prensa," *The Amnewpubas Bugle* (November 1931): 2. "Avila Adobe Again Rings with Gayety," *Los Angeles Times,* March 31, 1930. Estrada, "Sacred and Contested Space," 201–202, presents descriptions of street vending in the area before Olvera Street. Anthropologist Manuel Gamio hired an observer to gather these impressions.

54. Olvera Street contributed to the nascent cultural form of the theme park, where the object of consumption was the experience itself. Many scholars identify theme parks as a post–World War II phenomenon, the progeny of Coney Island and the world's fair. Olvera Street belonged to an intermediate phase, combining elements of those earlier institutions with a preservationist impulse. Other projects during this phase were John D. Rockefeller's Colonial Williamsburg and New Deal–sponsored projects like the Historic American Building Survey. In Sterling's plan, Olvera Street presaged the theme park with its thorough immersion, overlapping of public and private interests, careful image management, and, as much as possible, centralized organization and administration. This successful theming augured the development of even more unified and comprehensive amusement spaces to come in Southern California. Susan G. Davis, "The Theme Park: Global Industry and Cultural Form," *Media, Culture & Society* 18 (1996): 400, 403; Mike Wallace, *Mickey Mouse History and Other Essays on American Memory* (Philadelphia: Temple University Press, 1996), 9–15, 184–85; William J. Murtaugh, *Keeping Time: The History and Theory of Preservation in America* (Pittstown, N.J.: The Main Street Press, 1988), 35–38.

55. Natt Piper, "El Paseo de Los Angeles," *The Architect and Engineer* 107, no. 3 (December 1931): 33; "Olvera Market Opening Will Be Held Tomorrow," *Los Angeles Examiner*, April 19, 1930; see also "Bringing Back Our Yesterdays," *Southern California Business* 8, no. 7 (August 1929): 44; Forman Brown, *Olvera Street and the Avila Adobe* (Los Angeles: Times-Mirror Press, 1931), 15.

56. For analysis of the Padua Hills Theater, which persisted from 1931 to 1974, see Matt Garcia, *A World of Its Own: Race, Labor, and Citrus in the Making of Greater Los Angeles, 1900–1970* (Chapel Hill: University of North Carolina Press, 2001), ch. 4.

57. As David Gutiérrez states, "repatriation statistics, like most data concerning the ethnic Mexican population for this period, are highly unreliable." Still, by combining local figures from Los Angeles and other cities with data from the U.S. Labor Department's repatriation program, scholars estimate that anywhere from 350,000 to 600,000 people of Mexican descent returned to Mexico in the 1930s, whether by deportation, coercion, or choice. Gutiérrez also suggests that to characterize this migration as a "return" is a misnomer because "many of the U.S.-born children of Mexican immigrants had never seen Mexico." Francisco Balderrama and Raymond Rodríguez provide a thorough review of the sources for repatriation figures; the estimate they reach is 1 million. David G. Gutiérrez, *Walls and Mirrors: Mexican Americans, Mexican Immigrants, and the Politics of Ethnicity* (Berkeley: University of California Press, 1995), 72, 234 n.5; Francisco E. Balderrama and Raymond Rodríguez, *Decade of Betrayal: Mexican Repatriation in the 1930s* (Albuquerque: University of New Mexico Press, 1995), 55–64, 79–80, 120–22; see also Sánchez, *Becoming Mexican American*, 70–71, 210–17, 314 n. 3; Emory S. Bogardus, *The Mexicans in the United States* (Los Angeles: University of Southern California Press, 1934), 90; "Mexicans Taking Too Much Charity Here, Says Crail," *Los Angeles Examiner*, February 19, 1932; "1000 Mexicans Will Leave Here Monday,"

Los Angeles Examiner, August 15, 1931; "1200 Mexicans Go Back Home," *Los Angeles Examiner,* October 30, 1931.

58. Balderrama and Rodríguez, *Decade of Betrayal,* 57–58; Sánchez, *Becoming Mexican American,* 214. Balderrama and Rodríguez believe that the Plaza was chosen for "maximum psychological impact." Five Chinese people and one Japanese person were also caught in the dragnet.

59. Sterling quoted in Chapin Hall, "What Goes On?" *Los Angeles Times,* ca. 1931, June Sterling Park Collection, El Pueblo Archive; Mario Valadez, "Olvera Street—Its Beginnings and Growth," interview by Dean Kosotch, n.d., El Pueblo History General File, El Pueblo Archive; Faries, *Rememb'ring,* 112–13.

60. Hall, "What Goes On?" ca. 1931. Sterling attempted to purchase land in Elysian Park for such a purpose. Her request was rejected by the city, which was unwilling to remove its Smallpox Quarantine Hospital from that location. City Council Meeting Minutes, August 4, 1932, City Council Minutes Books, vol. 235, 638, CF 3147, Council Records. In rejecting repatriation officially, Sterling thus diverged from the decision of the Friends of the Mexican—a Pomona College–based Progressive group led by women reformers that had focused on Americanization—to support repatriation. Garcia, *A World of Their Own,* 106–20.

61. McWilliams, *Southern California Country,* 287. For a review of leftist activity at the Plaza in the early twentieth century, see Estrada, "Sacred and Contested Space," ch. 3.

62. "Hordes of Reds Battled in Fierce Riot at Plaza," *Los Angeles Times,* February 27, 1930; "Reds at Plaza Battle Police," *Los Angeles Times,* August 3, 1930; "Red Raid Jails 17," *Los Angeles Times,* September 2, 1930; Mark Wild, "The Political Citizen and the Communist Party in Depression-era Los Angeles," paper presented at the annual meeting of the Western History Association, Sacramento, Calif., October 1998; Sánchez, *Becoming Mexican American,* 71. In response both to increased tourism and to these outbreaks of disorder, the city stepped up its policing of the Plaza and installed "bum-proof" bricks to discourage "loitering and public protest." Estrada, "Sacred and Contested Space," 265.

63. Sterling quoted in Hall, "What Goes On," ca. 1931; "Plaza District Put Under Martial Law," *Los Angeles Times,* December 26, 1913.

64. As Michael Sorkin has written, "There are no demonstrations in Disneyland," and neither would Sterling tolerate such intrusions in her idyllic realm. Michael Sorkin, "Introduction: Variations on a Theme Park," in *Variations on a Theme Park: The New American City and the End of Public Space,* ed. Michael Sorkin (New York: The Noonday Press, 1992), xv. See also Susan G. Davis, *Spectacular Nature: Corporate Culture and the Sea World Experience* (Berkeley: University of California Press, 1997), 2–4.

65. LACOC Minutes, March 7, 1929.

66. Chandler quoted in Jean Bruce Poole and Tevvy Ball, *El Pueblo: The Historic Heart of Los Angeles* (Los Angeles: The Getty Conservation Institute and the J. Paul Getty Museum, 2002), 65.

67. Sterling, *Olvera Street* (1933), 20; Forman Brown, *Olvera Street and the Avila Adobe* (Los Angeles: Dobe Dollar Bookstore, 1930), 18; Brown, *Olvera*

Street (1931); *El Paseo: Olvera Guide Book* (Los Angeles: Clyde Brown's Abbey Print Shop, 1932); Piper, "El Paseo," 33.

68. Sterling, quoted in newspaper clipping, January 22, 1934, June Sterling Park Collection, El Pueblo Archive; Valadez, "Olvera Street."

69. Lee Shippey, "The Lee Side o' L.A.," *Los Angeles Times*, March 28, 1933; Gottlieb and Wolt, *Thinking Big*, 165–84. The *Examiner* even reported that Mexicans on repatriation trains were "smiling and apparently undismayed at their inability to make a living here." "1200 Mexicans Go Back."

70. "Sabada de Gloria Set by Olvera Craftsmen," *Los Angeles Times*, April 5, 1936; Lee Shippey, "Lee Side o' L.A.," *Los Angeles Times*, March 28, 1933.

71. "Olvera Market Opening Will Be Held Tomorrow," *Los Angeles Examiner*, April 19, 1930; "Restored Old L.A. Landmark Opens Today," *Los Angeles Examiner*, April 20, 1930.

72. *Los Angeles To-Day* (Los Angeles: Los Angeles Chamber of Commerce, 1927), 10; Chandler quoted in Gutiérrez, *Walls and Mirrors*, 47. As Mike Davis has written, Los Angeles "business elites . . . claimed that 1920s Southern California was a new kind of industrial society where Ford and Darwin, engineering and nature, were combined in a eugenic formula that eliminated the root causes of class conflict and inefficient production. Militant anti-unionism, together with scientific factory planning, low taxes, abundant electric power, warm weather, mass-produced bungalows and a racially-selected labor force, made Los Angeles a paradise of the open shop." And Chandler was its leading apostle. Davis, "Sunshine and the Open Shop: Ford and Darwin in 1920s Los Angeles," *Antipode* 29, no. 4 (1997), 358. For more about Chandler's role in the Los Angeles labor climate, see Davis, *City of Quartz*, ch. 2. For analysis of Mexican positions in the labor force, both imagined and real, see Sánchez, *Becoming Mexican American*, 96; Gutiérrez, *Walls and Mirrors*, 46–55; and, Balderrama and Rodríguez, *Decade of Betrayal*, 19. See also Arnoldo de León, *They Called Them Greasers: Anglo Attitudes Toward Mexicans in Texas, 1821–1900* (Austin: University of Texas Press, 1983), ch. 3, for the earlier origins of the Anglo image of Mexican laziness.

73. Balderrama and Rodríguez, *Decade of Betrayal*, 59; Gutiérrez, *Walls and Mirrors*, 99–107; D. H. Dinwoodie, "Deportation: The Immigration Service and the Chicano Labor Movement in the 1930s," *New Mexico Historical Review* 52, no. 3 (Summer 1977): 193–203.

74. Piper, "El Paseo de Los Angeles," 35–36.

75. Sterling, "Viva Mejico!" 2.

76. McWilliams, *North From Mexico*, 175–77.

77. Catherine Cocks, *Doing the Town: The Rise of Urban Tourism in the United States, 1850–1915* (Berkeley: University of California Press, 2001), 189–90.

78. "Señores y Señoras de la Prensa," 2; Ernest M. Pratt and Viroque Baker, "A Street of Memories," *Touring Topics* 23, no. 5 (May 1931): rotogravure; Harry Carr, *Los Angeles: City of Dreams* (New York: Appleton-Century, 1936), 9–10.

79. David Glassberg, *Sense of History: The Place of the Past in American Life* (Amherst: University of Massachusetts Press, 2001), 157–58.

80. Sterling, *Olvera Street* (1933), 19. On this function of building restoration as a restrictive interpretation of time, see Richard Handler and Eric Gable, *The New History in an Old Museum: Creating the Past at Colonial Williamsburg* (Durham, N.C.: Duke University Press, 1997), 222–23.

81. Some have suggested that I give Sterling too little credit for her role in preserving a history that might otherwise have been forgotten. As Estrada writes, "she prevented the complete erasure of the city's remaining Spanish, Mexican, and Early American architecture." He suggests that "for Sterling to have consciously engaged in historic preservation . . . thereby assigning the space some degree of historical continuity, would have weakened Kroop's [sic] argument for Anglo manipulation of time and space on Olvera Street." He argues for a view of Sterling "in context," understanding that she cannot be expected to escape the prejudices of her era. He then agrees with historian Kevin Starr's estimation that "Olvera Street might not be authentic Old California or even authentic Mexico, but it was better than the bulldozer." (Estrada, "Sacred and Contested Space," 264; Starr, *Material Dreams*, 205.) Yet Estrada here equates historic preservation with historic continuity, when his own analysis contradicts this point. He charges that the 1931 city sesquicentennial celebration was "a distortion of the city's beginnings" and that the "historical reenactment was a real and planned reaffirmation of who wielded power in 1931" (251, 253). Moreover, elsewhere he calls Olvera Street "a partisan view of the past" and a "homogenized, lobotomized presentation of mythic Mexico" (258, 260). That there are threads of continuity tangled within such admitted distortions is sure, but whether the mere fact of preservation, the better-than-the-bulldozer principle, outweighs the representation of that history—its structures, artifacts, and people, and its rearrangement according to present-day balances of power—which Estrada admits, is a proposition I highly doubt. If we rightly should take Sterling in her context, then we must see Olvera Street in its context as well, not as a neutral conduit of preservation but as one laden with enduring, troublesome assumptions that have proven difficult for many Southern California Anglos to shed in their understandings of both local history and contemporary race relations.

82. Christine Sterling to Mr. Wirsching, Board of Public Works, May 22, 1941; Virginia Goodhue to Jean Bruce Poole, January 18, 1985, Christine Sterling Correspondence File, El Pueblo Archive. On the connection of hand labor to an assumed premodern or primitive way of life, see Erika Bsumek, "Making 'Indian-Made': The Production, Consumption, and Legal Construction of Navajo Identity, 1880–1935," Ph.D. diss., Rutgers University, 2000.

83. "Sabada de Gloria"; *Aperitif* (Santa Barbara: n.p., 1935). Olvera Street joined a broader, national revival of Mexican arts and crafts, part of a fad for all things Mexican in the 1920s and 1930s. Pottery and other traditional crafts became popular among many American consumers, thus creating opportunities for Mexicans to gain income and even to develop careers as artisans. Providers of social services, from the famed Hull House in Chicago to the Spanish Colonial Arts Society in New Mexico, provided job training in arts and crafts for Mexican clients. Hull House even ran its own commercial kilns. Yet, as Charles Montgomery suggests, this focus on traditional artisanry led as often to

restricted job choices as it did to new possibilities; in Albuquerque, for example, vocational schools directed Mexicans to classes in weaving, tanning, and wood carving and shut them out of training in more modern occupations, such as welding, construction, carpentry, and auto repair. See Helen Delpar, *The Enormous Vogue of Things Mexican: Cultural Relations between the United States and Mexico, 1920–1935* (Tuscaloosa: University of Alabama Press, 1995); Cheryl R. Ganz and Margaret Strobel, eds., *Pots of Promise: Mexicans and Pottery at Hull House, 1920–40* (Urbana and Chicago: University of Illinois Press, 2004); Charles Montgomery, *The Spanish Redemption: Heritage, Power and Loss on New Mexico's Upper Rio Grande* (Berkeley: University of California Press, 2002), ch. 5.

84. For a discussion of rendering a people premodern by the display and consumption of their crafts as premodern artifacts, see Barbara Babcock and Marta Weigle, eds., *The Great Southwest of the Fred Harvey Company and the Santa Fe Railway* (Tucson: University of Arizona Press and The Heard Museum, 1996); Leah Dilworth, *Imagining Indians in the Southwest: Persistent Visions of a Primitive Past* (Washington, D.C.: Smithsonian Institution Press, 1996).

85. Harry Carr, "The Lancer," *Los Angeles Times,* December 24, 1930.

86. The 1930s witnessed a movement of artists, writers, photographers, and anthropologists that has often been called regionalism but is largely associated with this desire to save or recapture America's "folk" cultures. This movement came in part from a "fear that America's provincial customs were endangered" and also from a belief that betrayal of these roots by the elite business class and modernity had led to the tragedy of the Depression. Cultural commentators from painters like Thomas Hart Benton and Grant Wood (of *American Gothic* fame) to ethnographers like Zora Neale Hurston and Alan Lomax believed that in the common folk one could find the soul of America. This belief led to an interest in folk customs around the world as well. See Glassberg, *Sense of History,* 130; Warren Susman, ed., *Culture and Commitment, 1929–1945.* (New York: G. Braziller, 1973); Robert L. Dorman, *Revolt of the Provinces: The Regionalist Movement in America, 1920–1945* (Chapel Hill: University of North Carolina Press, 1993); Erika Doss, *Benton, Pollock and the Politics of Modernism: From Regionalism to Abstract Expressionism* (Chicago: University of Chicago Press, 1995).

87. The ideas of "picturesque urban peasants" and the "aestheticization of poverty" both come from Catherine Cocks's exploration of urban tourism in turn-of-the-century America. In particular, the "slumming tours" she describes, in which traditional, colorful, and sometimes shady ethnic lifestyles became exotic commodities, were a kind of precursor to Olvera Street. See Cocks, *Doing the Town,* 185–95.

88. Sterling quoted in, "The Round Point of the Plaza to Be Surrounded," *California Southland* 8, no. 83 (November 1926): 11; "El Paseo de Los Angeles," *The Amnewpubas Bugle* (November 1931): 2; Lee Shippey, "The Lee Side O' L.A.," *Los Angeles Times,* November 11, 1928. As Jackson Lears has demonstrated, antimodern expressions like the ones at Olvera Street, even when coupled with the disapproval of modern ugliness, with rare exception failed to become vehicles to critique progress. T. J. Jackson Lears, *No Place of Grace:*

Antimodernism and the Transformation of American Culture, 1880–1920 (Chicago: University of Chicago Press, 1981).

89. "Fiesta Brings Historic Glory," *Los Angeles Examiner,* March 25, 1934; [Los Compadres de la Calle Olvera], invitation, August 2, 1934, California Ephemeral Collection, University of California, Los Angeles, University Research Library, Special Collections (hereafter UCLA Special Collections). For other such costume commentary, see Lee Shippey, "The Lee Side o' L.A.," *Los Angeles Times,* December 9, 1932; "Olvera Fiesta Scheduled," *Los Angeles Times,* March 17, 1934; "Name Day Fiesta Held at Theater," *Los Angeles Times,* August 3, 1934; Harry Carr, "The Lancer," *Los Angeles Times,* August 4, 1934.

90. Chapin Hall, "Olvera Street," *Lary Ride Guide,* Los Angeles Railway Corp., September 15, 1934; Lee Shippey, "The Lee Side o' L.A.," *Los Angeles Times,* August 6, 1934; Western Costume Company, "Costuming Ourselves Into the Past," advertisement, *La Fiesta de Los Angeles: Official Program* (Los Angeles: La Fiesta de Los Angeles, 1931), n.p., James Marshall Miller Collection, UCLA Special Collections.

91. Scholars of blackface minstrelsy and of Indian costuming have shown that such disguises had the potential to be rebellious, but more commonly the temporary transference only reinforced the definition of normal. As Philip Deloria has written about playing Indian, "wearing a mask makes one self-conscious of a *real* 'me' underneath." Part of the significance of blackface was that it rubbed off, as black skin could not. Philip J. Deloria, *Playing Indian* (New Haven, Conn.: Yale University Press, 1998), 7. For more on Indian costuming, see Rayna Green, "The Tribe Called Wannabee: Playing Indian in America and Europe," *Folklore* 99 (1992): 30–55. For a discussion of blackface minstrelsy, see Eric Lott, *Love and Theft: Blackface Minstrelsy and the American Working Class* (New York: Oxford University Press, 1993); Alexander Saxton, *The Rise and Fall of the White Republic: Class Politics and Mass Culture in Nineteenth-Century America* (London: Verso, 1990); David Roediger, *The Wages of Whiteness: Race and the Making of the American Working Class* (London: Verso, 1991); and Susan G. Davis, *Parades and Power: Street Theatre in Nineteenth-Century Philadelphia* (Philadelphia: Temple University Press, 1986).

92. Brown, *Olvera Street* (1930), 17.

93. Sterling to City Council, May 16, 1929, emphasis added; Sterling quoted in "The Round Point," emphasis added; Christine Sterling, "A Touch of Old Spain: Olvera Street, Los Angeles, Cradle of Spanish History in California," *Arrowhead Magazine* (December 1931): 17–18, emphasis added; Irene Wilde, "El Paseo de Los Angeles," *Los Angeles Times,* n.d., emphasis added; "Bringing Back Our Yesterdays," emphasis added.

94. Again, Cocks's investigation of urban tourism has been instructive here. "The cultivation of historic associations enabled middling Americans to reassert cultural hegemony over parts of the city they felt they had lost to the influx of immigrants or the encroachments of business. At the same time it cemented a sense of both local and national pride now increasingly visible on the landscape." Cocks, *Doing the Town,* 185.

95. Lee Shippey, "The Lee Side o' L.A.," *Los Angeles Times,* June 15, 1932; Lee Shippey, "The Lee Side o' L.A.," *Los Angeles Times,* August 6, 1934. Padua

Hills audiences made similar remarks. As one *Los Angeles Times* review suggested, the performance was "the most genuine thing we've ever seen in the United States. It was all in Spanish, all presented by Mexicans and all quite natural. They didn't act or speak for the audience. They didn't seem to know there was an audience. They were just a group of lively young Mexicans having a good time." See Garcia, *A World of Their Own,* 142–43.

96. Marguerite Decker, "El Paseo de Los Angeles," in *El Paseo: Olvera Guide,* 4.

97. "Old Olvera Street Restaurant Described," *Los Angeles Record,* May 9, 1930.

98. Martin Walsh, "Black Angels," *Touring Topics* 19, no. 9 (September 1927): 21; De León, *They Called Them Greasers,* 37–42, 9–10. Recalling observations by Anglos in nineteenth-century Texas, De León explained that "the fandango, for instance, was identified with lewd passions and lasciviousness."

99. Harry Carr, "The Lancer," *Los Angeles Times,* November 25, 1928; see also Sánchez, *Becoming Mexican American,* 172; Faries, *Rememb'ring,* 108–109; "Judge to Visit Olvera Street"; "Historic Lane Now Clean."

100. "Olvera Street, Menaced by Ruling"; Decker, "El Paseo," 3; *Olvera Street News: The Magazine from the Birthplace of Los Angeles* 1, no.1 (August 1933): 1.

101. De León, *They Called Them Greasers,* 37–42, 9–10; Reginald Horsman, *Race and Manifest Destiny: The Origins of American Racial Anglo-Saxonism* (Cambridge, Mass.: Harvard University Press, 1981), 232–35. The perpetual desire for Mexican and Spanish women appears in popular sheet-music lyrics and cover art of the era. See Sam DeVincent Collection of Illustrated Sheet Music, Archives Center, National Museum of American History, Smithsonian Institution.

102. Sterling, *Olvera Street* (1947), 11, 14; see also "Latins to be Serenaded," *Los Angeles Times,* December 18, 1928; "Adobe Landmark to be Preserved," *Los Angeles Examiner,* February 15, 1929; California State Society Sons of the Revolution (Los Angeles), *The Bulletin* 2 (January 1929): 6

103. "City Captured by Americans!" *Los Angeles Times,* January 11, 1929; *Los Angeles Times,* May 29, 1930; Lott, *Love and Theft,* 62; see also Christine Sterling, letter to the editor, *Los Angeles Times,* January 10, 1929; "Historical House Rings with Music," *Los Angeles Times,* December 21, 1928.

104. Harry Carr, "The Lancer," *Los Angeles Times,* December 24, 1930; McGroarty, "The Plaza Beautiful," emphasis added.

105. The originator of the term *imperialist nostalgia,* Renato Rosaldo, sees these two elements as intrinsically linked: a demand for ongoing innovation entails a yearning for "more stable worlds, whether these reside in our own past, in other cultures, or in the conflation of the two." He compares this version of nostalgia to the way in which "people destroy their environment and then worship nature." In Olvera Street as well, the operations appear ironic but depend upon each other. Renato Rosaldo, "Imperialist Nostalgia," *Representations* 26, Special Issue: Memory and Counter-Memory, (Spring 1989): 107–108.

106. "Work-a-Day World 'Halts' at Plaza Fete," *Los Angeles Examiner,* September 6, 1933, emphasis added.

107. For a discussion of more recent controversies about the ethnic character of Olvera Street and the perspective of Chicano scholars involved in it, see Rodolfo Acuña, *Anything But Mexican: Chicanos in Contemporary Los Angeles* (London: Verso, 1996); and Estrada, "Sacred and Contested Space," ch. 5.

108. Plaza Mexican Methodist Episcopal Church, "Petition," March 18, 1929, CF 3210 (1929); Public Works Committee, "Memorandum," August 28, 1929, CF 4312 (1929), Council Records. The Methodist Church, built in 1925, competed with the traditional Plaza Catholic Church, particularly for the loyalty of immigrants. Designed ironically, or deliberately, in a florid, Goodhuesque Spanish style, it dwarfed La Placita in size and pomposity. It attracted a good number of followers, however, not for its architecture but for its outreach programs that provided extensive social services for Mexican immigrants, even if these services often came laden with motives of Americanization.

109. Plaza Community Center, "Petition," March 15, 1929, CF 3210 (1929), Council Records.

110. For work on the efforts of marginalized groups to reclaim urban spaces, see Dolores Hayden, *The Power of Place: Urban Landscapes as Public History* (Cambridge, Mass.: MIT Press, 1995); and Martha K. Norkunas, *The Politics of Public Memory: Tourism, History, and Ethnicity in Monterey, California* (Albany: State University of New York Press, 1993).

111. L. F. Bustamante, "Calle Tipica Mexicana en el Sonora Town," *La Opinión,* April 11, 1930; "Sigue el Lío de Olvera St.," *La Opinión,* April 26, 1930.

112. [Untitled photograph], 1–68, Olvera Street file, Photograph Collections, Seaver Center for Western History Research, Los Angeles County Museum of Natural History; "Se Celebro la Fundacion de Los Angeles," *La Opinión,* September 6, 1930. In its early years, Olvera Street was not a major center for Mexican celebration of events like Cinco de Mayo and Mexican Independence Day; it was absent from *La Opinión's* lists of places to go on these holidays. Rather, Olvera Street was a place for Anglos to go and celebrate these Mexican holidays.

113. "De Sociedad: La Inauguracion de 'La Golondrina,'" *La Opinión,* April 22, 1930; "De Sociedad: Una Fiesta en el 'Paseo de Los Angeles,'" *La Opinión,* April 20, 1930; "Casa La Golondrina, Mexican Cafe, 1850, in the First Wine Cellar, 35 Olvera," invitation, 1935, California Ephemeral Collection, UCLA Special Collections. De Bonzo came to Los Angeles from Mexico as a young child, later marrying an Italian immigrant. She opened Le Misión Café nearby on South Spring Street in 1924, which became popular and was frequented by numerous local boosters and city politicians. When the city targeted her block for demolition, her powerful patrons helped get compensation for her in the form of space in the Pelanconi Building. McGroarty, *California of the South,* V: 777–78; Estrada, "Sacred and Contested Space," 230–32, 311.

114. "Old Olvera Street Restaurant"; "Woman to Give Gala Olvera Street Dinner," *Los Angeles Record,* June 18, 1930; "Mexicans Open Cafe With Rites."

115. "Una Junta de Mexicanos en Olvera Street," [*La Opinión*], n.d., June Sterling Park Collection Scrapbook, El Pueblo Archive.

116. "Tampico Relief Fund President Named," *Los Angeles Examiner*, October 3, 1933; "$692 Produjeron los Festejos en Olvera," *La Opinión*, October 7, 1933; "Mexicans to Hold Yule Fete in Park," *Los Angeles Examiner*, December 4, 1933.

117. David Alfaro Siqueiros, *Mi Respuesta* (Mexico: n.p., 1960), 32; see also Shifra M. Goldman, "Siqueiros and Three Early Murals in Los Angeles," *Art Journal* 33, no. 4 (Summer 1974): 321–24, 327 n. 26; "Huge Mural, 82 Feet Long, To Be Unveiled," *Los Angeles Examiner*, October 8, 1932; "Banquete el Pintor Siqueiros," *La Opinión*, April 23, 1932. For Siqueiros's biography, mural techniques, and art criticism of his work, see Goldman, "Siqueiros," 321–27; Raquel Tibol, *Siqueiros: Introductor de Realidades* (Mexico: n.p., 1961); Raquel Tibol, *David Alfaro Siqueiros* (Mexico: n.p., 1969); Enrique Gaul, *Siqueiros*, trans. Emma Gutierrez Suarez (México: Galeria de Arte Misrachi, 1965). Ferenz was an unusual character and was an active Nazi propagandist in California. Though Siqueiros's Communist connections were public knowledge, Ferenz hired him anyway. Contemporaries called Ferenz an "opportunist," believing that he was more intrigued by the publicity the mural might generate for the art center and himself than put off by Siqueiros's politics. Estrada, "Sacred and Contested Space," 271.

118. Siqueiros quoted in Goldman, "Siqueiros," 324; Arthur Millier, "Power Unadorned Marks Olvera Street Fresco," *Los Angeles Times*, October 16, 1932.

119. Don Ryan, "Don Ryan's Parade Ground," *Los Angeles Illustrated Daily News*, October 11, 1932; see also "Fresco of Jungle Scene Hailed by Dean Cornwell as Start of New Move," *Los Angeles Times*, October 10, 1932; Herbert Jepson, "Los Angeles Art Community," interview, University of California, Los Angeles, Oral History Program, 1977, 41, 260–62.

120. Ryan, "Don Ryan's Parade Ground"; newspaper clipping, ca. 1932, June Sterling Park Collection, El Pueblo Archive; Jack Jones, "Disputed Mural May Reappear," *Los Angeles Times*, May 23, 1971; Sánchez, *Becoming Mexican American*, 317 n. 59; Walter Gutman, "News and Gossip," *Creative Art: A Magazine of Fine and Applied Art* 12 (January 1933): 75. Sterling's act was part of a larger backlash against Mexican and leftist artists in general. Some Los Angelenos disparaged the employment of non-American artists on public projects during the Depression. Siqueiros's mural is currently being restored. Madge Clover, *Saturday Night* (Los Angeles), October 15, 1932; *Christian Science Monitor* (April 27, 1935), quoted in Goldman, "Siqueiros," 323, 325; *California Arts & Architecture* (July–August 1932): 2; Marita Hernandez, "An Old City Scandal May Resurface," *Los Angeles Times*, October 27, 1989; Poole and Ball, *El Pueblo*, 89–95.

121. Gutiérrez, *Walls and Mirrors*, 11–15, 110–14; Sánchez, *Becoming Mexican American*, 245–47; Mario T. García, *Mexican Americans: Leadership, Ideology and Identity* (New Haven, Conn.: Yale University Press, 1989), 151–53; John Bright, "Las Mañanitas: A New Awakening for Mexicans in the United States," *Black and White* 1 (June 1939): 15. Much of El Congreso's politics emerged from a Southern California context, as did many of the convention's representatives, including Fierro. See Gutiérrez and Sánchez for detailed

analyses of El Congreso and its first national convention. For more about Luisa Moreno's involvement and other aspects of women's involvement in this radical movement, including work by Fierro, see Vicki L. Ruiz, *Cannery Women, Cannery Lives: Mexican Women, Unionization, and the California Food Processing Industry, 1930–1950* (Albuquerque: University of New Mexico Press, 1987); Vicki L. Ruiz, *From Out of the Shadows: Mexican Women in Twentieth-Century America* (New York: Oxford University Press, 1998).

122. Josefina Fierro, quoted in Bright, "Las Mañanitas," 14, emphasis added.

123. Sánchez, *Becoming Mexican American,* 226–29. Sánchez's narrative charts this politics of opposition as leading away from the Plaza. In fact, the Plaza area, which is a significant focus of his analysis of Mexican society and culture in his book up to this point, does not reappear in the text. While Sánchez's understanding of the "declining influence" of the Plaza-area residents demonstrates an important shift, the Plaza and Olvera Street clearly continued to be a symbolic center for the Mexican community, as El Congreso's choice of the Plaza for its rally confirmed.

124. David Gutiérrez, "Significant to Whom?: Mexican Americans and the History of the American West," *Western Historical Quarterly* 24, no. 4 (November 1993): 524; "Solemne Fiesto Hubo Ayer en la Placita"; Bustamante, "Calle Tipica."

125. Fierro quoted in Bright, "Las Mañanitas," 14.

126. Estrada, "Sacred and Contested Space," 356; Mary P. Ryan, "Looking for the Public in Time and Space: The Case of the LA Plaza, from the 18th century to the Present," paper presented at The Transformation of Public Culture: Assessing the Politics of Diversity, Democracy, and Community in the United States, symposium, Miami University of Ohio, March 5, 2004. My understanding of the connection of public spaces and exclusion also borrows from Bryant Simon, *Boardwalk of Dreams: Atlantic City and the Fate of Urban America* (New York: Oxford University Press, 2004).

127. In his dissertation, Estrada includes a reminiscence and analysis of his experience on a childhood field trip to Olvera Street. Estrada, "Sacred and Contested Space," 1–2.

CONCLUSION

1. Lisa Fugard, "Writer on the Road: The Mission Trail," *New York Times Magazine,* March 3, 2002. Thanks to Kathy Peiss for this citation.

2. Logan Jenkins, "Donated Bells Rope in Ringing Endorsement," *San Diego Union-Tribune,* March 15, 1999; Daniel Hernandez, "Mexican Marketplace Evokes Tinges of Home," *Los Angeles Times,* September 19, 2002. Thanks to Theresa Smith for the latter citation. For additional information on the recent efforts of the Women's Club, see also Lola Sherman, "Bells Seen as Way to Go on 'The King's Road,'" *San Diego Union-Tribune,* March 11, 1998; Logan Jenkins, "It's Time to Ring the Bell for an Emblem of California," *San Diego Union-Tribune,* March 11, 1998; "El Camino Real Bell Dedicated," *La Prensa San Diego,* June 26, 1998; Betty Barnacle, "Campbell Unveils Mission

Bell Replica: Stretching History of El Camino Real," *San Jose Mercury News,* July 12, 1998; Barbara Brill, "Ivey Ranch Students Help Restore Fading Historic El Camino Real Bell Marker," *North County Times* [San Diego], October 13, 2000; Michael Cabanatuan, "Mission Bells Mark the Road Again," *San Francisco Chronicle,* November 11, 2004; Max Kurillo and Erline Tuttle, *California's El Camino Real and its Historic Bells* (San Diego: Sunbelt Publications, 2000), 39–48.

3. Sandy Bien quoted in Tony Perry and Louis Sahagun, "Rich Enclave Values Privacy," *Los Angeles Times,* June 5, 2002; Perry and Sahagun, "Rich Enclave."

4. Loren Miller, "Not My Fault," *California Eagle,* September 4, 1931, 8.

5. Mike Davis describes the split in Los Angeles imagery as "the master dialectic of sunshine and *noir.*" Davis, *City of Quartz: Excavating the Future in Los Angeles* (London: Verso, 1990), 15–97. A great deal of literature exists on the literary and cinematic genre of noir, but for discussions of its relation to local culture and the Spanish past, see William Alexander McClung, *Landscapes of Desire: Anglo Mythologies of Los Angeles* (Berkeley: University of California Press, 2000), 48–65; William Estrada, "Sacred and Contested Space: The Los Angeles Plaza," Ph.D. diss, University of California, Los Angeles, 2003, 206–207, 251–52; J. U. Peters, "The Los Angeles Anti-Myth," in *Essays on California Writers,* eds. Charles L. Crow and Kevin Starr (Bowling Green, Ohio: Bowling Green State University Press, 1978), 21–32; David L. Ulin, *Writing Los Angeles: A Literary Anthology* (New York: The Library of America, 2002). For telling original examples of this view, see Louis Adamic, *The Truth about Los Angeles* (Girard, Kansas: Haldeman-Julius Publications, 1927); Louis Adamic, *Laughing in the Jungle* (New York: Harper, 1932); Raymond Chandler, *The Big Sleep* (1939; reprint, New York: Vintage Crime, 1992).

6. McWilliams published numerous volumes on California. Those that investigate the Spanish myth most famously are *Southern California Country: An Island on the Land* (New York: Duell, Sloan & Pearce, 1946); and *California: The Great Exception* (New York: Current Books, 1949). His *Factories in the Fields: The Story of Migratory Farm Labor in California* (Boston: Little, Brown, 1939) was part of a national exposé of the dreadful conditions in the state's agricultural industry. McWilliams's work joined the chorus of critics that included John Steinbeck, *The Harvest Gypsies: On the Road to the Grapes of Wrath* (1936; Berkeley, Calif.: Heyday Books, 1988); and Dorothea Lange and Paul S. Taylor, *An American Exodus: A Record of Human Erosion* (New York: Reynal & Hitchcock, 1939).

7. Mike Davis, *Ecology of Fear: Los Angeles and the Imagination of Disaster* (New York: Vintage Books, 1998), 12.

8. For histories of twentieth-century Indian activism, see Peter Iverson, *We Are Still Here: American Indians in the Twentieth Century* (Wheeling, Ill.: Harlan-Davidson, 1998); Paul Chaat Smith and Paul Allen Warrior, *Like a Hurricane: The Indian Movement from Alcatraz to Wounded Knee* (New York: The New Press, 1997); Joane Nagel, *American Indian Ethnic Renewal: Red Power and the Resurgence of Identity and Culture* (New York: Oxford University Press, 1997); Stephen Cornell, *Return of the Native: American Indian Political*

Resurgence (New York: Oxford University Press, 1990). For histories of the Chicano movement, its antecedents, and its continuing influence, see Ernesto Chavez, *¡Mi Raza Primero! (My People First!): Nationalism, Identity, and Insurgency in the Chicano Movement in Los Angeles, 1966–1978* (Berkeley: University of California Press, 2002); Chon A. Noriega, Eric R. Avila, and Karen Mary Davalos, *The Chicano Studies Reader: An Anthology of Aztlan, 1970–2000* (Berkeley: University of California Press, 2001); Vicki L. Ruiz, *From Out of the Shadows: Mexican Women in Twentieth-Century America* (New York: Oxford University Press, 1999), 72–152; David G. Gutiérrez, *Walls and Mirrors: Mexican Americans, Mexican Immigrants, and the Politics of Ethnicity* (Berkeley: University of California Press, 1995), 117–216; Mario T. García, *Mexican Americans: Leadership, Ideology and Identity, 1930–1960* (New Haven, Conn.: Yale University Press, 1991).

9. "Sonoma Mission to Commemorate Local Indians," *Got CALICHE*, April 1999, http://www.swanet.org/zarchives/gotcaliche/alldailyeditions/99apr/myjo40199.html, January 20, 2005. For further examples of recent Indian efforts to gain recognition at mission sites, see "New Church-Indian Divide," *Los Angeles Times*, November 27, 2002; and Margie Mason, "Displaced Tribe Seeks Credit for Mission Role," *San Diego Union-Tribune*, February 11, 2001.

10. Velez quoted in "Mexican Marketplace." *Guaraches* are traditional leather sandals and the *molcajete* is a stone mortar for grinding corn. For a discussion of the efforts of Mexican scholars and locals to gain leadership roles at Olvera Street, see Rodolfo F. Acuña, *Anything But Mexican: Chicanos in Contemporary Los Angeles* (London: Verso, 1996), 26–30. Restoration of the Siqueiros mural has been contentious and is ongoing, with work by the Getty Preservation Foundation. Various citywide commemorations and exhibits of Siqueiros's work in Los Angeles have helped preserve his legacy in the area. Jean Bruce Poole and Tevvy Ball, *El Pueblo: The Historic Heart of Los Angeles* (Los Angeles: The Getty Preservation Institute and the J. Paul Getty Museum, 2002), 61–82. For examples of recent Mexican attempts to reclaim other such historic spaces, see Jeanne F. Brooks, "Whose History Shall Old Town Display?" *San Diego Union-Tribune*, April 12, 1998.

11. For in-depth treatment of this controversy, see Acuña, *Anything but Mexican*, 19–42. Dolores Hayden has chronicled a number of instances in which Los Angelenos of varying races have worked to reclaim public spaces. See her *The Power of Place: Urban Landscapes as Public History* (Cambridge, Mass.: MIT Press, 1997).

12. Several scholars have noted that this built-in forgetfulness echoes monuments' power not to compel memory but to discharge the obligation to remember. As Robert Musil has suggested, "There is nothing in this world as invisible as a monument." Repetition in particular dilutes the impetus to remember; or in Liliane Weissberg's phrase, "memory can be drowned out by the vast number of allusions to the past." For this discourse, see Musil, "Monuments," in *Posthumous Papers of a Living Author* (Hygiene, Colo.: Eridanos Press, 1987), 64; Weissberg, "Memory Confined," in Dan Ben-Amos and Liliane Weissberg, eds., *Cultural Memory and the Construction of Identity* (Detroit: Wayne State University Press, 1999), 45–76; Maya Nadkarni, "The Death of Socialism and

the Afterlife of its Monuments: Making and Marketing the Past in Budapest's Statue Park Museum," in Katharine Hodgkin and Susannah Radstone, eds., *Contested Pasts: The Politics of Memory* (London: Routledge, 2003), 193–207; Andreas Huyssen, "Monumental Seduction," in Mieke Bal et. al., eds., *Acts of Memory: Cultural Recall in the Present* (Hanover, N.H.: Dartmouth College and University Press of New England, 1999), 191–207; Michel-Rolph Trouillot, *Silencing the Past: Power and the Production of History* (Boston: Beacon Press, 1995), 48–59; James E. Young, *The Texture of Memory: Holocaust Memorials and Meaning* (New Haven, Conn.: Yale University Press, 1993), 5.

Index

Phillips, Kate, 285–86n35
Picher, Anna, 53, 63, 292n29
Pickford, Mary, 159–60, 180, 281–82n1
Pico, Ysidora, 25
Picturesque Pala (James), 302n120
pilgrimages: and *Ramona*, 36–41, 37, 46, 50; and Spanish missions, 85–88, 299n95
Pinkerton detectives, 126–27, 126
Pitt, Leonard, 34, 275–76n15
place, 2, 5, 272n3
places as stages, 13–14, 280–81n35
Plains Indians, 9, 148, 152
Plan de San Diego, 112
Plaza (Los Angeles): and commercial interests, 212–14, 217–20, 218, 222–23, 330nn7,8, 333n23; and ethnic Mexicans, 208, 210–11, 227, 248, 253, 266; as public space, 212, 225, 259–60; and radicalism, 232–33, 241, 254–58, 256, 338n62, 345n120, 345–46n121, 346n123; and repatriation, 231–32, 241, 338n58
Plaza Art Center (Los Angeles), 254–55, 256, 345n117
Plaza Catholic Church (Los Angeles), 65, 67, 68, 218, 344n108
Plaza Community Center (Los Angeles), 252
Plaza de Los Angeles, Inc., 216–17, 219, 224, 332–33n21
Plaza Mexican Methodist Episcopal Church (Los Angeles), 235, 251–52, 344n108
Plummer, John A., 335n38
Pomeroy, Earl, 300n104
Poole, Jean Bruce, 336n52
Poor Little Rich Girl (Gates), 297n76
Popular Homecraft, 297n78
population statistics: for California Indians, 14, 30, 81–84, 82, 87, 155, 298nn86–88; for Californios, 26–27; for ethnic Mexicans, 230–31, 257, 337–38n57; for Los Angeles, 219, 230–31, 333n26; for San Diego, 105–7, 110–11, 155
Porter, John, 215, 331n14
Portland cement, 322n26
Portolá, Gaspar de, 115, 123
Portolá Festival (San Francisco), 308n29
Post, Emily, 119, 127–28, 143
Pressmen's Union, 110
"pretend pueblo," 147, 154
primitivism, 133, 137–46, 142, 312n63, 315nn80–82, 316nn87,88, 317n96
progress, 3–4, 7–8, 20, 43, 51; and El Camino Real, 66, 73, 84, 89, 91;

and Olvera Street, 250; and Panama-California Exposition, 115, 118, 129, 132–36, 140, 156
Progressive Era, 11, 56, 65–66, 293n31
property rights: and Olvera Street, 212–13, 215, 331nn14,15; and *Ramona*, 39; and Rancho Santa Fe, 163, 179, 181, 190, 192–93, 198, 203–4
Protective Covenant (Rancho Santa Fe), 190, 196, 197, 198, 203, 327n88
Protestantism, 85–88, 96, 299–300n96, 300n100, 300–301n106
public memory, 1–3, 271–72n2, 272–73n4, 279n29; in nineteenth-century California, 27–28, 284n21; and Olvera Street, 212, 226
public/private partnerships, 70, 212–19, 218, 220, 223–24, 226, 331n12, 332–33n21
public-relief programs, 231–32
public space, 6, 212, 225, 259–60, 264, 267
Pueblo Indians, 139–54, 298n88, 299n93; and modernity, 146–54, 317n96; and primitivism, 137–46, 142, 312n63, 315nn81,82, 316nn87,88, 317n96
puesteros, 234, 237, 238, 239, 243, 247, 251–54, 266
puestos, 216, 222, 233–34, 235, 237, 238, 239, 260
Pullen, John F., 335n38

Queen Ramona, 114, 115

racial division, 6–7, 9–11, 13, 30, 57, 278n24, 279n25; and built environment, 14, 280–81n35; and Olvera Street, 230; and Panama-California Exposition, 116, 308n29; and *Ramona*, 21; and Rancho Santa Fe, 160–61, 163, 190, 198–204, 327n88, 328n89, 329n100. See also ethnic division
radicalism, 111–12, 232–33, 241, 254–58, 256, 306n17, 338n62, 345n120, 345–46n121, 346n123
railroads. See names of railroads
Ramona (film), 159, 281–82n1
Ramona (Jackson), 19, 30, 34, 45, 281–82n1, 288n60; and California Indians, 30–35, 285n27, 285–86n35, 286n36; and Californios, 20–23, 31–35, 42, 44–46; synopsis of, 20–23, 283n7; and tourism, 35–41, 37, 38, 44, 286n40, 287n46
Ramona's Marriage Place, 36–37, 37, 50

Text: 10/13 Sabon
Display: Sabon
Indexer: Sharon Sweeney
Compositor: International Typesetting and Composition